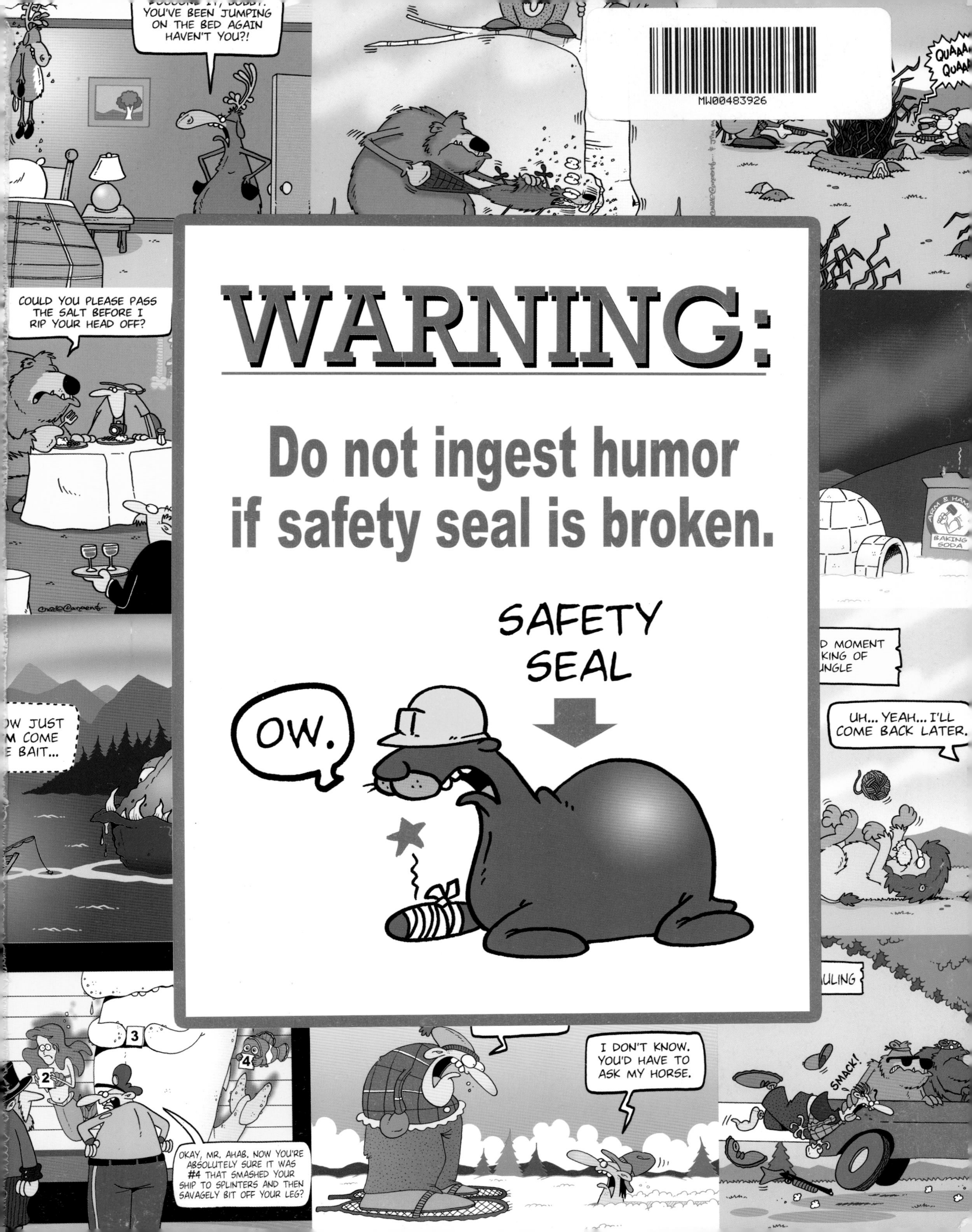
YOU'VE BEEN JUMPING ON THE BED AGAIN HAVEN'T YOU?!
COULD YOU PLEASE PASS THE SALT BEFORE I RIP YOUR HEAD OFF?
WARNING:
Do not ingest humor if safety seal is broken.
SAFETY SEAL
OW.
UH... YEAH... I'LL COME BACK LATER.
BAKING SODA
I DON'T KNOW. YOU'D HAVE TO ASK MY HORSE.
OKAY, MR. AHAB. NOW YOU'RE ABSOLUTELY SURE IT WAS #4 THAT SMASHED YOUR SHIP TO SPLINTERS AND THEN SAVAGELY BIT OFF YOUR LEG?
SMACK!

CHAD CARPENTER'S

TUNDRA

ORGANICALLY GROWN HUMOR

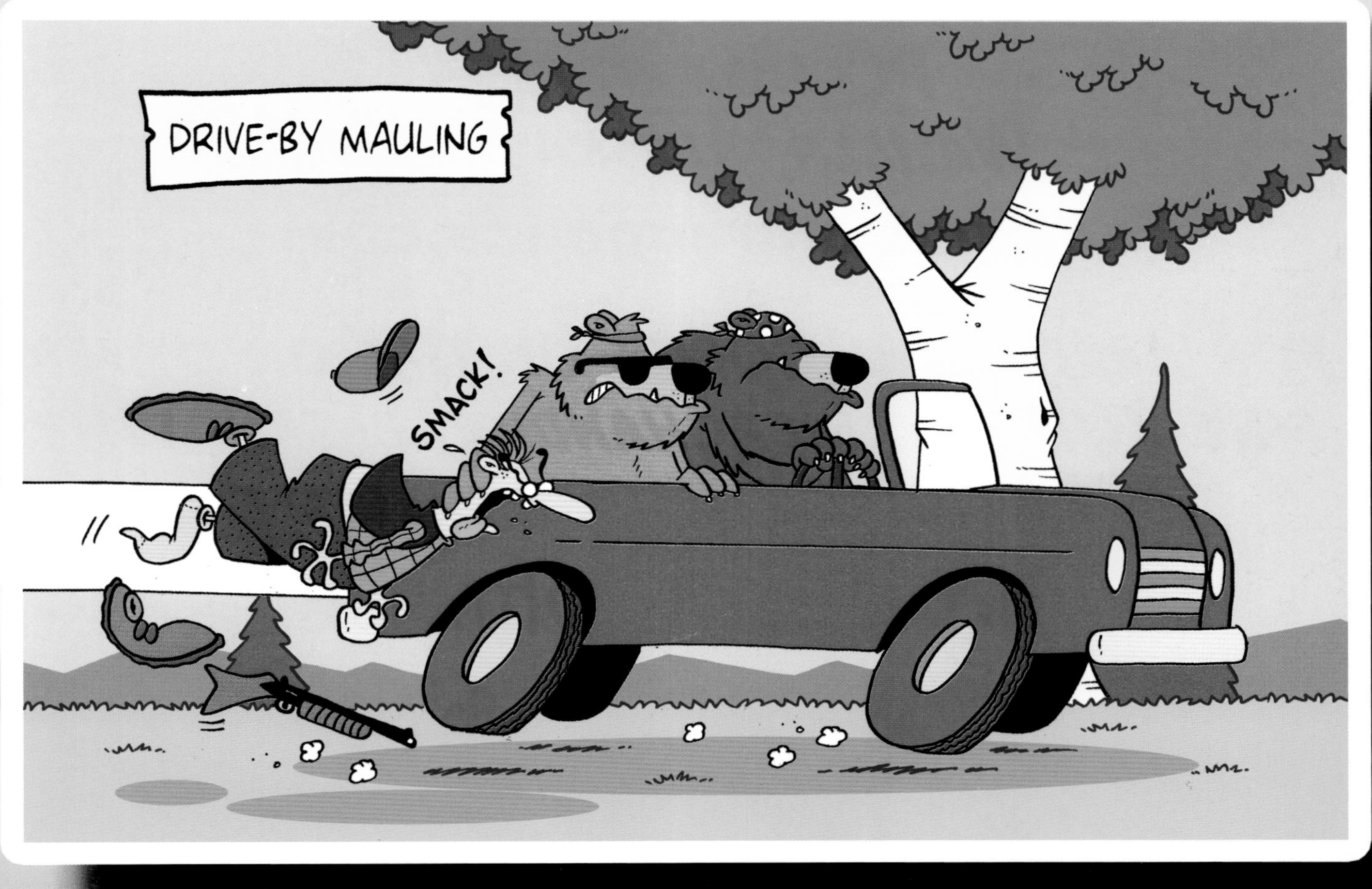
DRIVE-BY MAULING
SMACK!

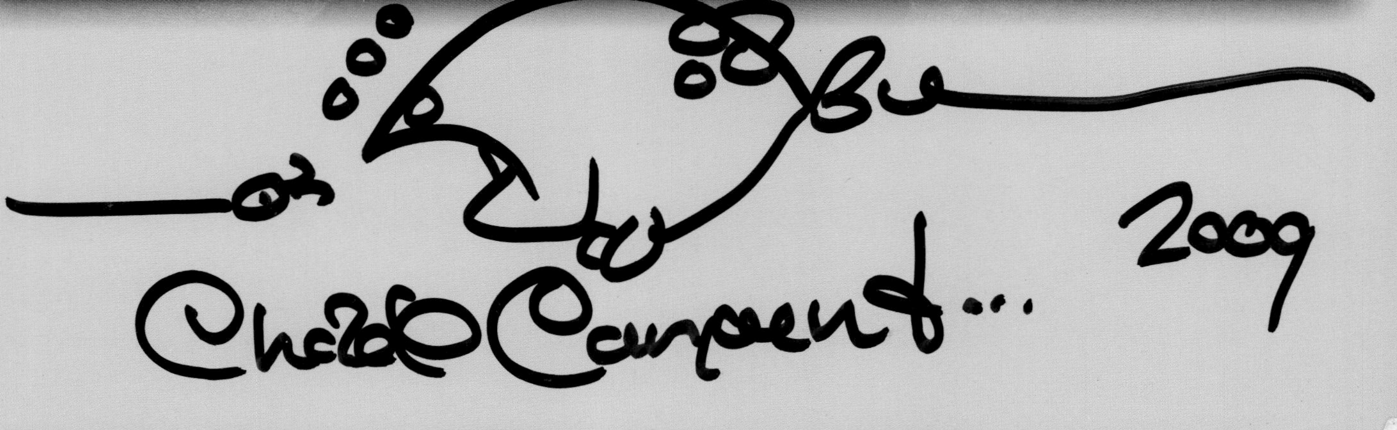
Chad Carpenter...
2009

TUNDRA

ORGANICALLY GROWN HUMOR
COPYRIGHT ©2009 BY CHAD CARPENTER
COLORED BY KAREN CARPENTER

PUBLISHED BY
TUNDRA & ASSOCIATES, INC.
PO BOX 871354
WASILLA, ALASKA 99687
info@tundracomics.com

FOR ADDITIONAL COPIES OF THIS OR OTHER FINE **TUNDRA** MERCHANDISE, PLEASE VISIT THE OFFICIAL **TUNDRA** WEBSITE AT:

www.tundracomics.com

Library of Congress Control Number: 2009901253
First Printing April 2009
ISBN: 978-0-9816291-2-4

Printed by Samhwa Printing Co., Ltd., Seoul, Korea
through **Alaska Print Brokers**

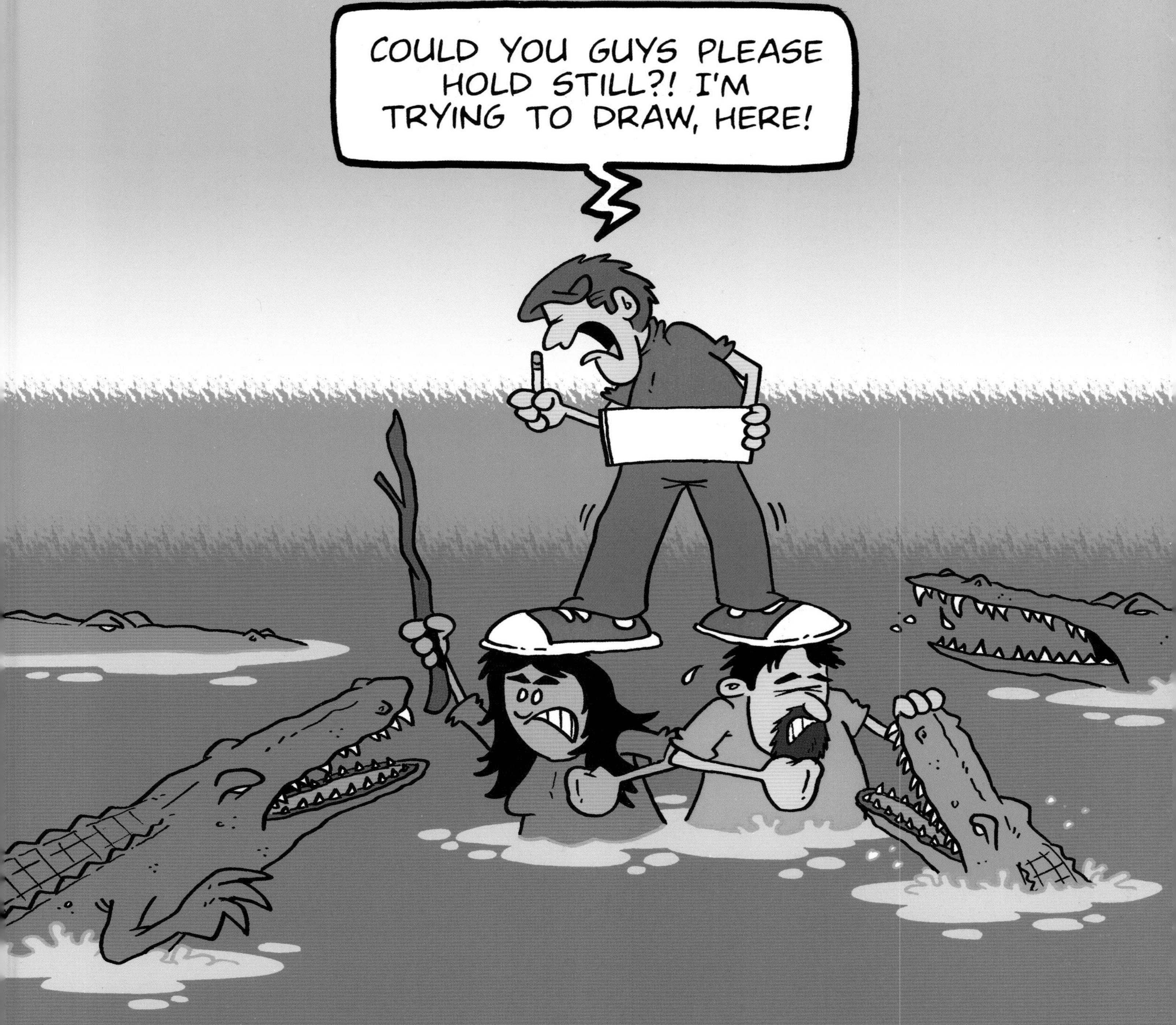
COULD YOU GUYS PLEASE HOLD STILL?! I'M TRYING TO DRAW, HERE!

I WOULD LIKE TO DEDICATE THIS BOOK TO MY BEAUTIFUL WIFE KAREN AND MY NOT-SO-BEAUTIFUL MARKETING DIRECTOR, BILL KELLOGG. IF IT WASN'T FOR THE TWO OF THEM DOING ALL THE THINGS I DON'T HAVE THE TALENT FOR, I WOULDN'T HAVE BEEN ABLE TO AVOID A REAL JOB FOR SO LONG.

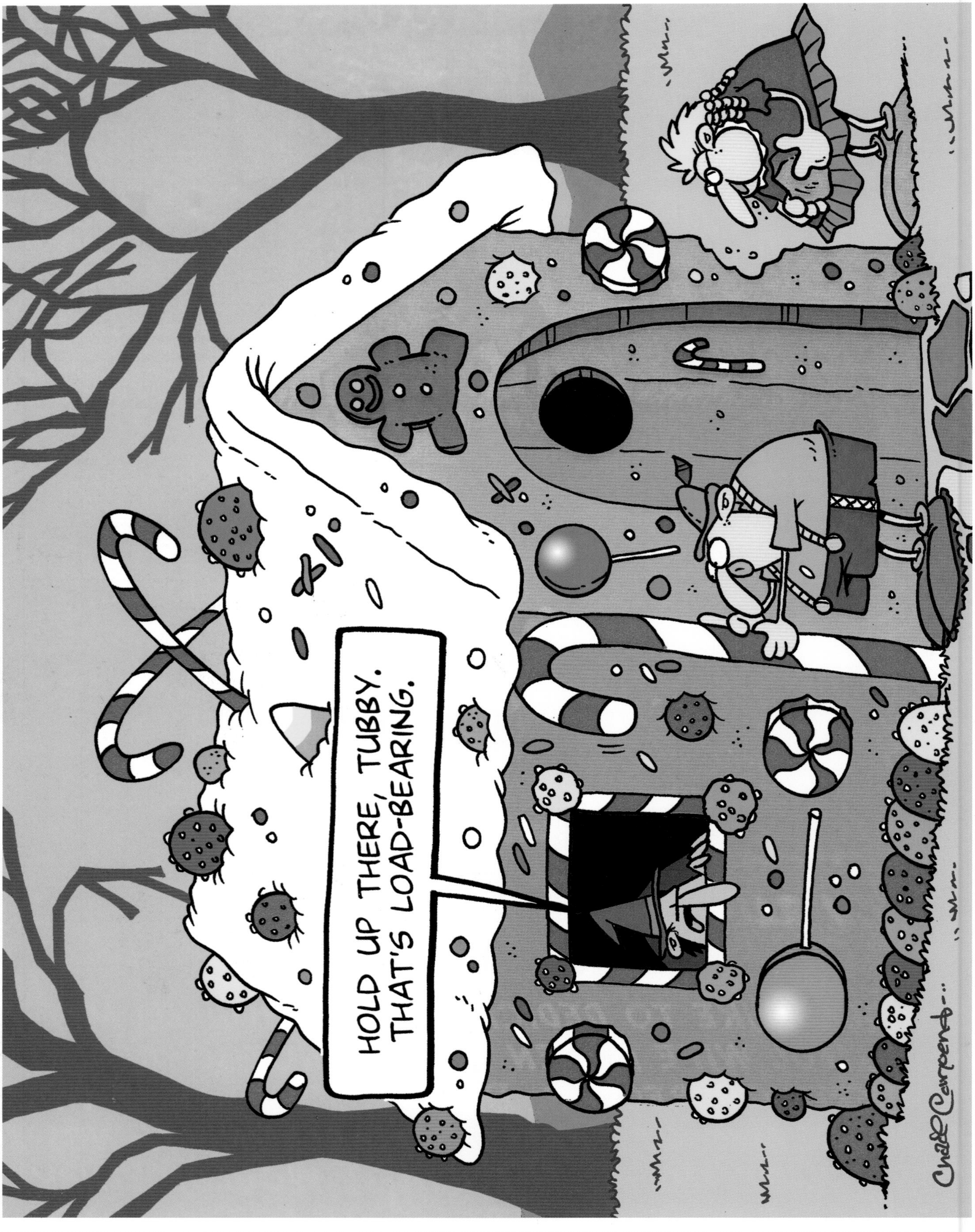
HOLD UP THERE, TUBBY.
THAT'S LOAD-BEARING.

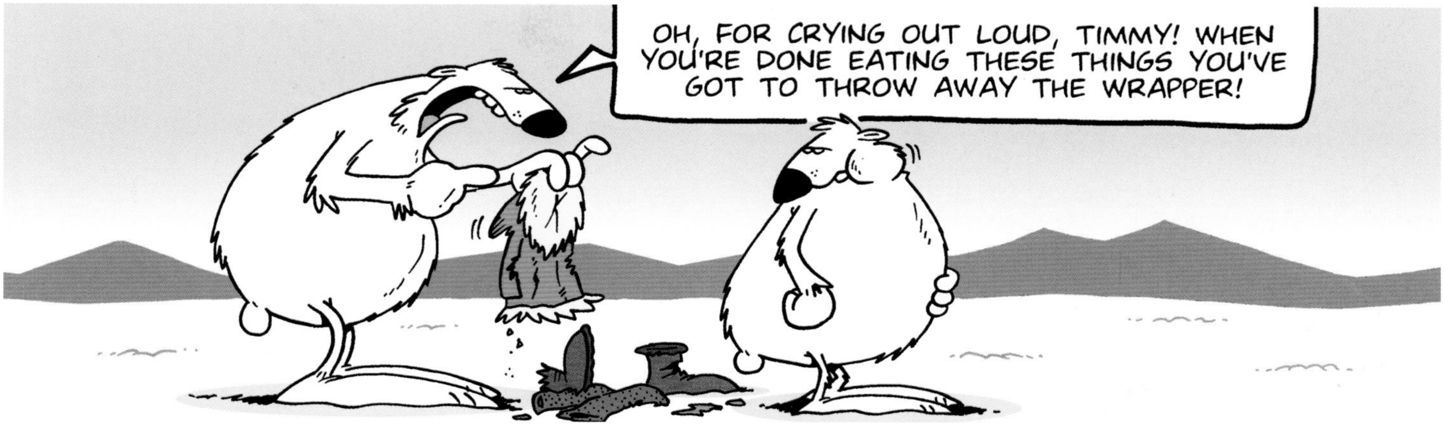
OH, FOR CRYING OUT LOUD, TIMMY! WHEN YOU'RE DONE EATING THESE THINGS YOU'VE GOT TO THROW AWAY THE WRAPPER!

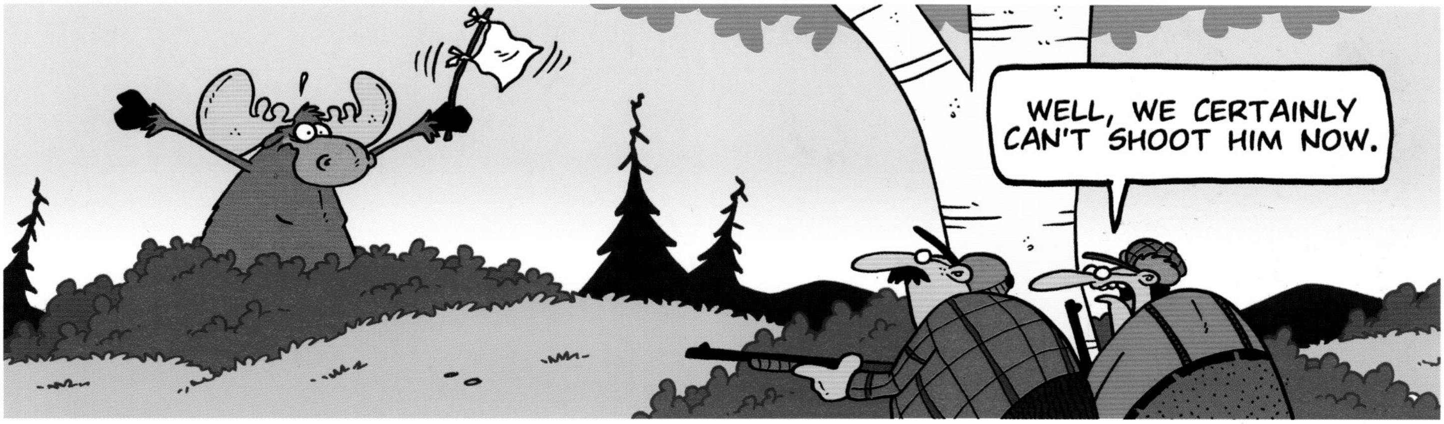
WELL, WE CERTAINLY CAN'T SHOOT HIM NOW.

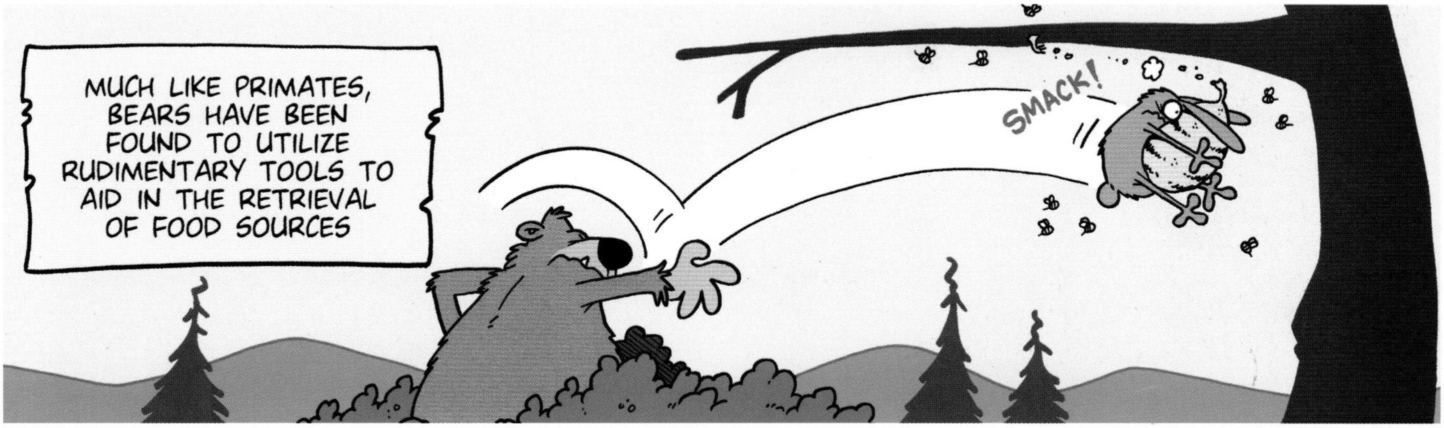
MUCH LIKE PRIMATES, BEARS HAVE BEEN FOUND TO UTILIZE RUDIMENTARY TOOLS TO AID IN THE RETRIEVAL OF FOOD SOURCES
SMACK!

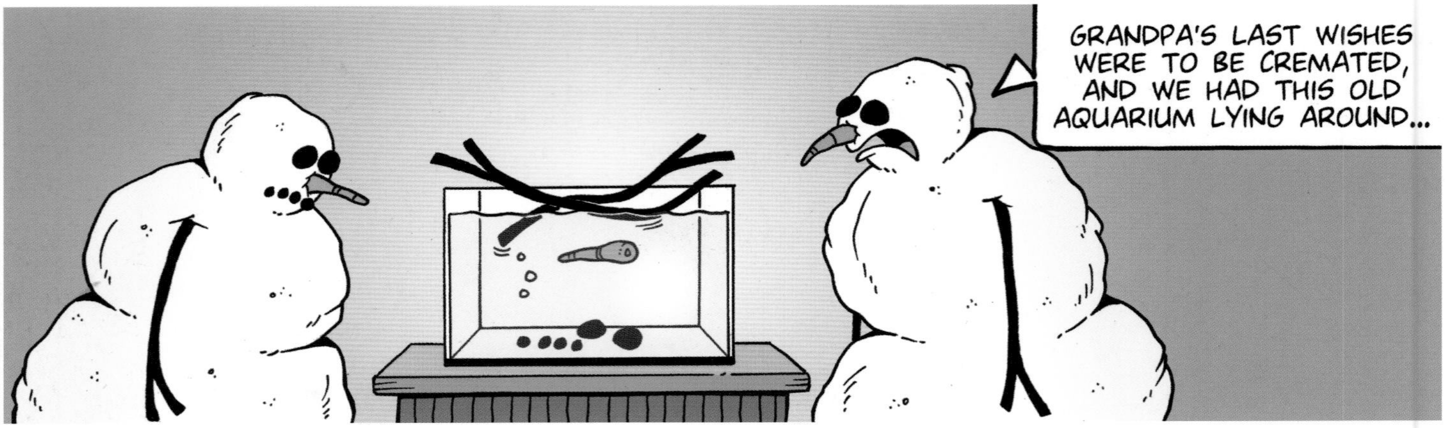
GRANDPA'S LAST WISHES WERE TO BE CREMATED, AND WE HAD THIS OLD AQUARIUM LYING AROUND...

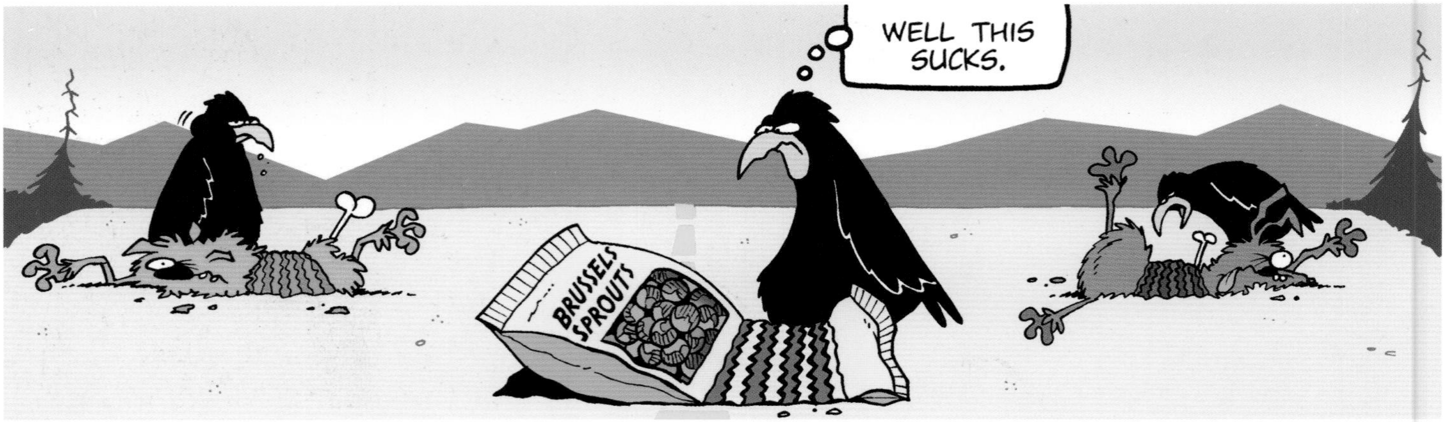
WELL THIS SUCKS.
BRUSSELS SPROUTS

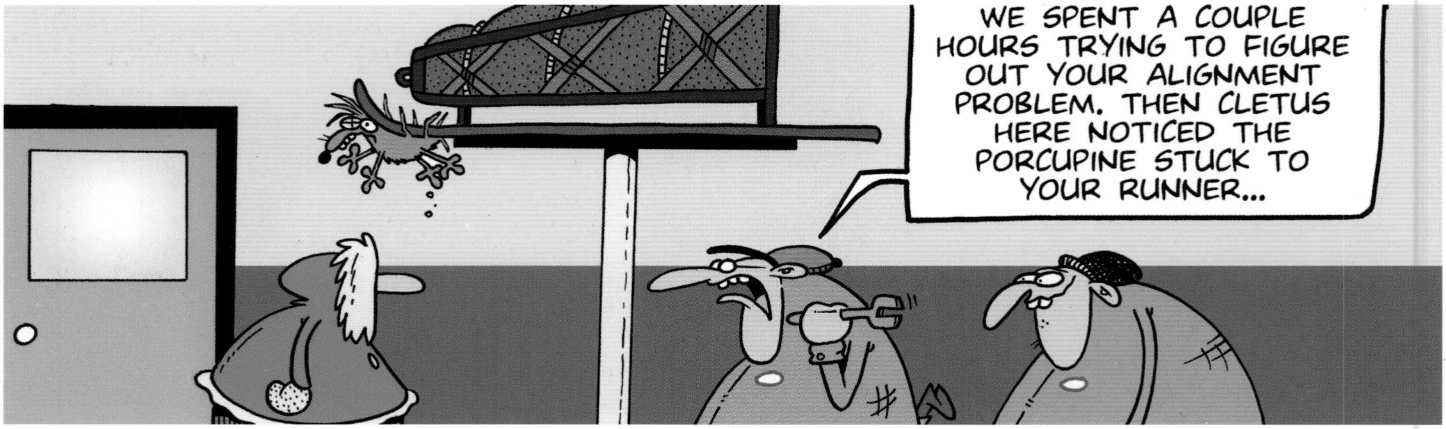
WE SPENT A COUPLE HOURS TRYING TO FIGURE OUT YOUR ALIGNMENT PROBLEM. THEN CLETUS HERE NOTICED THE PORCUPINE STUCK TO YOUR RUNNER...

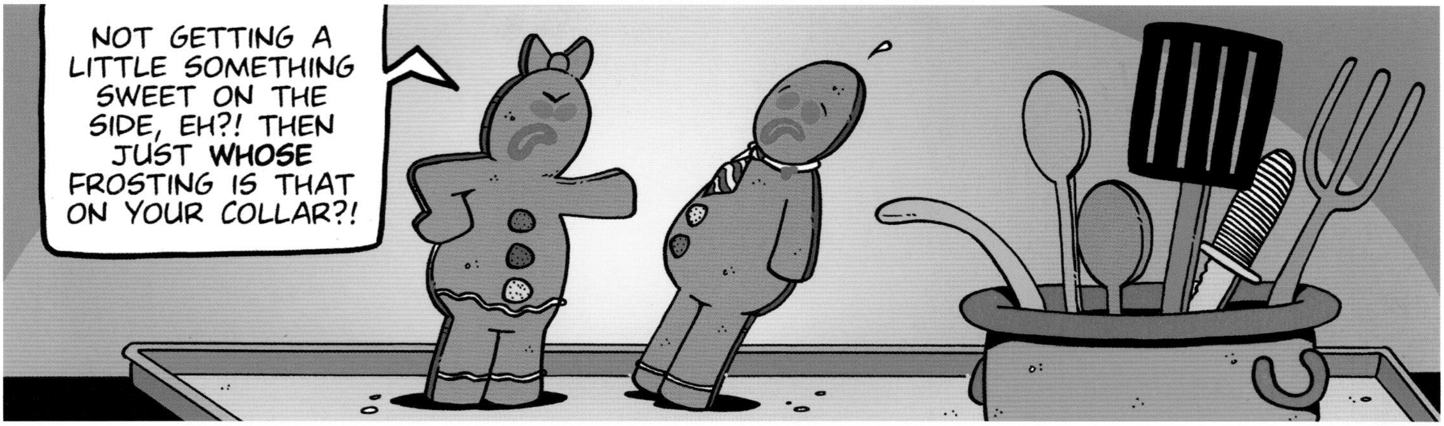
NOT GETTING A LITTLE SOMETHING SWEET ON THE SIDE, EH?! THEN JUST **WHOSE** FROSTING IS THAT ON YOUR COLLAR?!

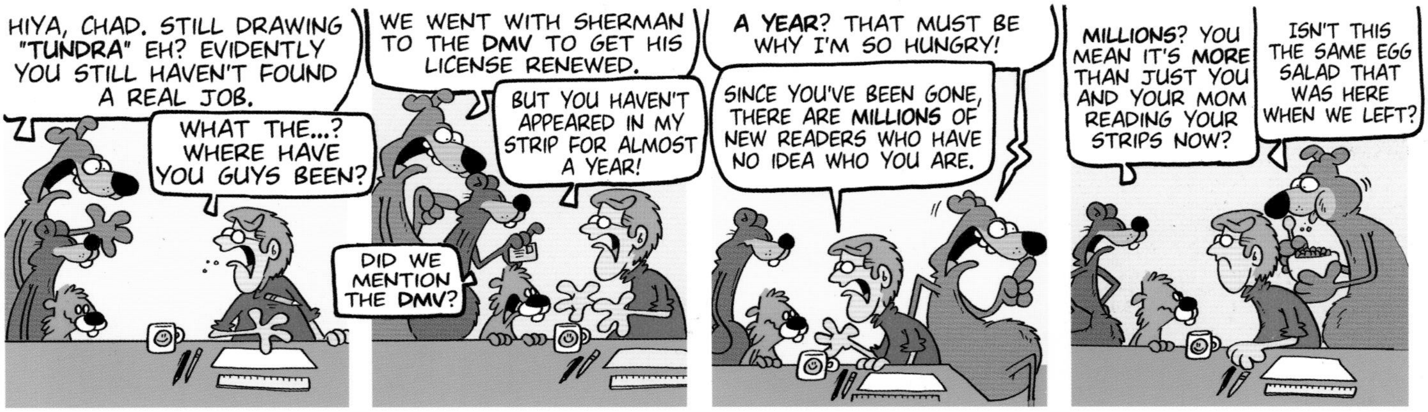
HIYA, CHAD. STILL DRAWING "**TUNDRA**" EH? EVIDENTLY YOU STILL HAVEN'T FOUND A REAL JOB.
WHAT THE...? WHERE HAVE YOU GUYS BEEN?
WE WENT WITH SHERMAN TO THE **DMV** TO GET HIS LICENSE RENEWED.
BUT YOU HAVEN'T APPEARED IN MY STRIP FOR ALMOST A YEAR!
DID WE MENTION THE **DMV**?
A YEAR? THAT MUST BE WHY I'M SO HUNGRY!
SINCE YOU'VE BEEN GONE, THERE ARE **MILLIONS** OF NEW READERS WHO HAVE NO IDEA WHO YOU ARE.
MILLIONS? YOU MEAN IT'S **MORE** THAN JUST YOU AND YOUR MOM READING YOUR STRIPS NOW?
ISN'T THIS THE SAME EGG SALAD THAT WAS HERE WHEN WE LEFT?

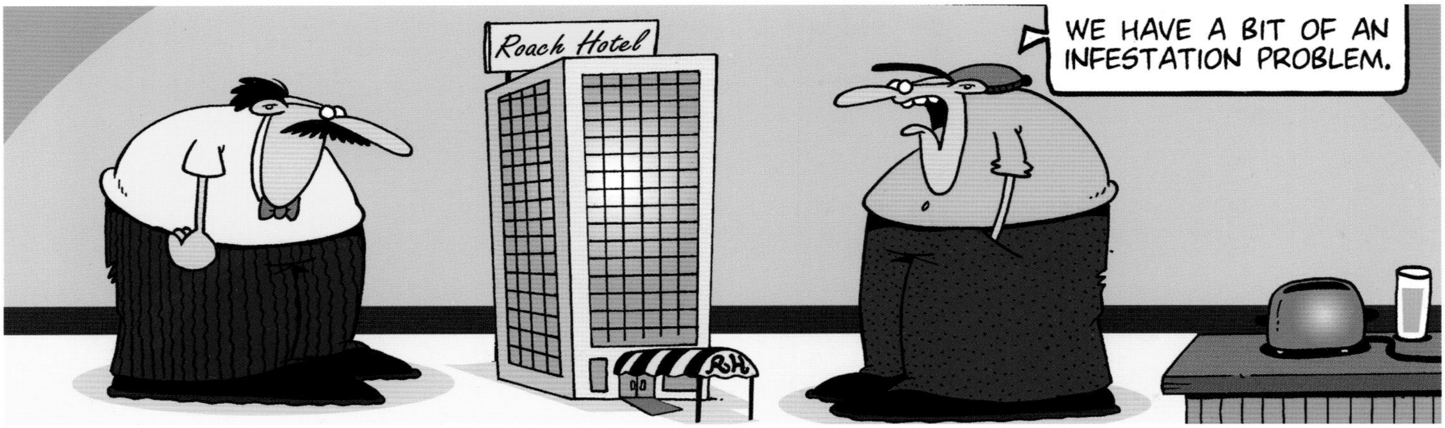
Roach Hotel
WE HAVE A BIT OF AN INFESTATION PROBLEM.
RH

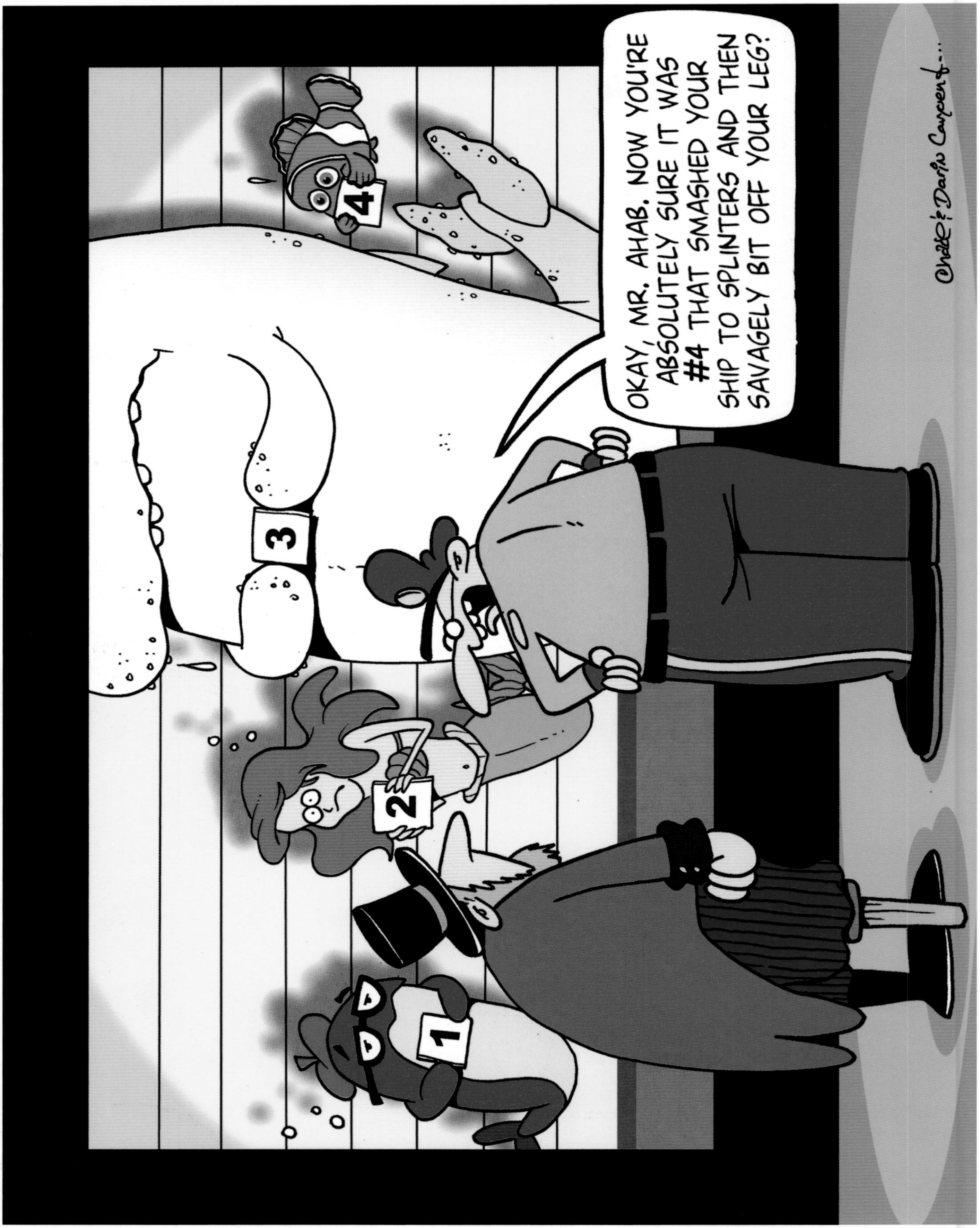
OKAY, MR. AHAB. NOW YOU'RE ABSOLUTELY SURE IT WAS #4 THAT SMASHED YOUR SHIP TO SPLINTERS AND THEN SAVAGELY BIT OFF YOUR LEG?

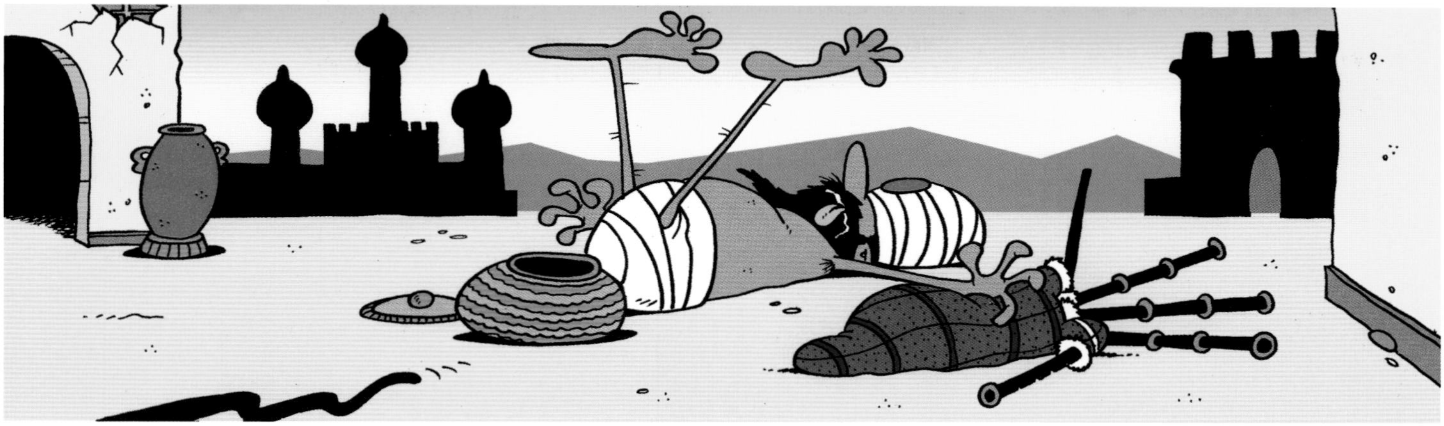

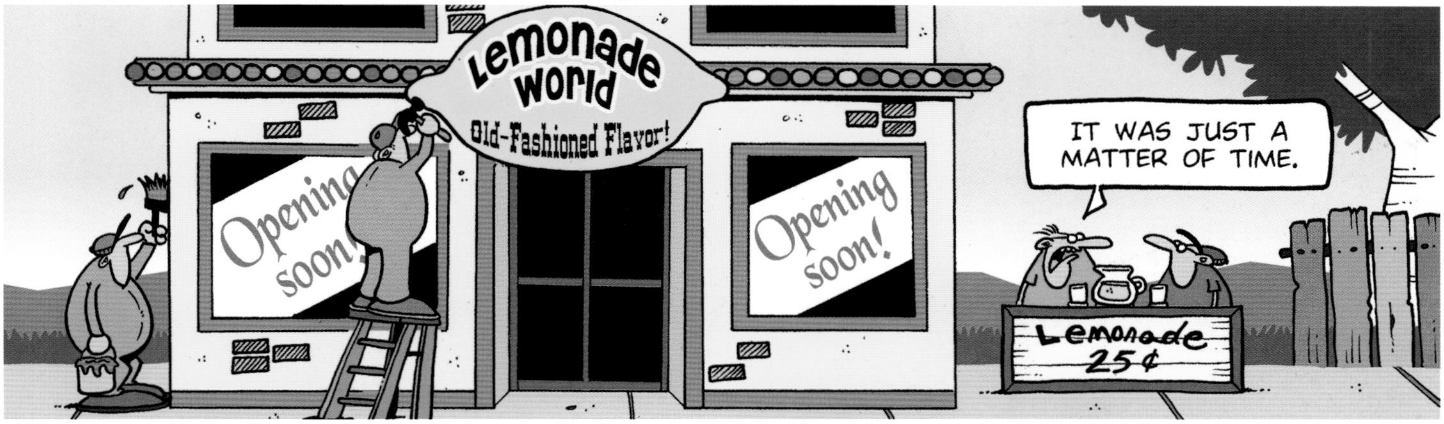
Lemonade World
Old-Fashioned Flavor!
Opening soon!
Opening soon!
IT WAS JUST A MATTER OF TIME.
Lemonade 25¢

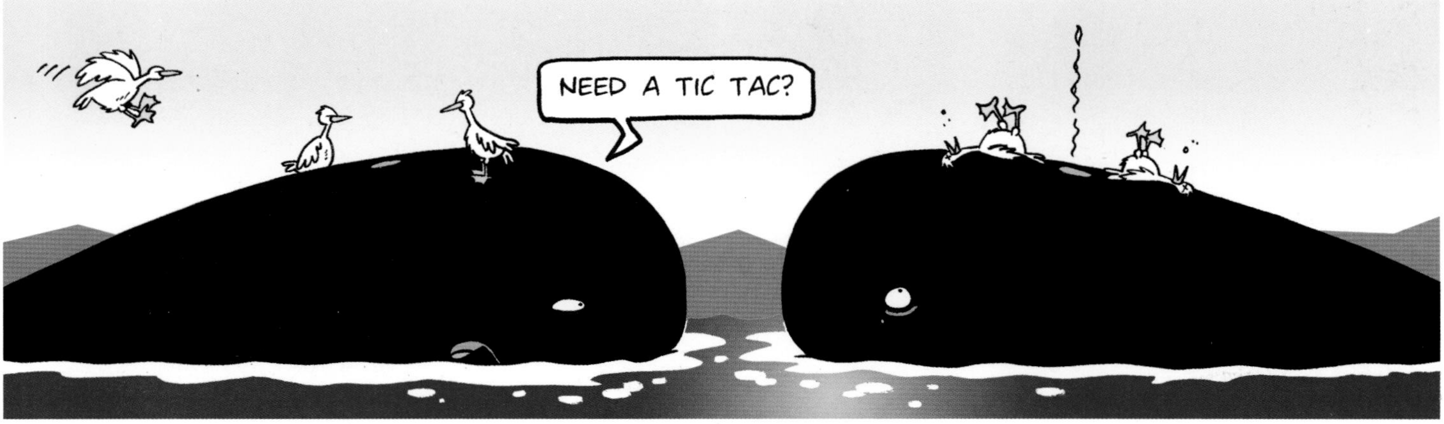
NEED A TIC TAC?

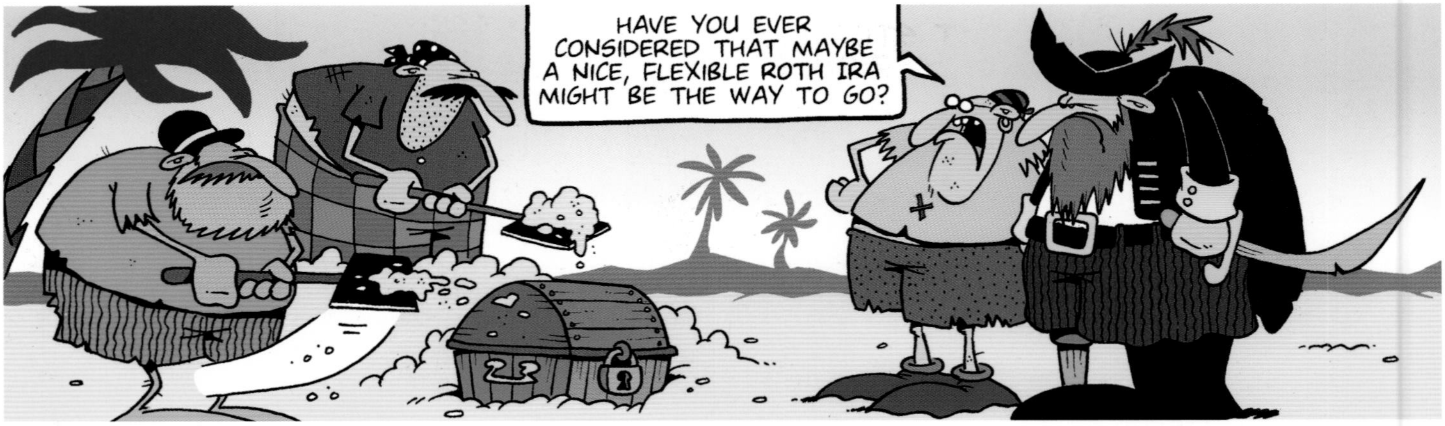
HAVE YOU EVER CONSIDERED THAT MAYBE A NICE, FLEXIBLE ROTH IRA MIGHT BE THE WAY TO GO?

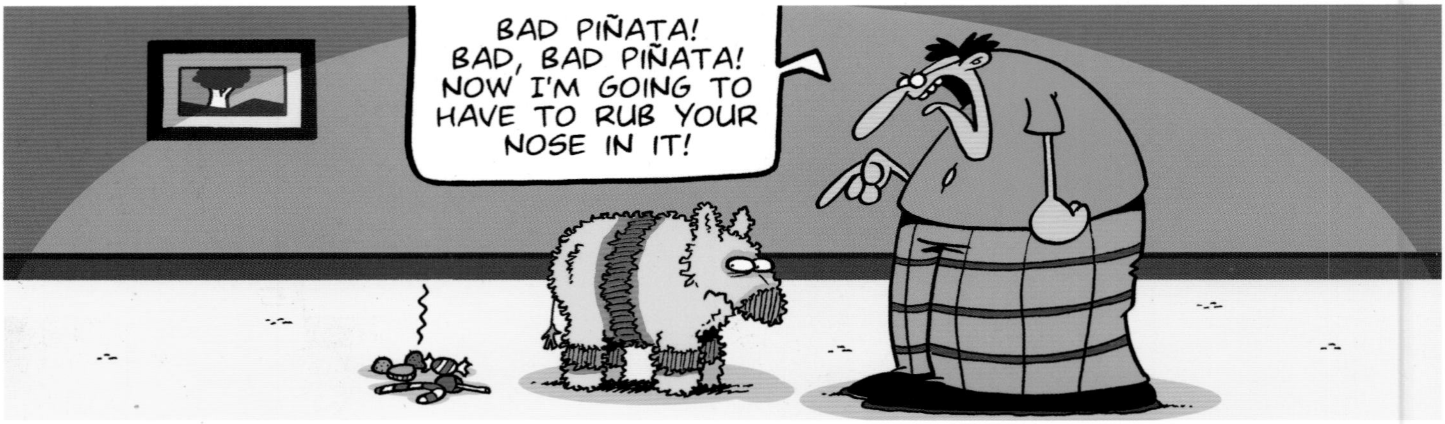
BAD PIÑATA! BAD, BAD PIÑATA! NOW I'M GOING TO HAVE TO RUB YOUR NOSE IN IT!

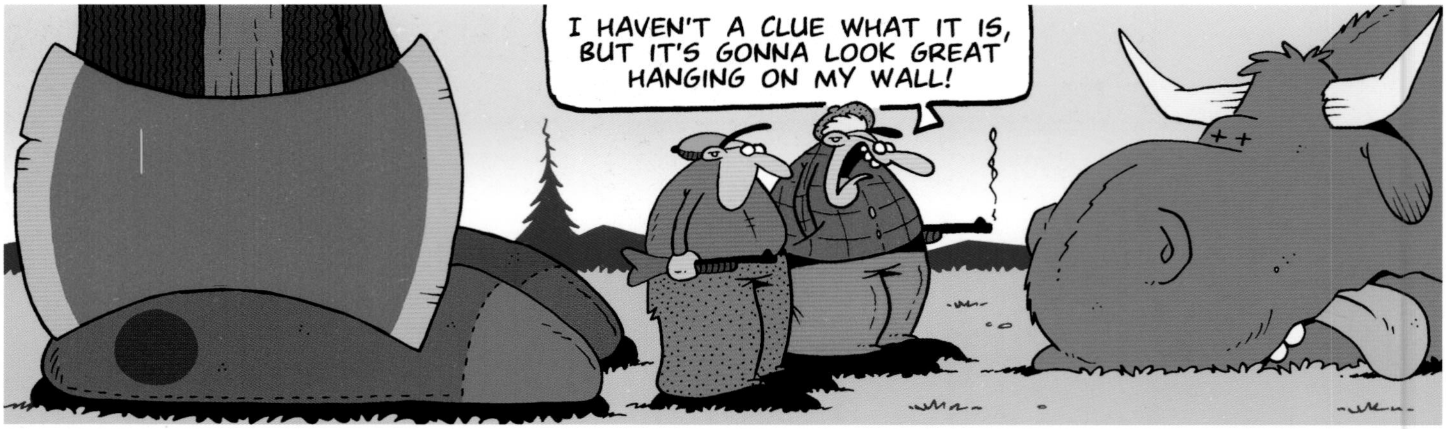
I HAVEN'T A CLUE WHAT IT IS, BUT IT'S GONNA LOOK GREAT HANGING ON MY WALL!

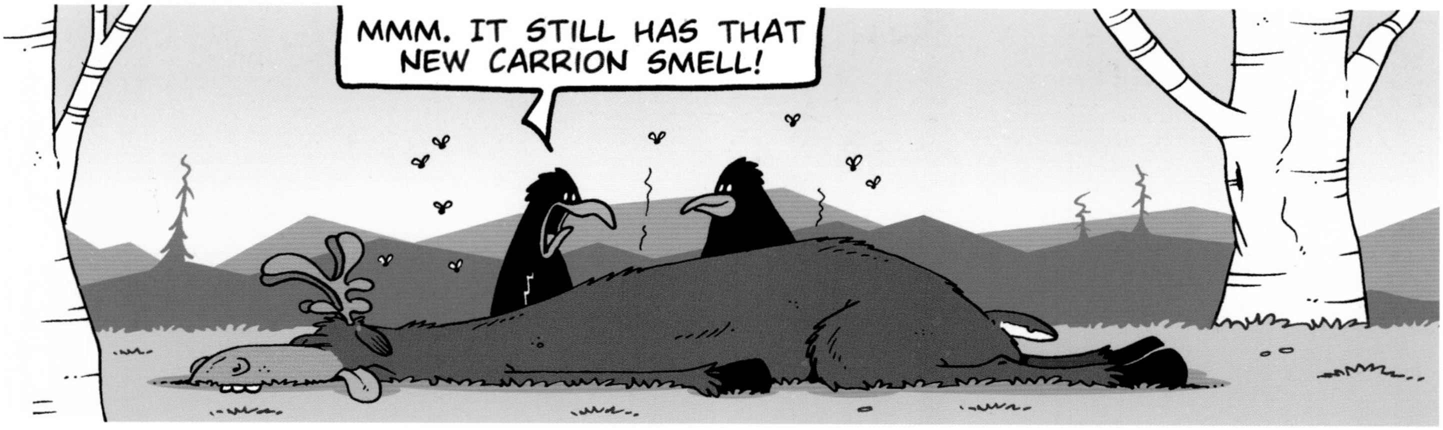
MMM. IT STILL HAS THAT NEW CARRION SMELL!

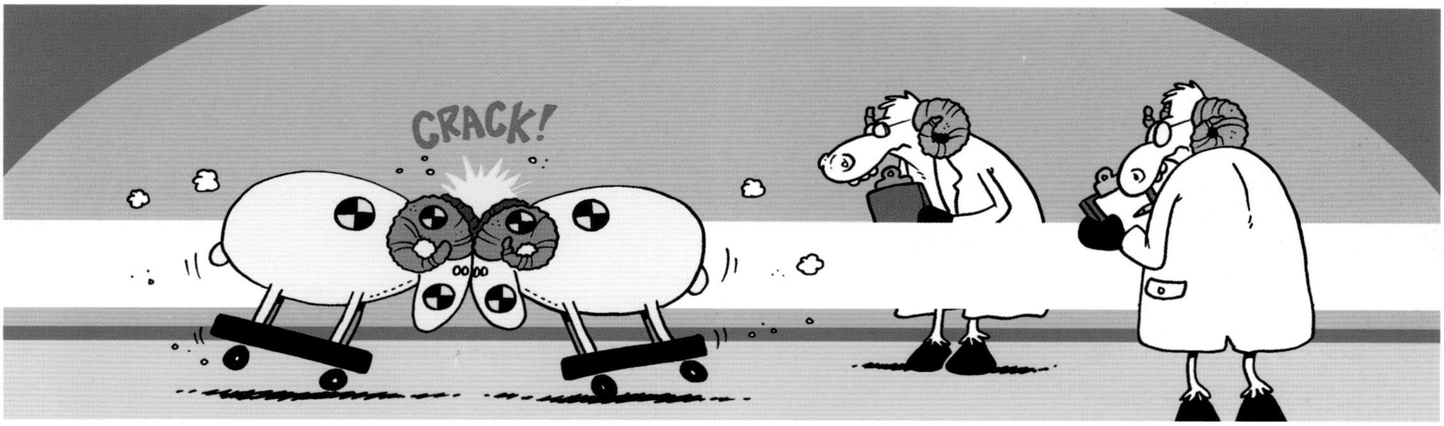
CRACK!

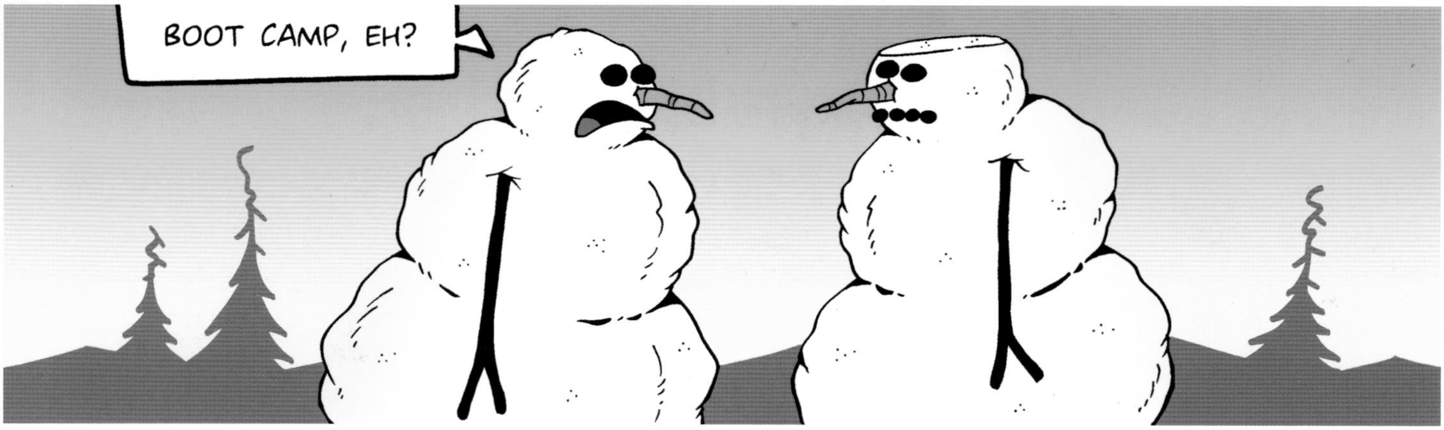
BOOT CAMP, EH?

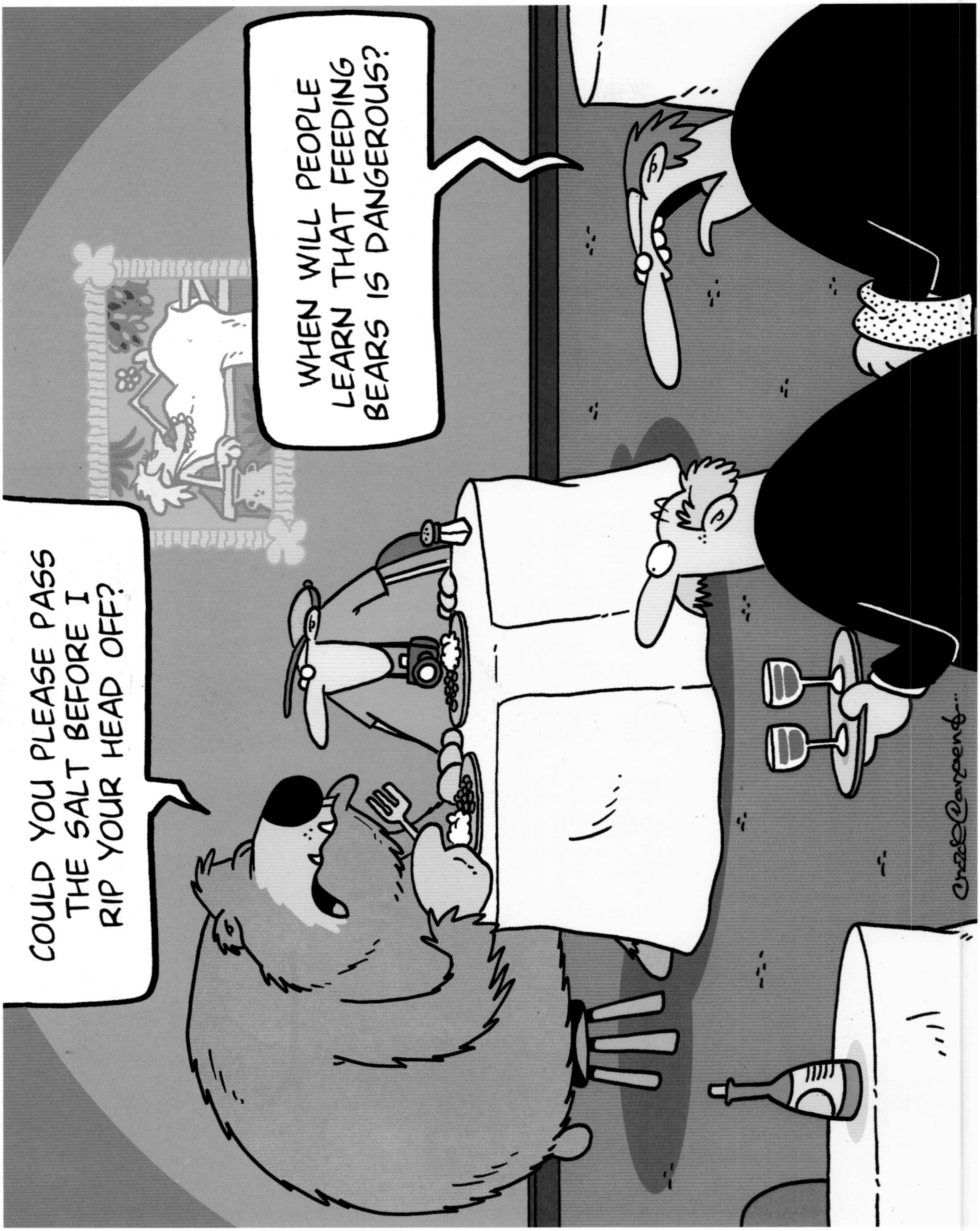
COULD YOU PLEASE PASS THE SALT BEFORE I RIP YOUR HEAD OFF?
WHEN WILL PEOPLE LEARN THAT FEEDING BEARS IS DANGEROUS?

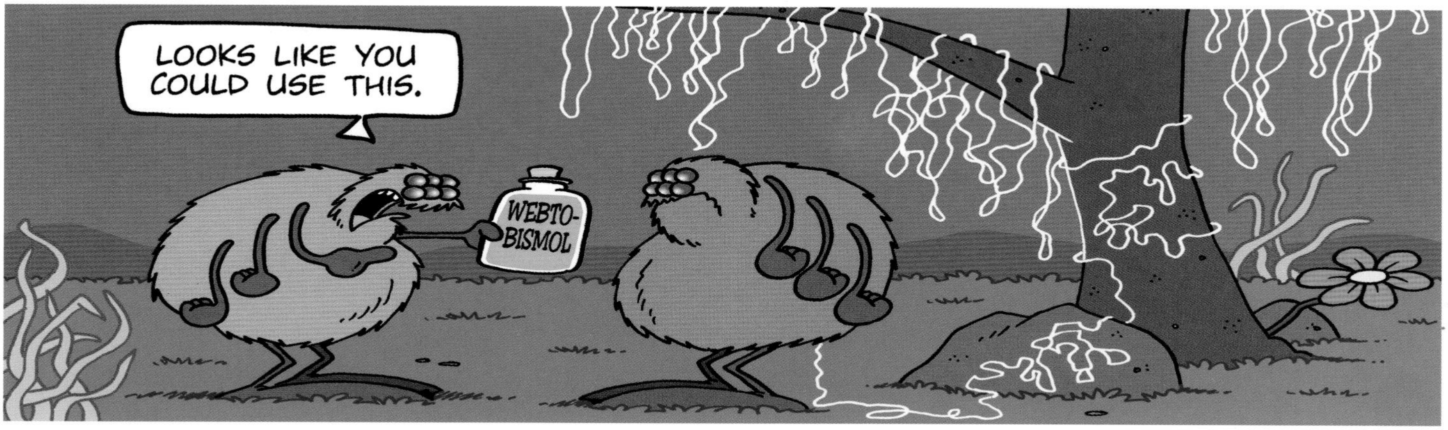
LOOKS LIKE YOU COULD USE THIS.
WEBTO-BISMOL

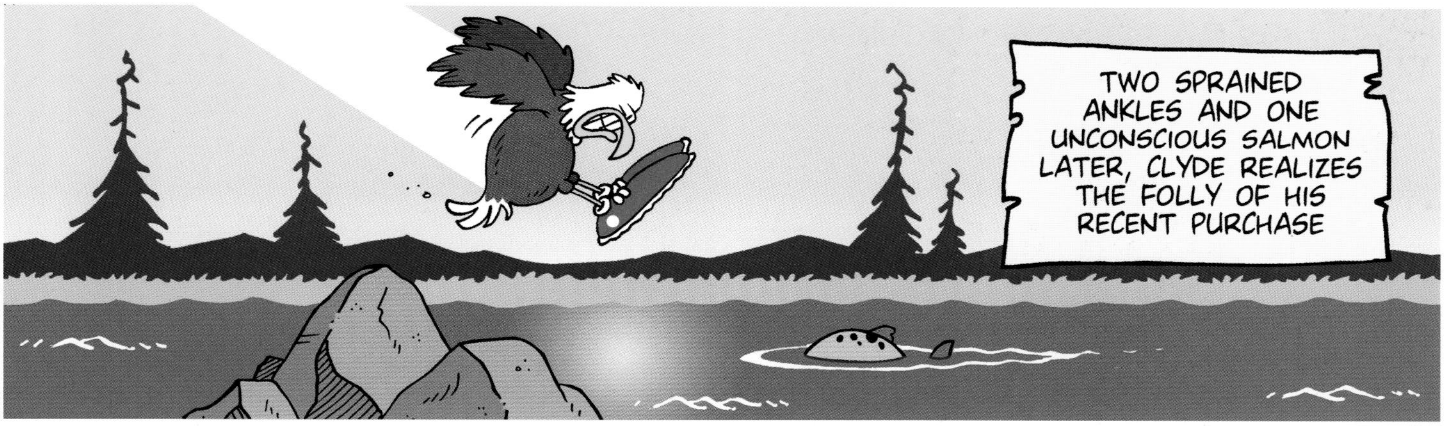
TWO SPRAINED ANKLES AND ONE UNCONSCIOUS SALMON LATER, CLYDE REALIZES THE FOLLY OF HIS RECENT PURCHASE

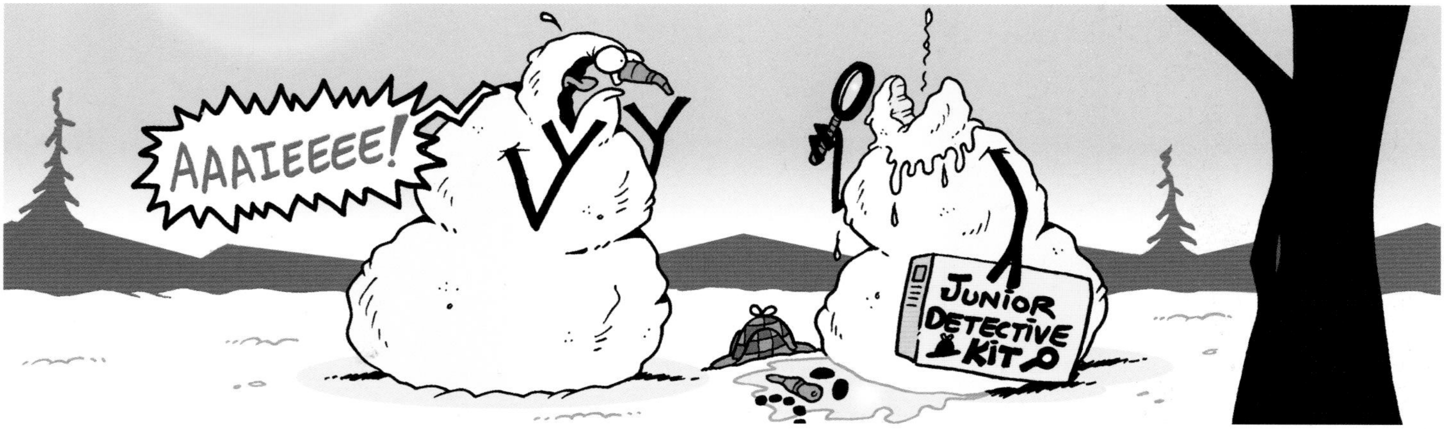
AAAIEEEE!
JUNIOR DETECTIVE KIT

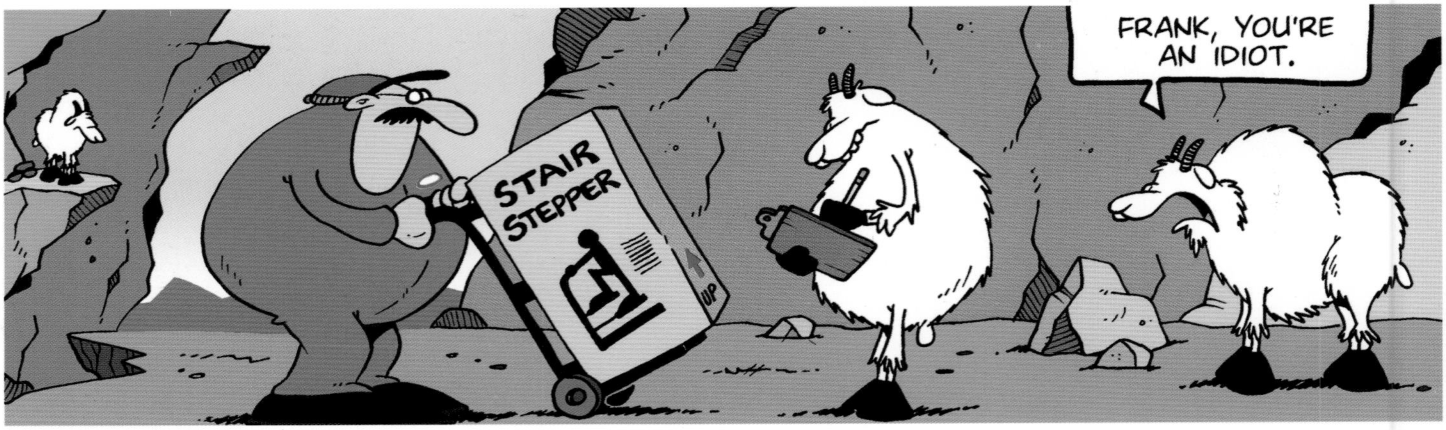
STAIR STEPPER
UP
FRANK, YOU'RE AN IDIOT.

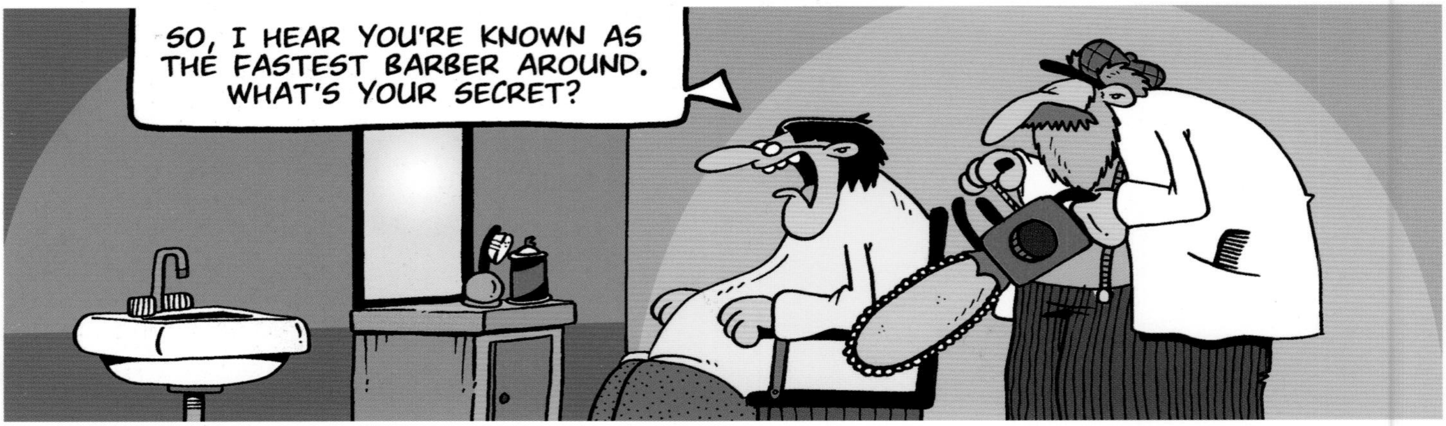
SO, I HEAR YOU'RE KNOWN AS THE FASTEST BARBER AROUND. WHAT'S YOUR SECRET?

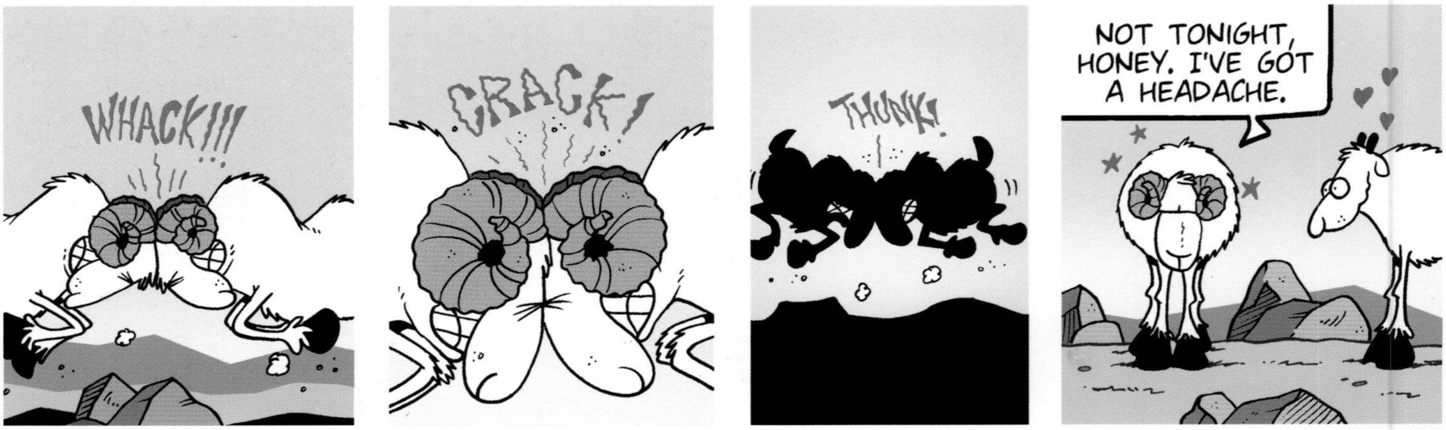
WHACK!!!
CRACK!
THUNK!
NOT TONIGHT, HONEY. I'VE GOT A HEADACHE.

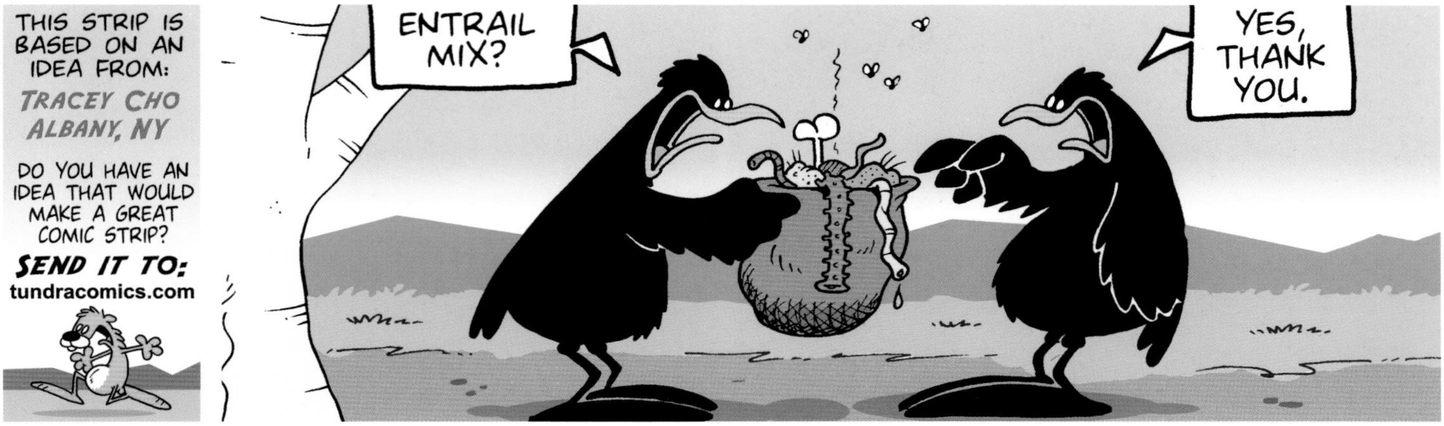
THIS STRIP IS BASED ON AN IDEA FROM:
TRACEY CHO
ALBANY, NY
DO YOU HAVE AN IDEA THAT WOULD MAKE A GREAT COMIC STRIP?
SEND IT TO:
tundracomics.com
ENTRAIL MIX?
YES, THANK YOU.

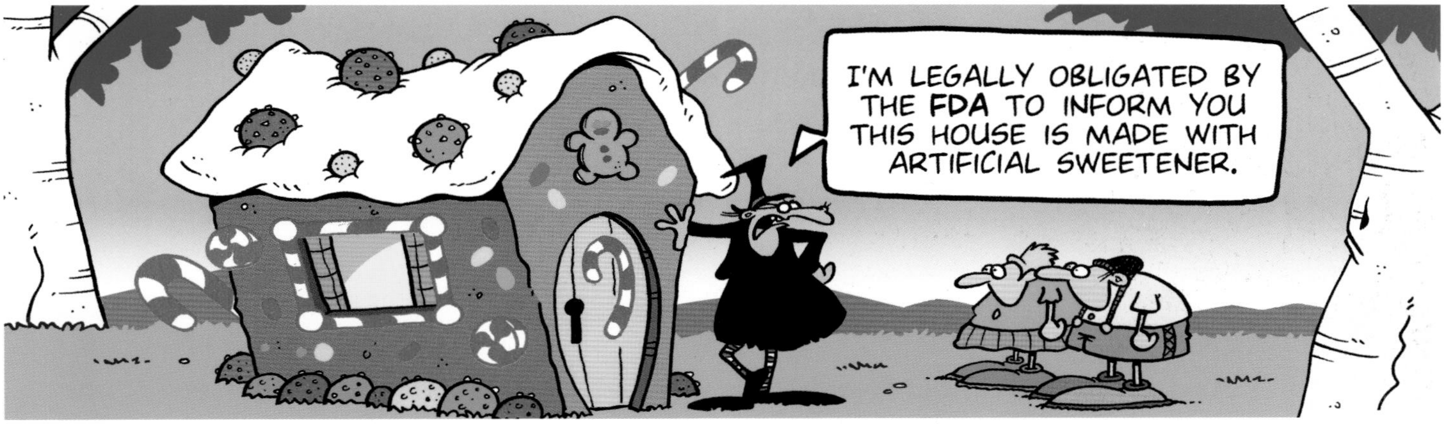
I'M LEGALLY OBLIGATED BY THE FDA TO INFORM YOU THIS HOUSE IS MADE WITH ARTIFICIAL SWEETENER.

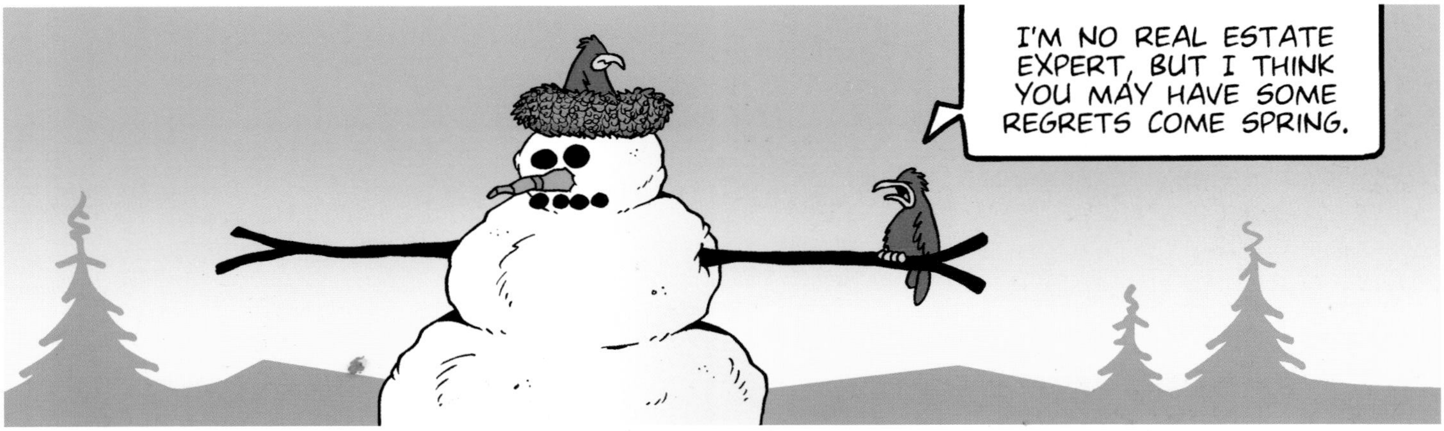
I'M NO REAL ESTATE EXPERT, BUT I THINK YOU MAY HAVE SOME REGRETS COME SPRING.

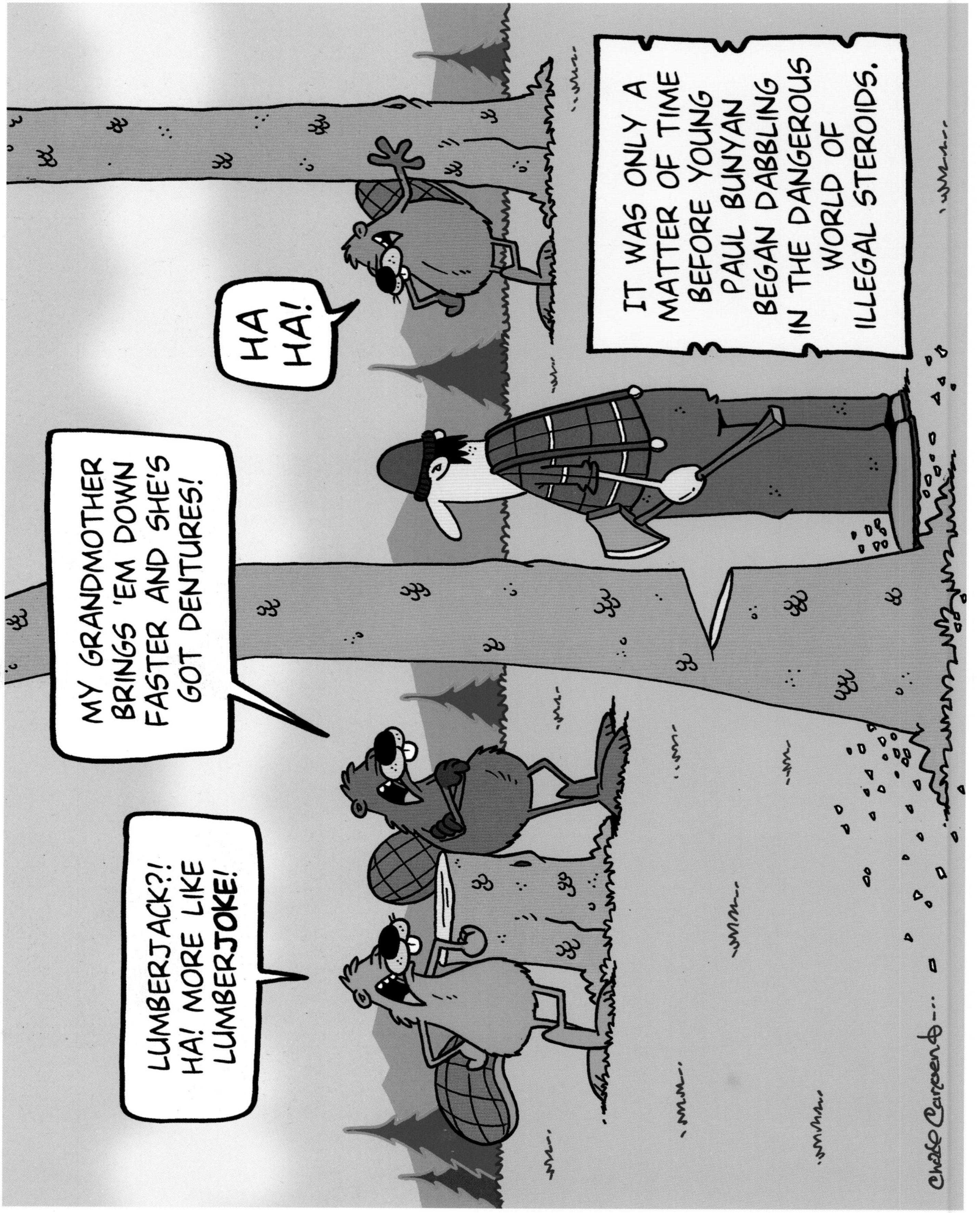
LUMBERJACK?! HA! MORE LIKE LUMBERJOKE!
MY GRANDMOTHER BRINGS 'EM DOWN FASTER AND SHE'S GOT DENTURES!
HA HA!
IT WAS ONLY A MATTER OF TIME BEFORE YOUNG PAUL BUNYAN BEGAN DABBLING IN THE DANGEROUS WORLD OF ILLEGAL STEROIDS.
Chad Carpenter

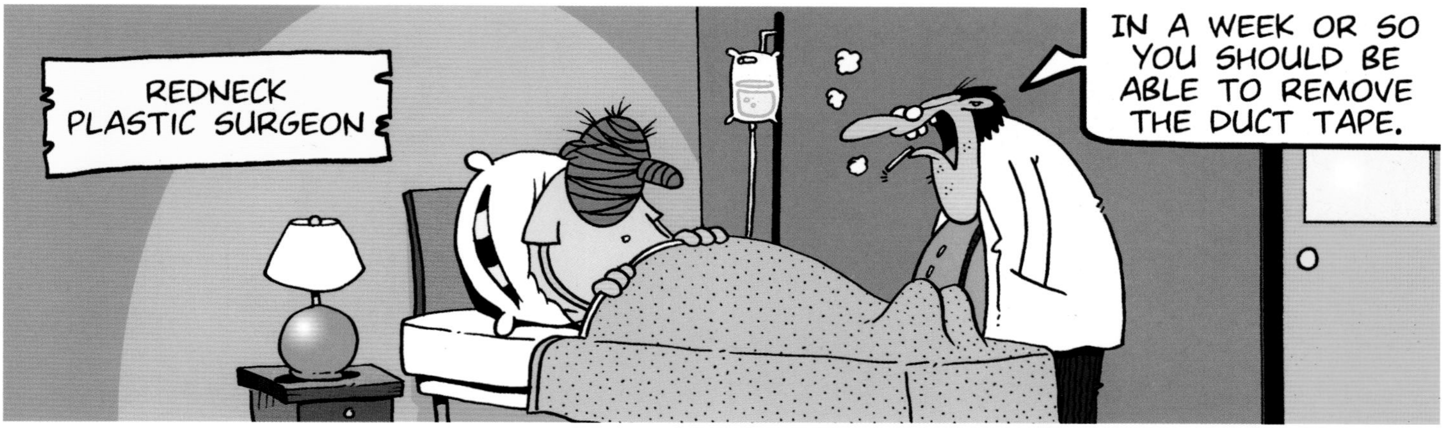
REDNECK PLASTIC SURGEON
IN A WEEK OR SO YOU SHOULD BE ABLE TO REMOVE THE DUCT TAPE.

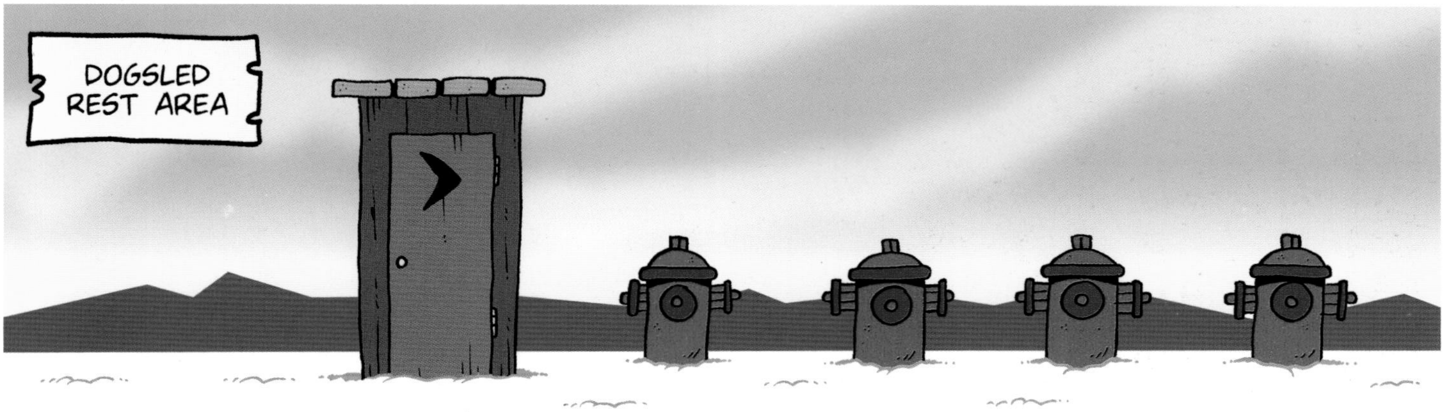
DOGSLED REST AREA

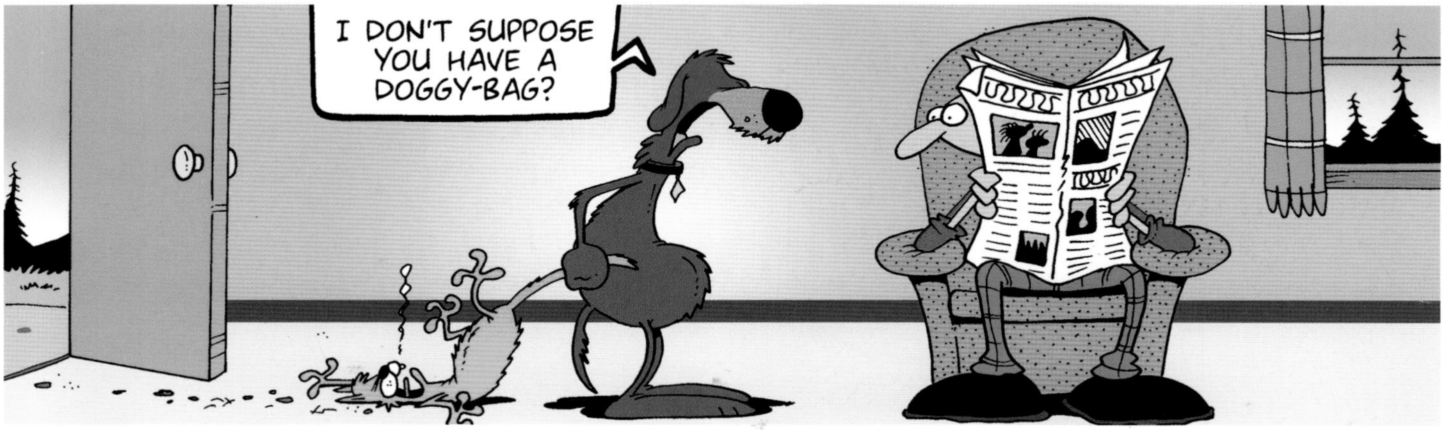
I DON'T SUPPOSE YOU HAVE A DOGGY-BAG?

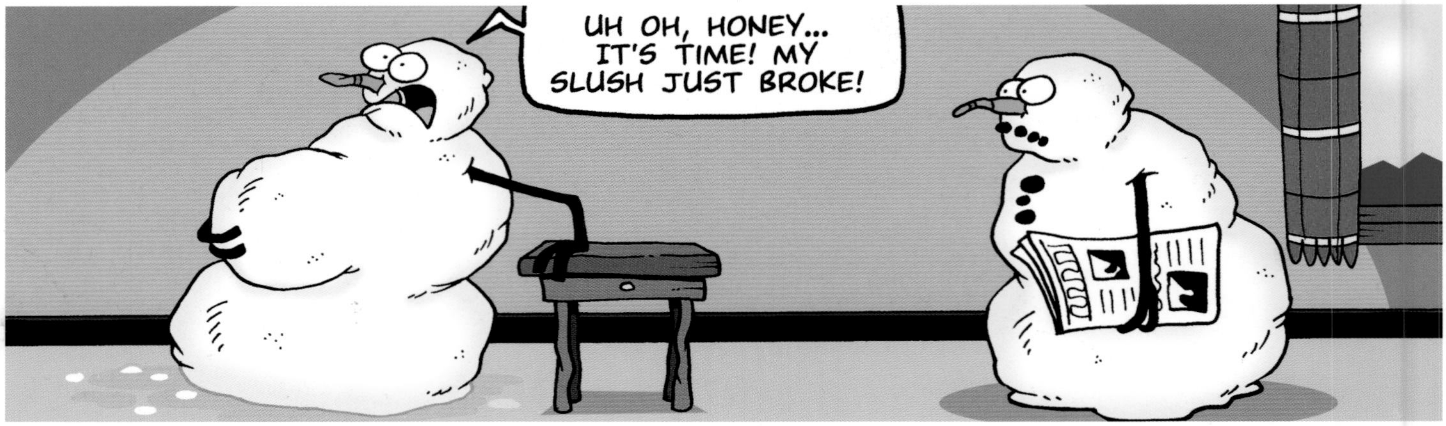
UH OH, HONEY...
IT'S TIME! MY
SLUSH JUST BROKE!

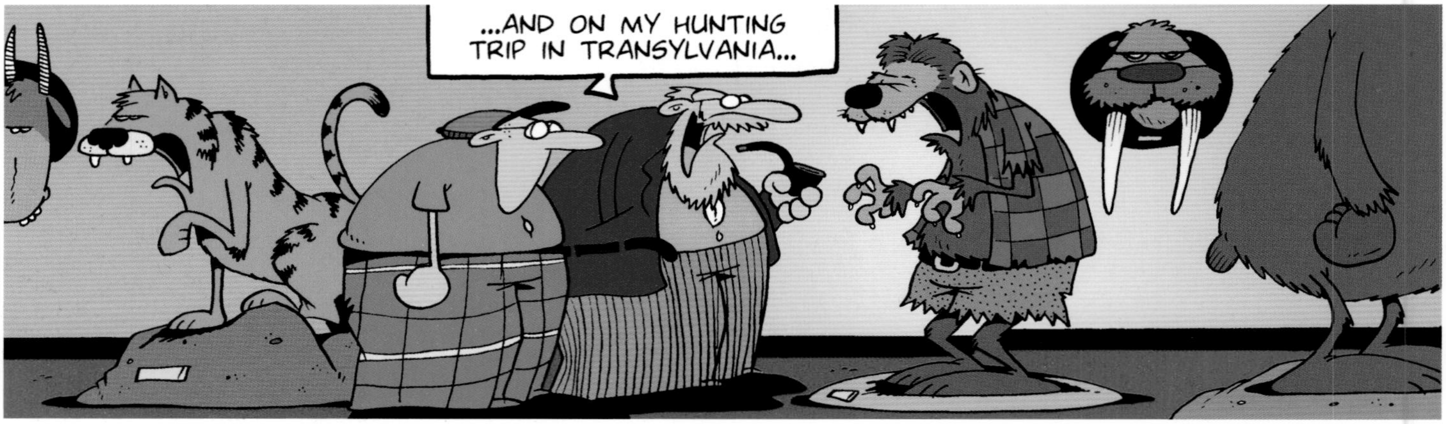
...AND ON MY HUNTING
TRIP IN TRANSYLVANIA...

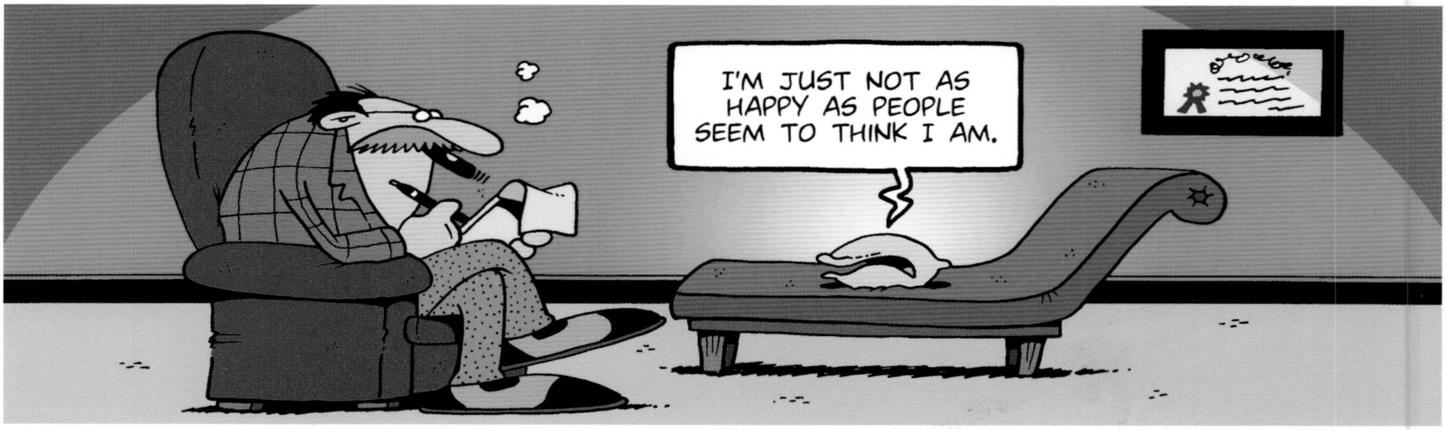
I'M JUST NOT AS
HAPPY AS PEOPLE
SEEM TO THINK I AM.

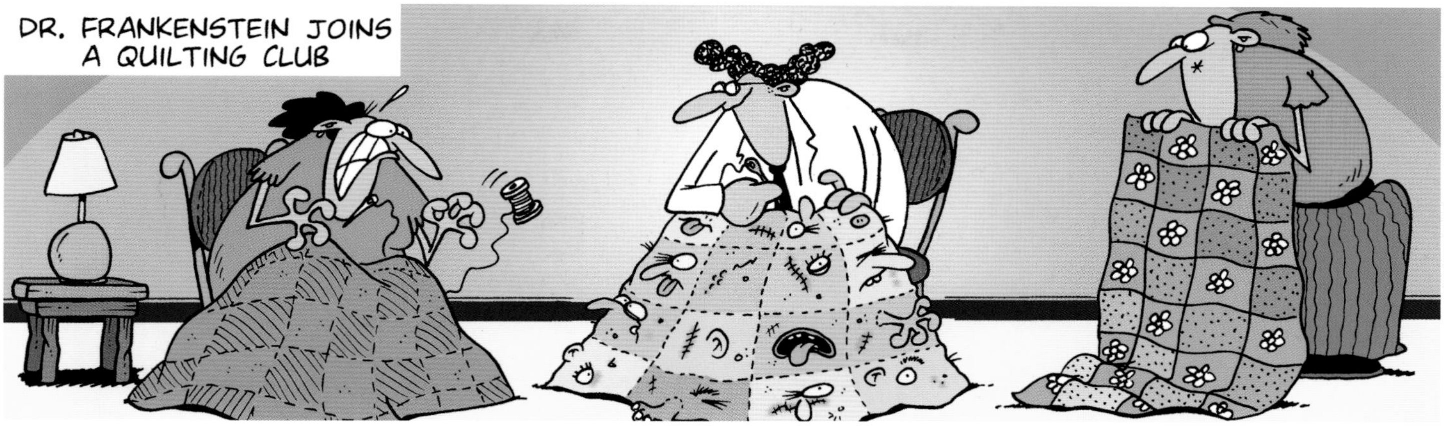
DR. FRANKENSTEIN JOINS A QUILTING CLUB

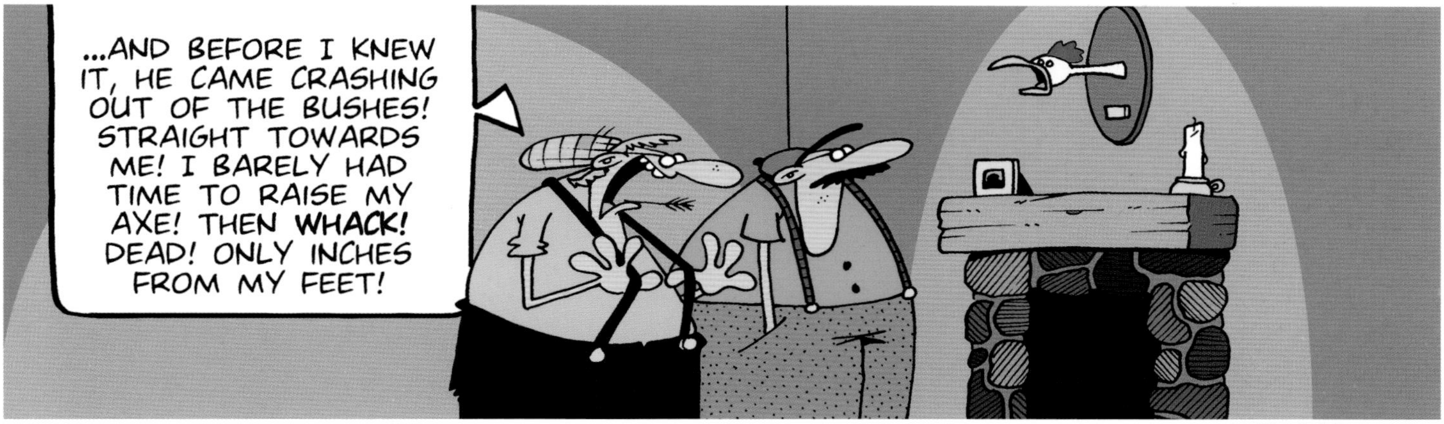
...AND BEFORE I KNEW IT, HE CAME CRASHING OUT OF THE BUSHES! STRAIGHT TOWARDS ME! I BARELY HAD TIME TO RAISE MY AXE! THEN **WHACK!** DEAD! ONLY INCHES FROM MY FEET!

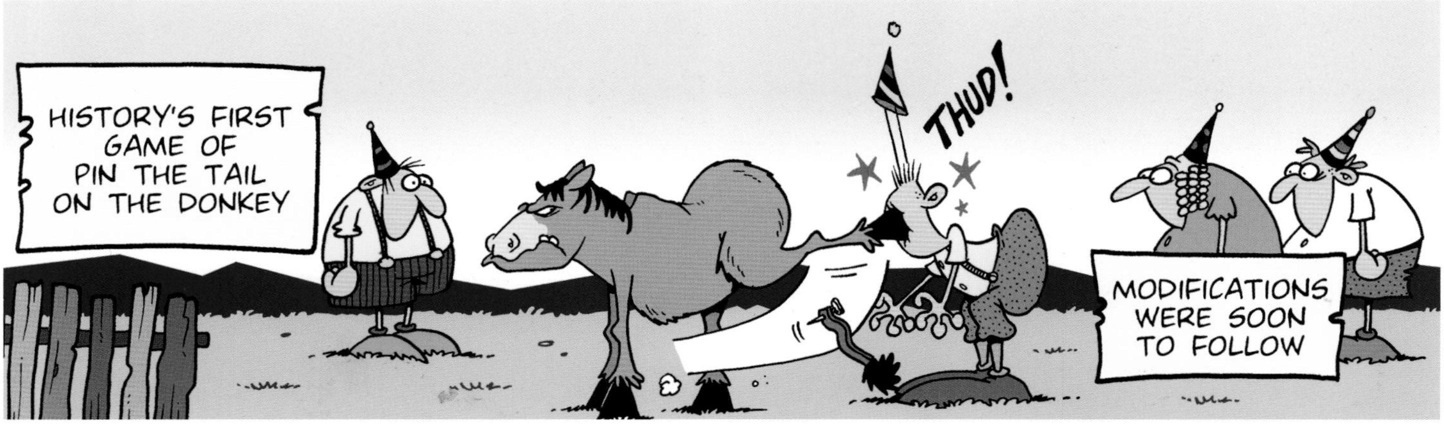
HISTORY'S FIRST GAME OF PIN THE TAIL ON THE DONKEY
THUD!
MODIFICATIONS WERE SOON TO FOLLOW

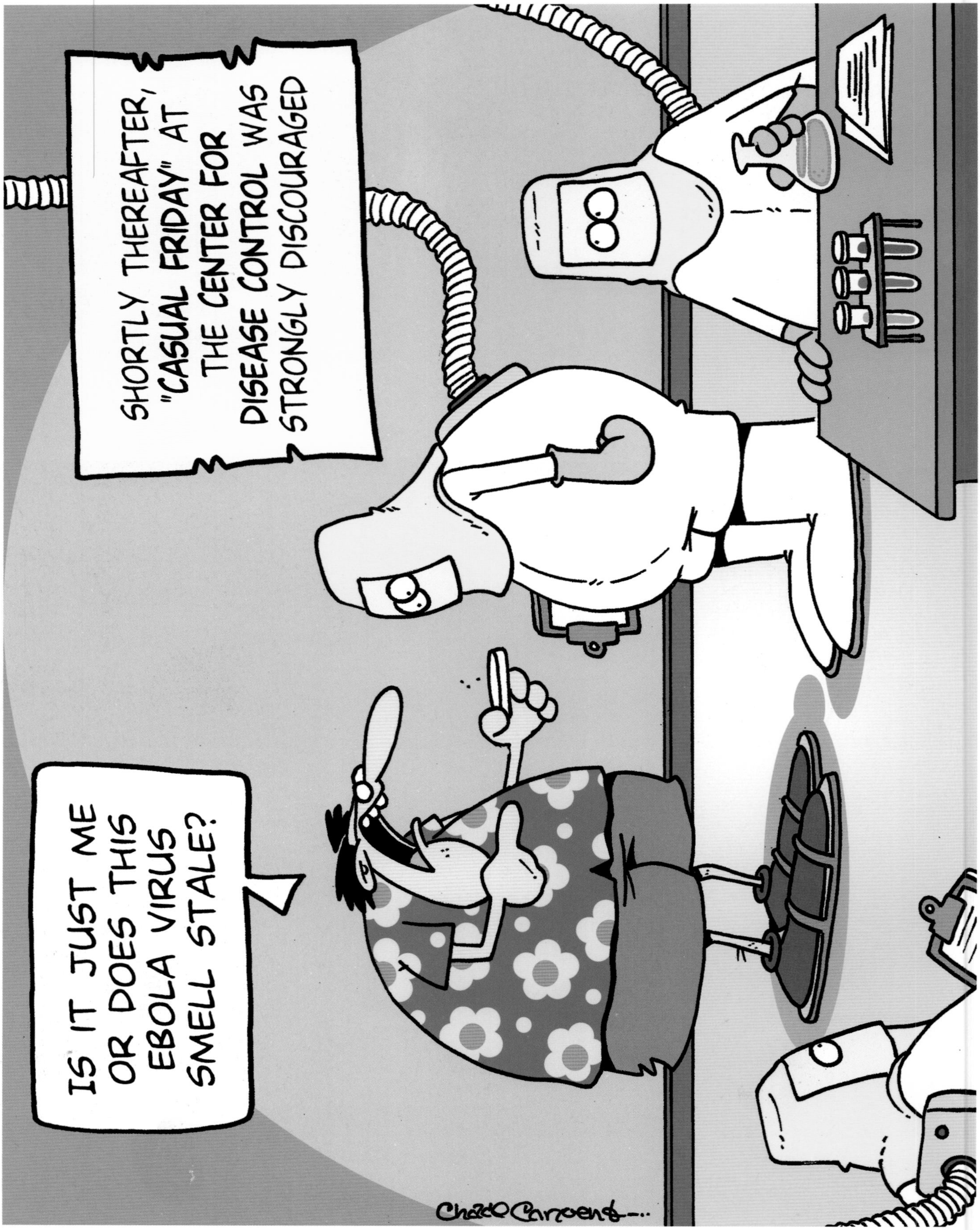
IS IT JUST ME OR DOES THIS EBOLA VIRUS SMELL STALE?
SHORTLY THEREAFTER, "CASUAL FRIDAY" AT THE CENTER FOR DISEASE CONTROL WAS STRONGLY DISCOURAGED

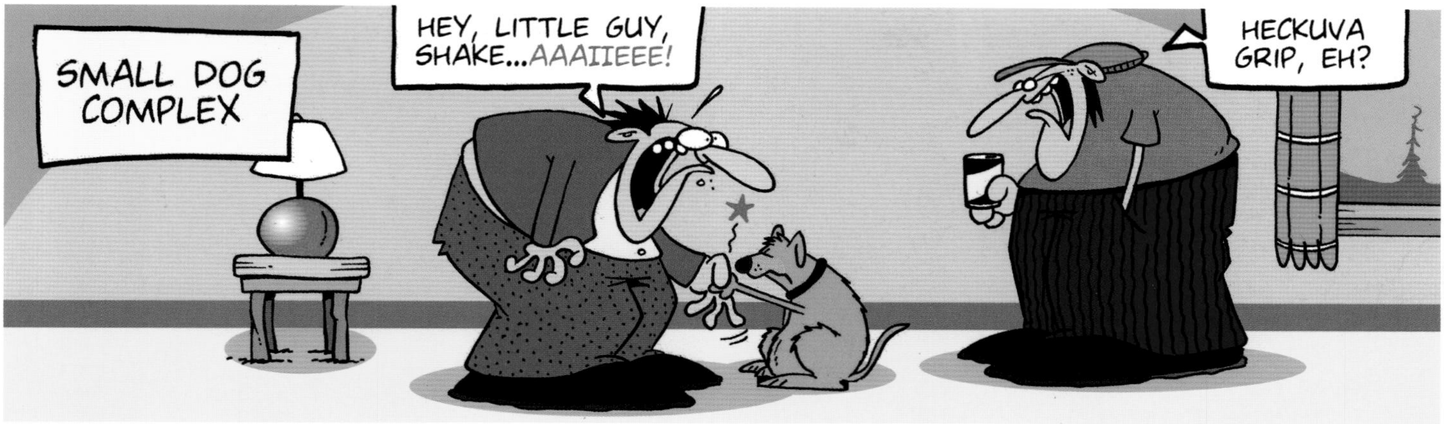
SMALL DOG COMPLEX
HEY, LITTLE GUY, SHAKE...AAAIIEEE!
HECKUVA GRIP, EH?

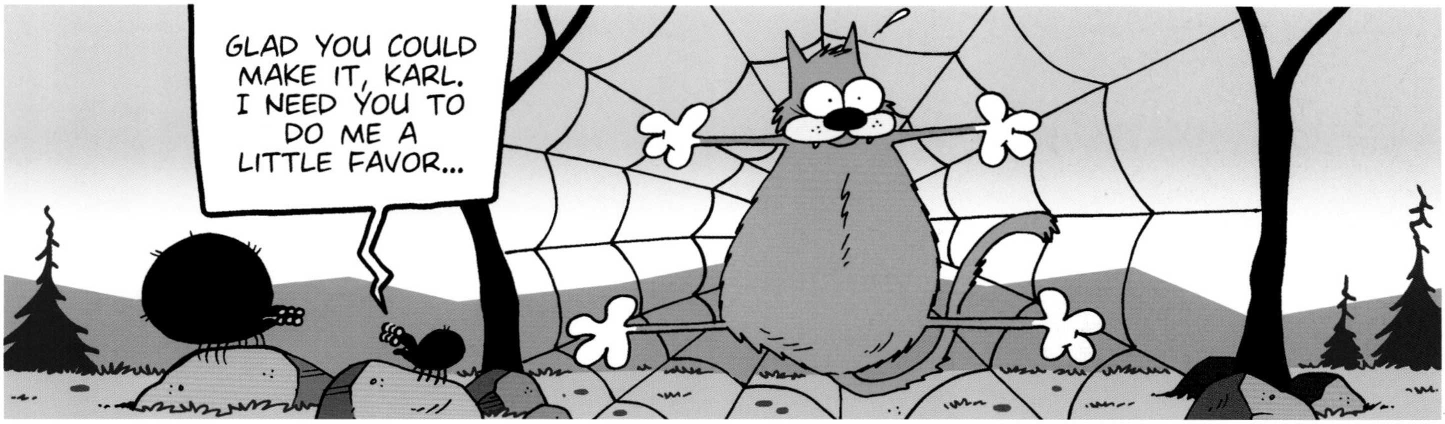
GLAD YOU COULD MAKE IT, KARL. I NEED YOU TO DO ME A LITTLE FAVOR...

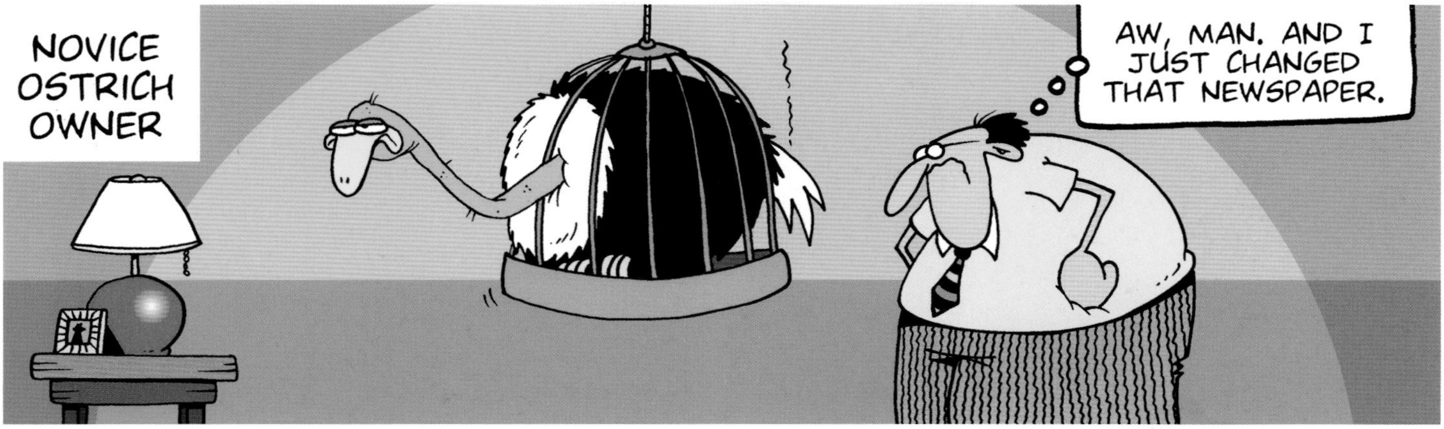
NOVICE OSTRICH OWNER
AW, MAN. AND I JUST CHANGED THAT NEWSPAPER.

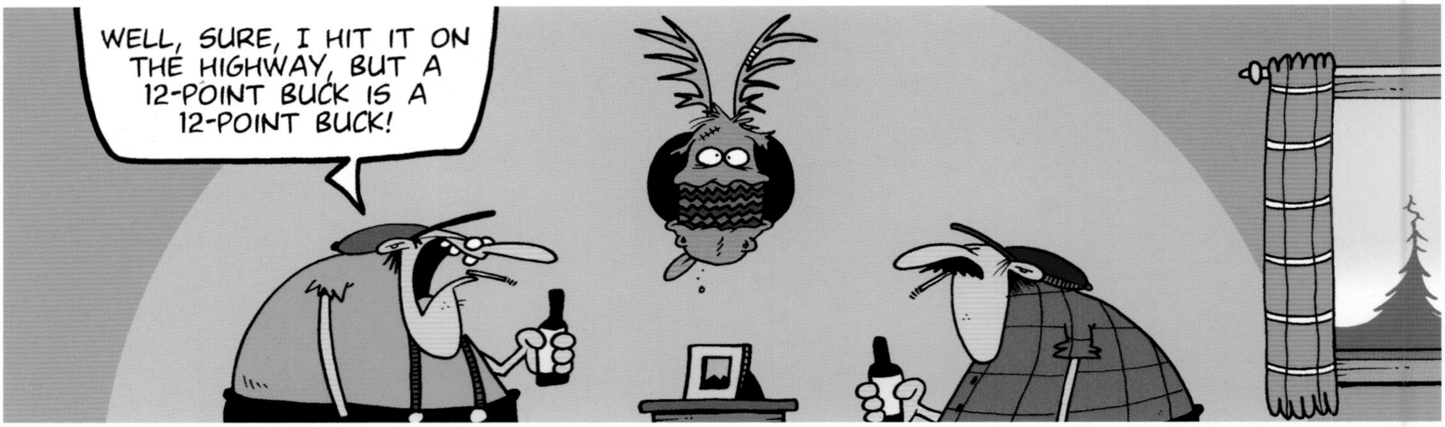
WELL, SURE, I HIT IT ON THE HIGHWAY, BUT A 12-POINT BUCK IS A 12-POINT BUCK!

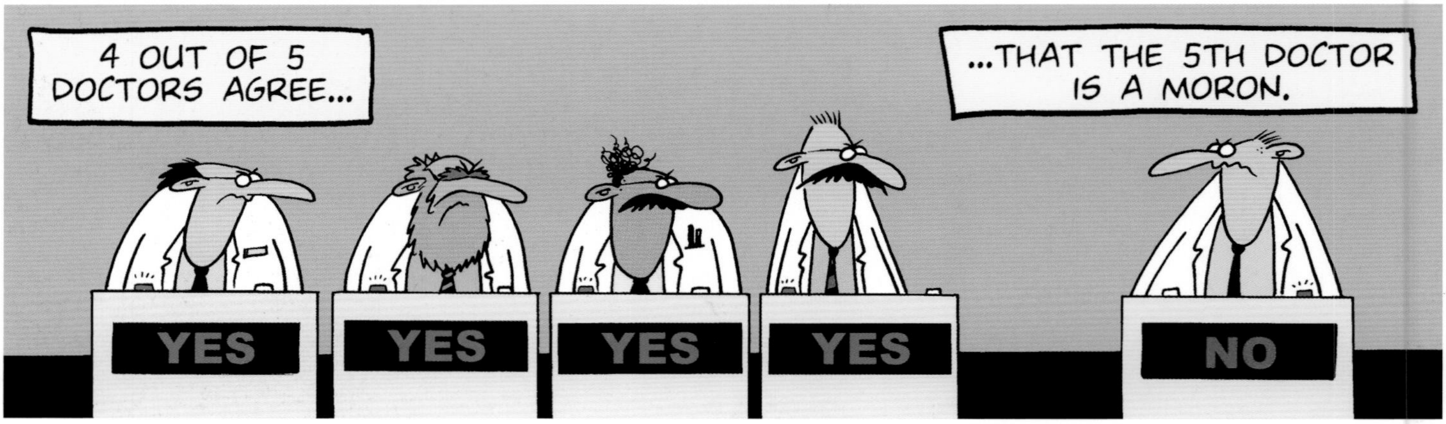
4 OUT OF 5 DOCTORS AGREE...
...THAT THE 5TH DOCTOR IS A MORON.
YES
YES
YES
YES
NO

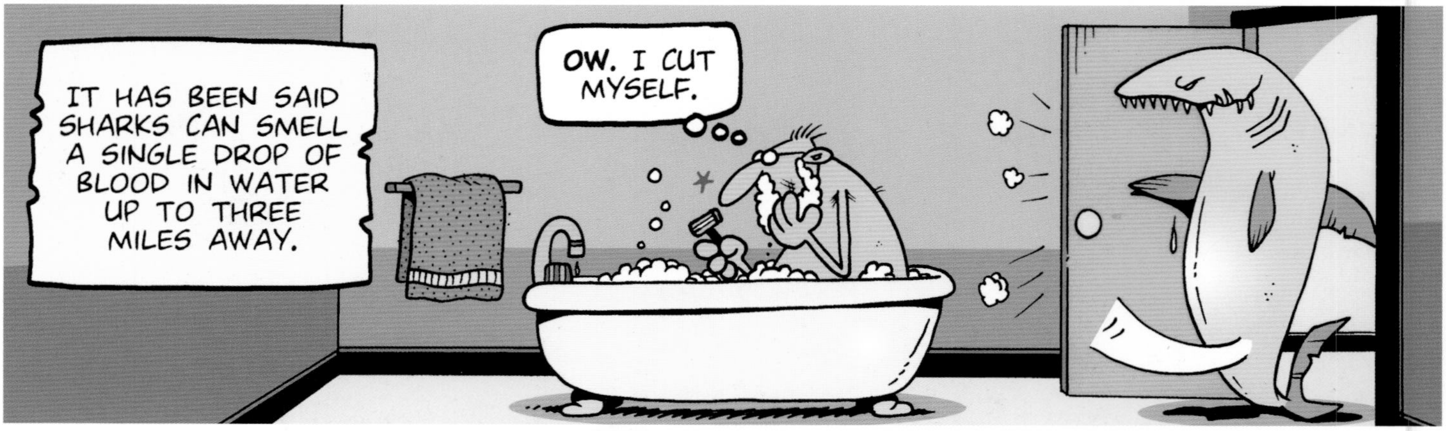
IT HAS BEEN SAID SHARKS CAN SMELL A SINGLE DROP OF BLOOD IN WATER UP TO THREE MILES AWAY.
OW. I CUT MYSELF.

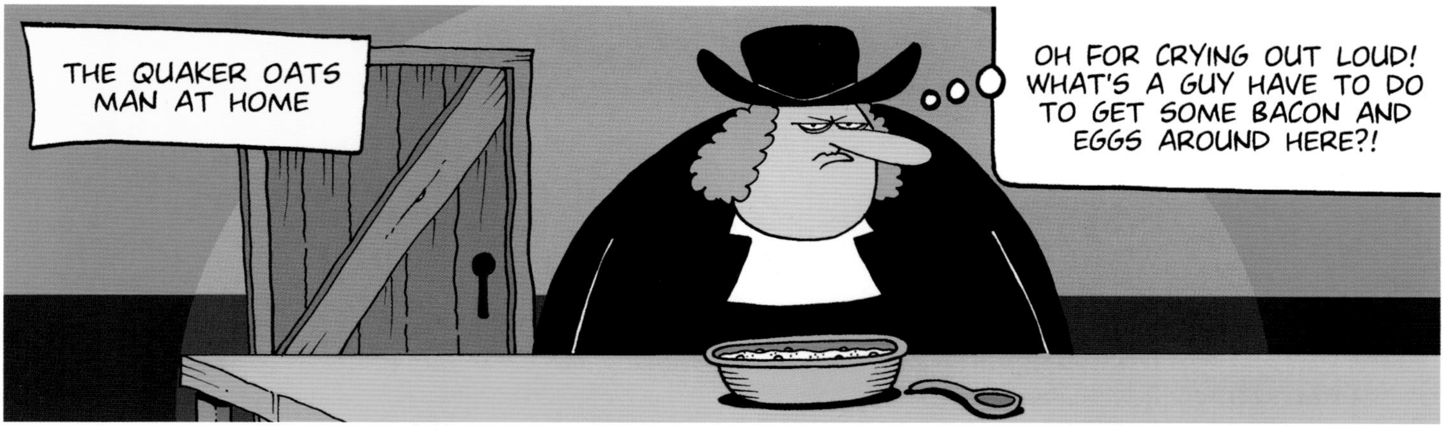
THE QUAKER OATS MAN AT HOME
OH FOR CRYING OUT LOUD! WHAT'S A GUY HAVE TO DO TO GET SOME BACON AND EGGS AROUND HERE?!

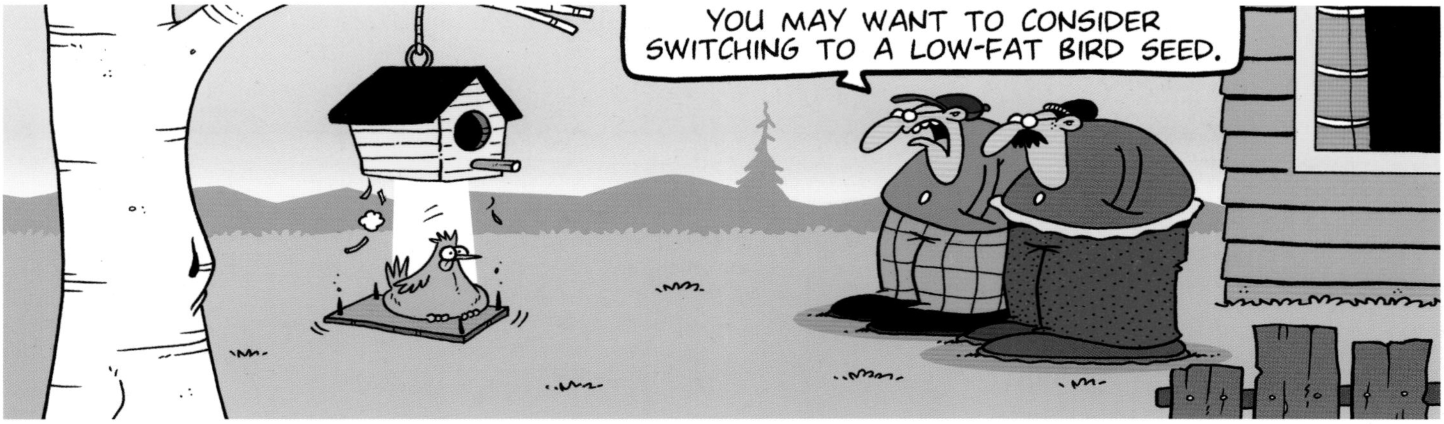
YOU MAY WANT TO CONSIDER SWITCHING TO A LOW-FAT BIRD SEED.

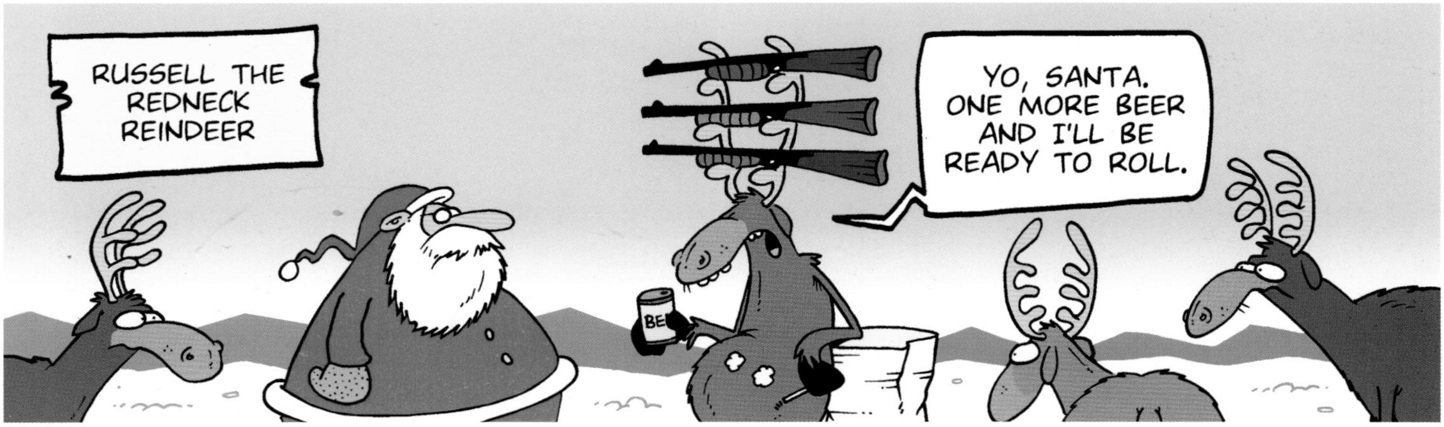
RUSSELL THE REDNECK REINDEER
YO, SANTA. ONE MORE BEER AND I'LL BE READY TO ROLL.

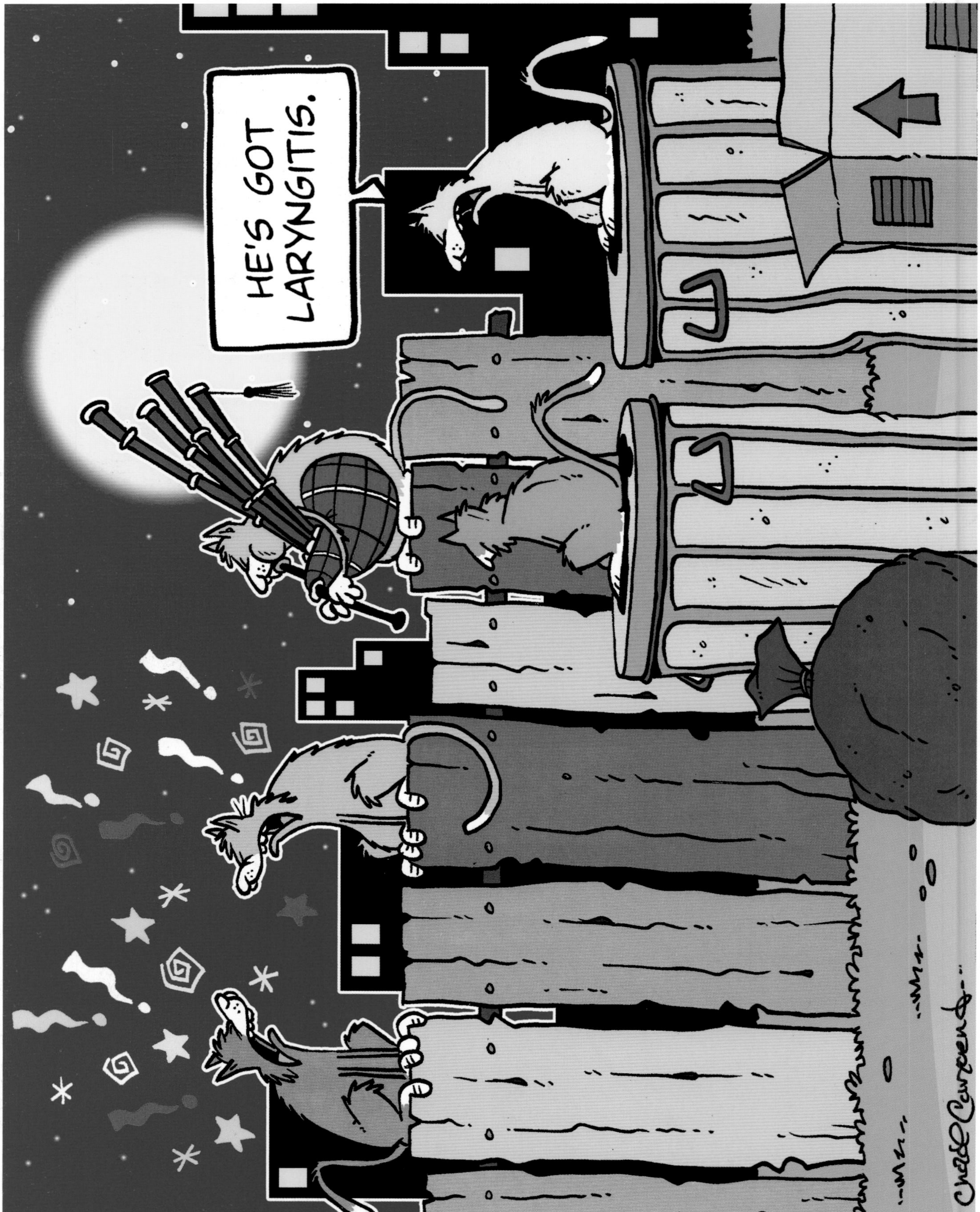
HE'S GOT LARYNGITIS.

THIS STRIP IS BASED ON AN IDEA FROM:

TROY TIBBETTS
FAIRBANKS, AK

DO YOU HAVE AN IDEA THAT WOULD MAKE A GREAT COMIC STRIP?

SEND IT TO:
tundracomics.com

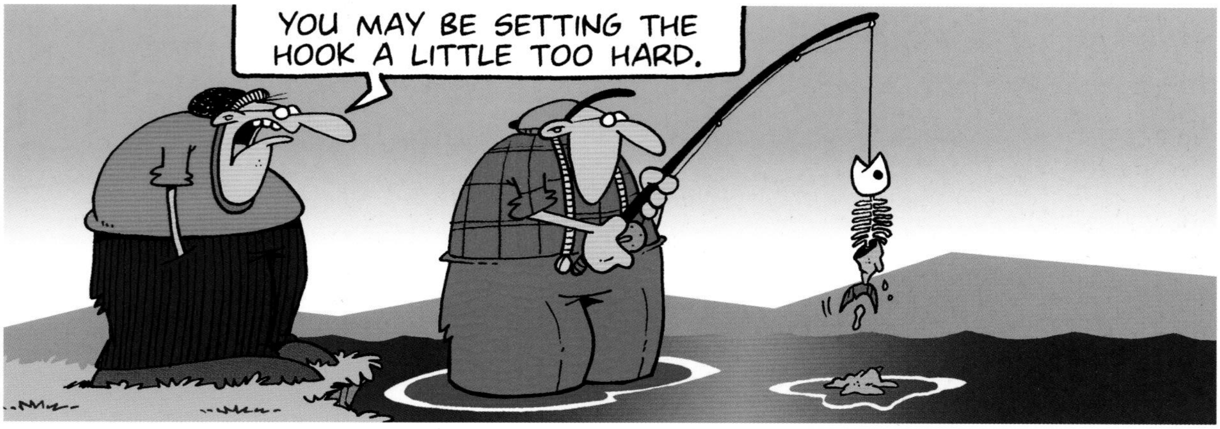
YOU MAY BE SETTING THE HOOK A LITTLE TOO HARD.

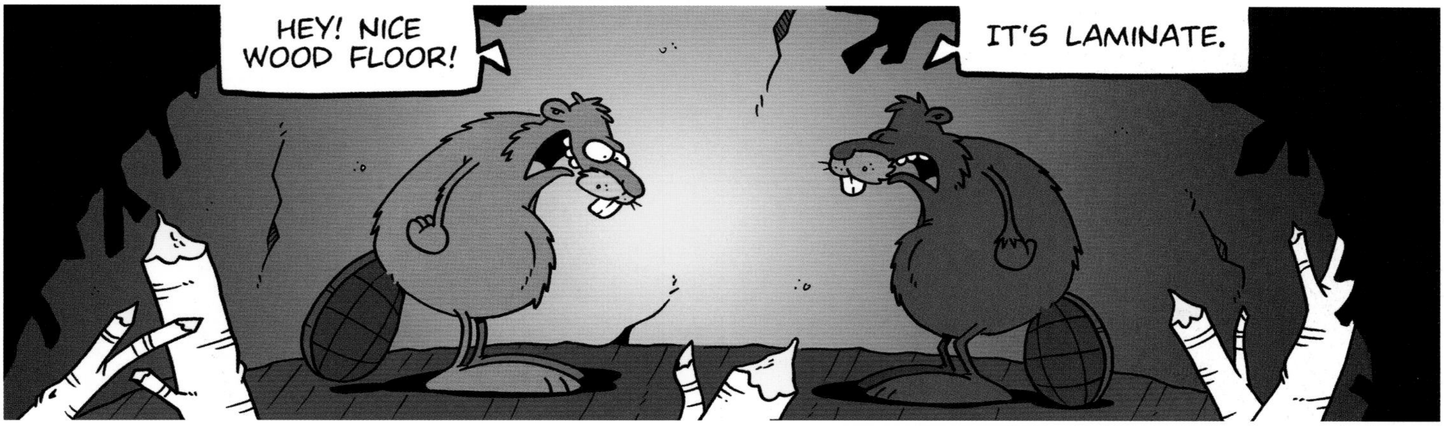
HEY! NICE WOOD FLOOR!
IT'S LAMINATE.

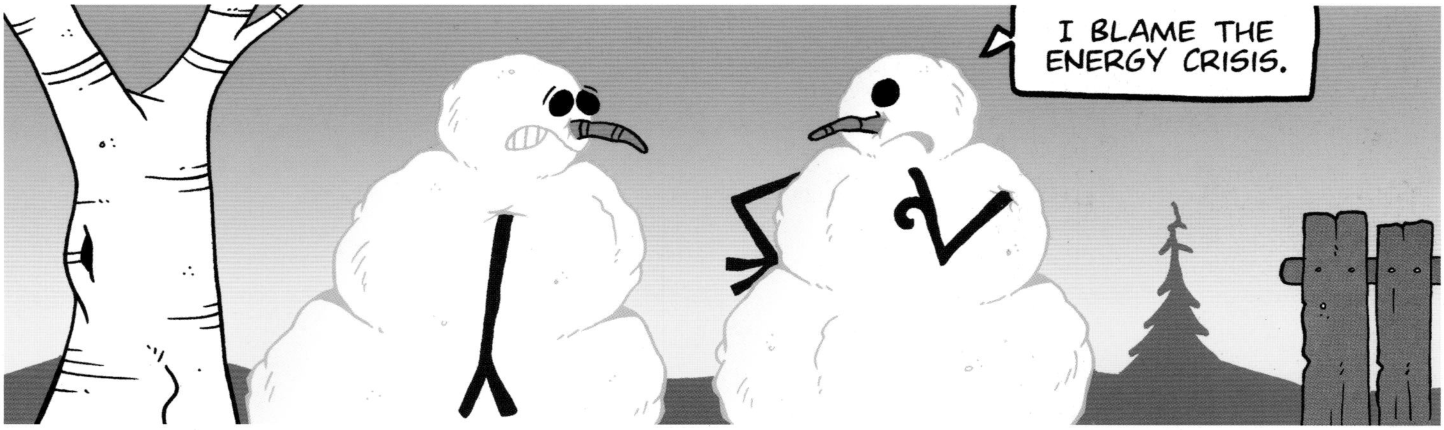
I BLAME THE ENERGY CRISIS.

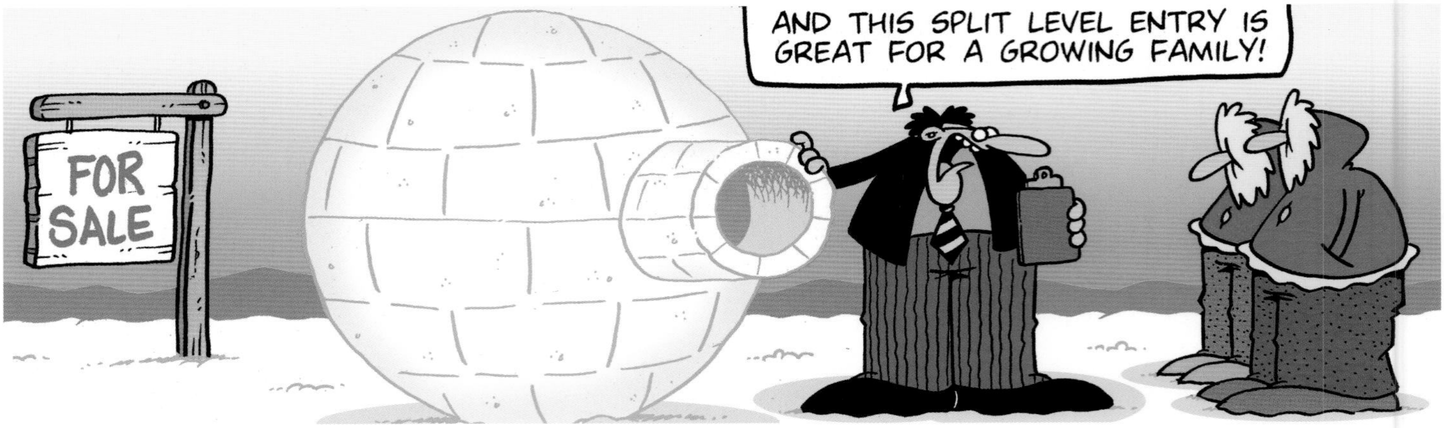
FOR SALE
AND THIS SPLIT LEVEL ENTRY IS GREAT FOR A GROWING FAMILY!

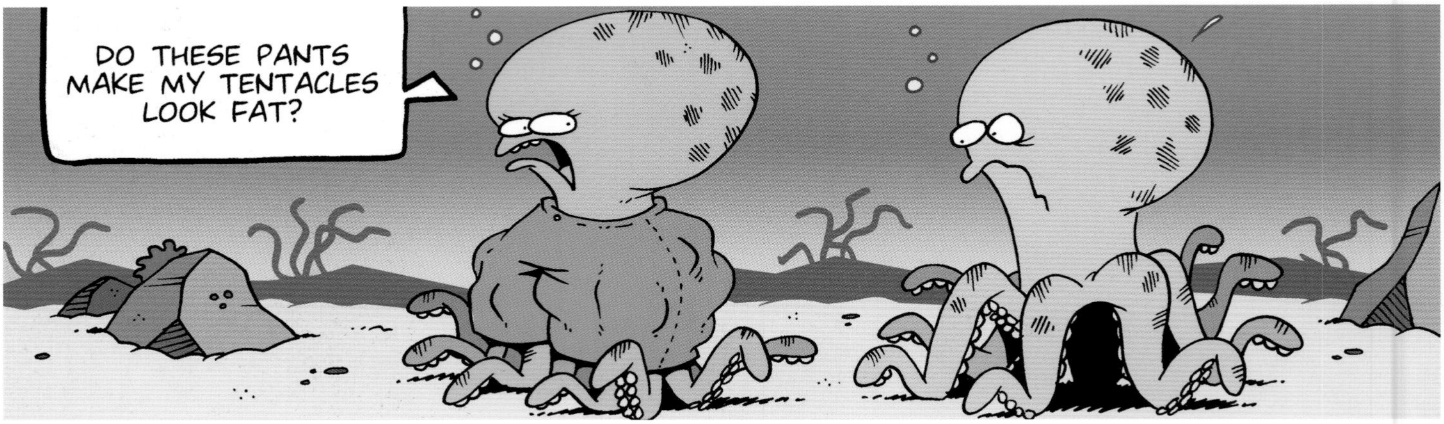
DO THESE PANTS MAKE MY TENTACLES LOOK FAT?

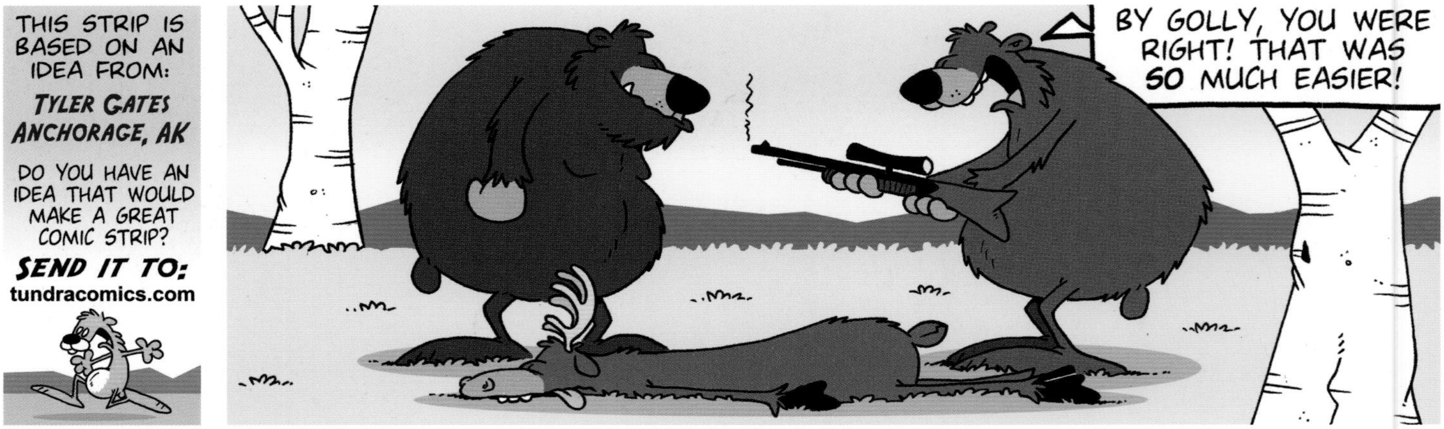
THIS STRIP IS BASED ON AN IDEA FROM:
TYLER GATES ANCHORAGE, AK
DO YOU HAVE AN IDEA THAT WOULD MAKE A GREAT COMIC STRIP?
SEND IT TO:
tundracomics.com
BY GOLLY, YOU WERE RIGHT! THAT WAS SO MUCH EASIER!

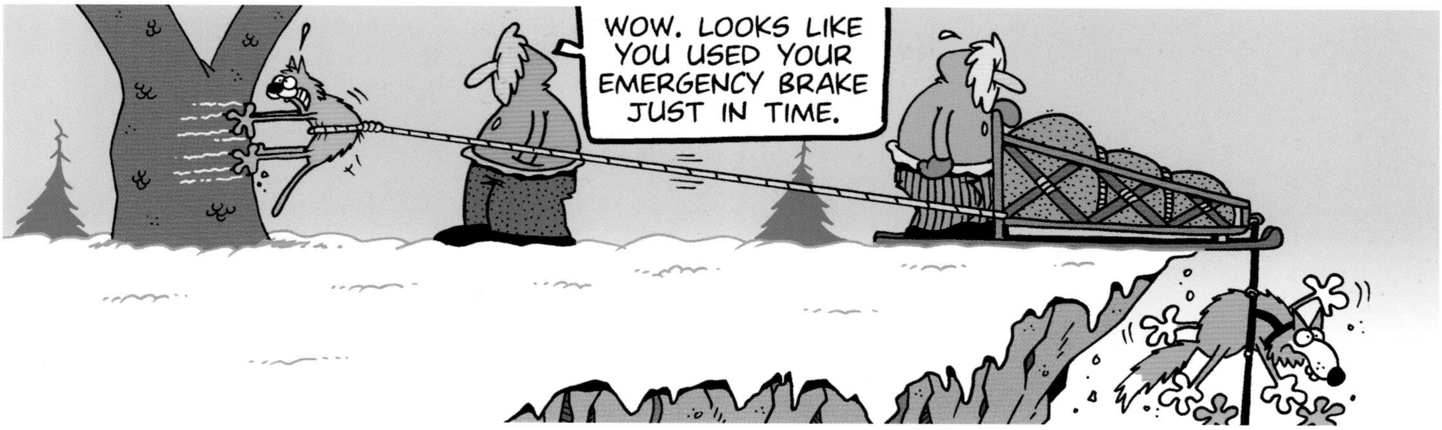
WOW. LOOKS LIKE YOU USED YOUR EMERGENCY BRAKE JUST IN TIME.

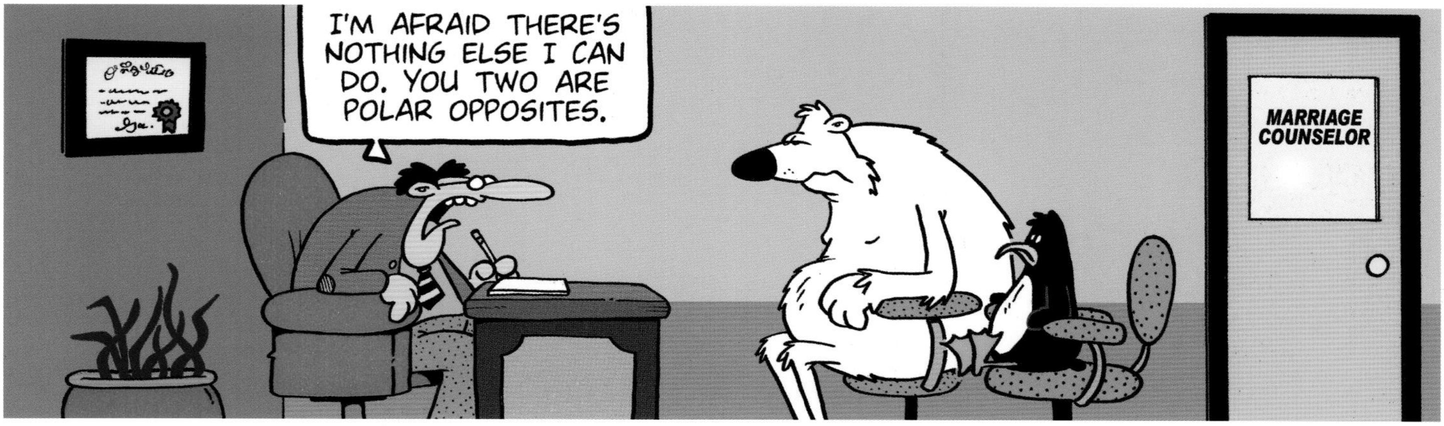
I'M AFRAID THERE'S NOTHING ELSE I CAN DO. YOU TWO ARE POLAR OPPOSITES.
MARRIAGE COUNSELOR

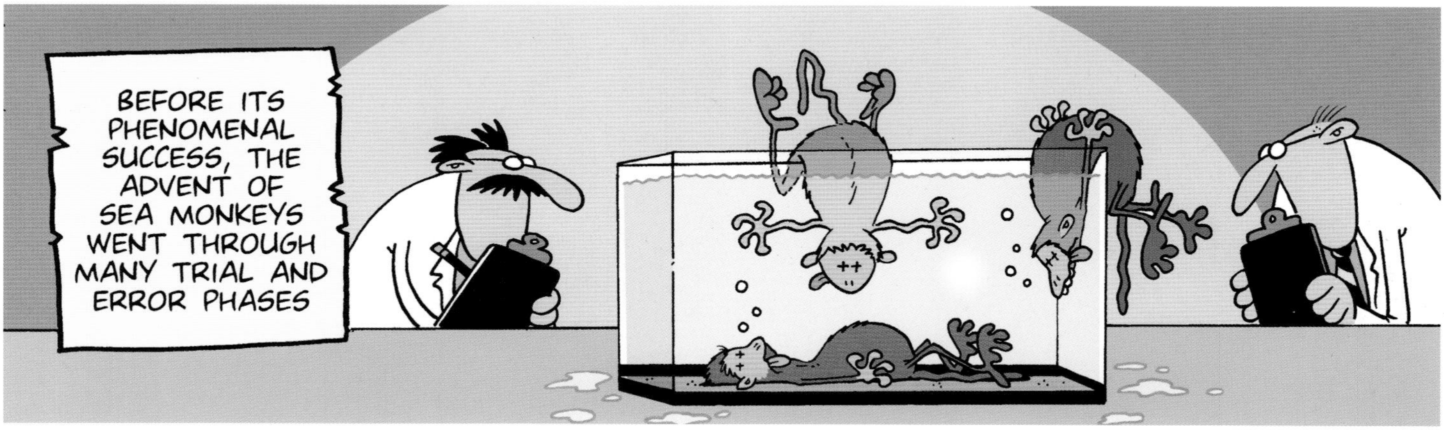
BEFORE ITS PHENOMENAL SUCCESS, THE ADVENT OF SEA MONKEYS WENT THROUGH MANY TRIAL AND ERROR PHASES

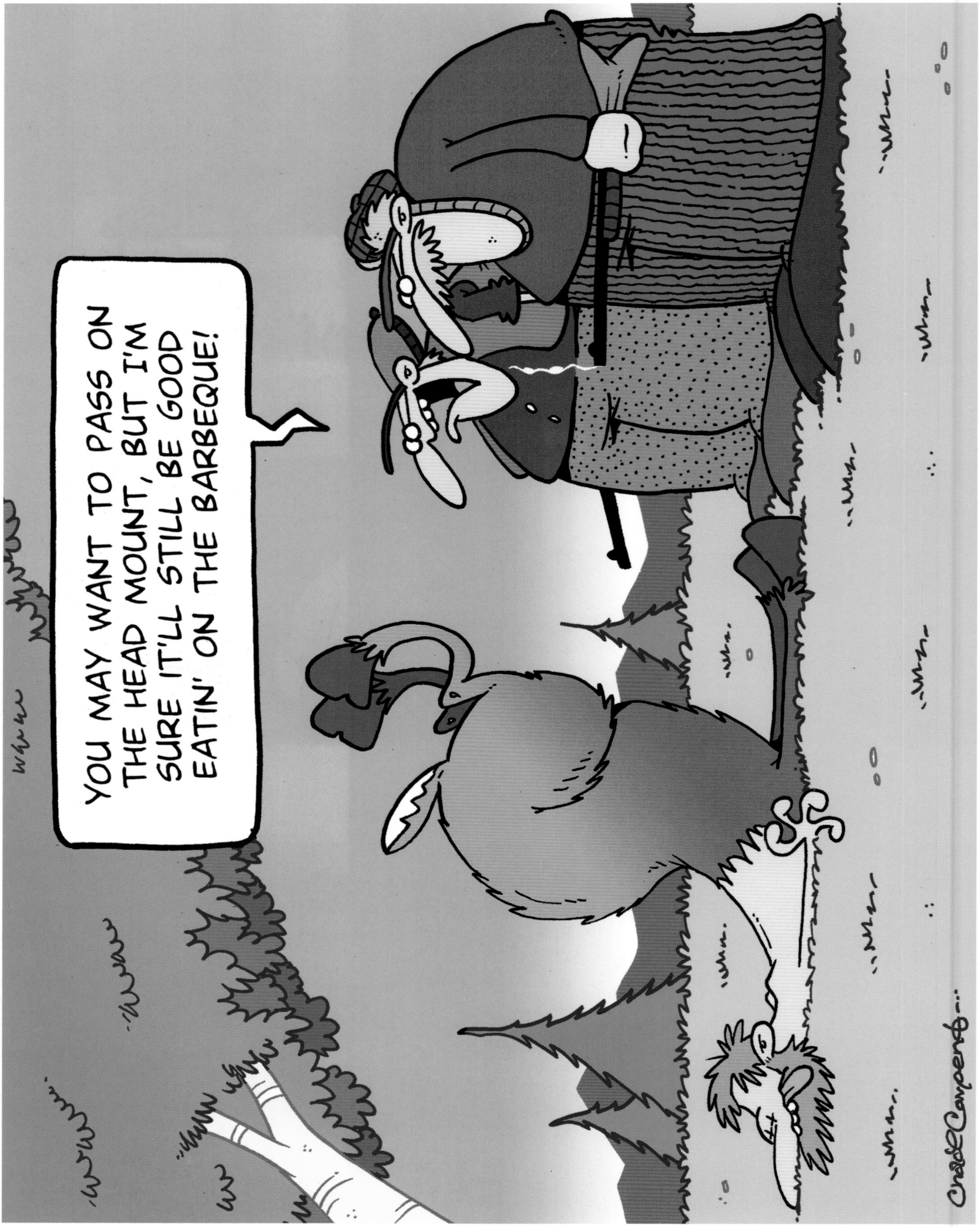
YOU MAY WANT TO PASS ON THE HEAD MOUNT, BUT I'M SURE IT'LL STILL BE GOOD EATIN' ON THE BARBEQUE!

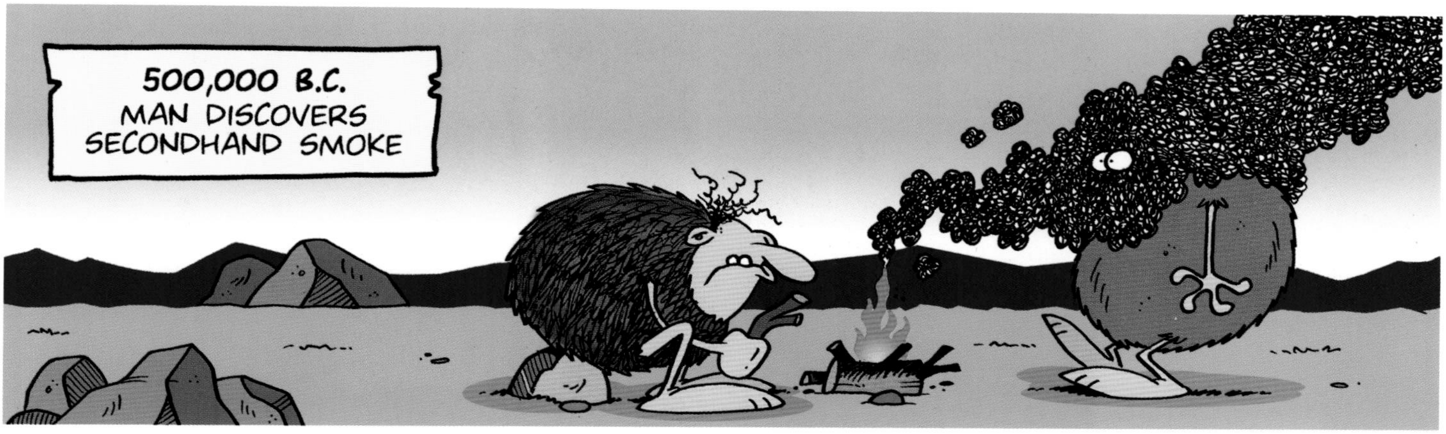
500,000 B.C.
MAN DISCOVERS SECONDHAND SMOKE

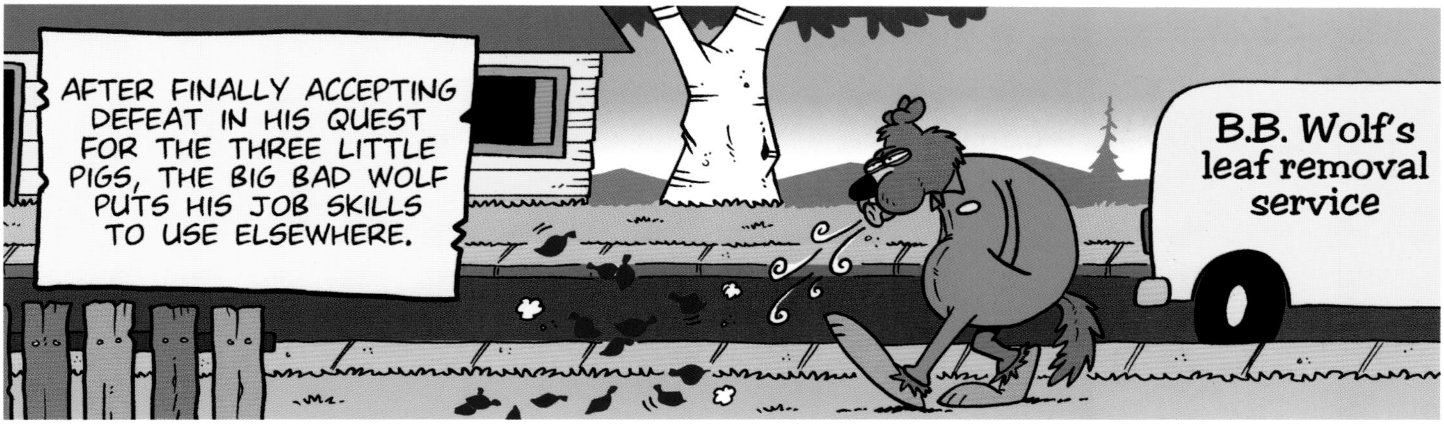
AFTER FINALLY ACCEPTING DEFEAT IN HIS QUEST FOR THE THREE LITTLE PIGS, THE BIG BAD WOLF PUTS HIS JOB SKILLS TO USE ELSEWHERE.
B.B. Wolf's leaf removal service

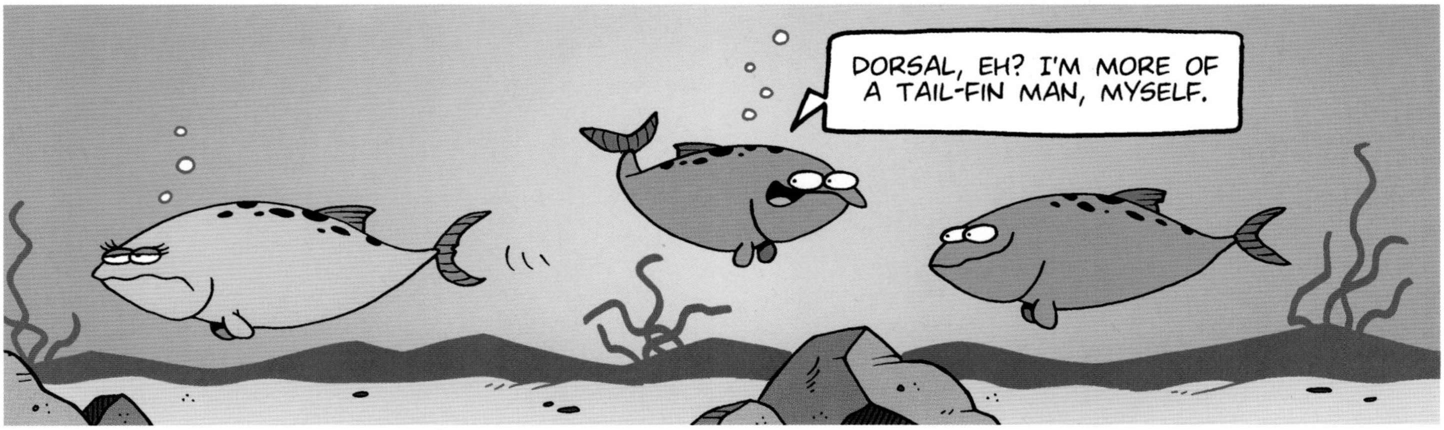
DORSAL, EH? I'M MORE OF A TAIL-FIN MAN, MYSELF.

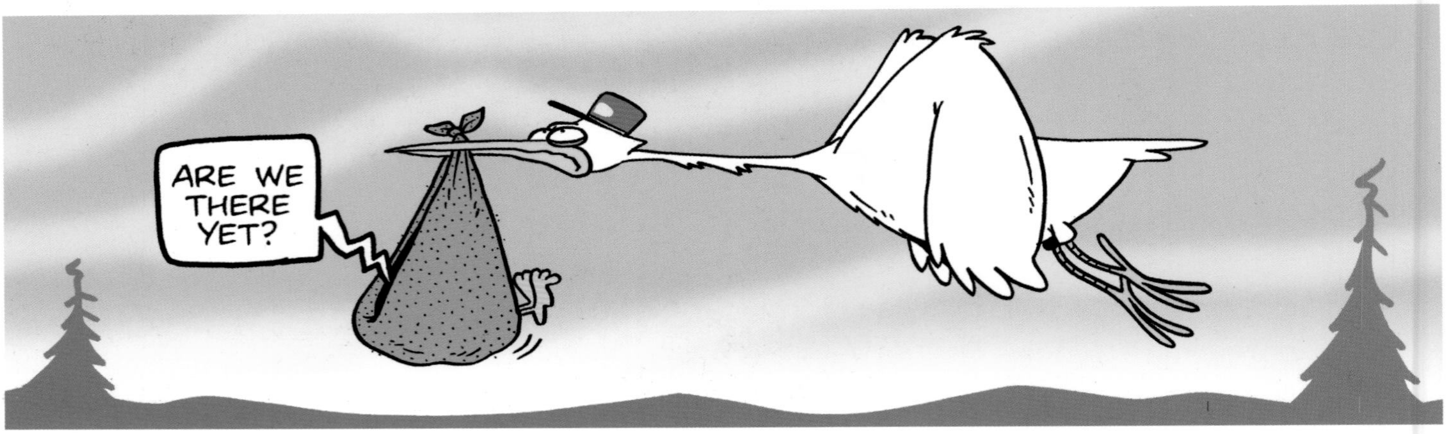
ARE WE THERE YET?

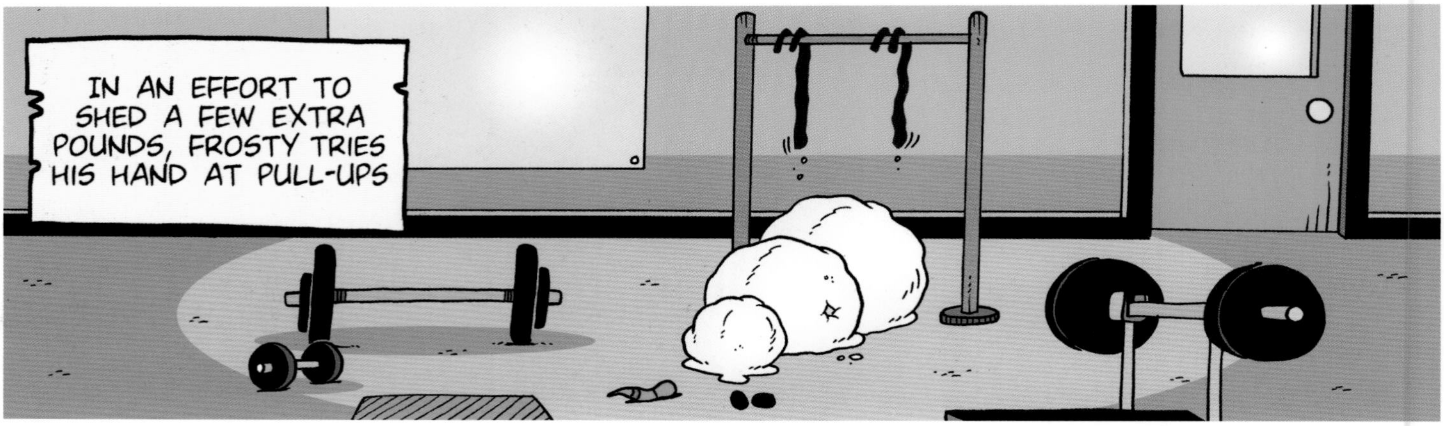
IN AN EFFORT TO SHED A FEW EXTRA POUNDS, FROSTY TRIES HIS HAND AT PULL-UPS

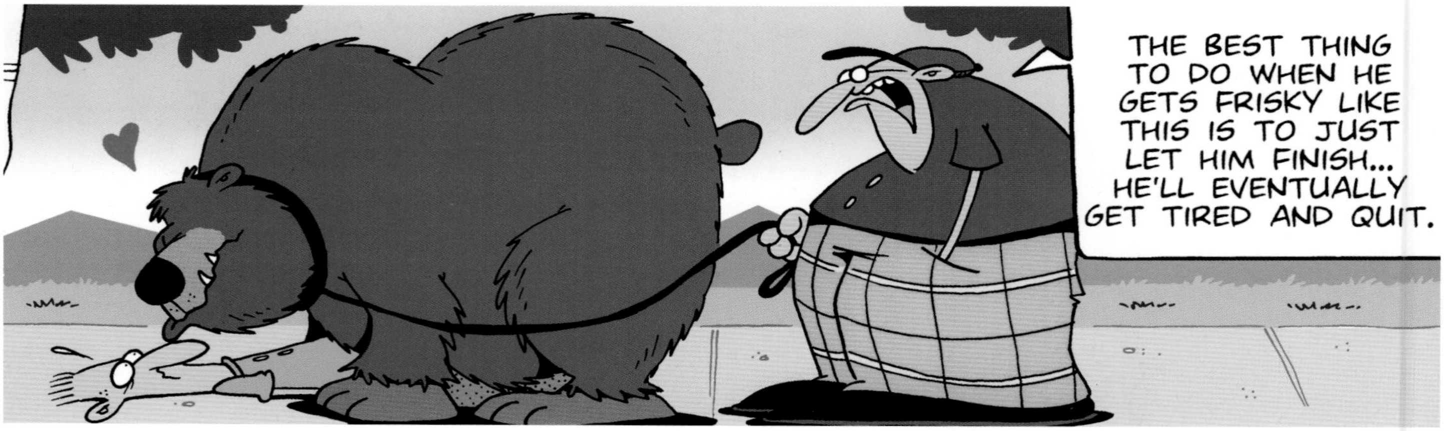
THE BEST THING TO DO WHEN HE GETS FRISKY LIKE THIS IS TO JUST LET HIM FINISH... HE'LL EVENTUALLY GET TIRED AND QUIT.

THIS STRIP IS BASED ON AN IDEA FROM:

HARLOW KODD
ST. PETE, FL

DO YOU HAVE AN IDEA THAT WOULD MAKE A GREAT COMIC STRIP?

SEND IT TO:
tundracomics.com

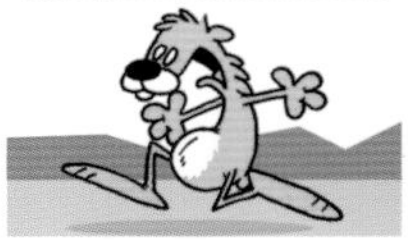

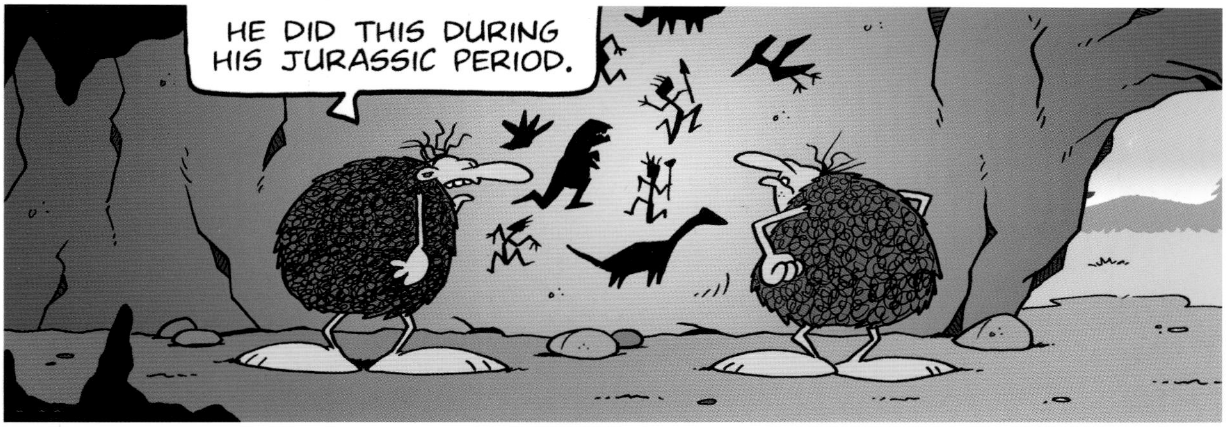
HE DID THIS DURING HIS JURASSIC PERIOD.

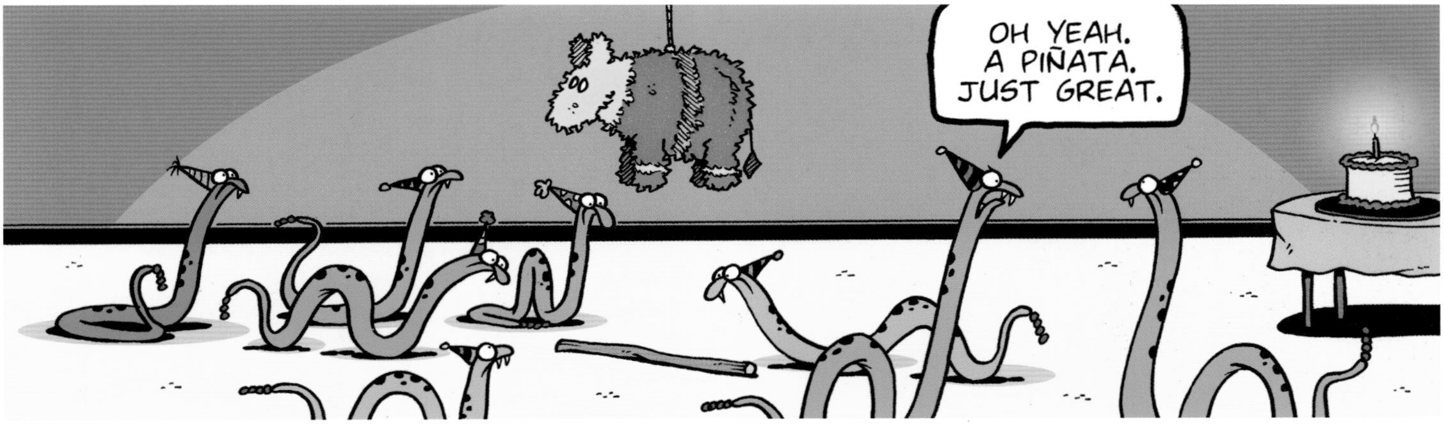
OH YEAH. A PIÑATA. JUST GREAT.

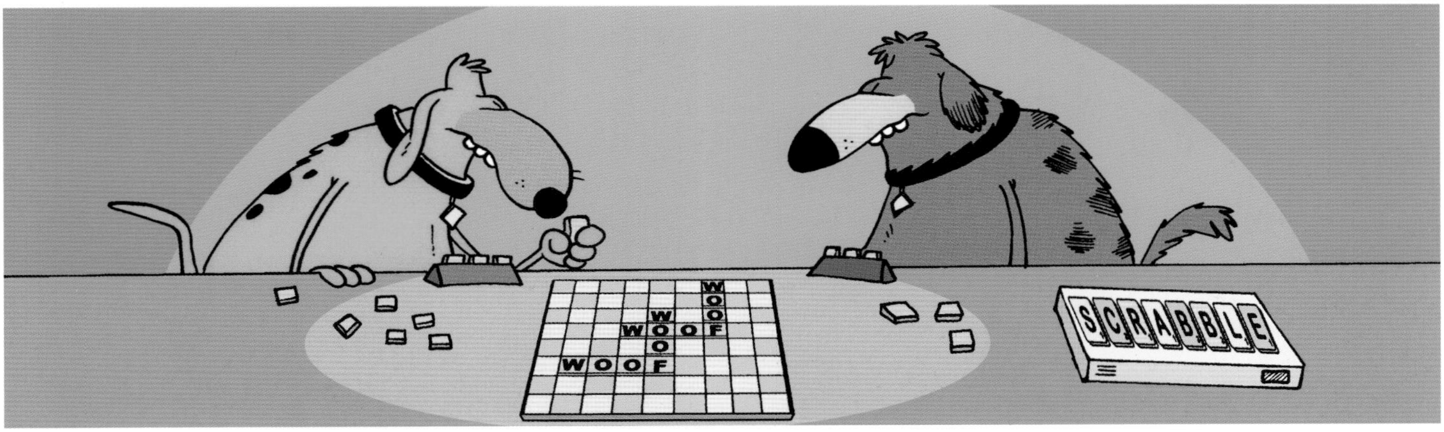
WOOF
WOOF
WOOF
WOOF
WOOF
SCRABBLE

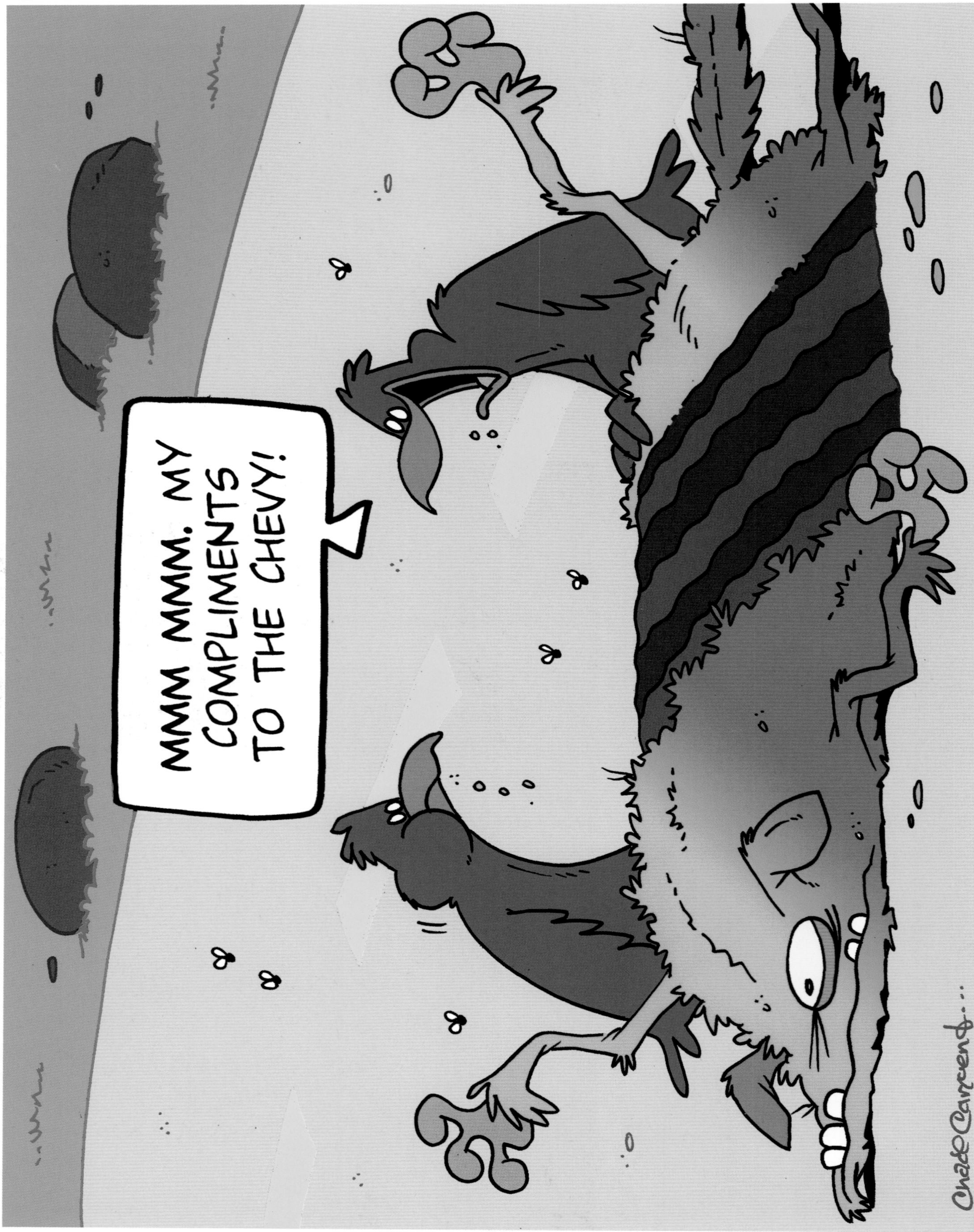
MMM MMM. MY COMPLIMENTS TO THE CHEVY!
Chad Carpenter...

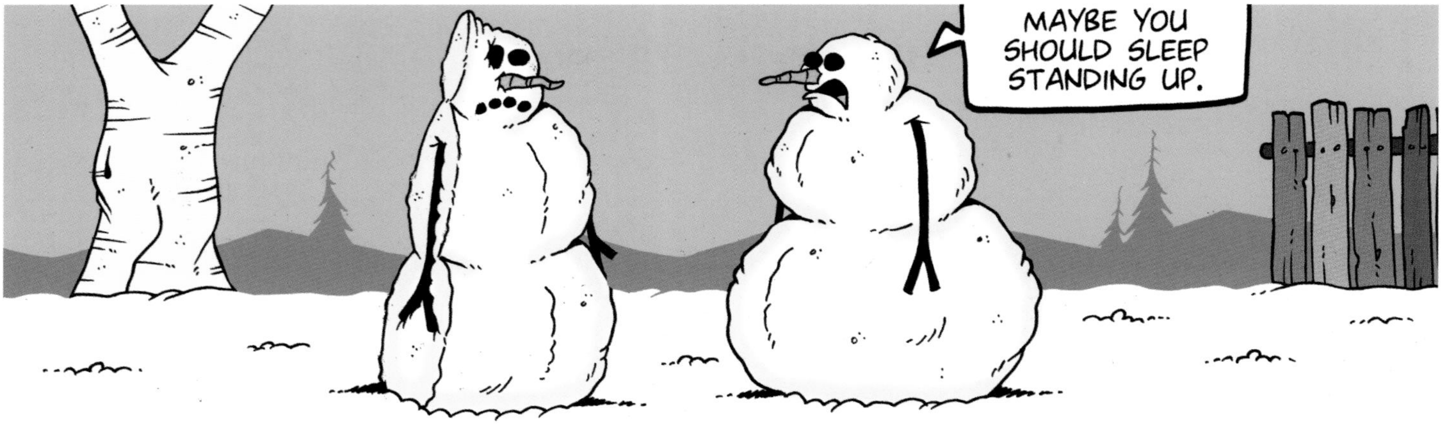
MAYBE YOU SHOULD SLEEP STANDING UP.

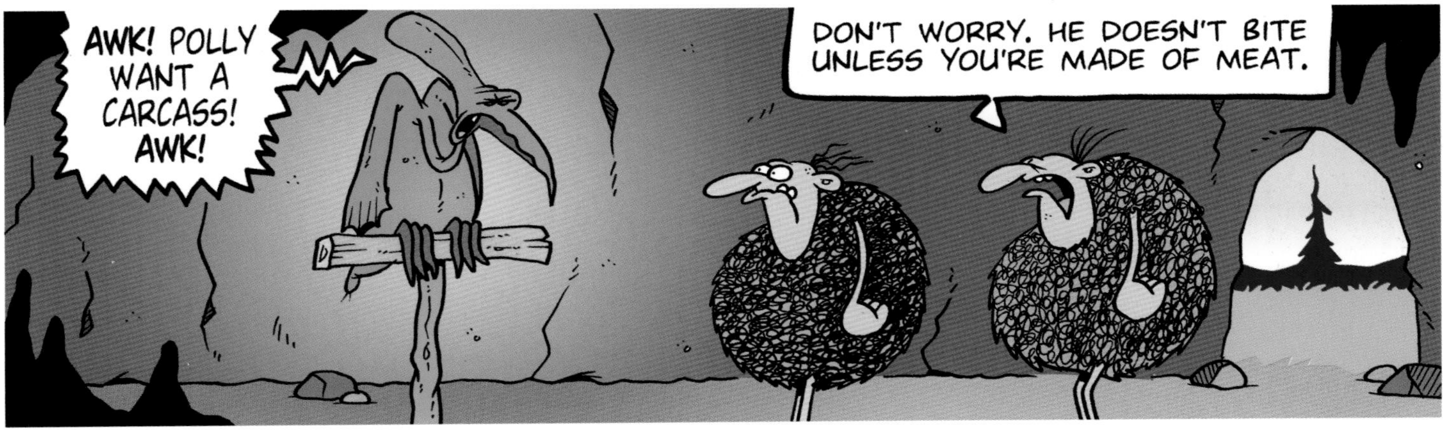
AWK! POLLY WANT A CARCASS! AWK!
DON'T WORRY. HE DOESN'T BITE UNLESS YOU'RE MADE OF MEAT.

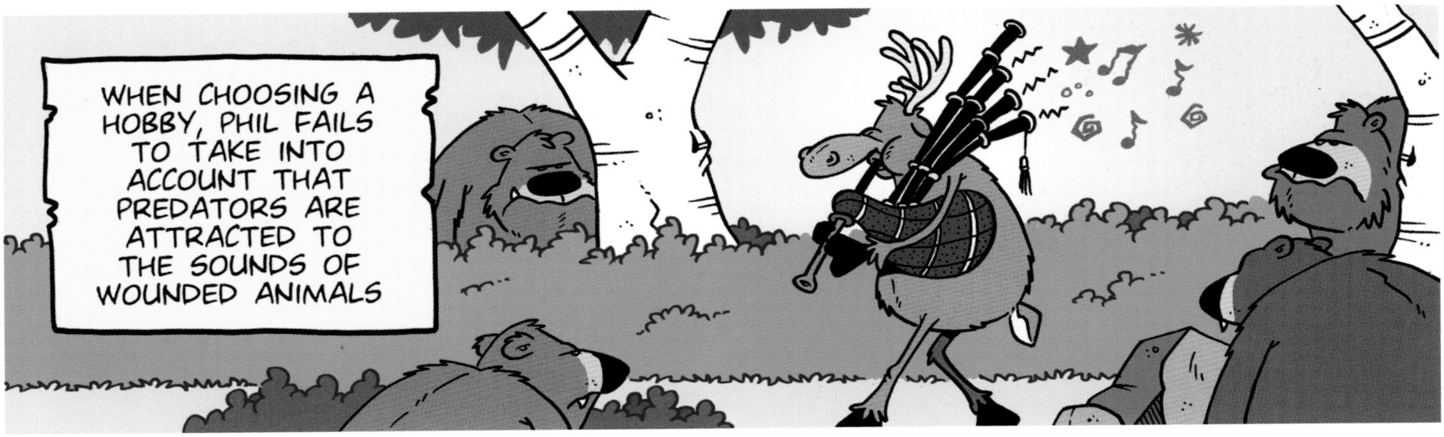
WHEN CHOOSING A HOBBY, PHIL FAILS TO TAKE INTO ACCOUNT THAT PREDATORS ARE ATTRACTED TO THE SOUNDS OF WOUNDED ANIMALS

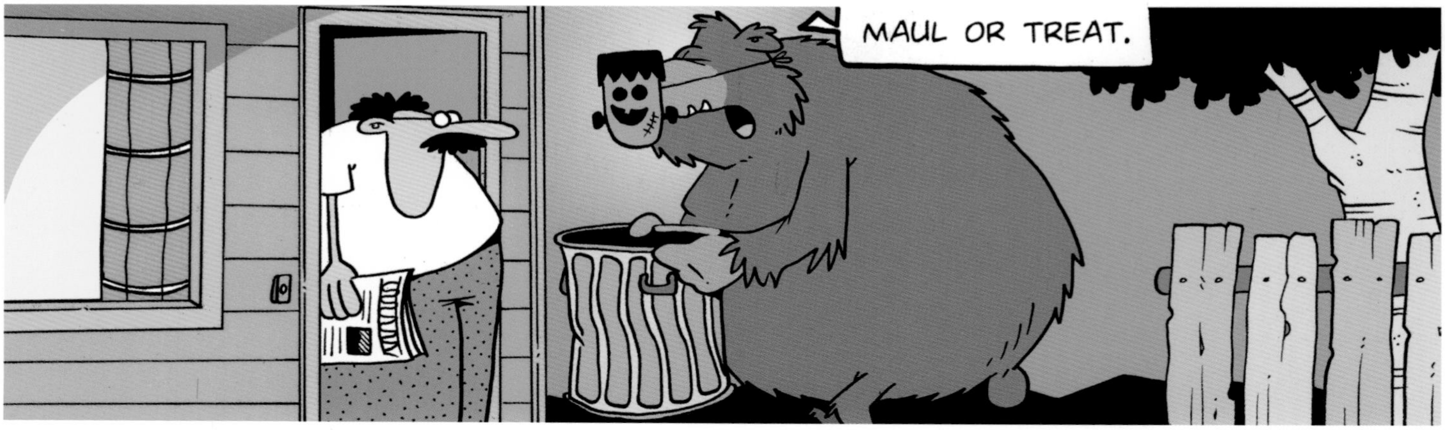
MAUL OR TREAT.

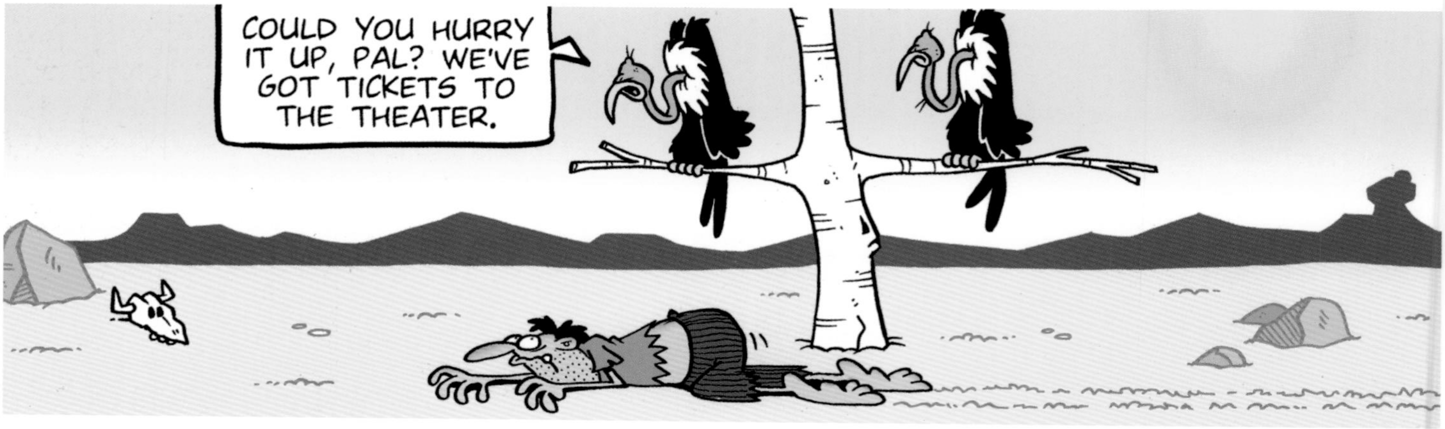
COULD YOU HURRY IT UP, PAL? WE'VE GOT TICKETS TO THE THEATER.

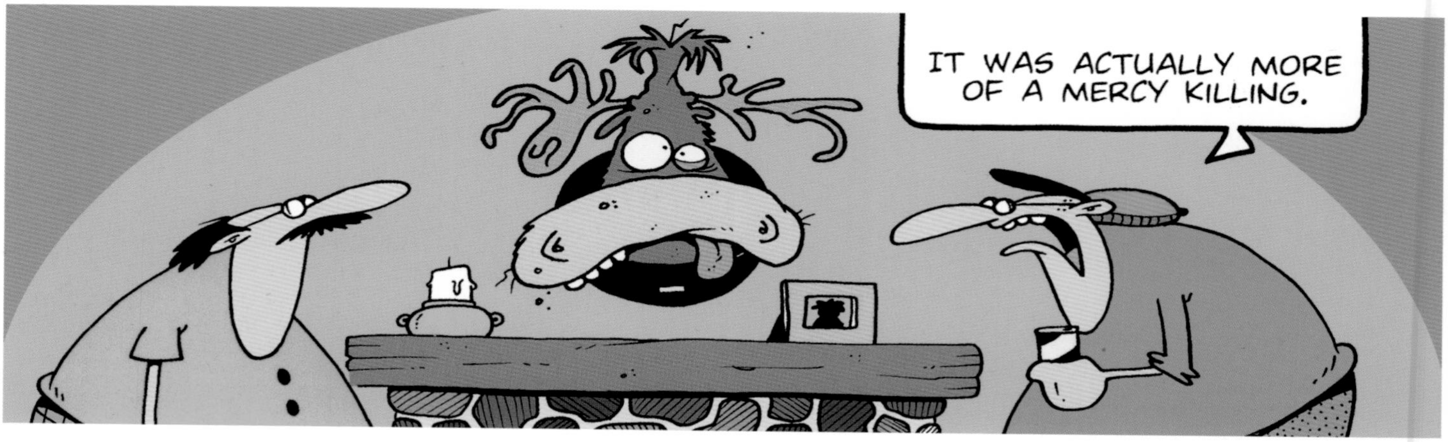
IT WAS ACTUALLY MORE OF A MERCY KILLING.

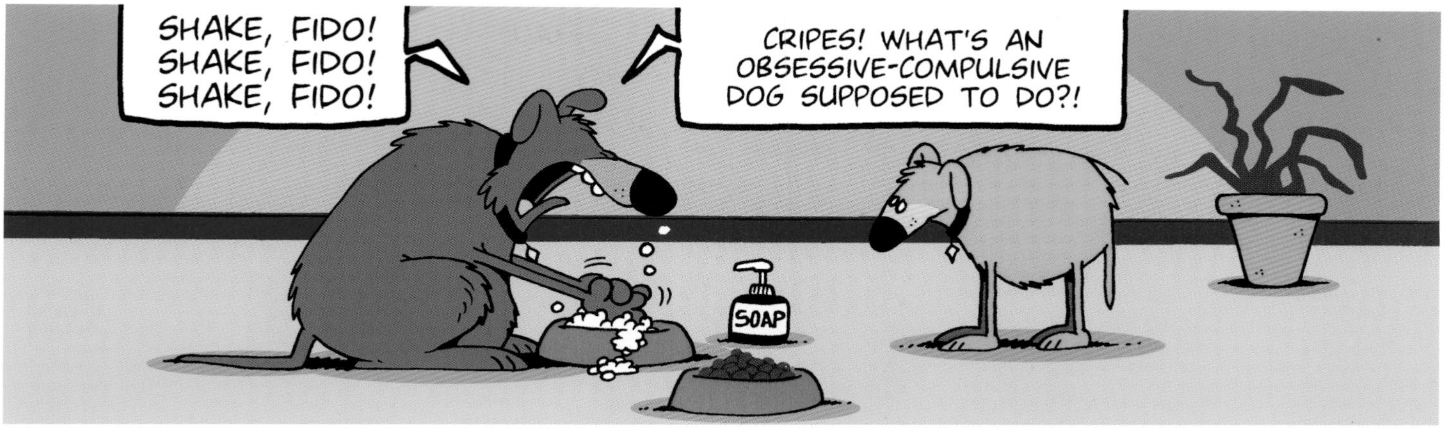
SHAKE, FIDO!
SHAKE, FIDO!
SHAKE, FIDO!
CRIPES! WHAT'S AN OBSESSIVE-COMPULSIVE DOG SUPPOSED TO DO?!
SOAP

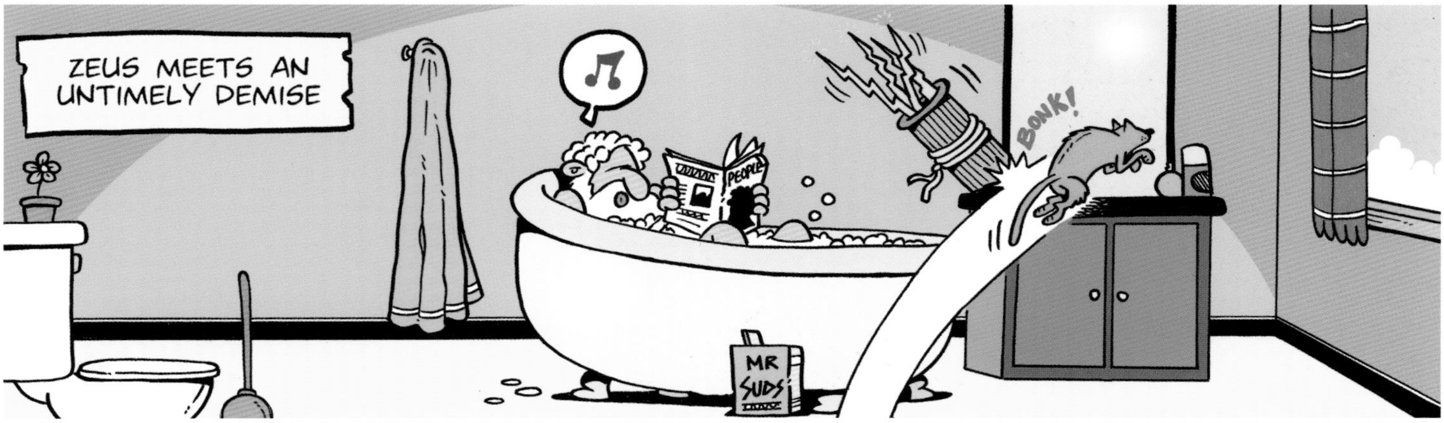
ZEUS MEETS AN UNTIMELY DEMISE
PEOPLE
BONK!
MR SUDS

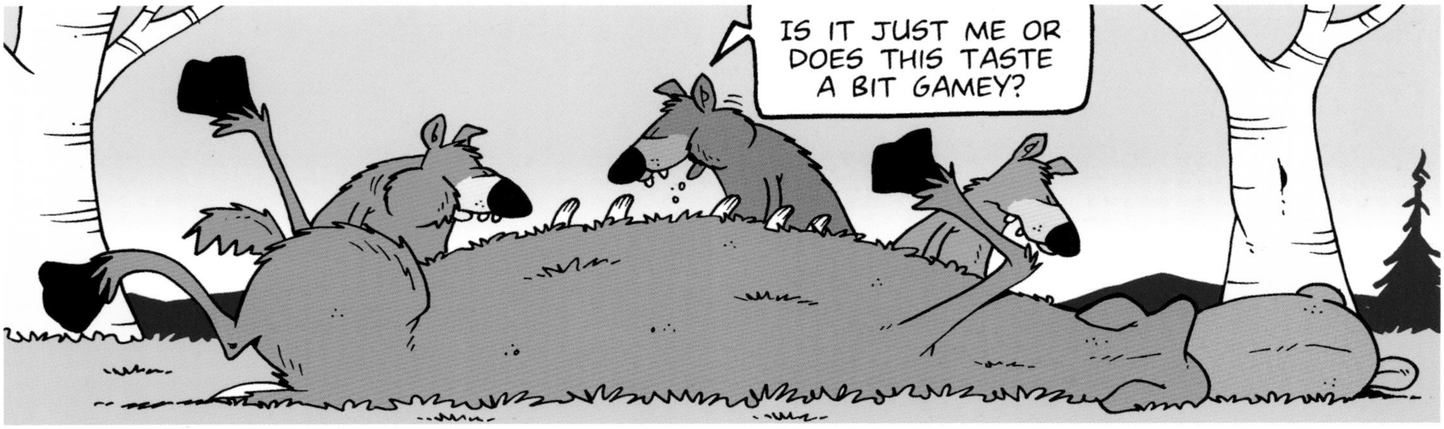
IS IT JUST ME OR DOES THIS TASTE A BIT GAMEY?

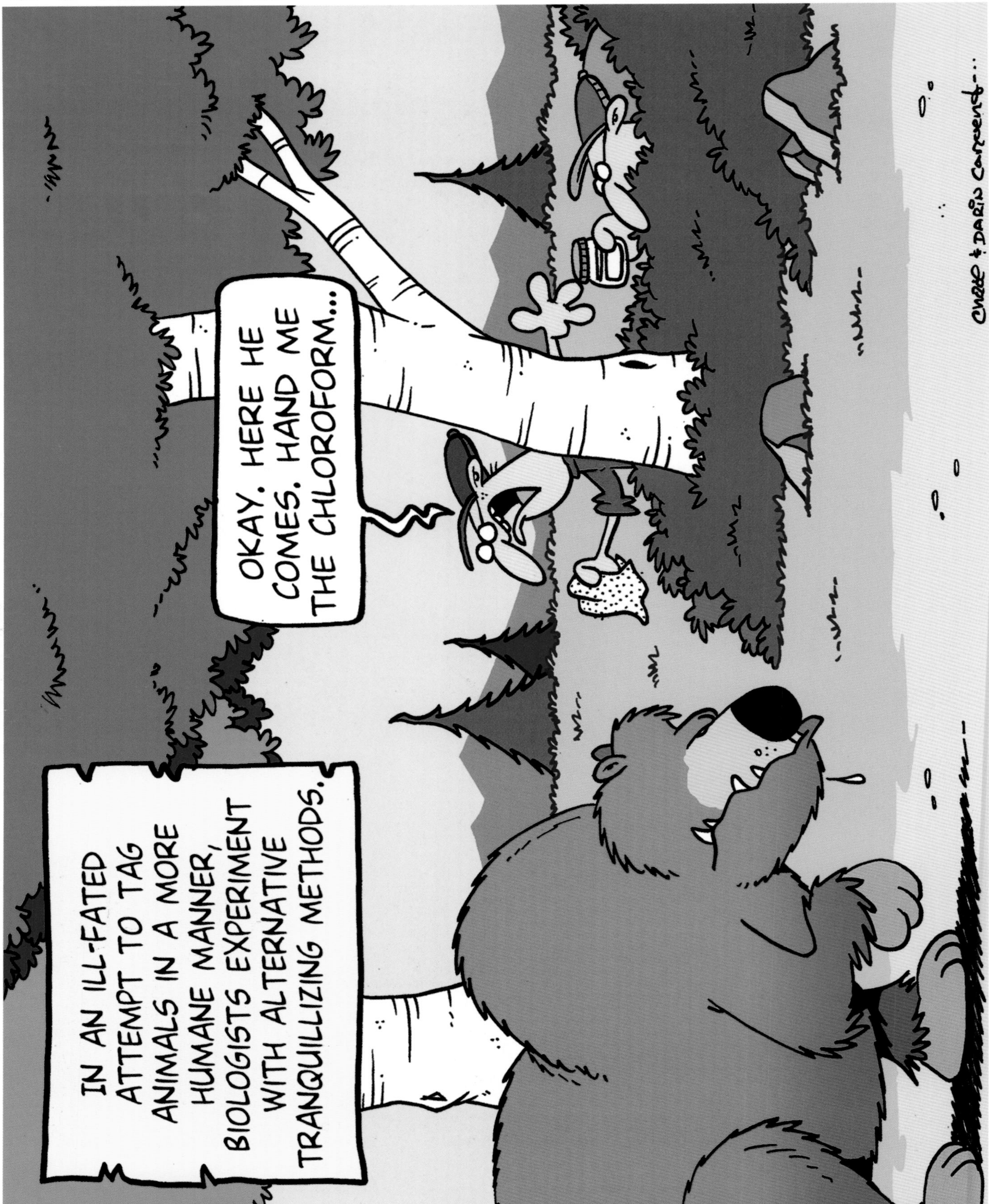
IN AN ILL-FATED ATTEMPT TO TAG ANIMALS IN A MORE HUMANE MANNER, BIOLOGISTS EXPERIMENT WITH ALTERNATIVE TRANQUILLIZING METHODS.
OKAY. HERE HE COMES. HAND ME THE CHLOROFORM...

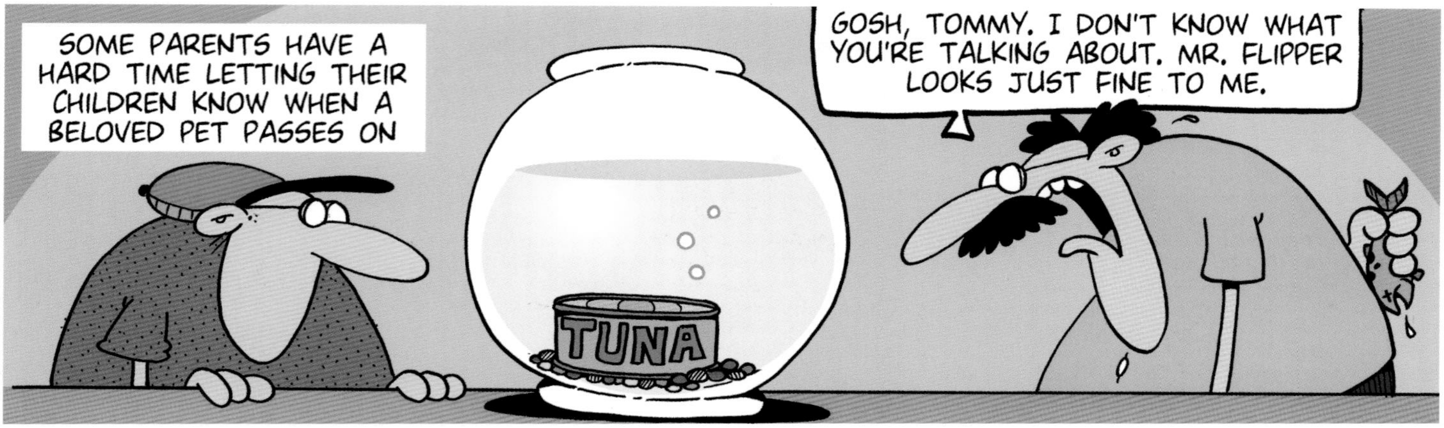
SOME PARENTS HAVE A HARD TIME LETTING THEIR CHILDREN KNOW WHEN A BELOVED PET PASSES ON
GOSH, TOMMY. I DON'T KNOW WHAT YOU'RE TALKING ABOUT. MR. FLIPPER LOOKS JUST FINE TO ME.
TUNA

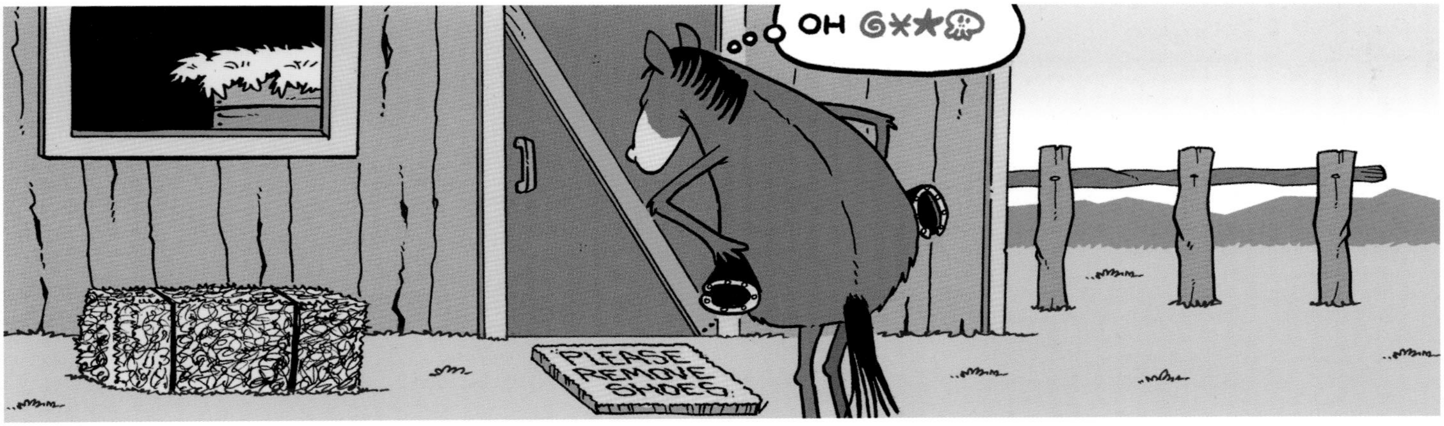
OH
PLEASE REMOVE SHOES

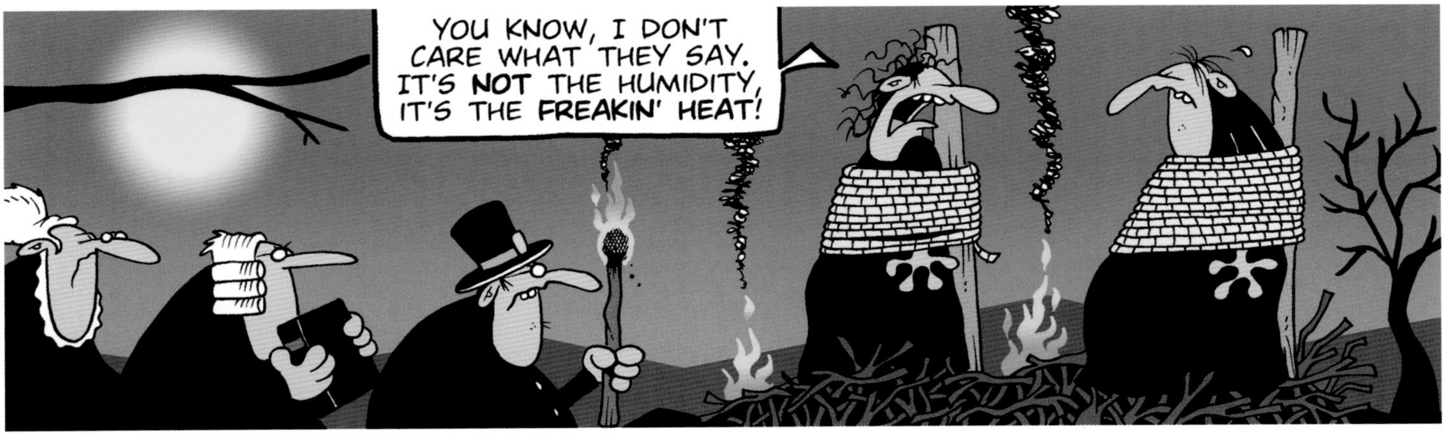
YOU KNOW, I DON'T CARE WHAT THEY SAY. IT'S **NOT** THE HUMIDITY, IT'S THE **FREAKIN' HEAT**!

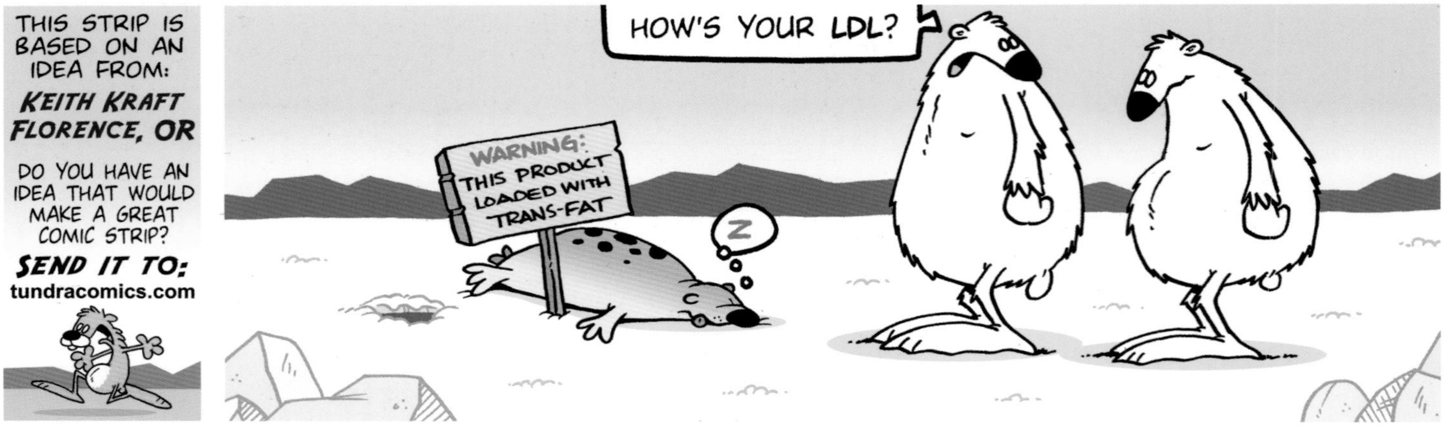
THIS STRIP IS BASED ON AN IDEA FROM:
KEITH KRAFT FLORENCE, OR
DO YOU HAVE AN IDEA THAT WOULD MAKE A GREAT COMIC STRIP?
SEND IT TO: tundracomics.com
WARNING: THIS PRODUCT LOADED WITH TRANS-FAT
Z
HOW'S YOUR LDL?

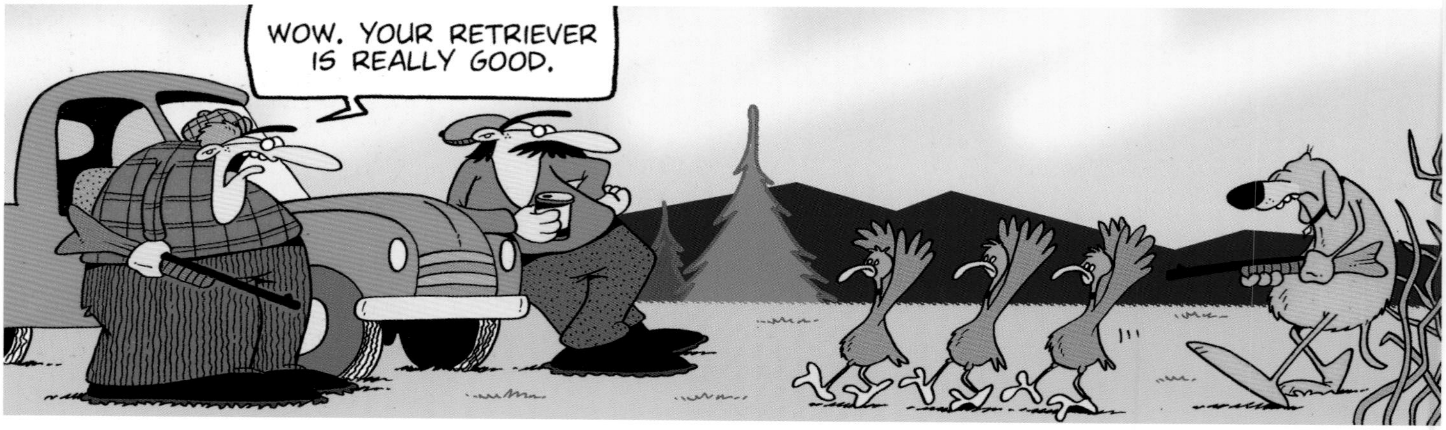
WOW. YOUR RETRIEVER IS REALLY GOOD.

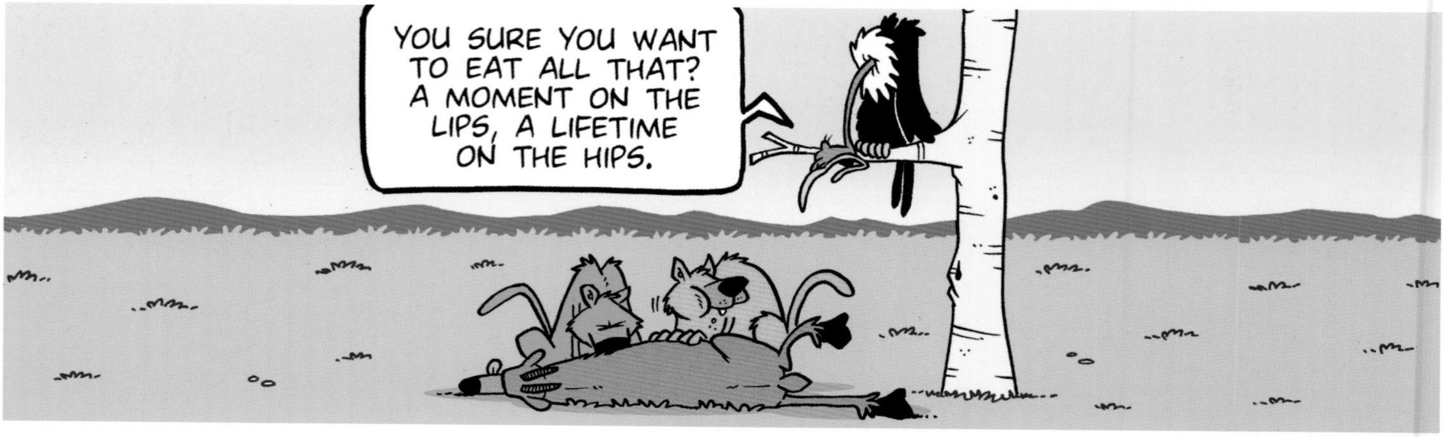
YOU SURE YOU WANT TO EAT ALL THAT? A MOMENT ON THE LIPS, A LIFETIME ON THE HIPS.

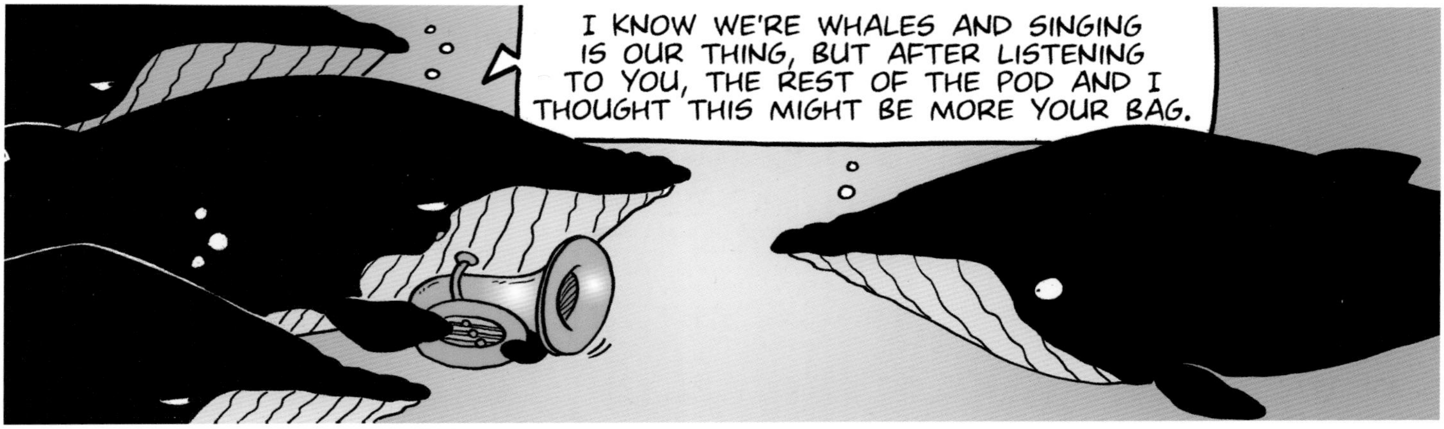
I KNOW WE'RE WHALES AND SINGING IS OUR THING, BUT AFTER LISTENING TO YOU, THE REST OF THE POD AND I THOUGHT THIS MIGHT BE MORE YOUR BAG.

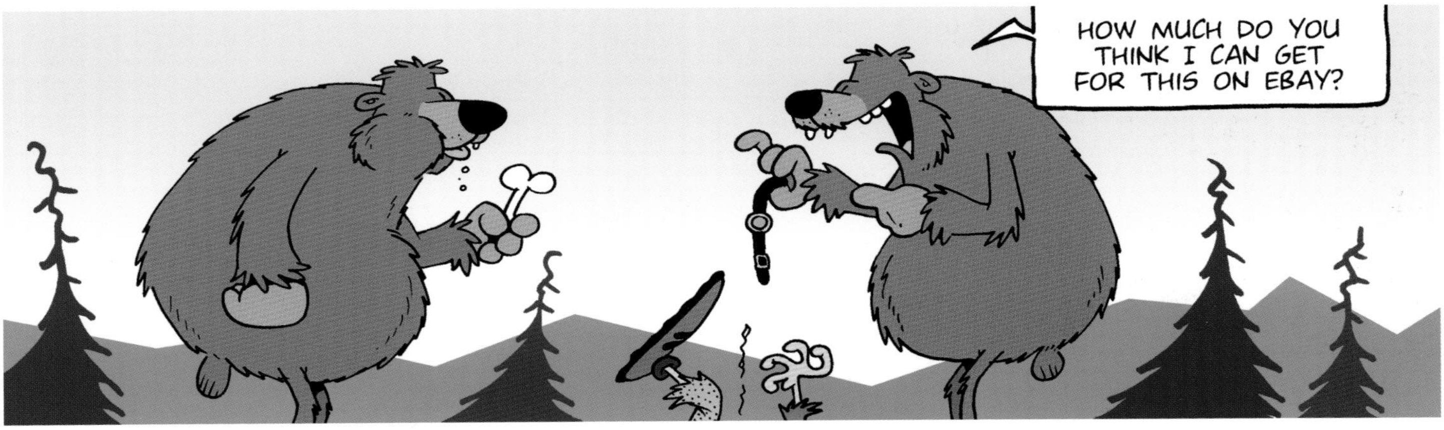
HOW MUCH DO YOU THINK I CAN GET FOR THIS ON EBAY?

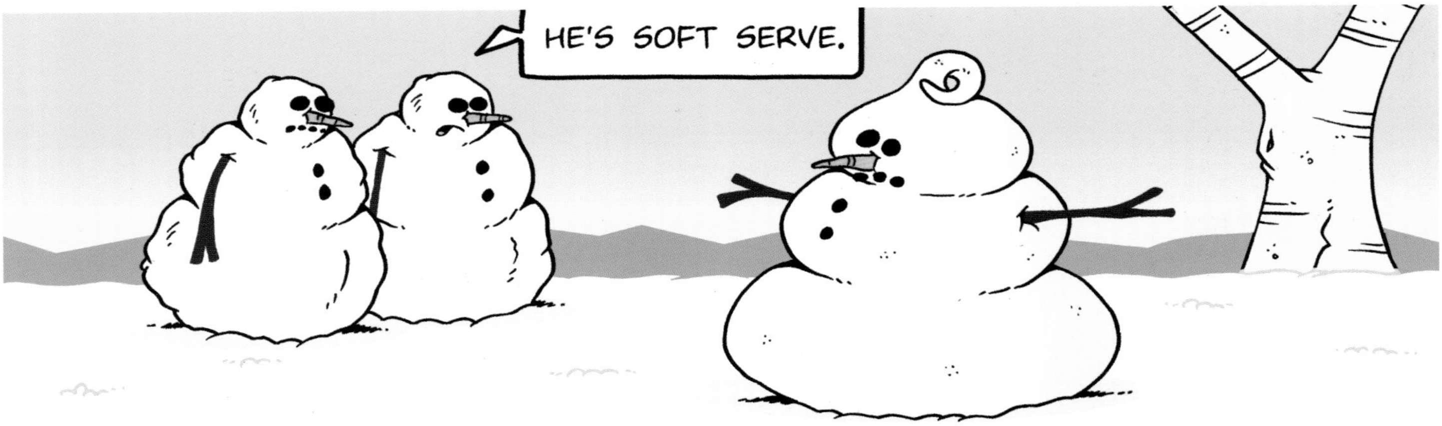
HE'S SOFT SERVE.

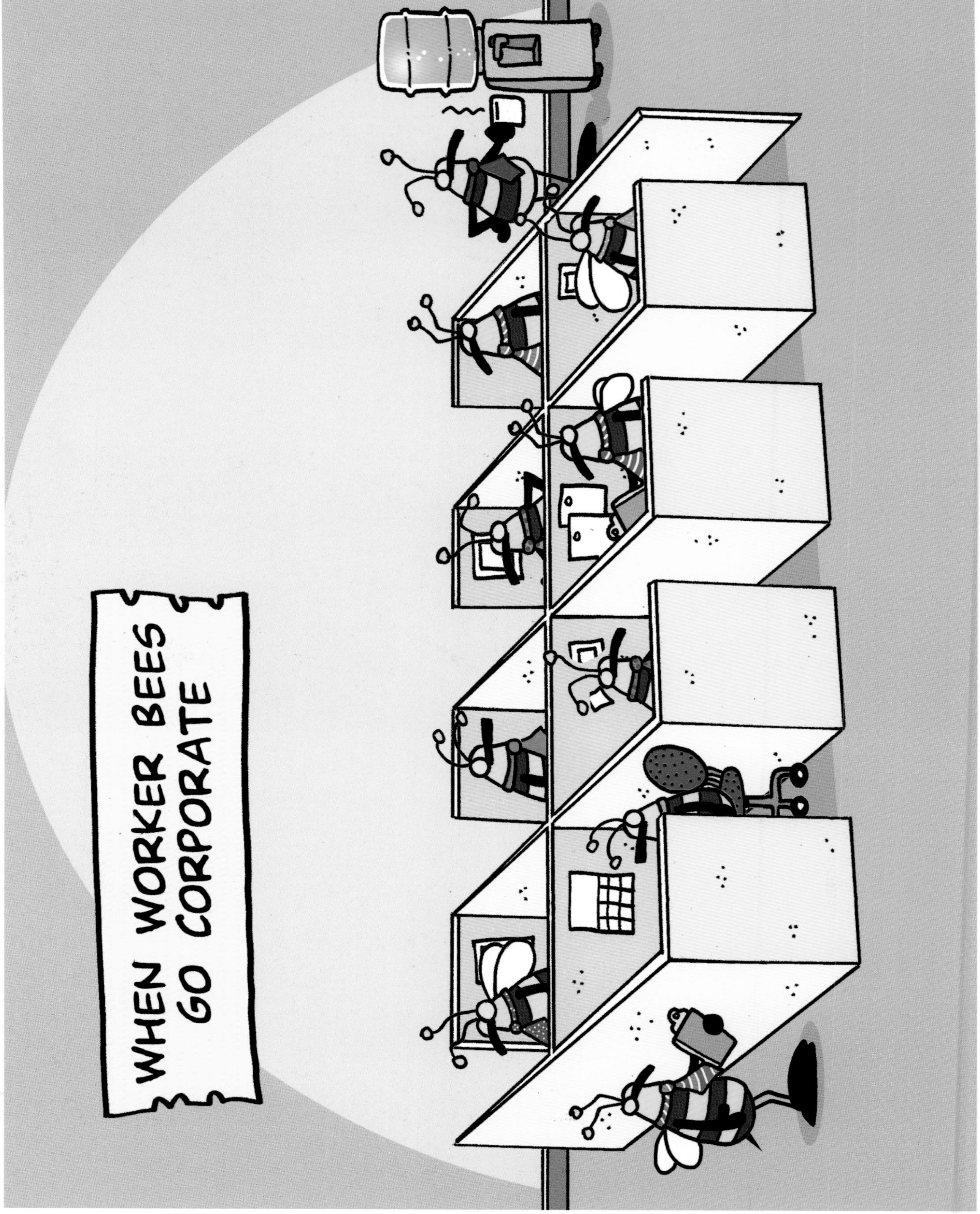
WHEN WORKER BEES
GO CORPORATE

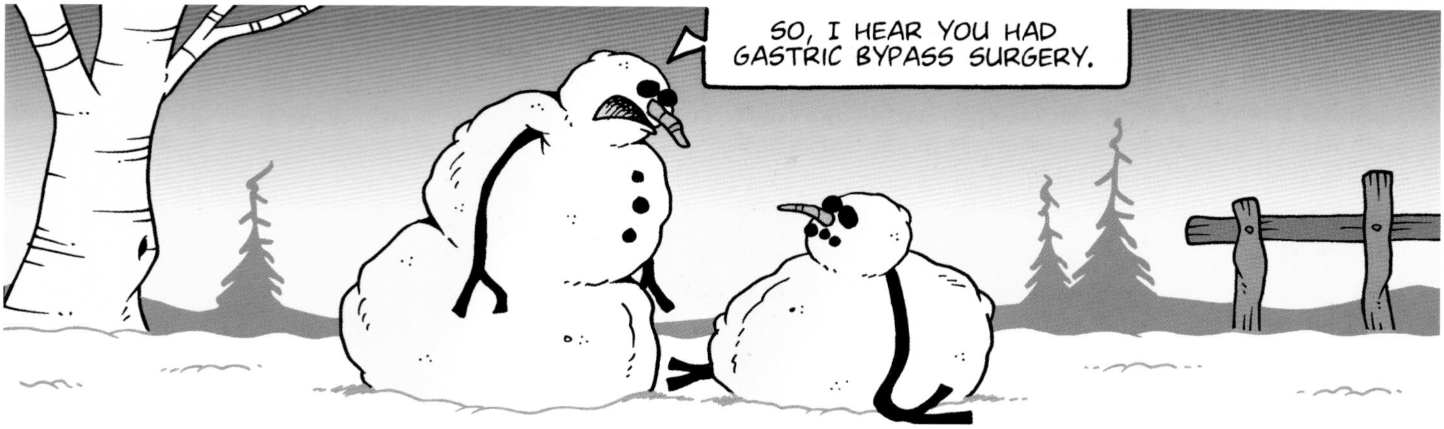
SO, I HEAR YOU HAD GASTRIC BYPASS SURGERY.

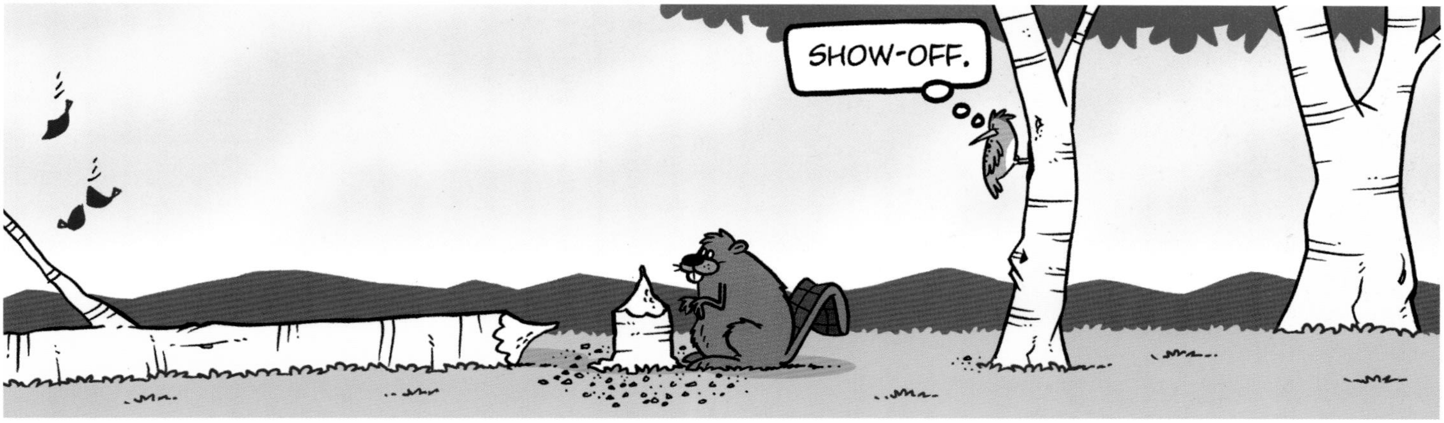
SHOW-OFF.

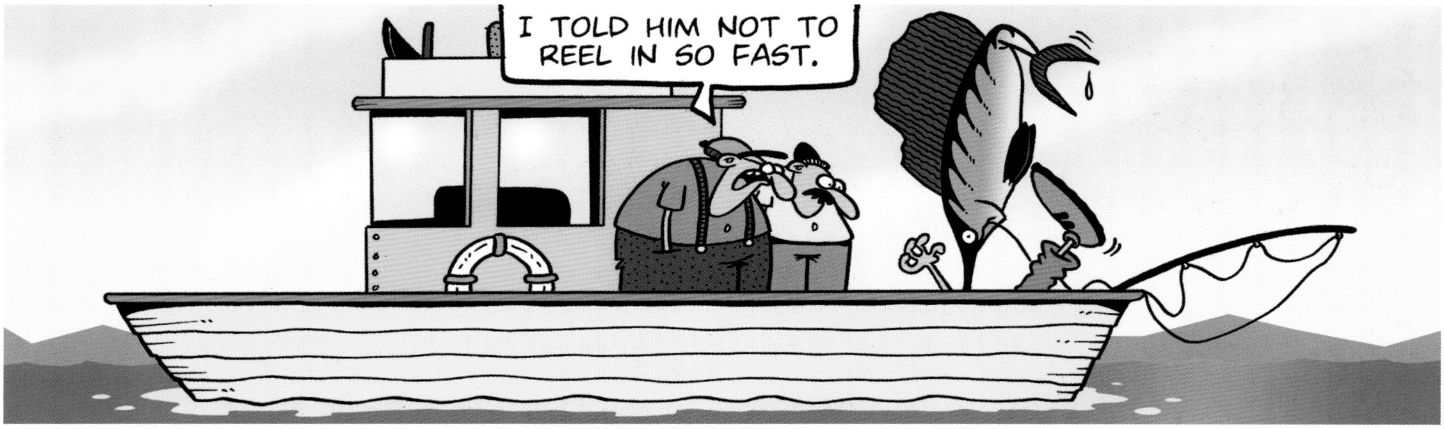
I TOLD HIM NOT TO REEL IN SO FAST.

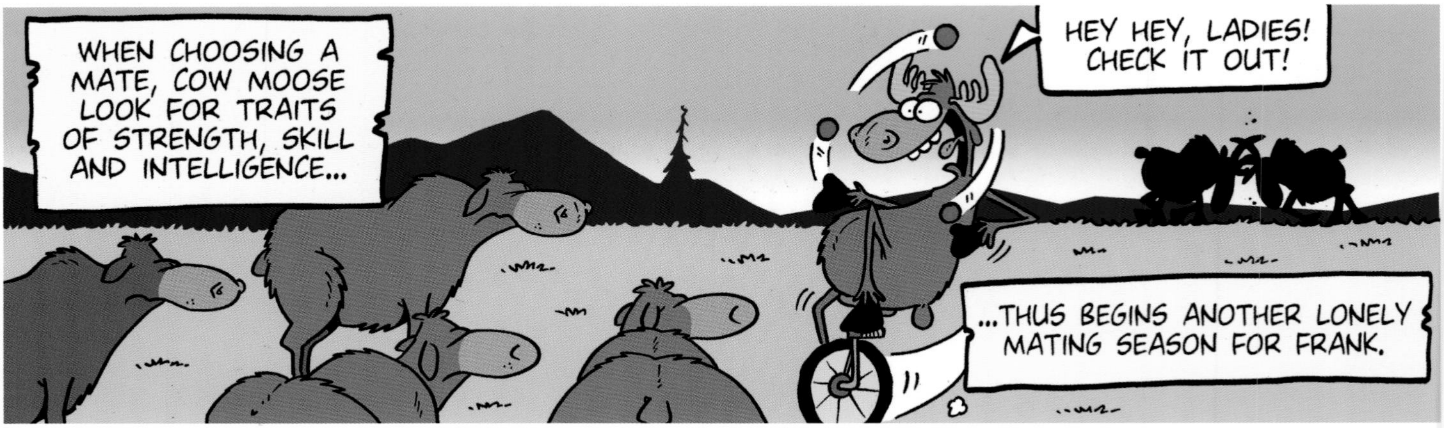
WHEN CHOOSING A MATE, COW MOOSE LOOK FOR TRAITS OF STRENGTH, SKILL AND INTELLIGENCE...
HEY HEY, LADIES! CHECK IT OUT!
...THUS BEGINS ANOTHER LONELY MATING SEASON FOR FRANK.

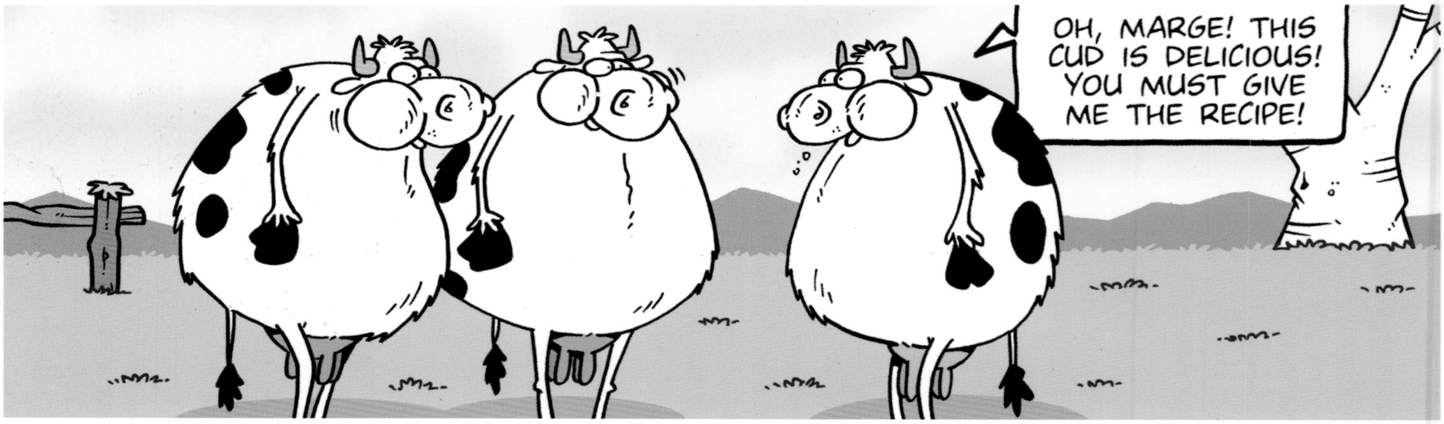
OH, MARGE! THIS CUD IS DELICIOUS! YOU MUST GIVE ME THE RECIPE!

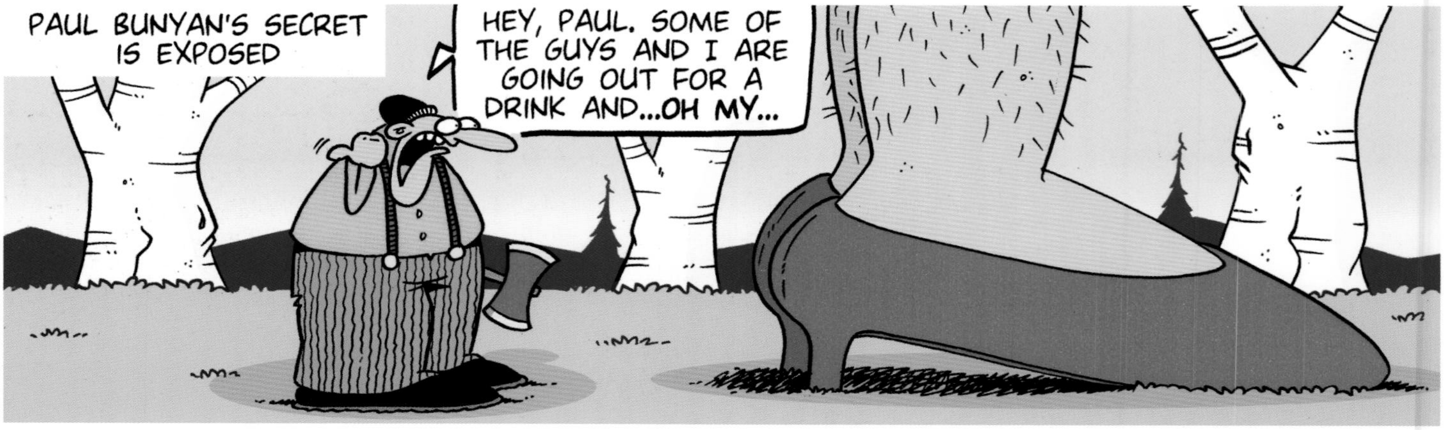
PAUL BUNYAN'S SECRET IS EXPOSED
HEY, PAUL. SOME OF THE GUYS AND I ARE GOING OUT FOR A DRINK AND...OH MY...

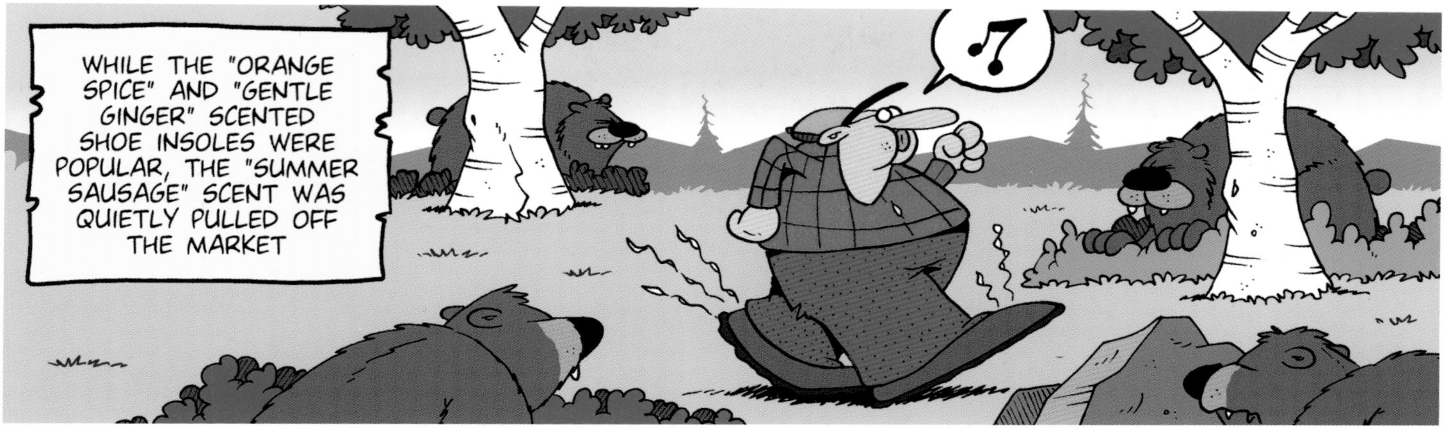
WHILE THE "ORANGE SPICE" AND "GENTLE GINGER" SCENTED SHOE INSOLES WERE POPULAR, THE "SUMMER SAUSAGE" SCENT WAS QUIETLY PULLED OFF THE MARKET

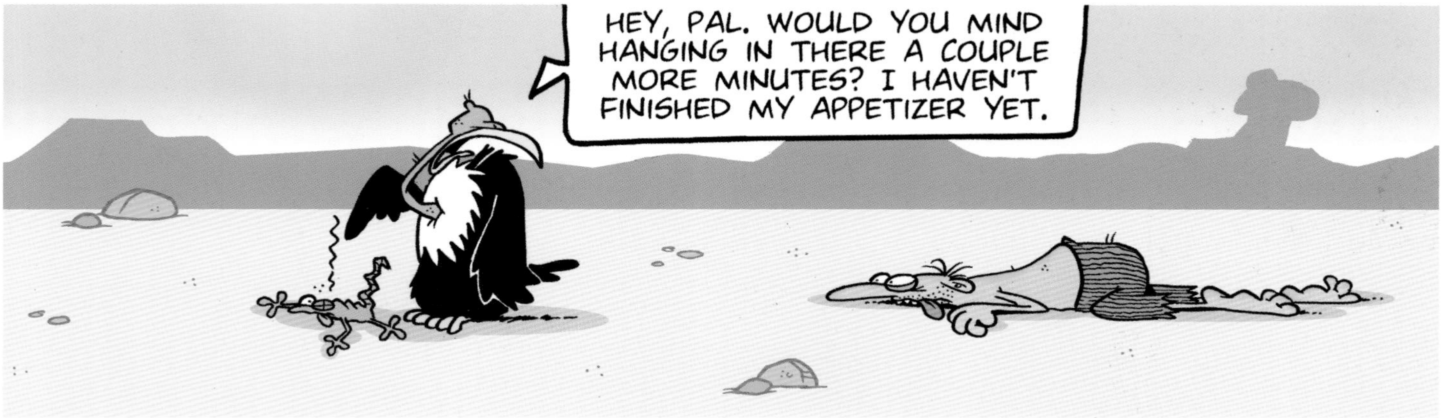
HEY, PAL. WOULD YOU MIND HANGING IN THERE A COUPLE MORE MINUTES? I HAVEN'T FINISHED MY APPETIZER YET.

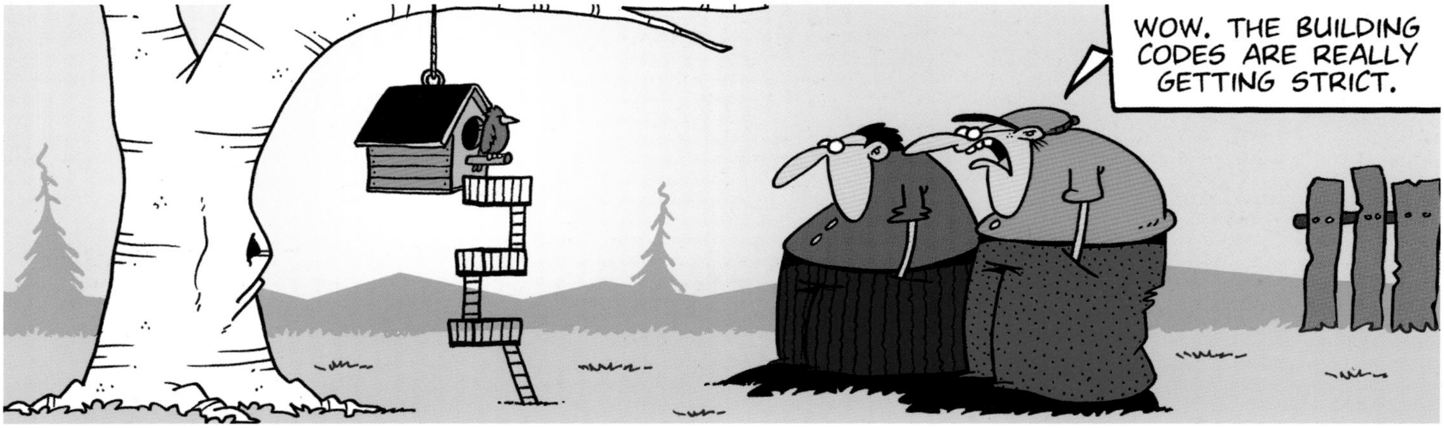
WOW. THE BUILDING CODES ARE REALLY GETTING STRICT.

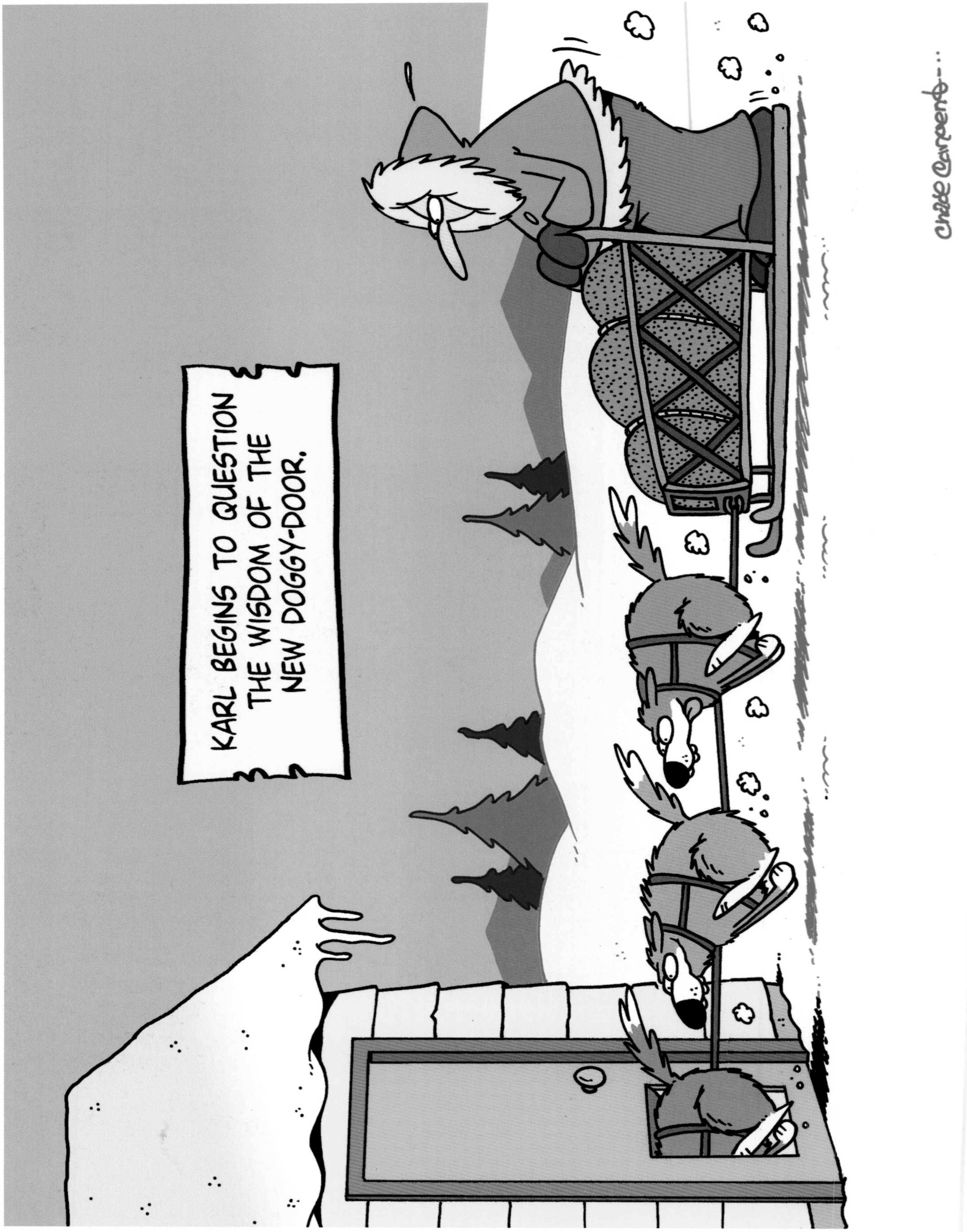
KARL BEGINS TO QUESTION THE WISDOM OF THE NEW DOGGY-DOOR.

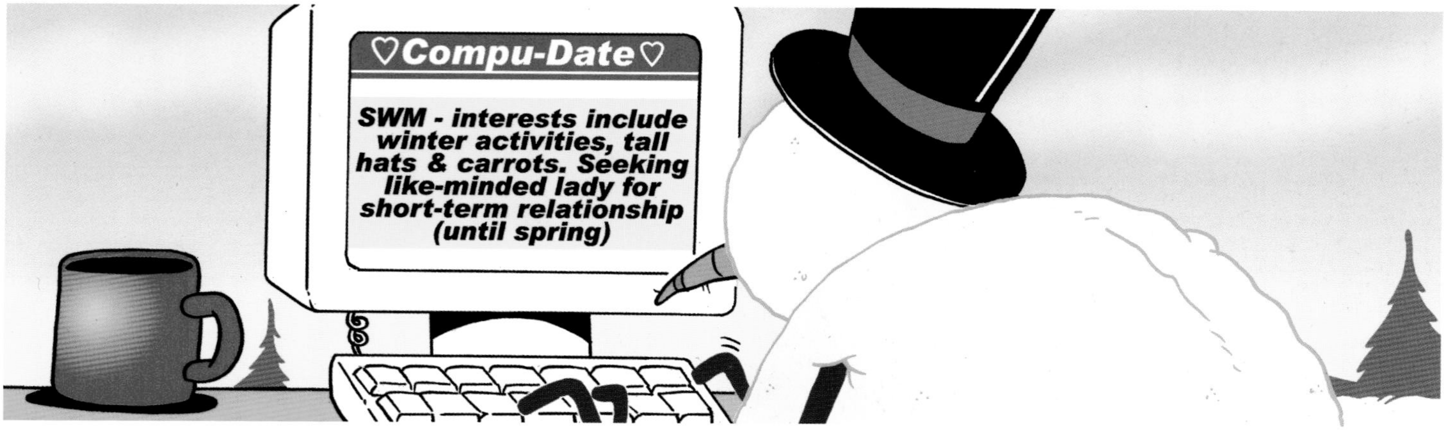
♡Compu-Date♡
SWM - interests include winter activities, tall hats & carrots. Seeking like-minded lady for short-term relationship (until spring)

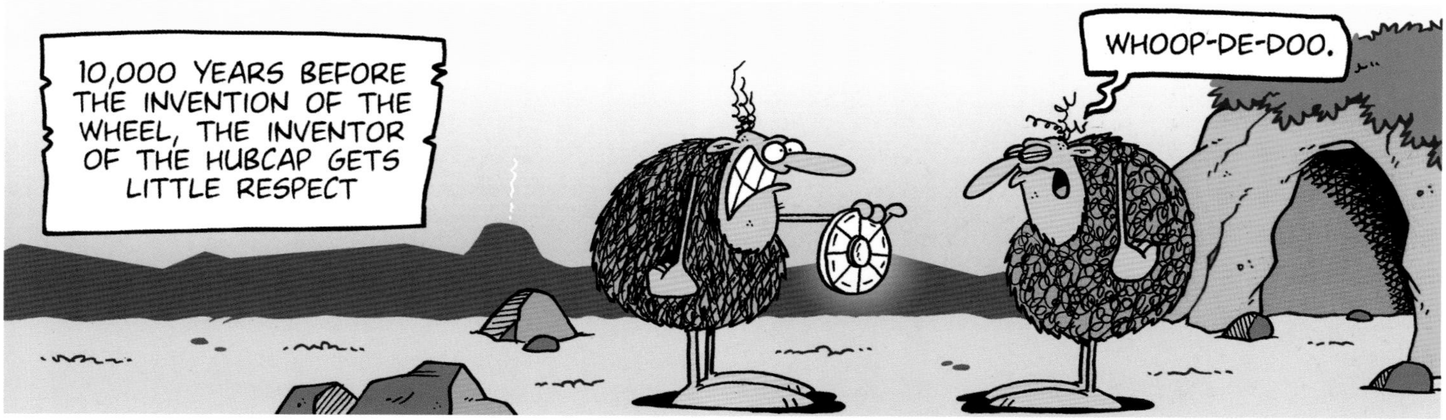
10,000 YEARS BEFORE THE INVENTION OF THE WHEEL, THE INVENTOR OF THE HUBCAP GETS LITTLE RESPECT
WHOOP-DE-DOO.

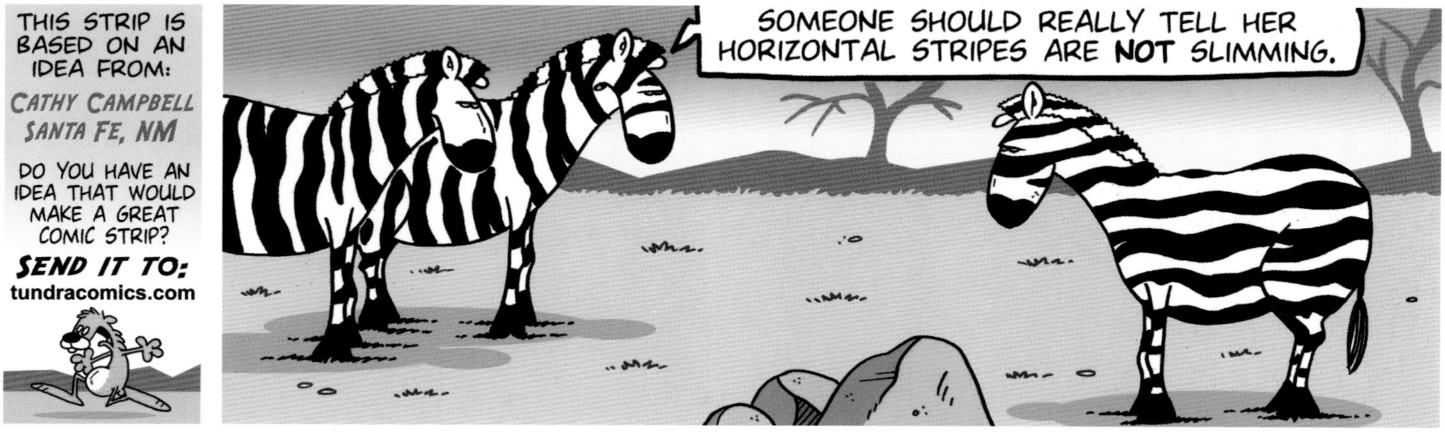
THIS STRIP IS BASED ON AN IDEA FROM:
CATHY CAMPBELL SANTA FE, NM
DO YOU HAVE AN IDEA THAT WOULD MAKE A GREAT COMIC STRIP?
SEND IT TO:
tundracomics.com
SOMEONE SHOULD REALLY TELL HER HORIZONTAL STRIPES ARE NOT SLIMMING.

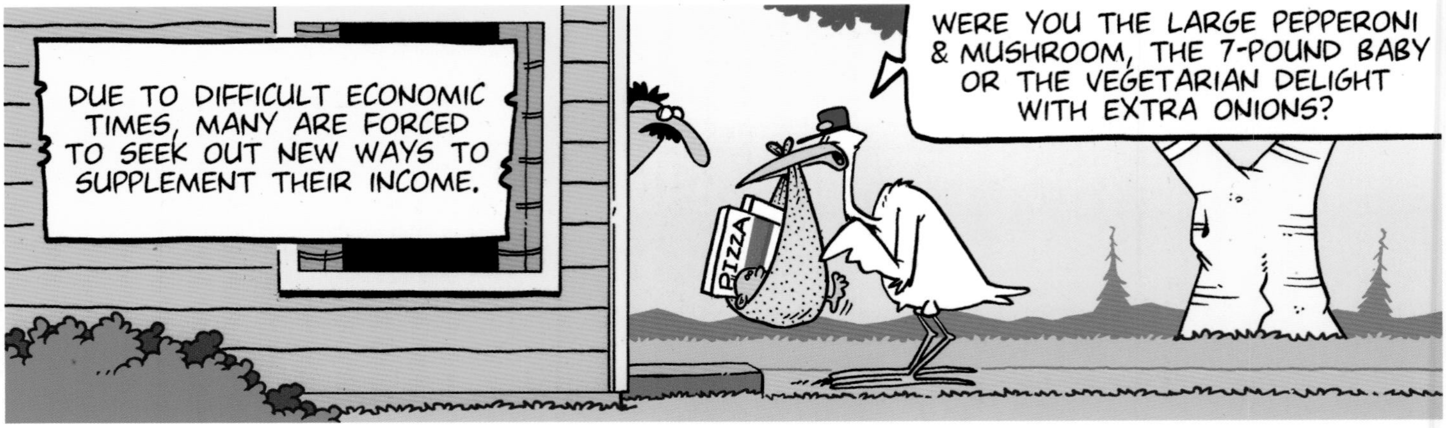
DUE TO DIFFICULT ECONOMIC TIMES, MANY ARE FORCED TO SEEK OUT NEW WAYS TO SUPPLEMENT THEIR INCOME.
WERE YOU THE LARGE PEPPERONI & MUSHROOM, THE 7-POUND BABY OR THE VEGETARIAN DELIGHT WITH EXTRA ONIONS?
PIZZA

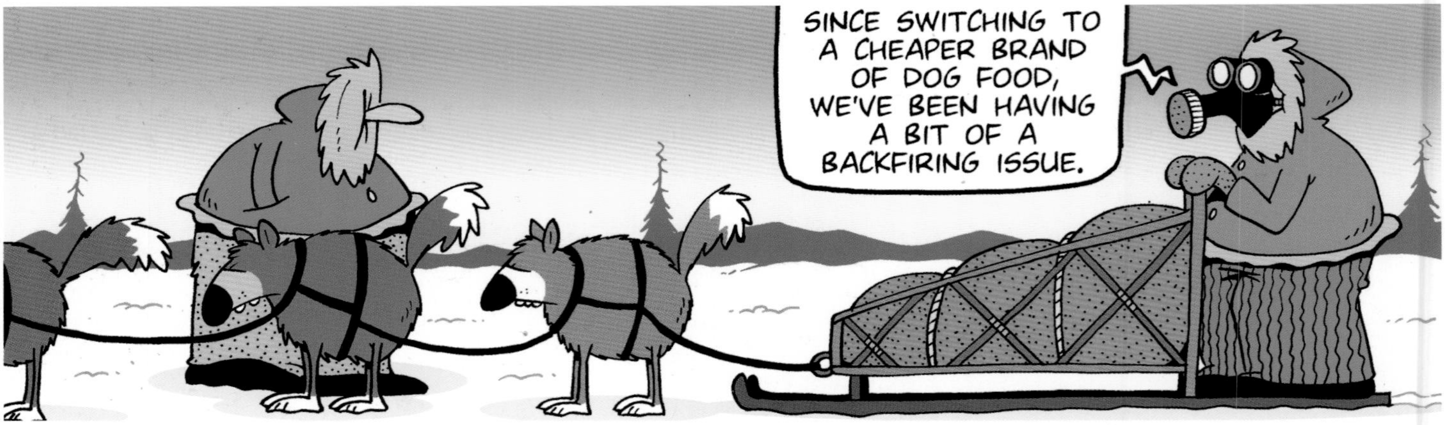
SINCE SWITCHING TO A CHEAPER BRAND OF DOG FOOD, WE'VE BEEN HAVING A BIT OF A BACKFIRING ISSUE.

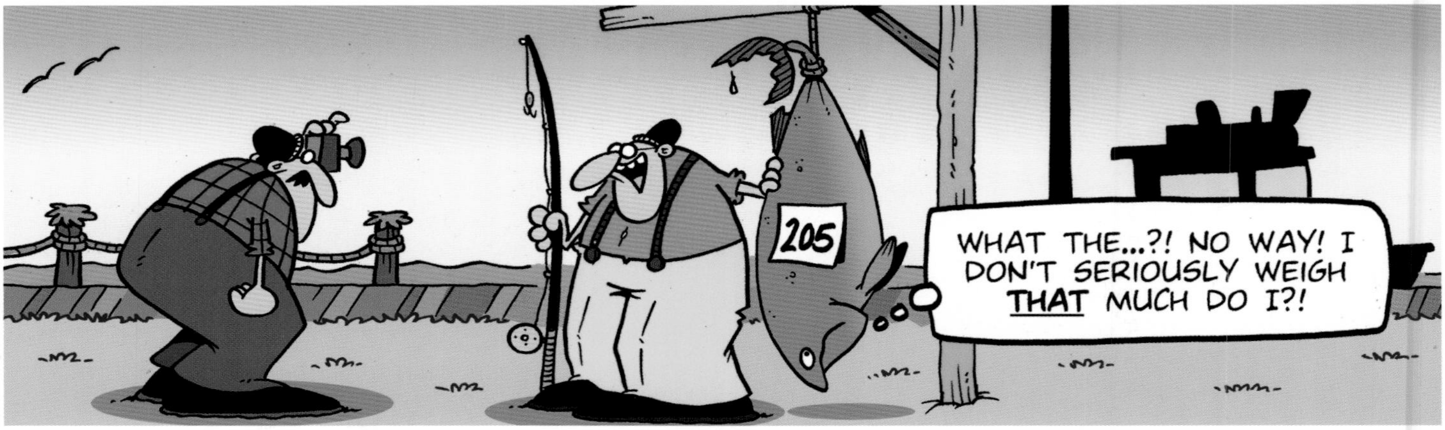
205
WHAT THE...?! NO WAY! I DON'T SERIOUSLY WEIGH THAT MUCH DO I?!

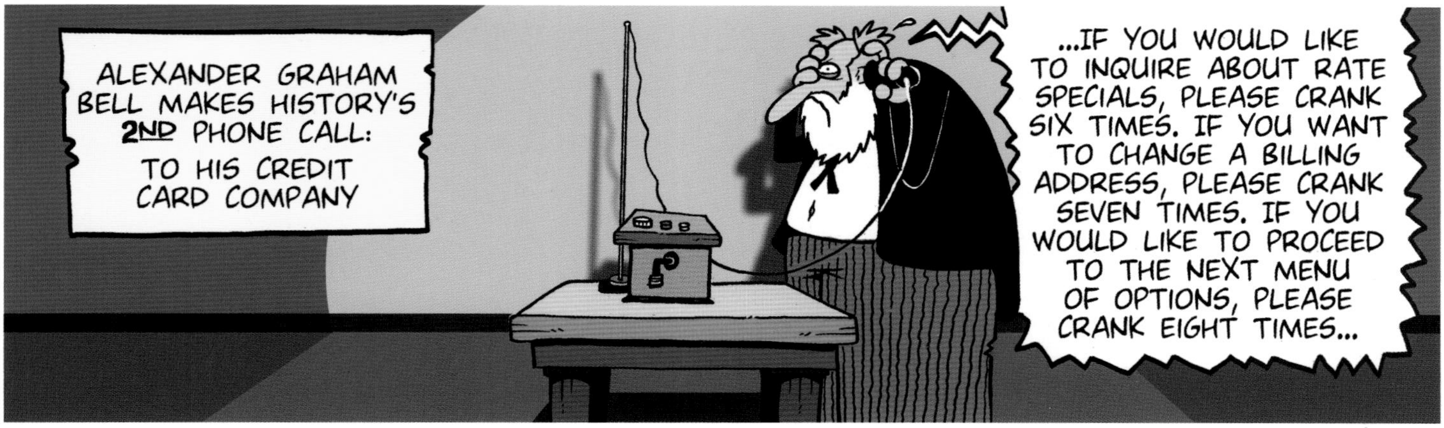
ALEXANDER GRAHAM BELL MAKES HISTORY'S 2ND PHONE CALL:
TO HIS CREDIT CARD COMPANY
...IF YOU WOULD LIKE TO INQUIRE ABOUT RATE SPECIALS, PLEASE CRANK SIX TIMES. IF YOU WANT TO CHANGE A BILLING ADDRESS, PLEASE CRANK SEVEN TIMES. IF YOU WOULD LIKE TO PROCEED TO THE NEXT MENU OF OPTIONS, PLEASE CRANK EIGHT TIMES...

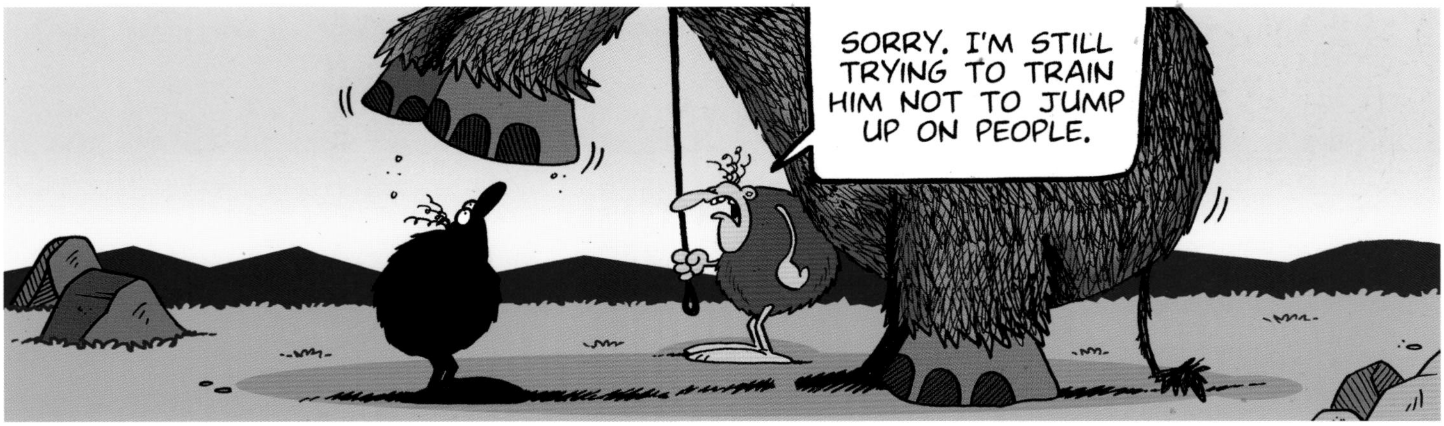
SORRY. I'M STILL TRYING TO TRAIN HIM NOT TO JUMP UP ON PEOPLE.

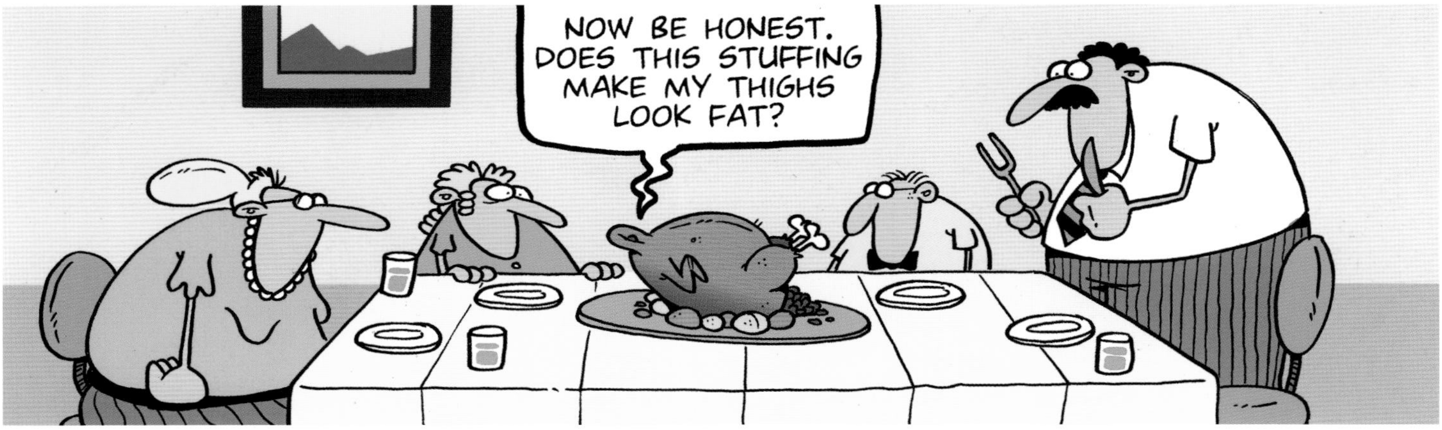
NOW BE HONEST. DOES THIS STUFFING MAKE MY THIGHS LOOK FAT?

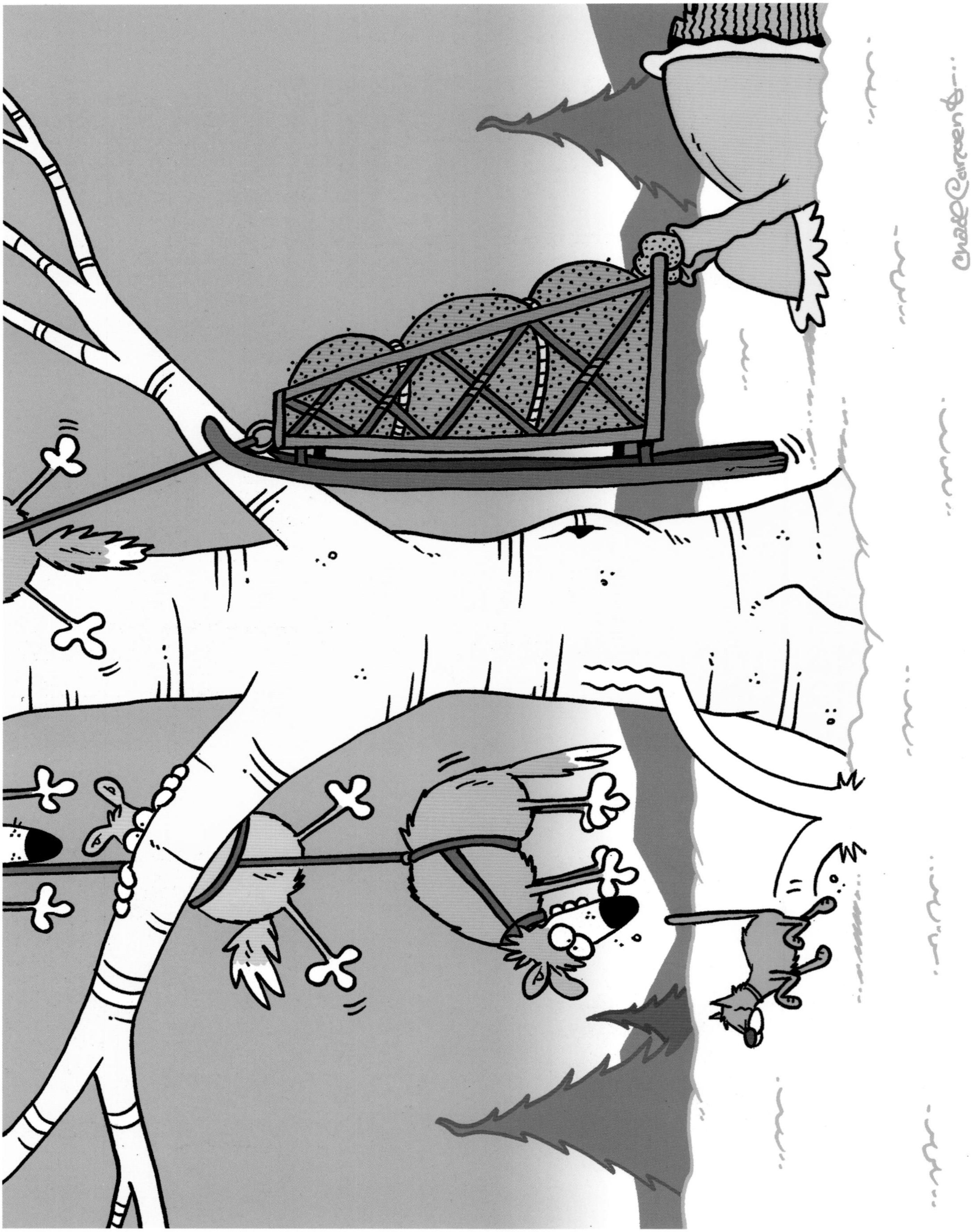
Chad Carpenter

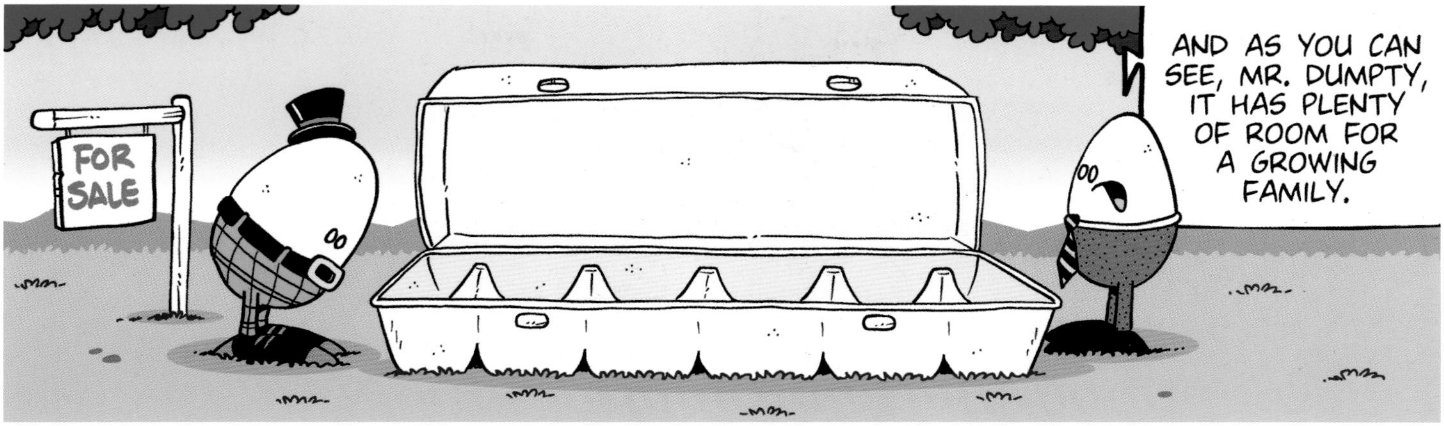
FOR SALE
AND AS YOU CAN SEE, MR. DUMPTY, IT HAS PLENTY OF ROOM FOR A GROWING FAMILY.

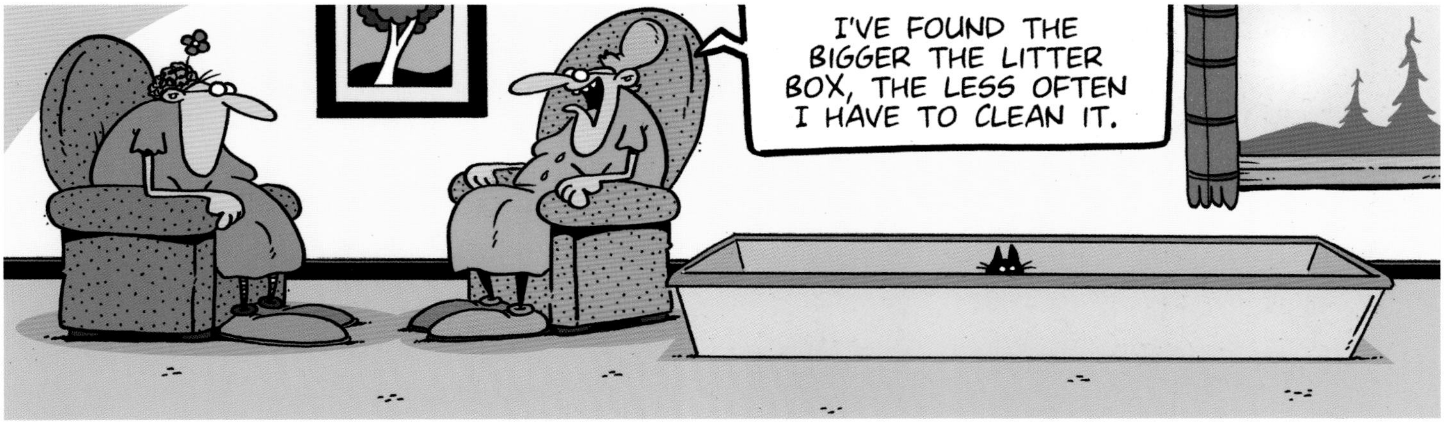
I'VE FOUND THE BIGGER THE LITTER BOX, THE LESS OFTEN I HAVE TO CLEAN IT.

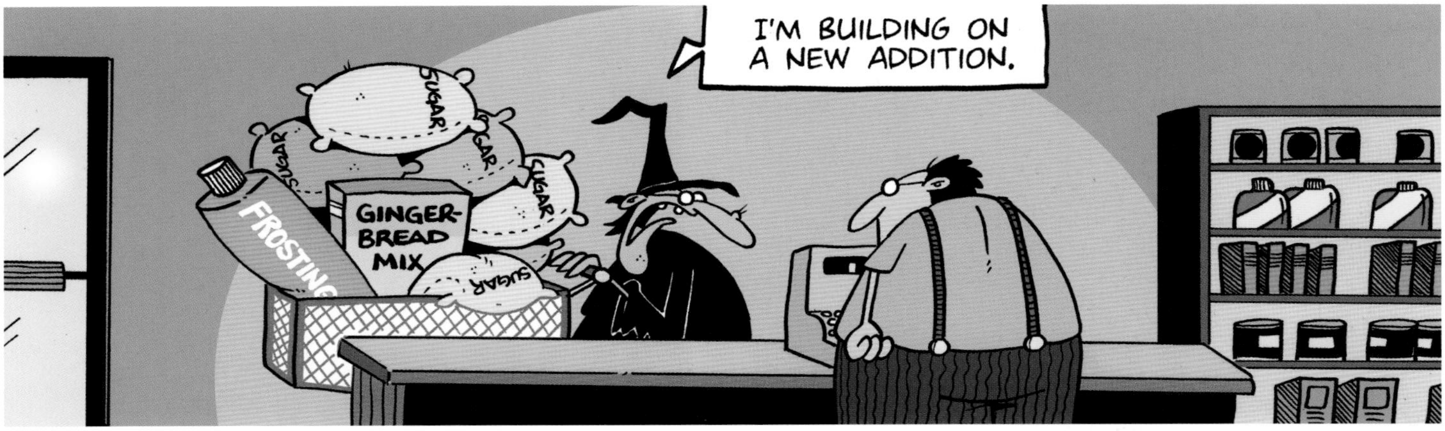
I'M BUILDING ON A NEW ADDITION.
SUGAR
FROSTING
GINGER-BREAD MIX

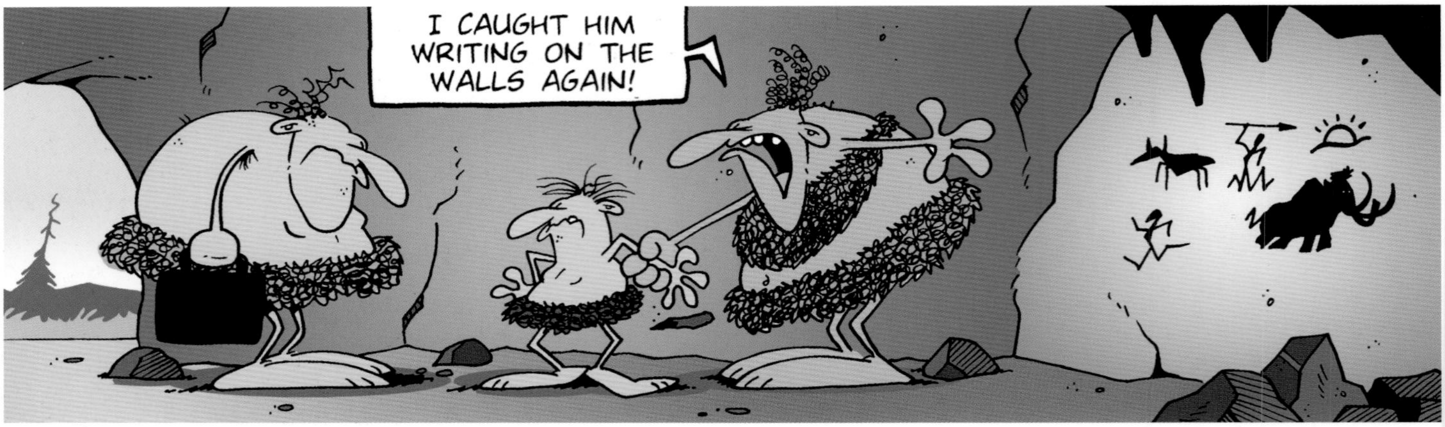
I CAUGHT HIM WRITING ON THE WALLS AGAIN!

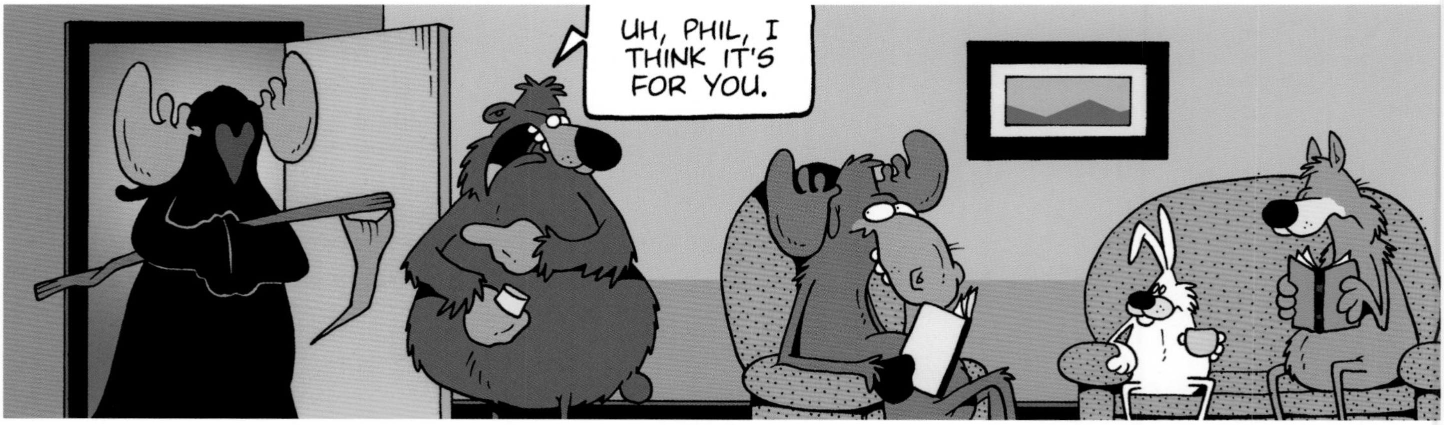
UH, PHIL, I THINK IT'S FOR YOU.

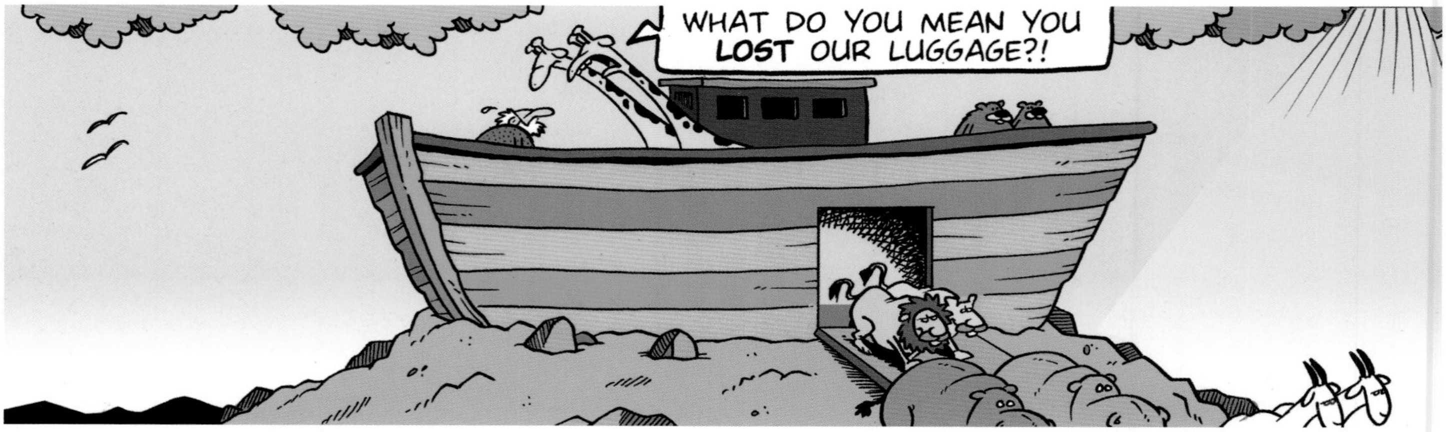
WHAT DO YOU MEAN YOU **LOST** OUR LUGGAGE?!

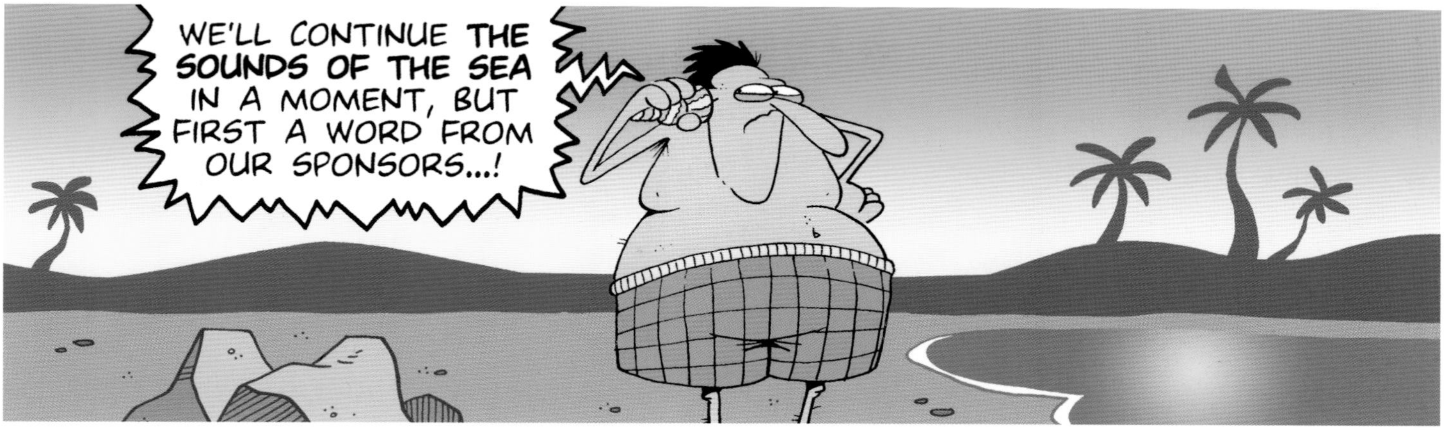
WE'LL CONTINUE THE SOUNDS OF THE SEA IN A MOMENT, BUT FIRST A WORD FROM OUR SPONSORS...!

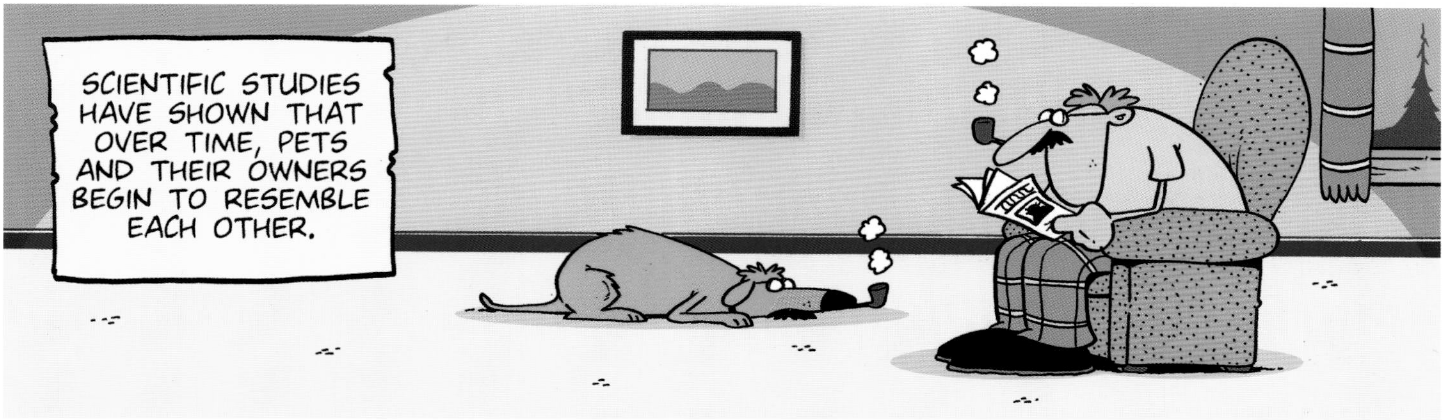
SCIENTIFIC STUDIES HAVE SHOWN THAT OVER TIME, PETS AND THEIR OWNERS BEGIN TO RESEMBLE EACH OTHER.

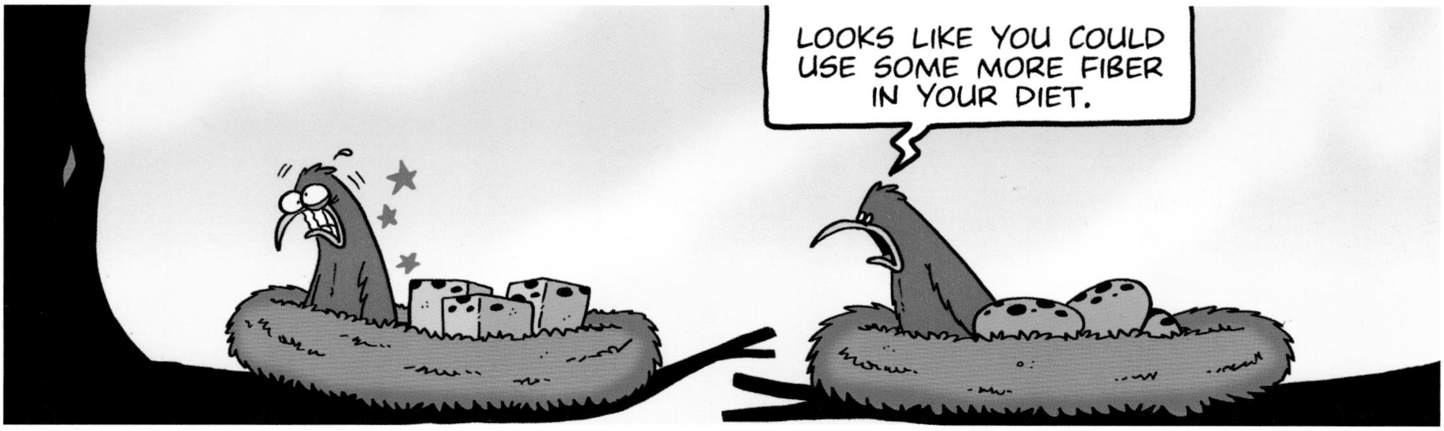
LOOKS LIKE YOU COULD USE SOME MORE FIBER IN YOUR DIET.

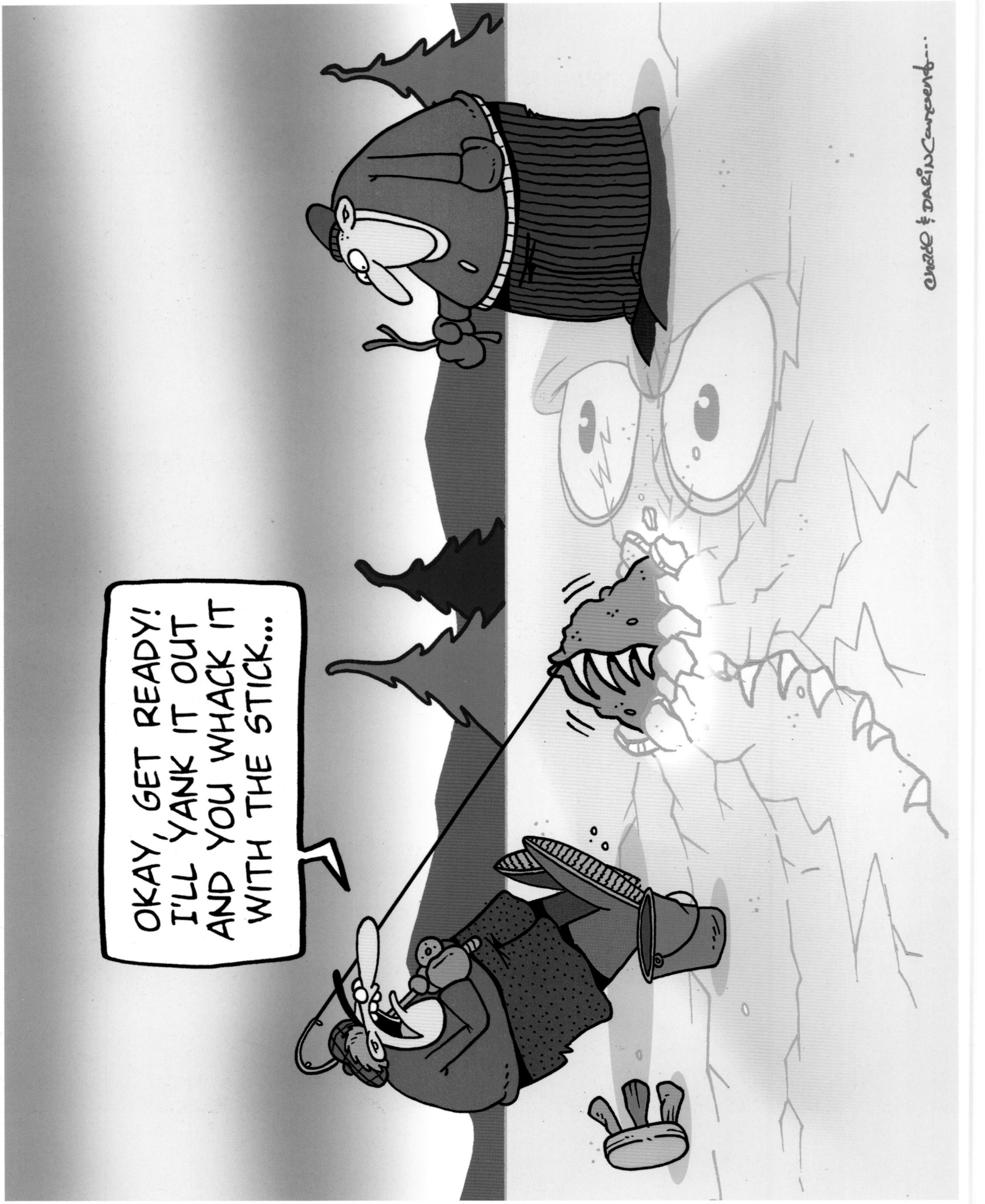
OKAY, GET READY! I'LL YANK IT OUT AND YOU WHACK IT WITH THE STICK...

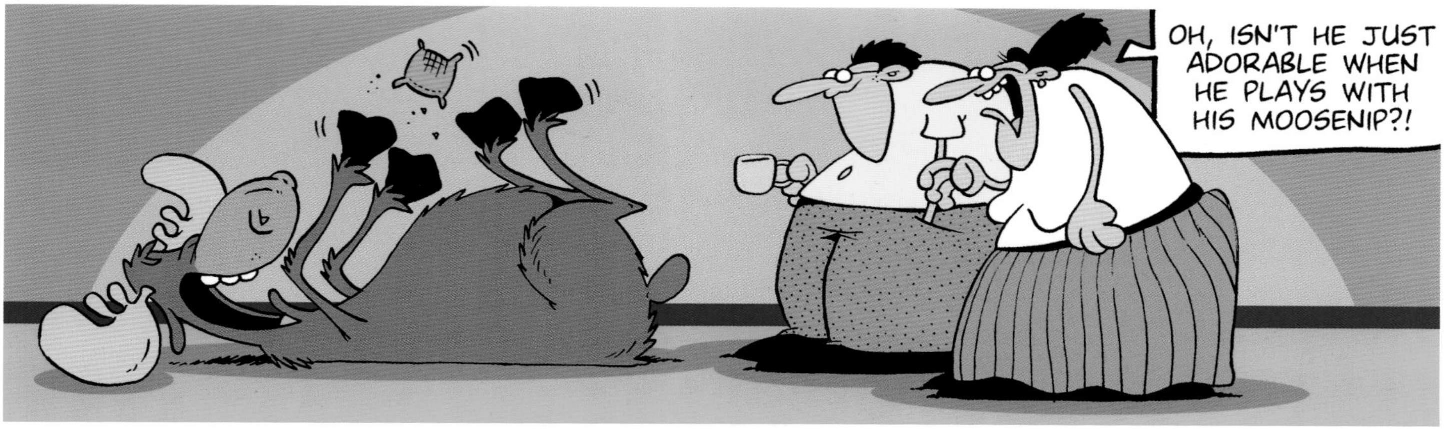
OH, ISN'T HE JUST ADORABLE WHEN HE PLAYS WITH HIS MOOSENIP?!

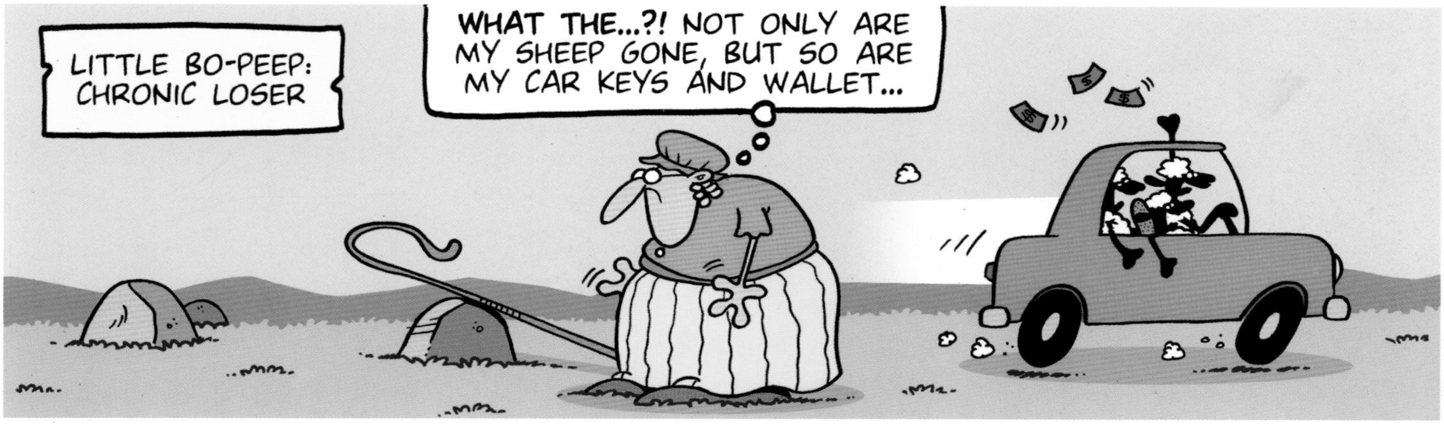
LITTLE BO-PEEP: CHRONIC LOSER
WHAT THE...?! NOT ONLY ARE MY SHEEP GONE, BUT SO ARE MY CAR KEYS AND WALLET...

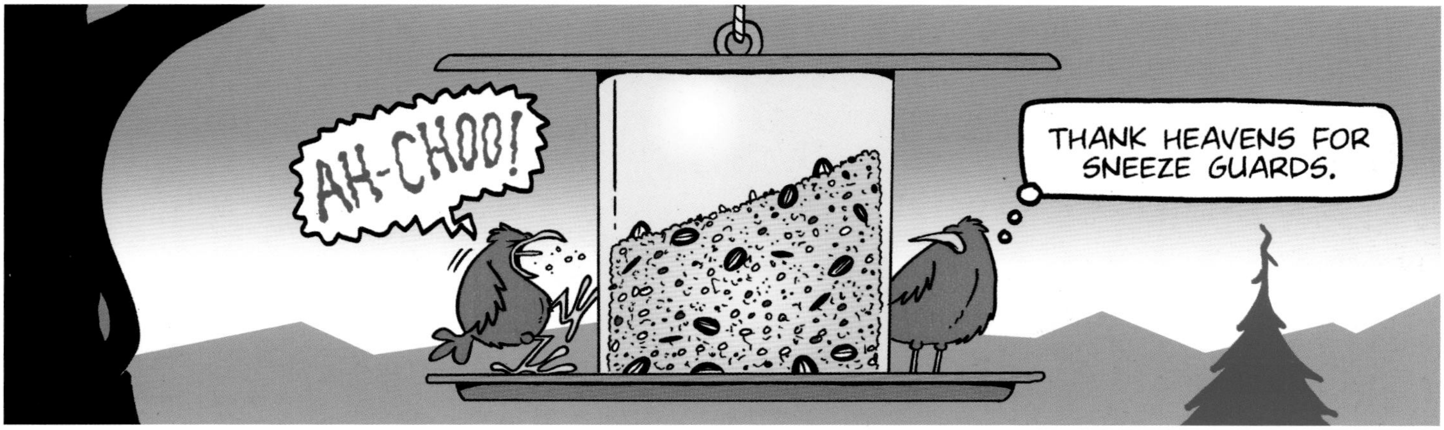
AH-CHOO!
THANK HEAVENS FOR SNEEZE GUARDS.

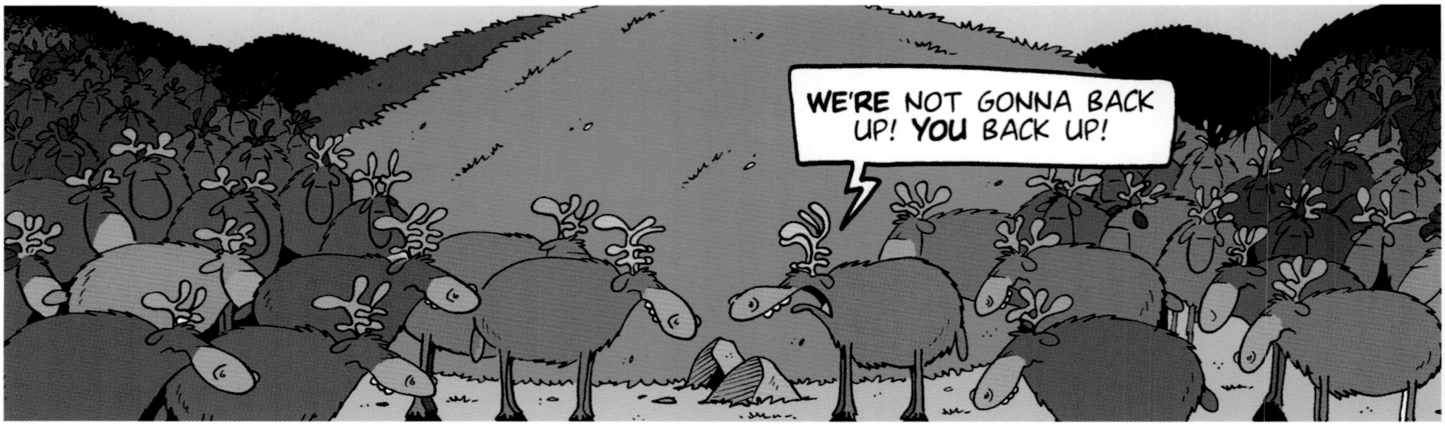
WE'RE NOT GONNA BACK UP! YOU BACK UP!

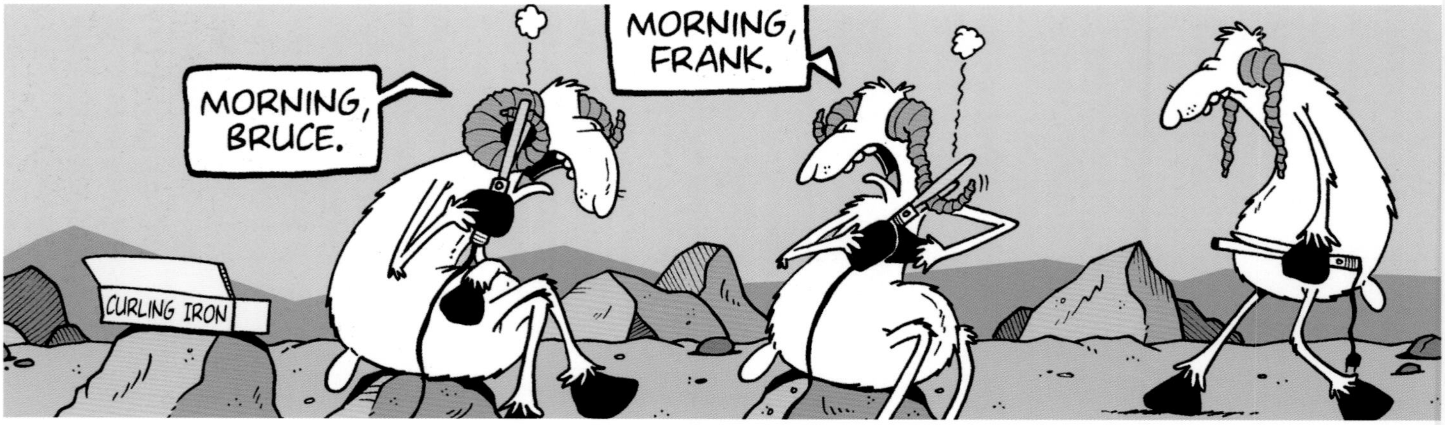
MORNING, BRUCE.
MORNING, FRANK.
CURLING IRON

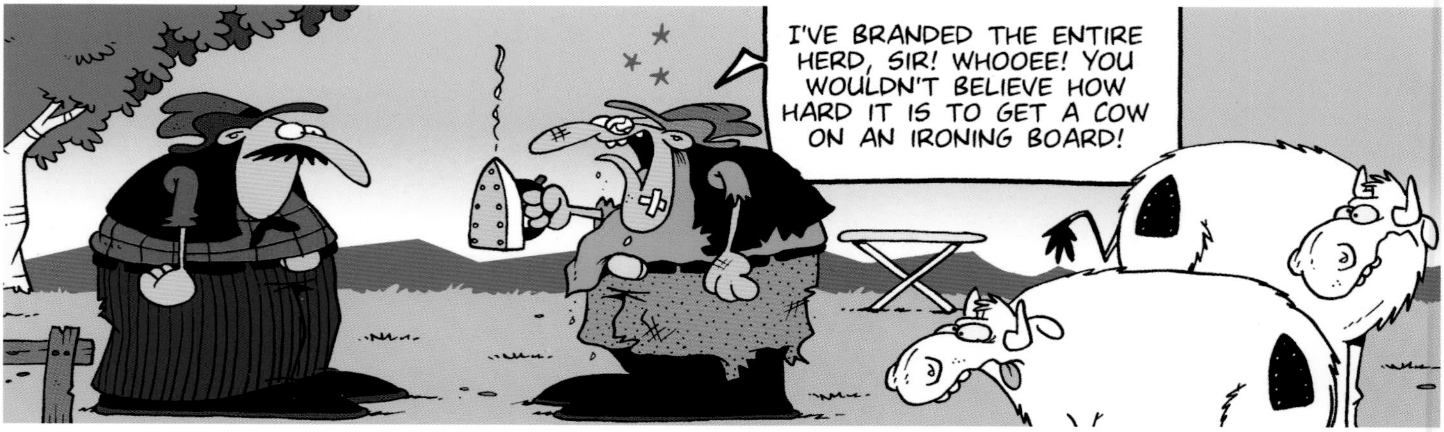
I'VE BRANDED THE ENTIRE HERD, SIR! WHOOEE! YOU WOULDN'T BELIEVE HOW HARD IT IS TO GET A COW ON AN IRONING BOARD!

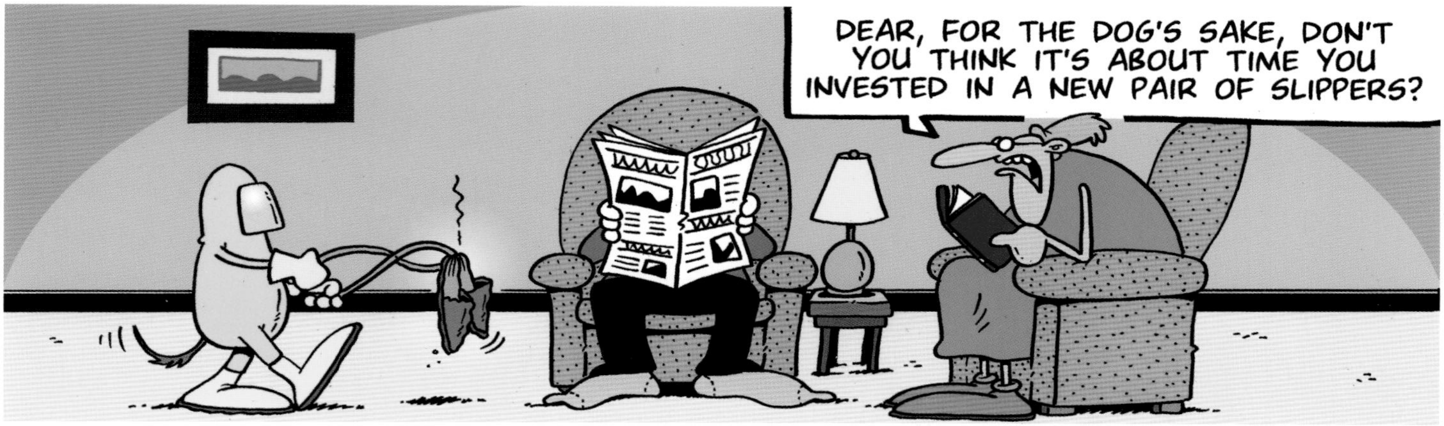
DEAR, FOR THE DOG'S SAKE, DON'T YOU THINK IT'S ABOUT TIME YOU INVESTED IN A NEW PAIR OF SLIPPERS?

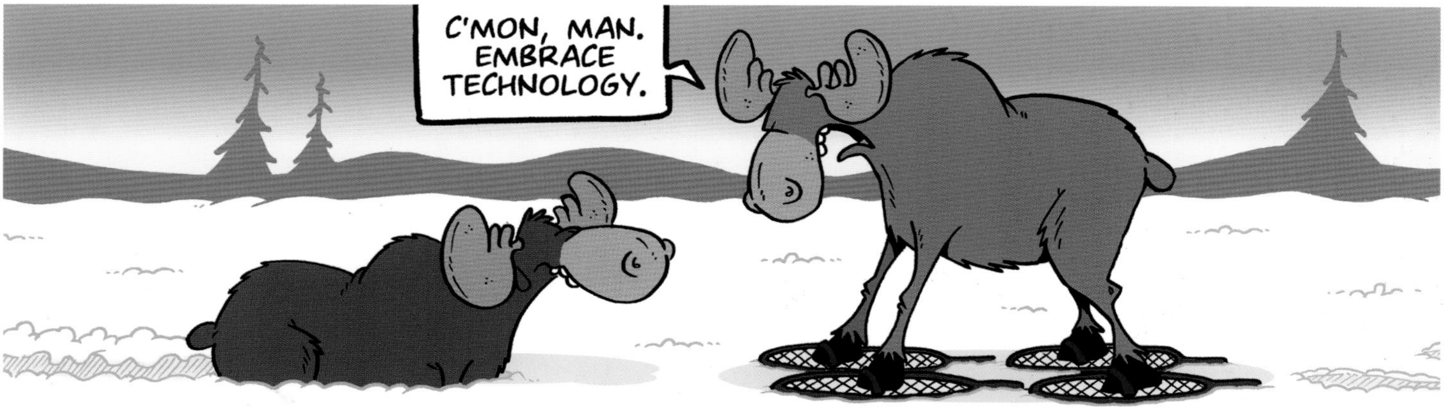
C'MON, MAN. EMBRACE TECHNOLOGY.

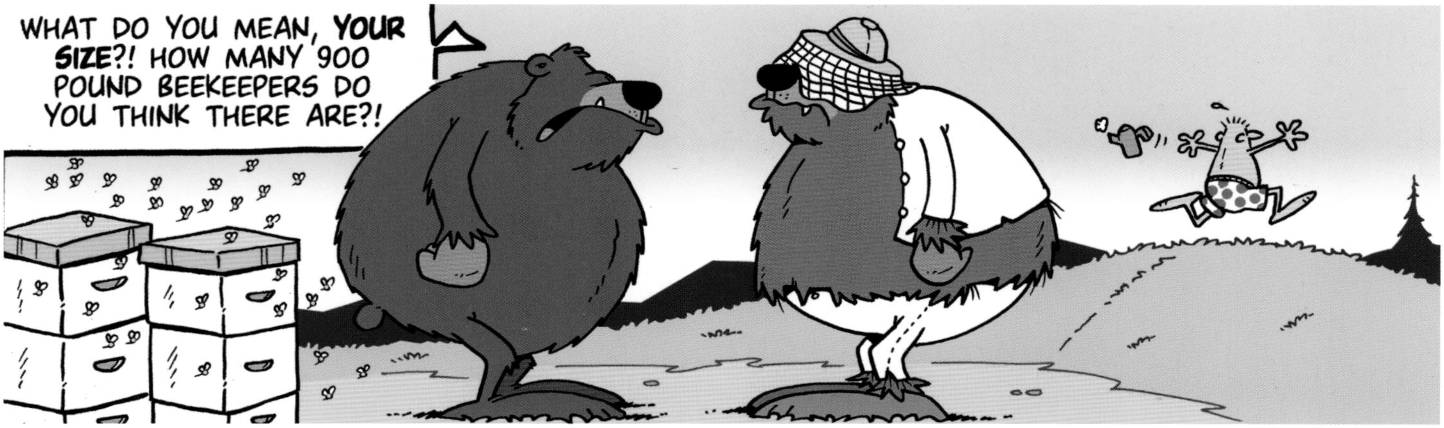
WHAT DO YOU MEAN, **YOUR SIZE**?! HOW MANY 900 POUND BEEKEEPERS DO YOU THINK THERE ARE?!

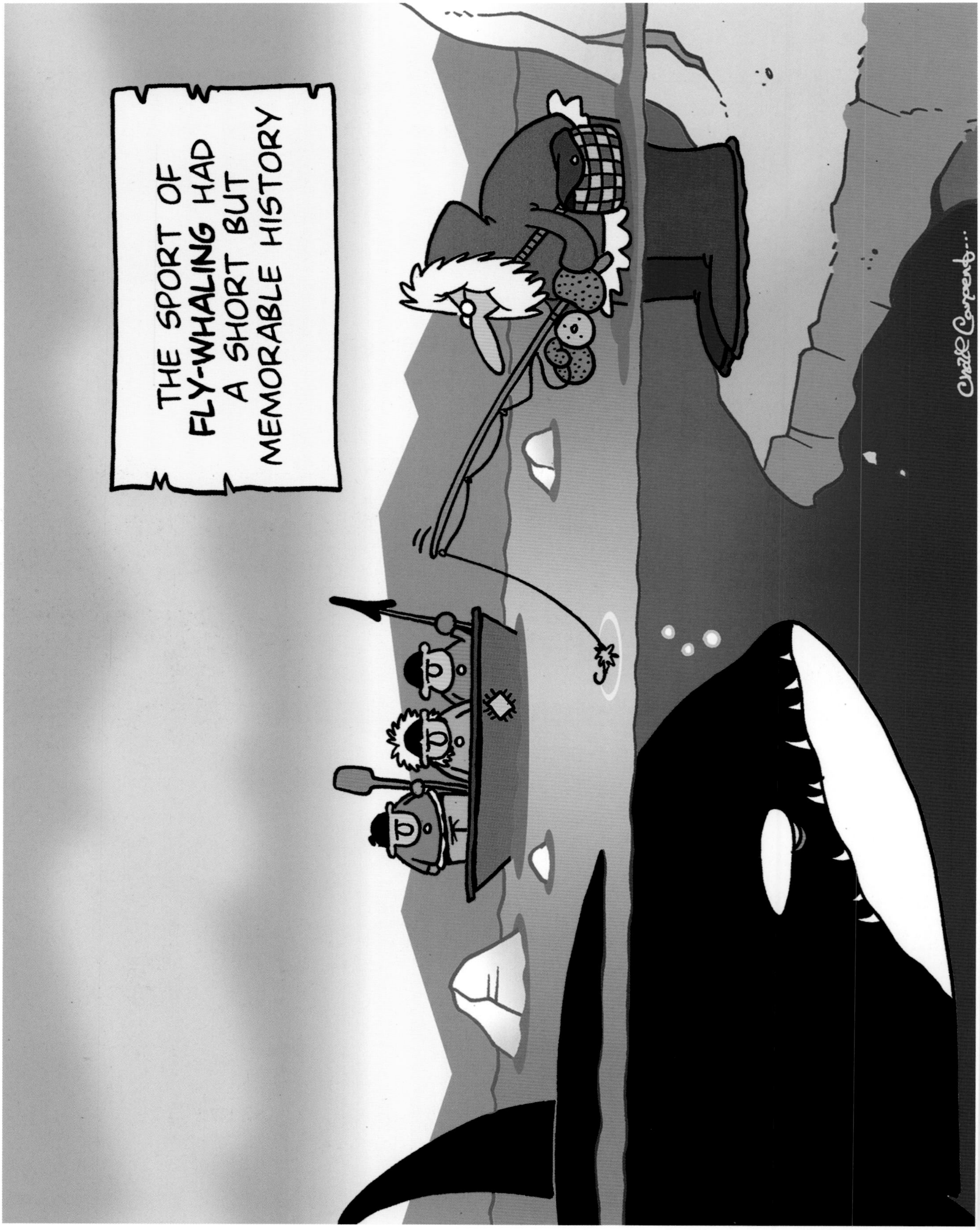
THE SPORT OF FLY-WHALING HAD A SHORT BUT MEMORABLE HISTORY

THIS STRIP IS BASED ON AN IDEA FROM:

ELORA CARPENTER
NORTH POLE, AK

DO YOU HAVE AN IDEA THAT WOULD MAKE A GREAT COMIC STRIP?

SEND IT TO:
tundracomics.com

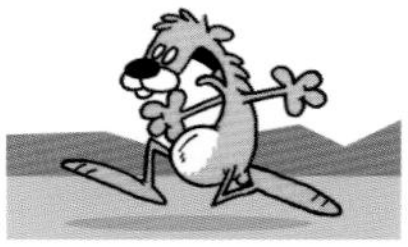

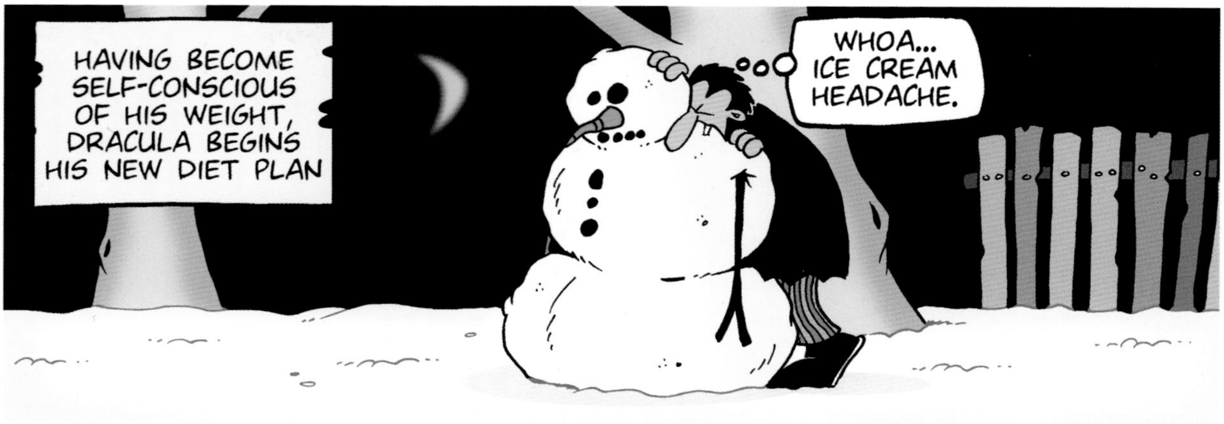
HAVING BECOME SELF-CONSCIOUS OF HIS WEIGHT, DRACULA BEGINS HIS NEW DIET PLAN
WHOA... ICE CREAM HEADACHE.

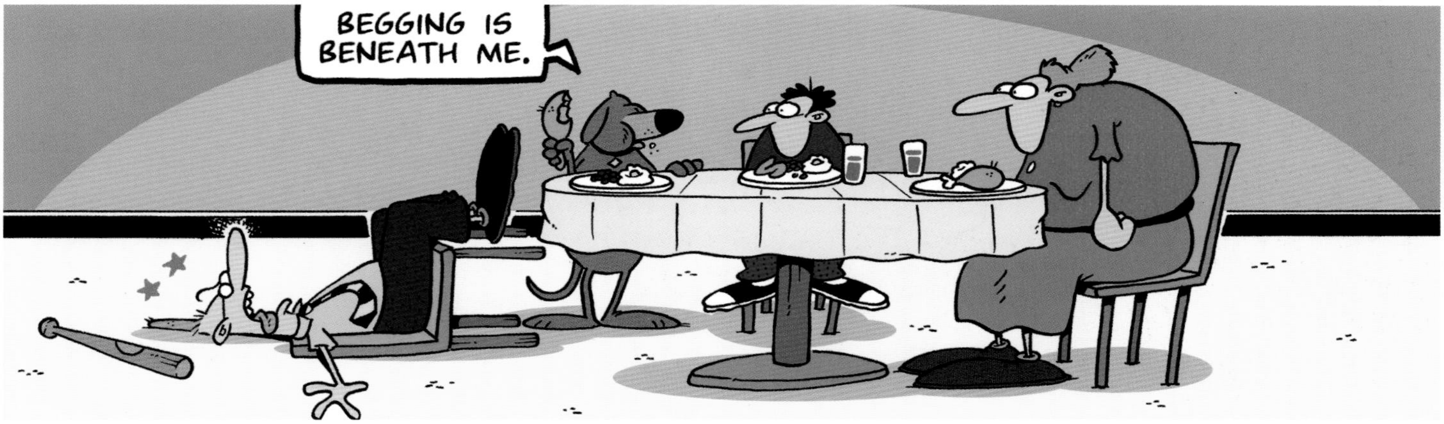
BEGGING IS BENEATH ME.

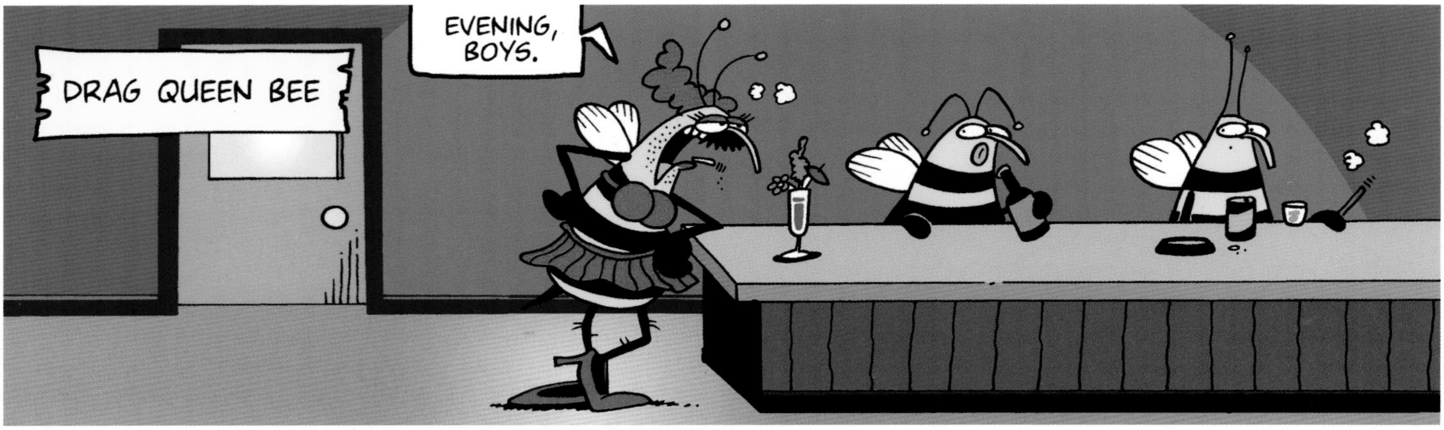
DRAG QUEEN BEE
EVENING, BOYS.

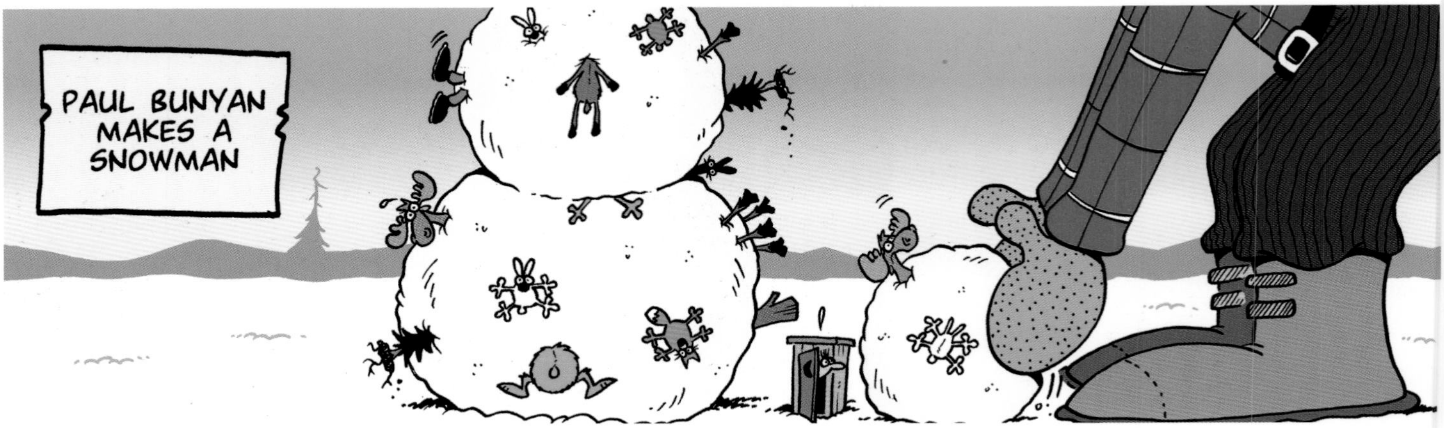
PAUL BUNYAN MAKES A SNOWMAN

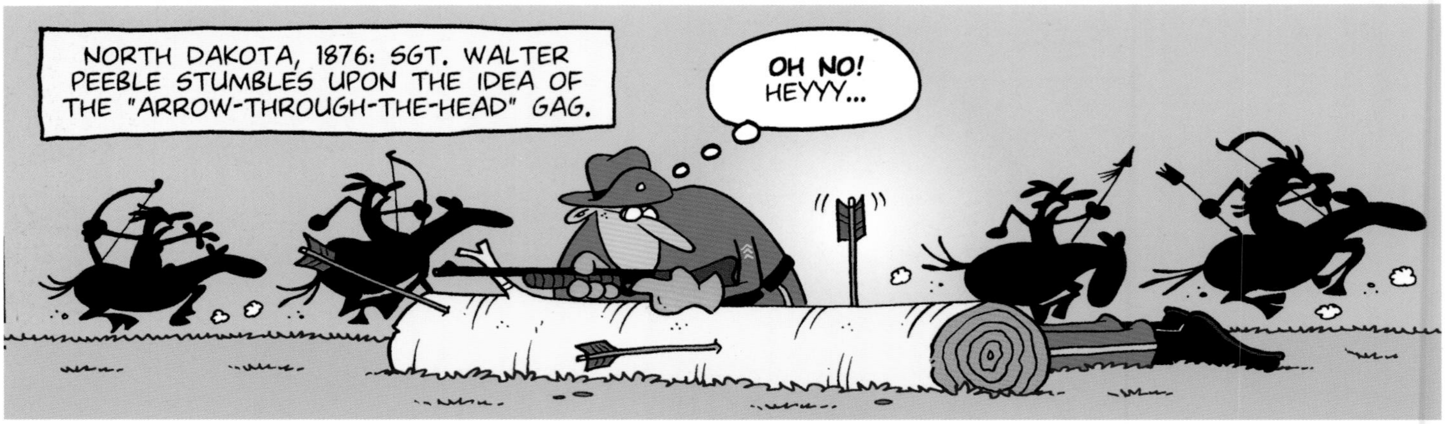
NORTH DAKOTA, 1876: SGT. WALTER PEEBLE STUMBLES UPON THE IDEA OF THE "ARROW-THROUGH-THE-HEAD" GAG.
OH NO! HEYYY...

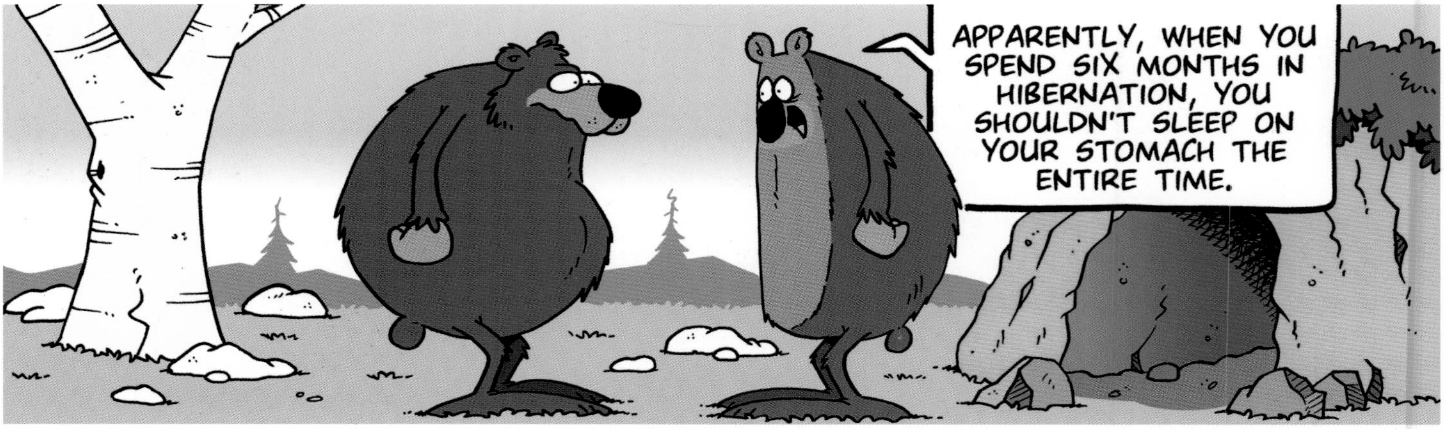
APPARENTLY, WHEN YOU SPEND SIX MONTHS IN HIBERNATION, YOU SHOULDN'T SLEEP ON YOUR STOMACH THE ENTIRE TIME.

THIS STRIP IS BASED ON AN IDEA FROM:
RUSSELL CHILTON
WILLOW, AK

DO YOU HAVE AN IDEA THAT WOULD MAKE A GREAT COMIC STRIP?

SEND IT TO:
tundracomics.com

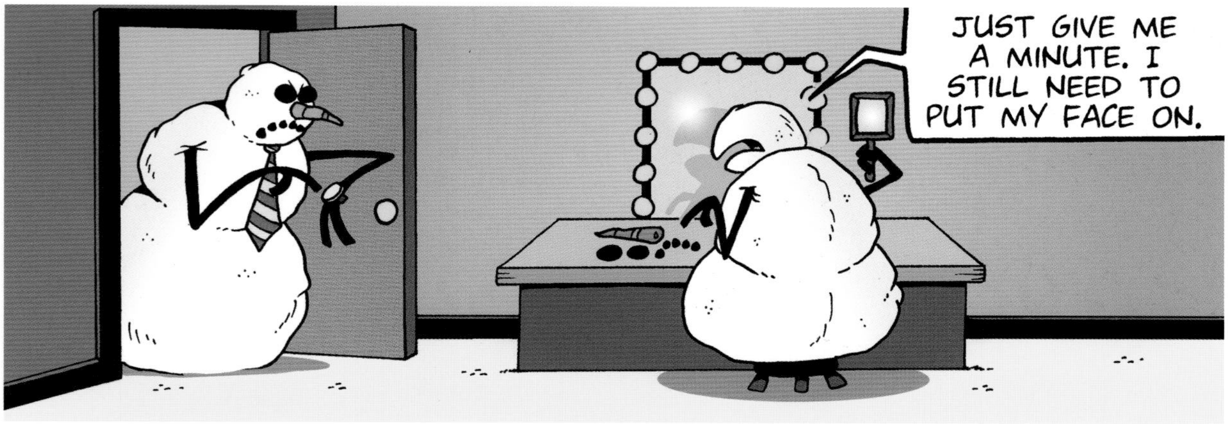
JUST GIVE ME A MINUTE. I STILL NEED TO PUT MY FACE ON.

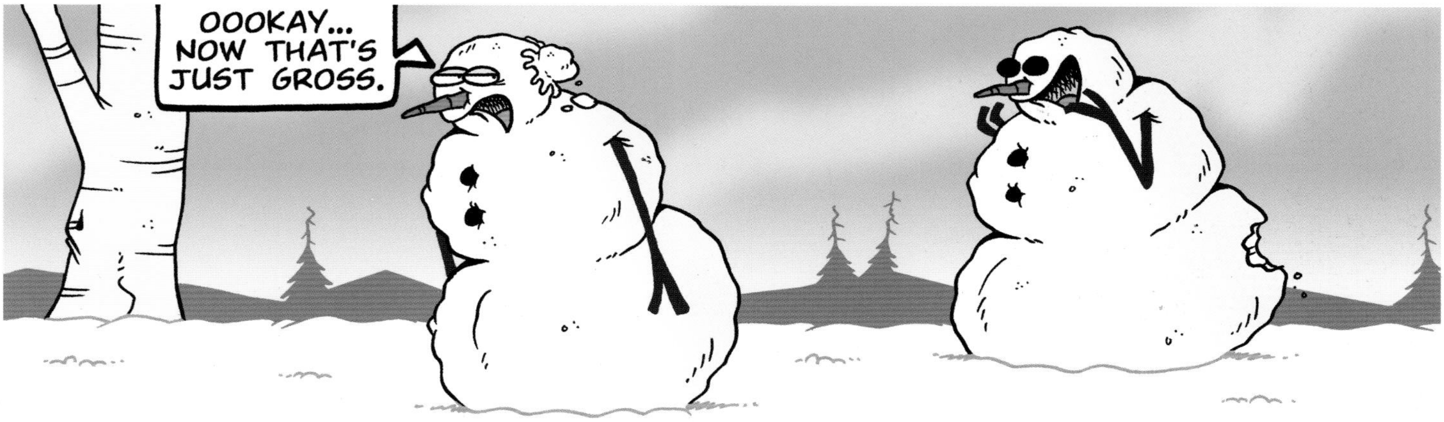
OOOKAY... NOW THAT'S JUST GROSS.

THIS STRIP IS BASED ON AN IDEA FROM:
ANDY OVERBAY
FAIRBANKS, AK

DO YOU HAVE AN IDEA THAT WOULD MAKE A GREAT COMIC STRIP?

SEND IT TO:
tundracomics.com

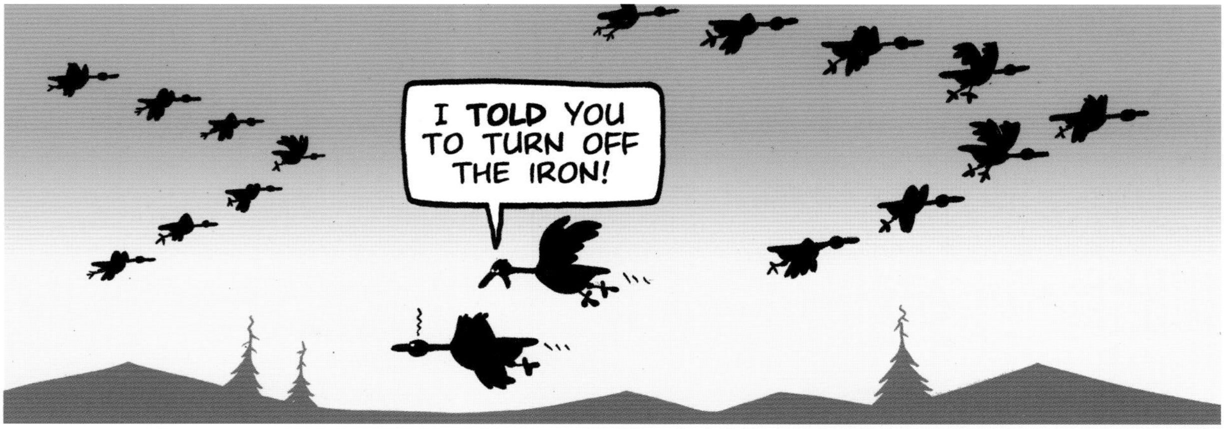
I **TOLD** YOU TO TURN OFF THE IRON!

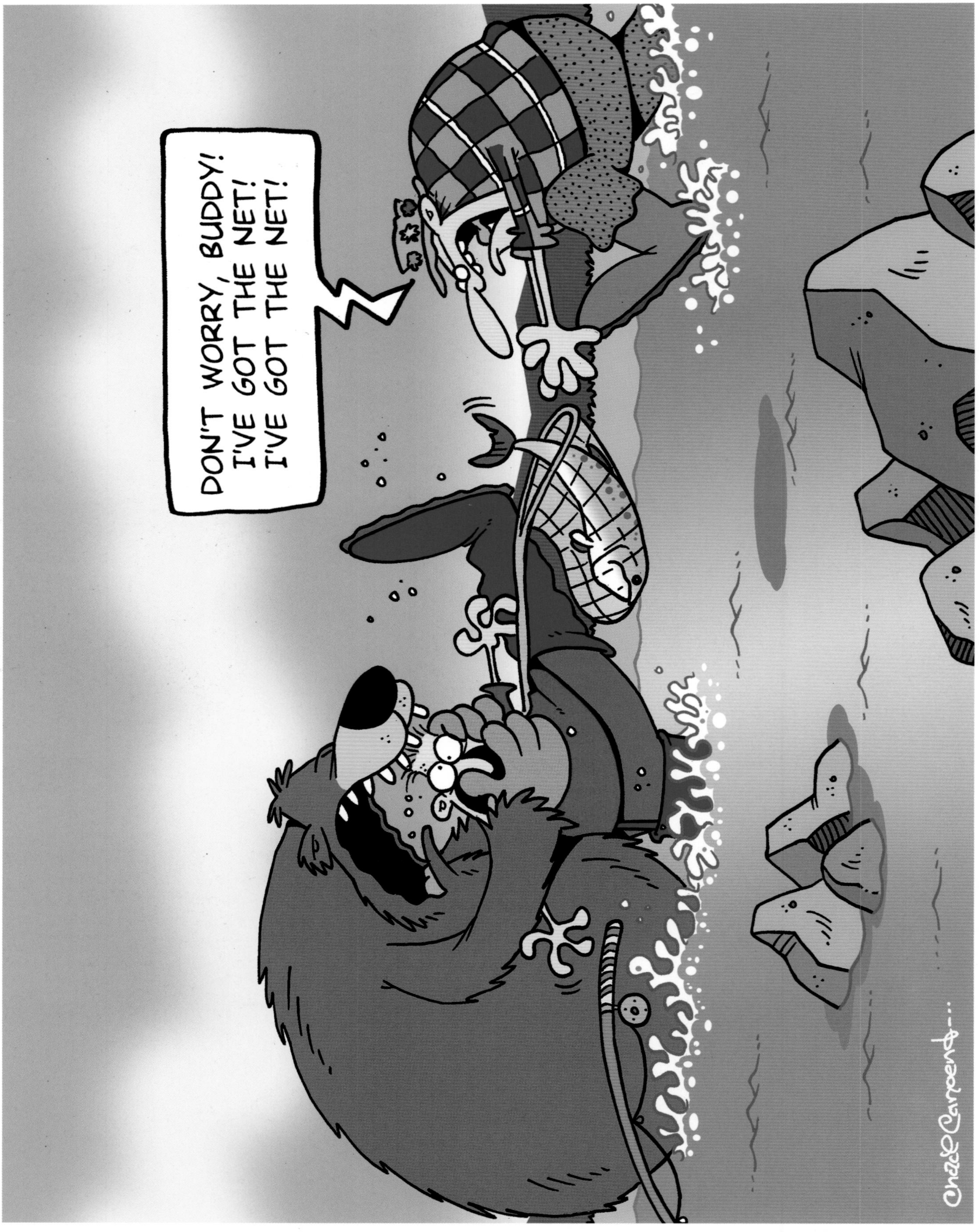
DON'T WORRY, BUDDY!
I'VE GOT THE NET!
I'VE GOT THE NET!

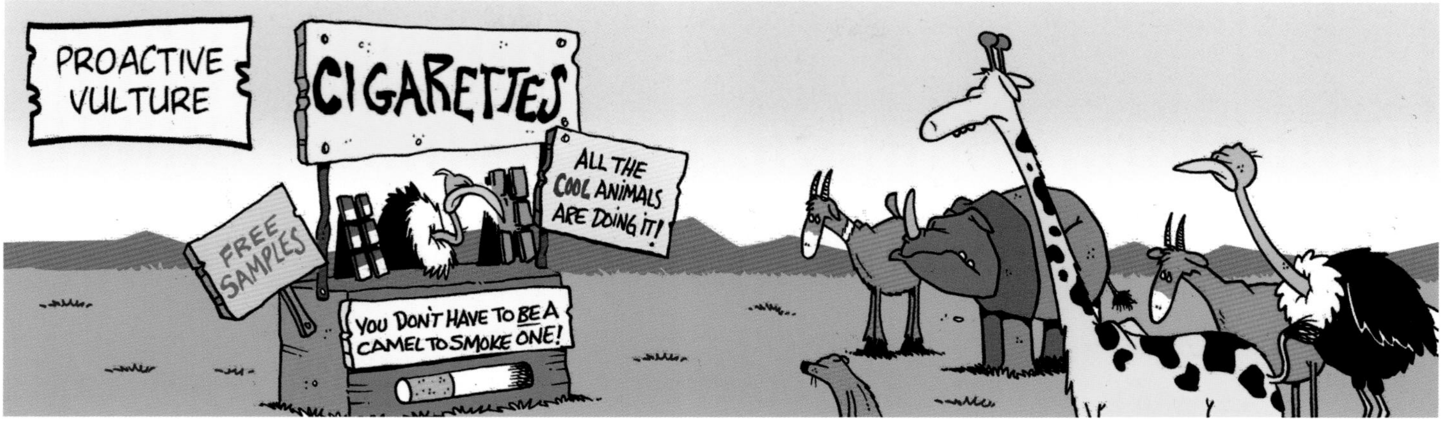
PROACTIVE VULTURE
CIGARETTES
FREE SAMPLES
ALL THE COOL ANIMALS ARE DOING IT!
YOU DON'T HAVE TO BE A CAMEL TO SMOKE ONE!

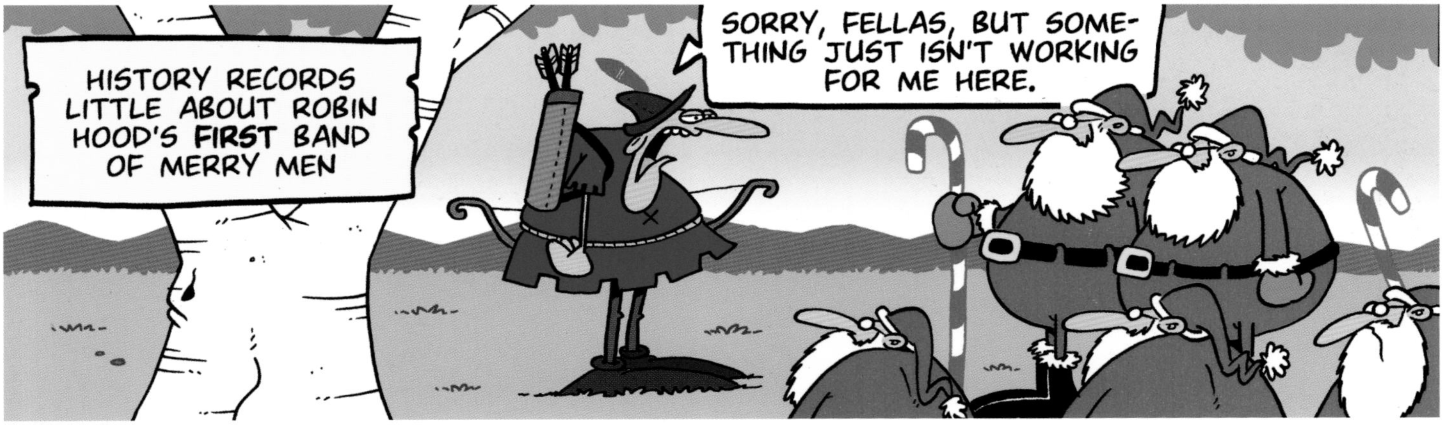
HISTORY RECORDS LITTLE ABOUT ROBIN HOOD'S FIRST BAND OF MERRY MEN
SORRY, FELLAS, BUT SOME-THING JUST ISN'T WORKING FOR ME HERE.

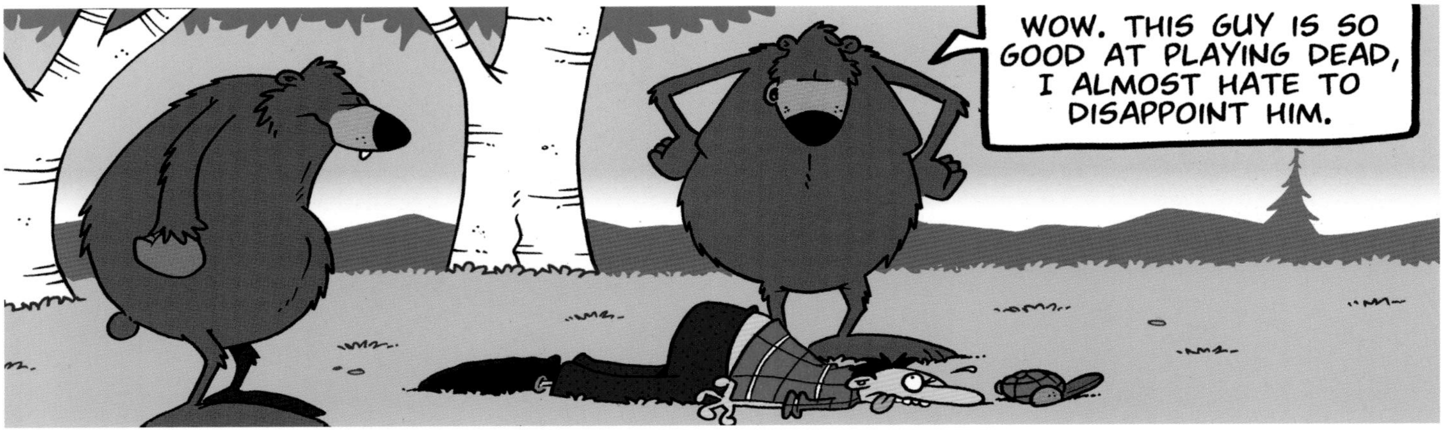
WOW. THIS GUY IS SO GOOD AT PLAYING DEAD, I ALMOST HATE TO DISAPPOINT HIM.

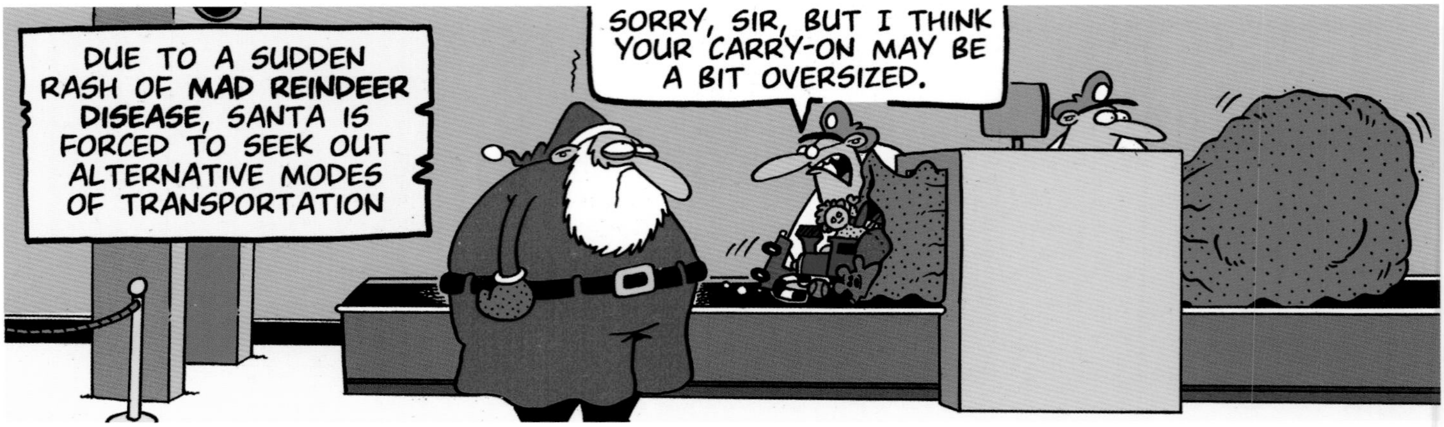
DUE TO A SUDDEN RASH OF MAD REINDEER DISEASE, SANTA IS FORCED TO SEEK OUT ALTERNATIVE MODES OF TRANSPORTATION
SORRY, SIR, BUT I THINK YOUR CARRY-ON MAY BE A BIT OVERSIZED.

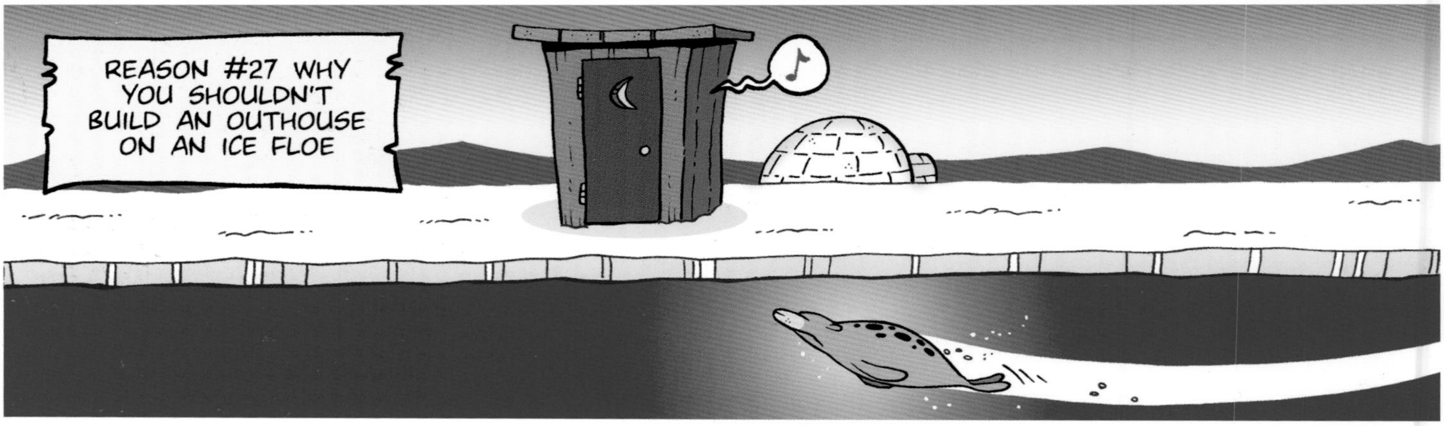
REASON #27 WHY YOU SHOULDN'T BUILD AN OUTHOUSE ON AN ICE FLOE

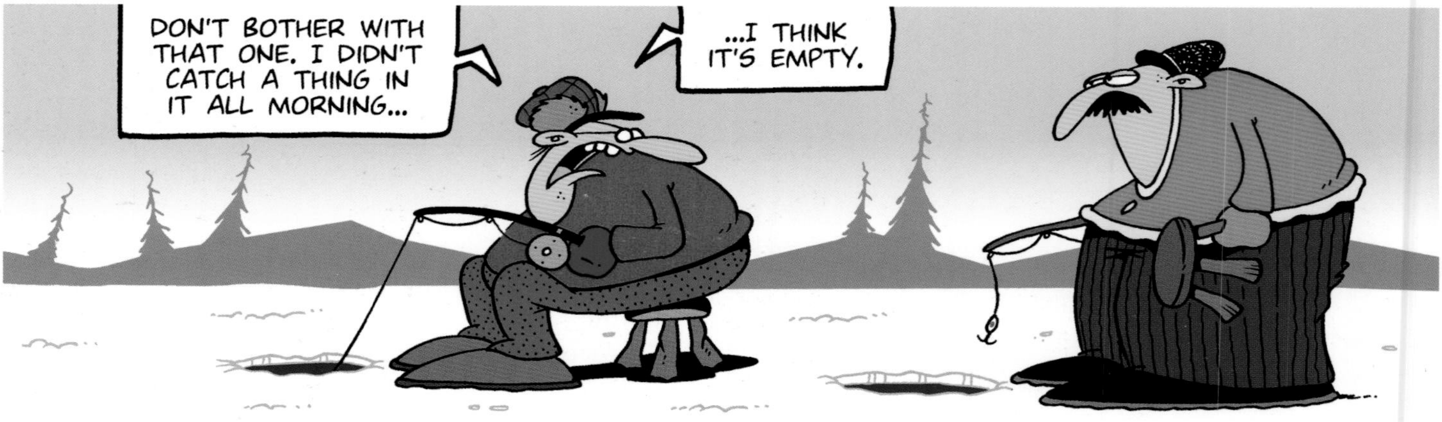
DON'T BOTHER WITH THAT ONE. I DIDN'T CATCH A THING IN IT ALL MORNING...
...I THINK IT'S EMPTY.

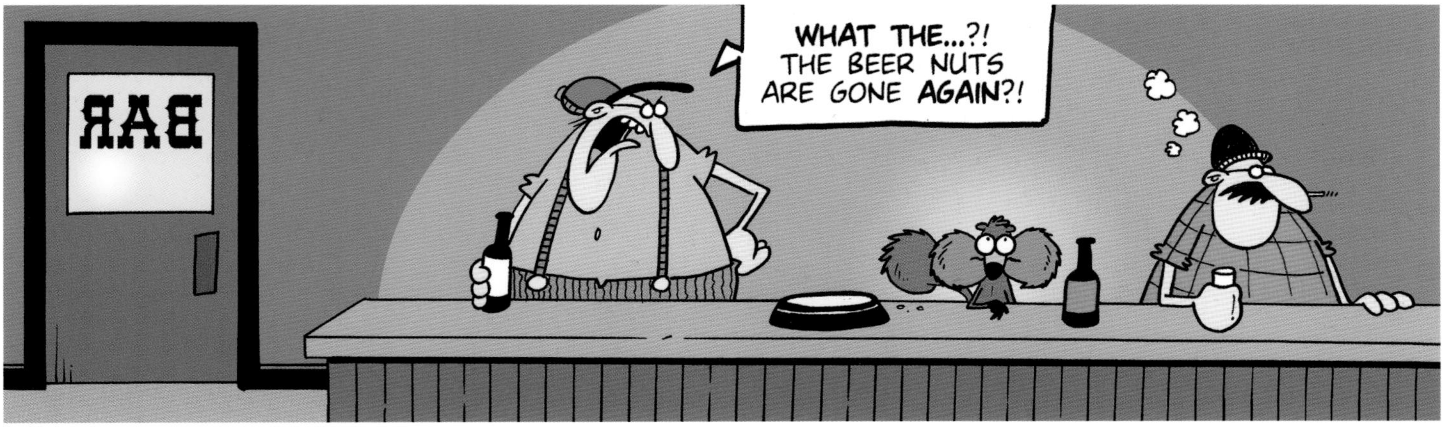
RAB
WHAT THE...?! THE BEER NUTS ARE GONE AGAIN?!

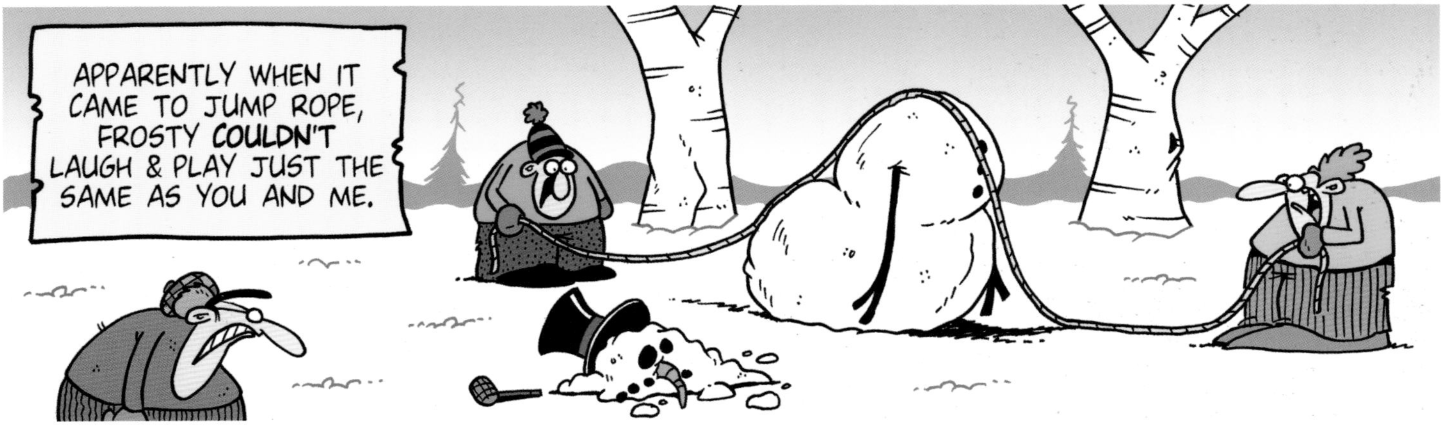
APPARENTLY WHEN IT CAME TO JUMP ROPE, FROSTY COULDN'T LAUGH & PLAY JUST THE SAME AS YOU AND ME.

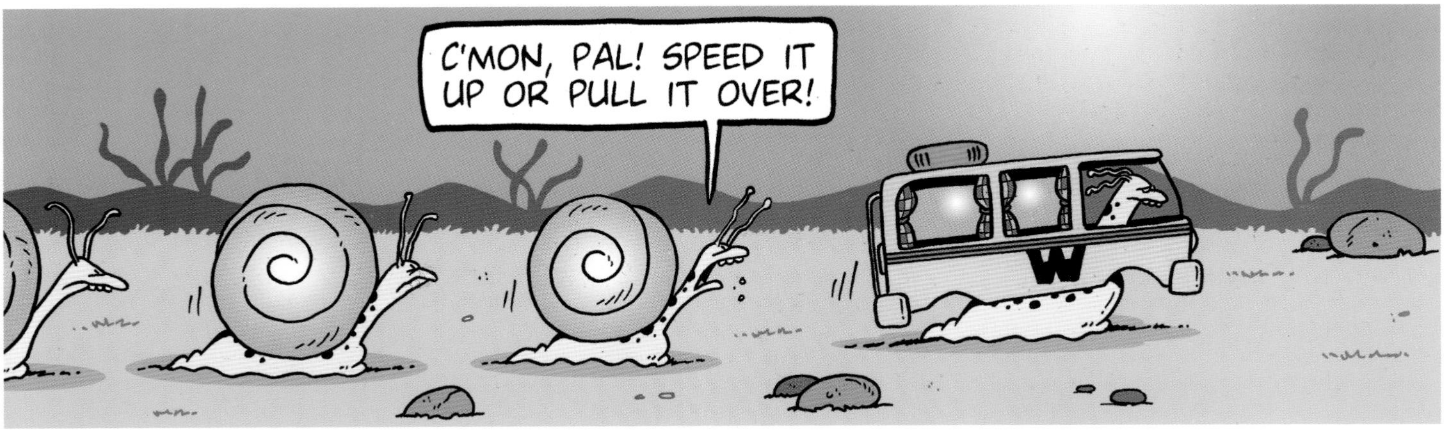
C'MON, PAL! SPEED IT UP OR PULL IT OVER!
W

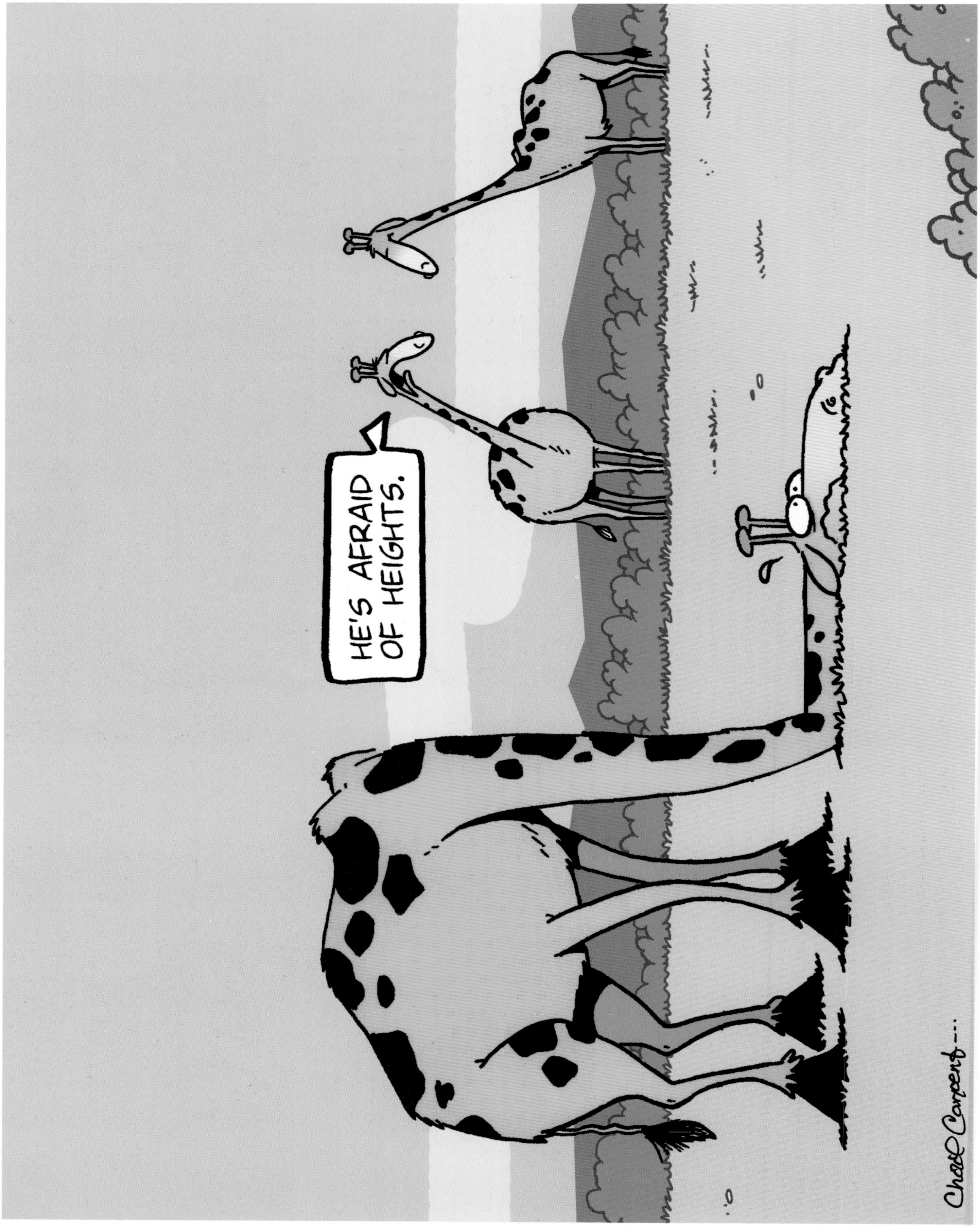
HE'S AFRAID
OF HEIGHTS.

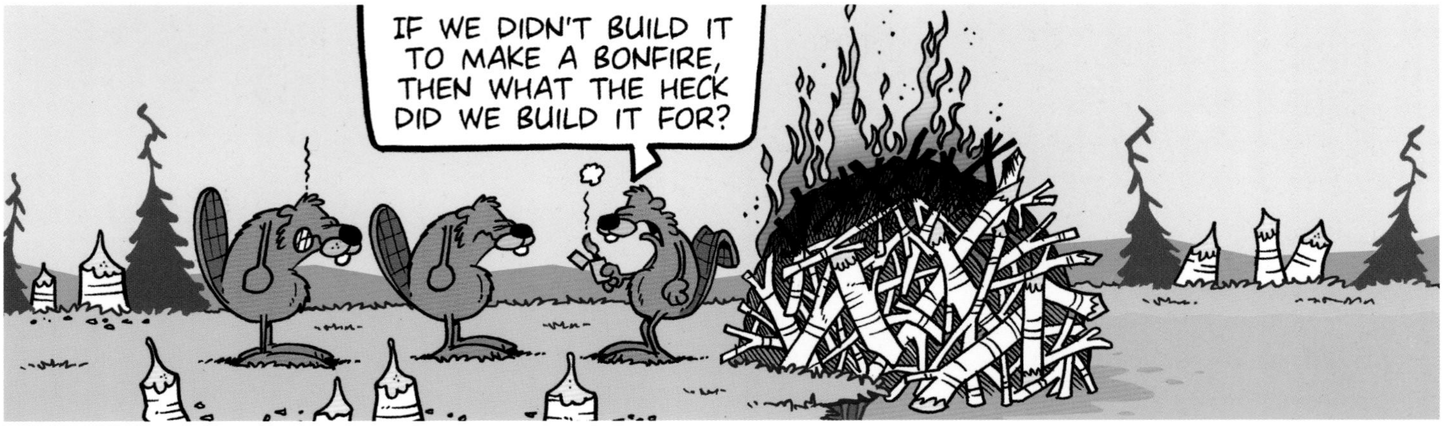
IF WE DIDN'T BUILD IT TO MAKE A BONFIRE, THEN WHAT THE HECK DID WE BUILD IT FOR?

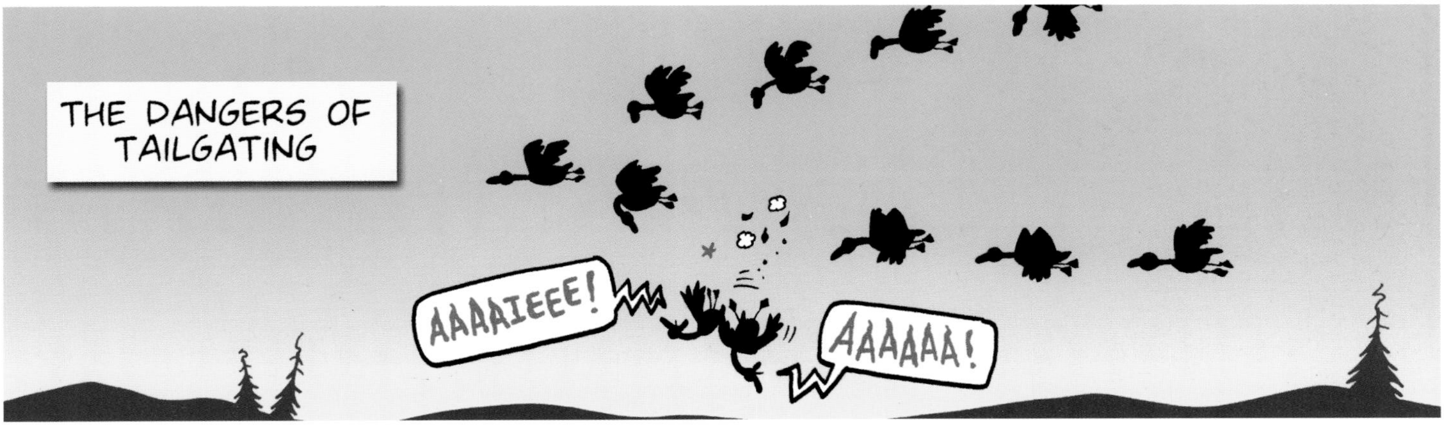
THE DANGERS OF TAILGATING
AAAAIEEE!
AAAAAA!

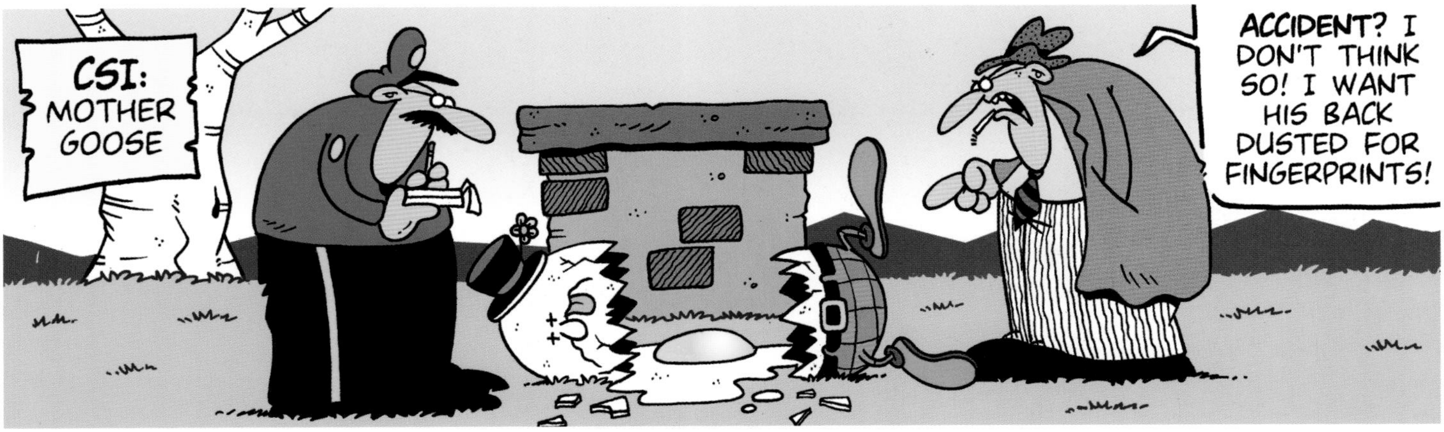
CSI: MOTHER GOOSE
ACCIDENT? I DON'T THINK SO! I WANT HIS BACK DUSTED FOR FINGERPRINTS!

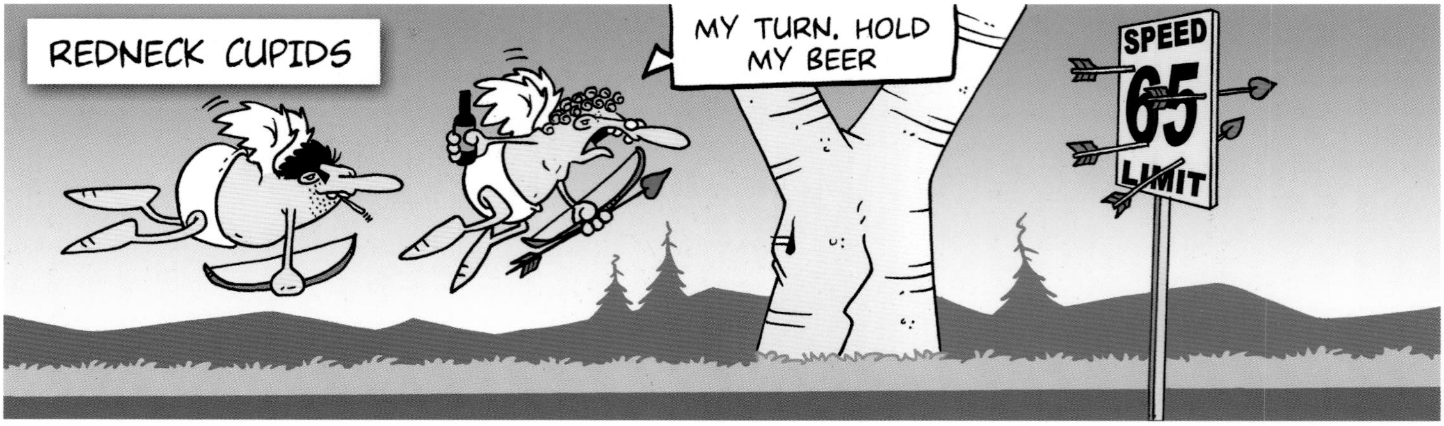
REDNECK CUPIDS
MY TURN. HOLD MY BEER
SPEED 65 LIMIT

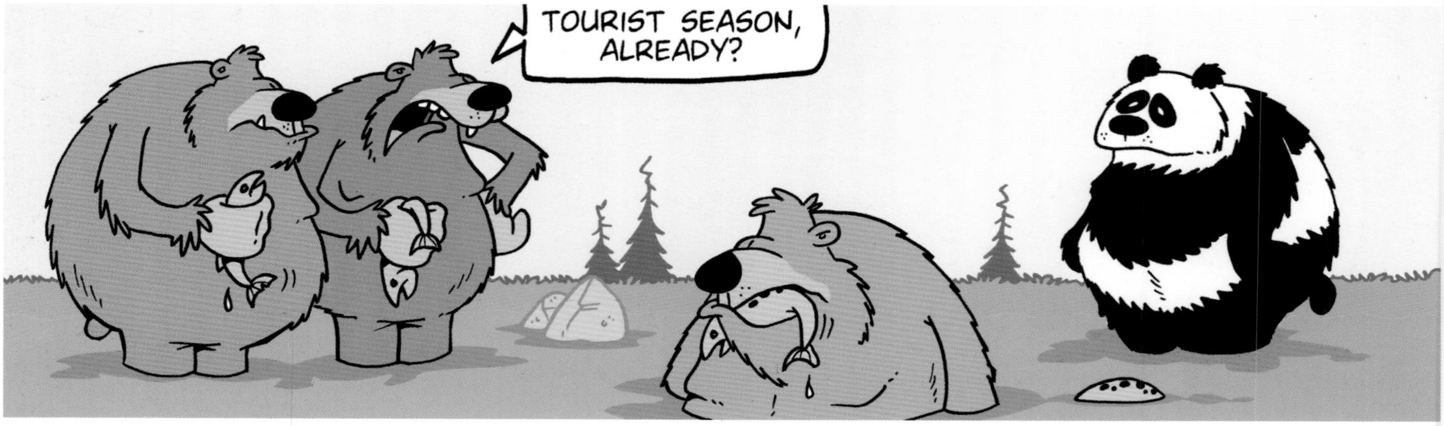
TOURIST SEASON, ALREADY?

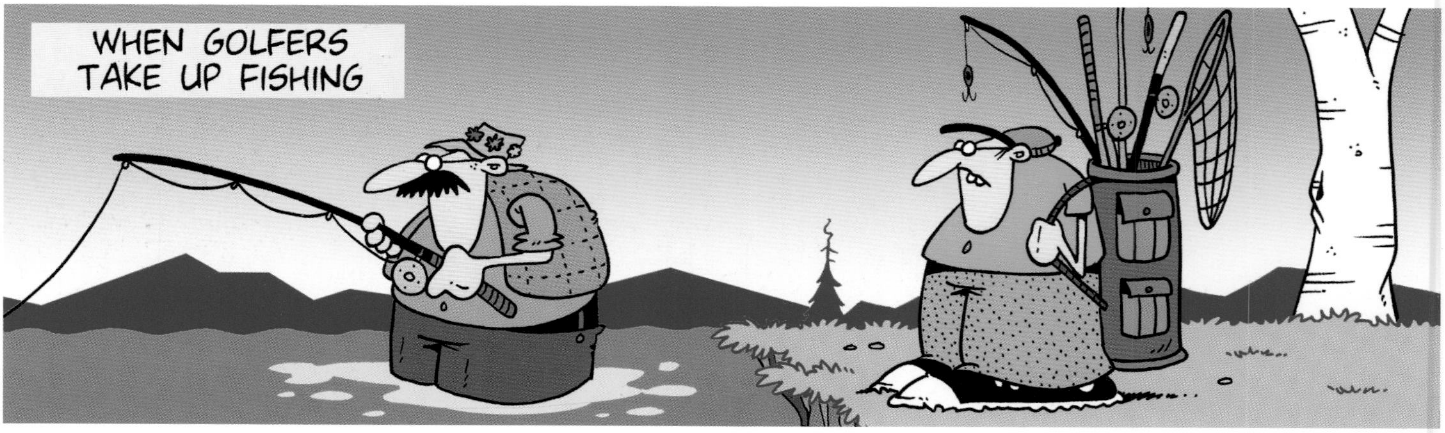
WHEN GOLFERS TAKE UP FISHING

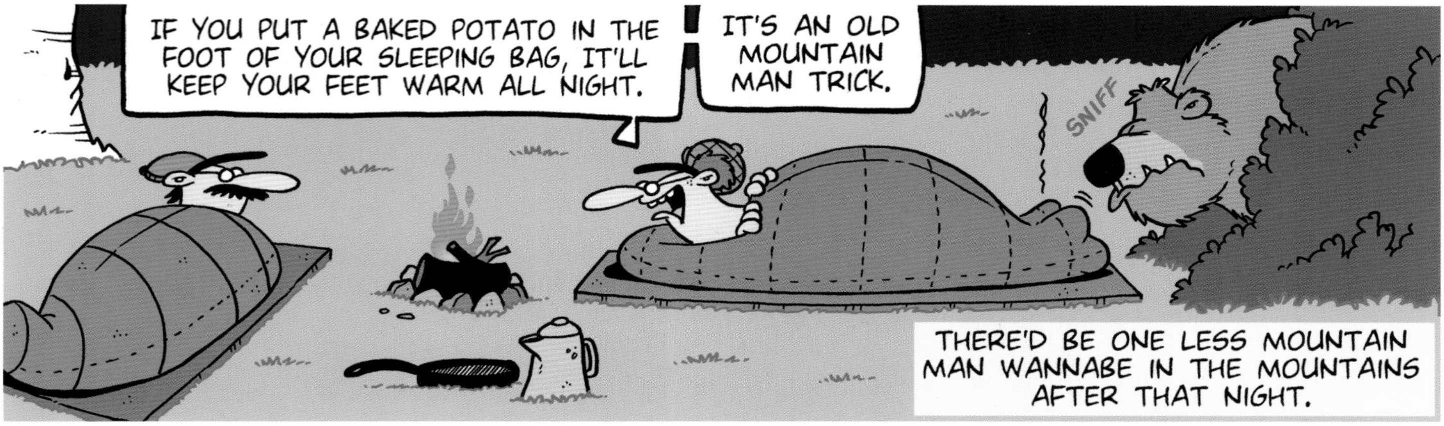
IF YOU PUT A BAKED POTATO IN THE FOOT OF YOUR SLEEPING BAG, IT'LL KEEP YOUR FEET WARM ALL NIGHT.
IT'S AN OLD MOUNTAIN MAN TRICK.
SNIFF
THERE'D BE ONE LESS MOUNTAIN MAN WANNABE IN THE MOUNTAINS AFTER THAT NIGHT.

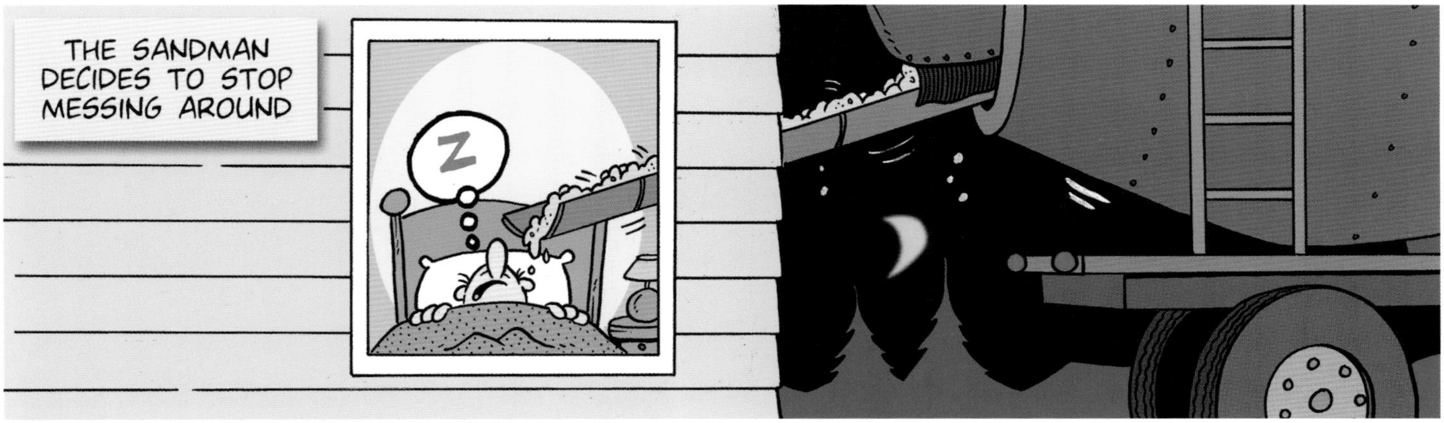
THE SANDMAN DECIDES TO STOP MESSING AROUND
Z

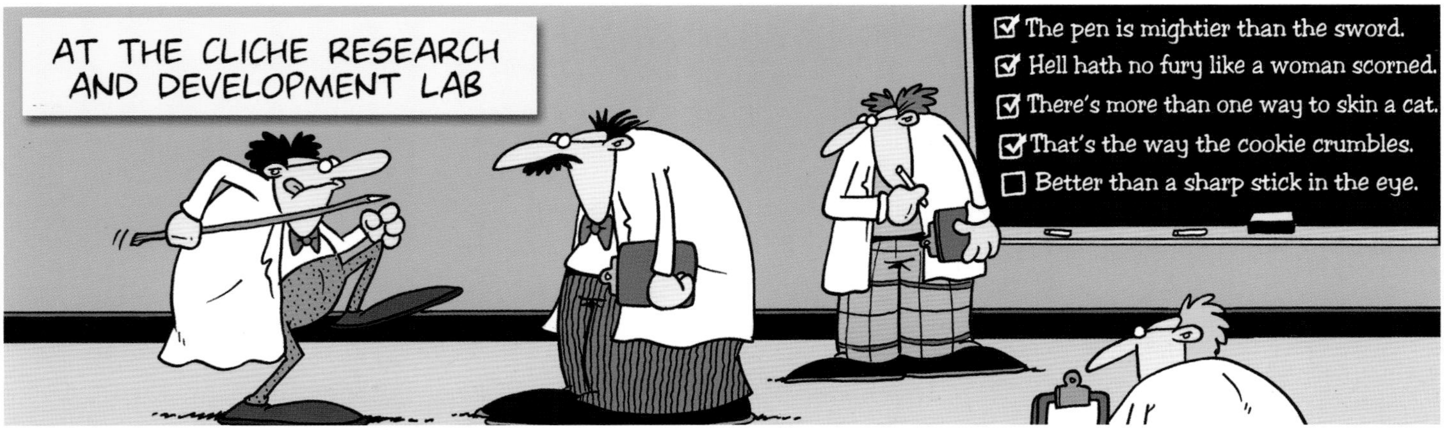
AT THE CLICHE RESEARCH AND DEVELOPMENT LAB
The pen is mightier than the sword.
Hell hath no fury like a woman scorned.
There's more than one way to skin a cat.
That's the way the cookie crumbles.
Better than a sharp stick in the eye.

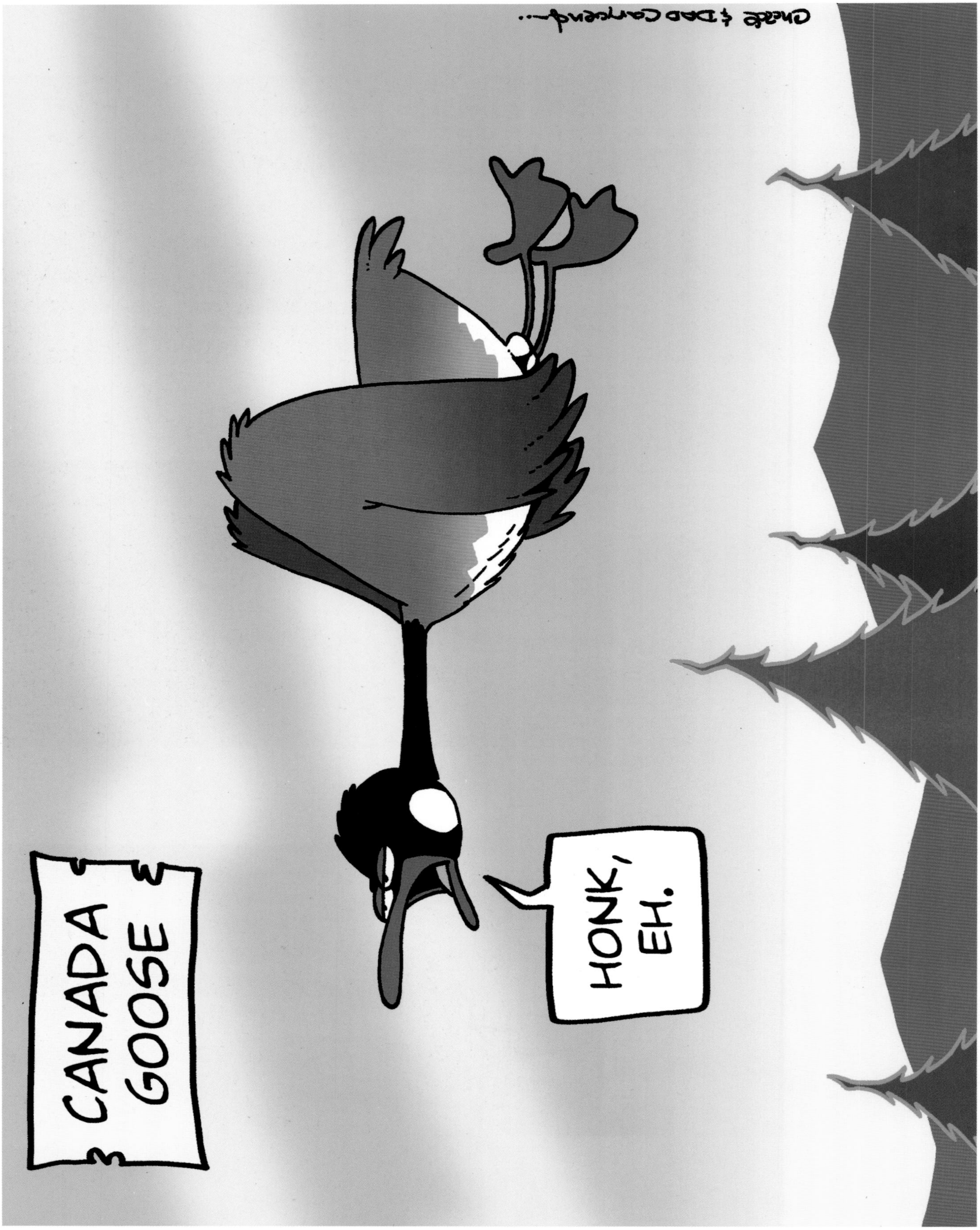
CANADA GOOSE
HONK, EH.

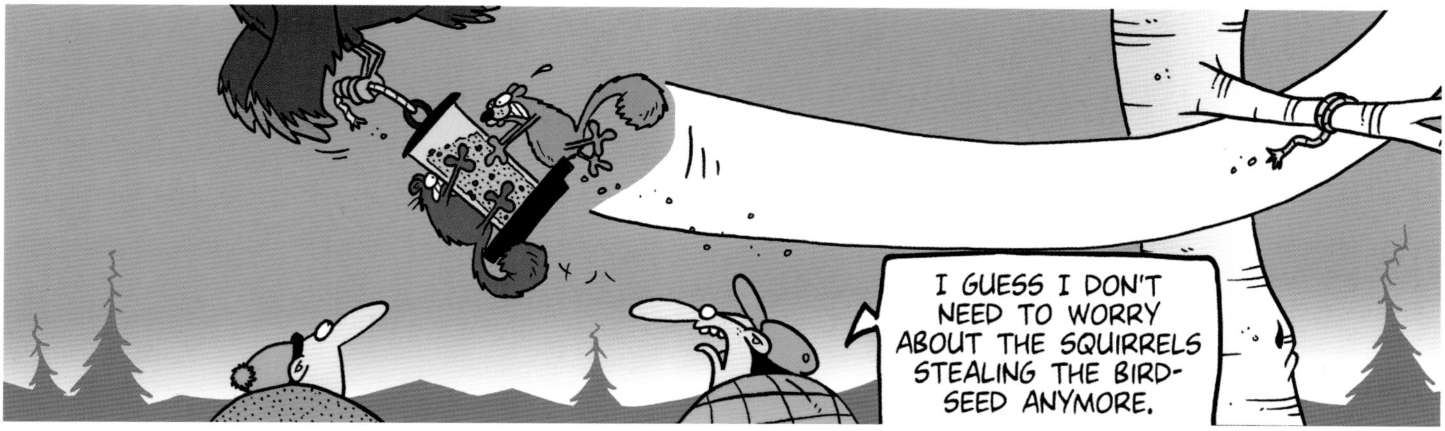
I GUESS I DON'T NEED TO WORRY ABOUT THE SQUIRRELS STEALING THE BIRD-SEED ANYMORE.

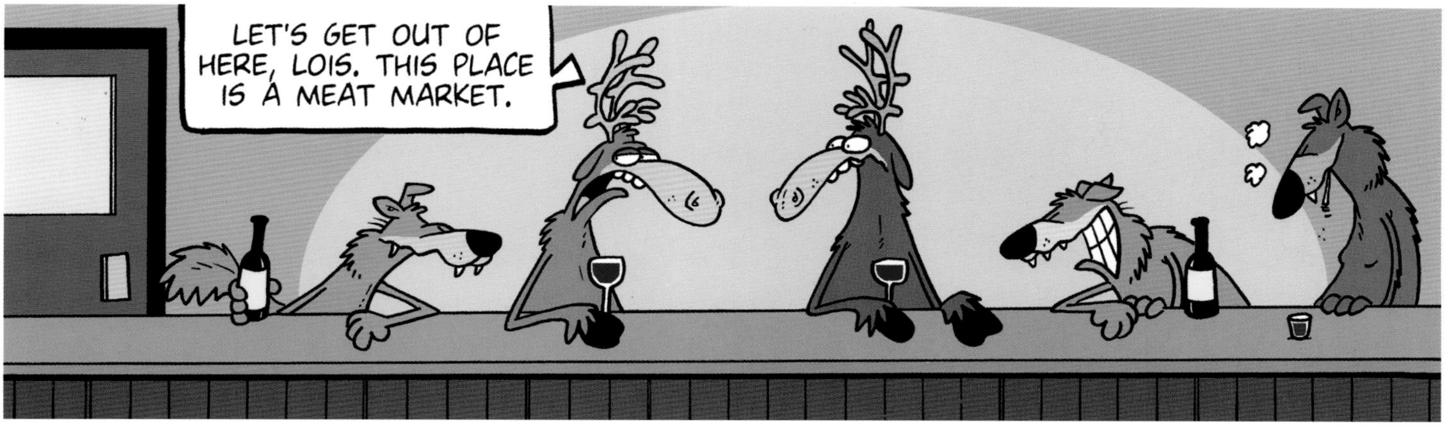
LET'S GET OUT OF HERE, LOIS. THIS PLACE IS A MEAT MARKET.

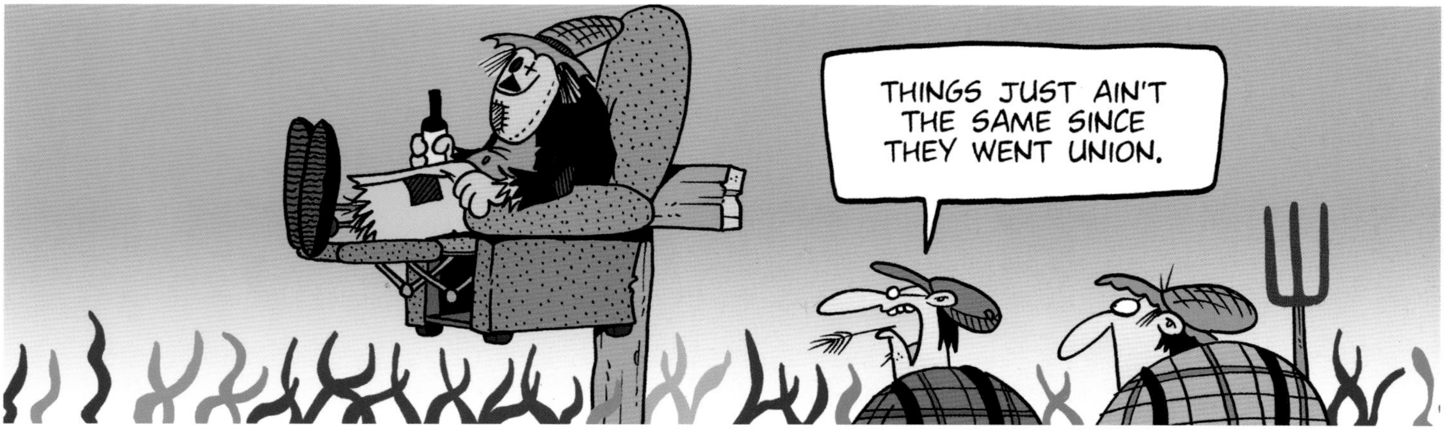
THINGS JUST AIN'T THE SAME SINCE THEY WENT UNION.

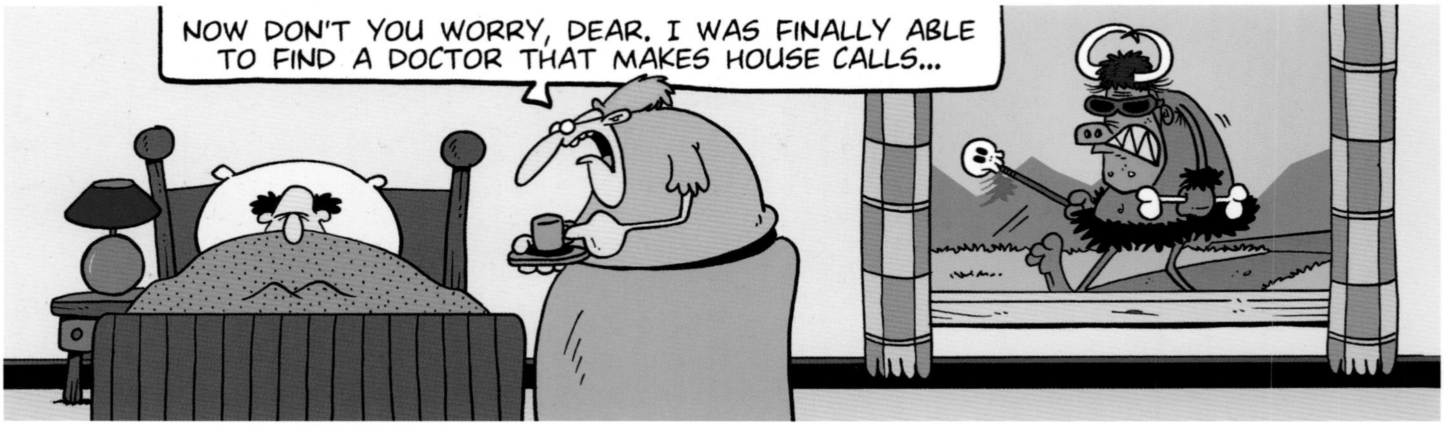
NOW DON'T YOU WORRY, DEAR. I WAS FINALLY ABLE TO FIND A DOCTOR THAT MAKES HOUSE CALLS...

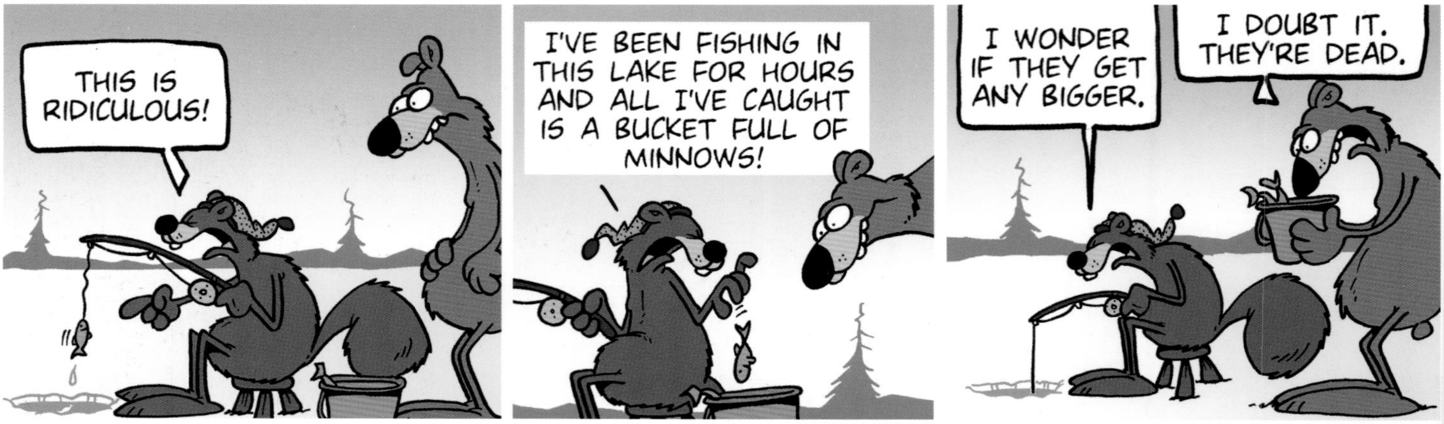
THIS IS RIDICULOUS!
I'VE BEEN FISHING IN THIS LAKE FOR HOURS AND ALL I'VE CAUGHT IS A BUCKET FULL OF MINNOWS!
I WONDER IF THEY GET ANY BIGGER.
I DOUBT IT. THEY'RE DEAD.

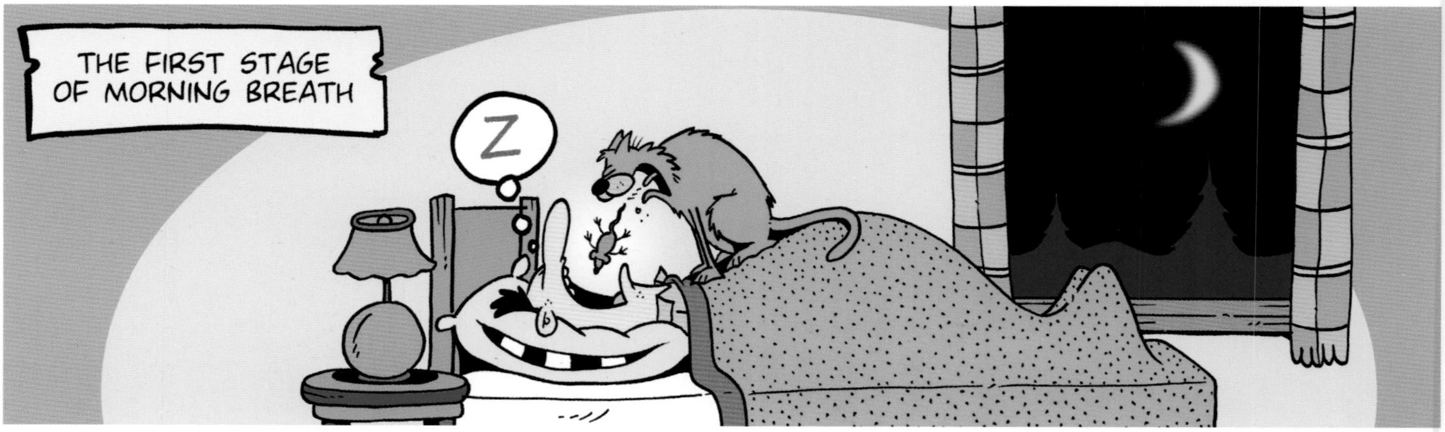
THE FIRST STAGE OF MORNING BREATH
Z

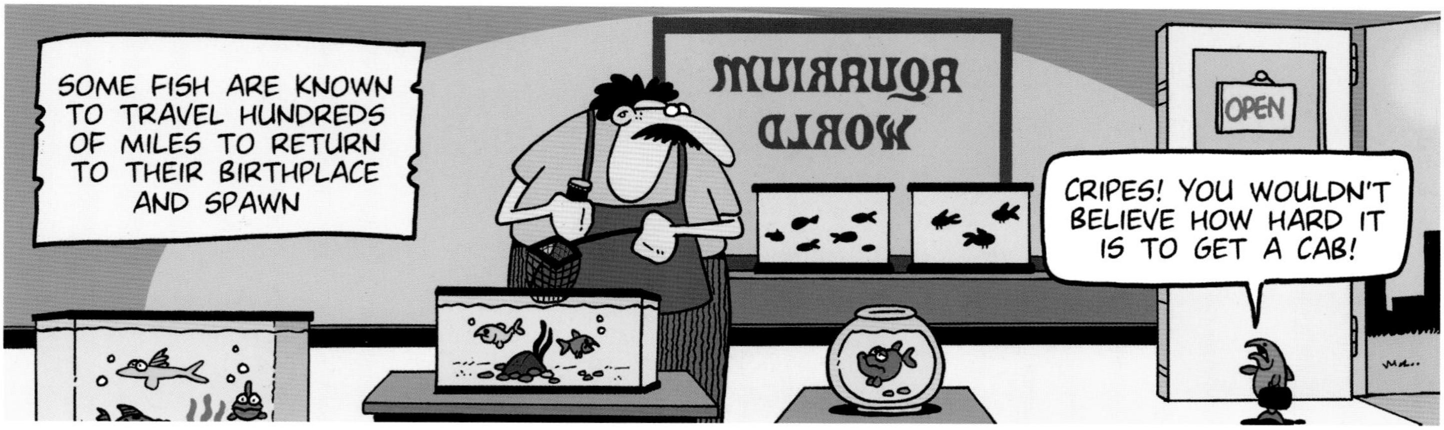
SOME FISH ARE KNOWN TO TRAVEL HUNDREDS OF MILES TO RETURN TO THEIR BIRTHPLACE AND SPAWN
OPEN
CRIPES! YOU WOULDN'T BELIEVE HOW HARD IT IS TO GET A CAB!

THIS STRIP IS BASED ON AN IDEA FROM:

T.R. BROWN
BOULDER, CO

DO YOU HAVE AN IDEA THAT WOULD MAKE A GREAT COMIC STRIP?

SEND IT TO:
tundracomics.com

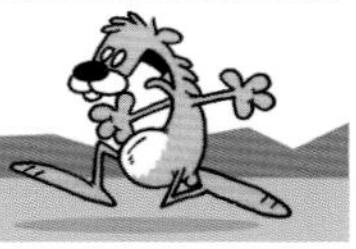

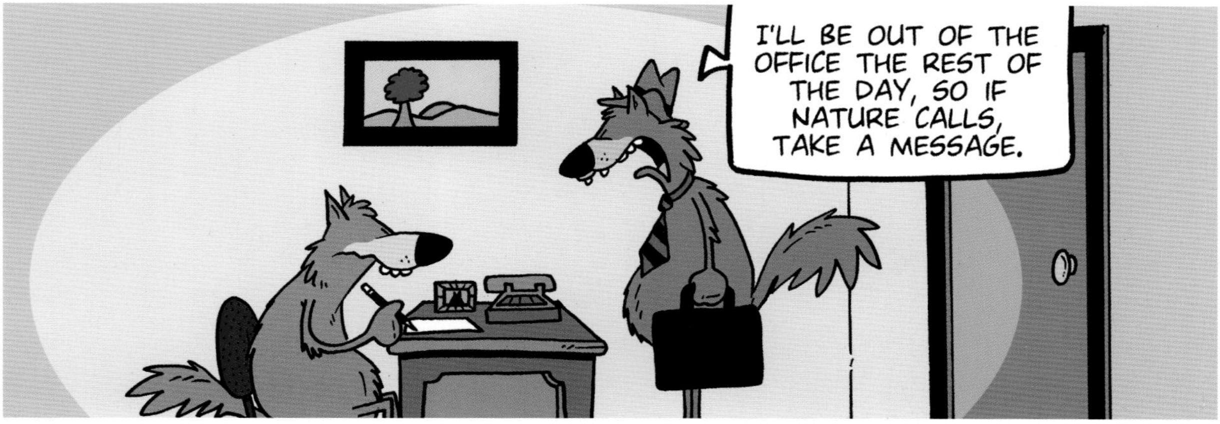
I'LL BE OUT OF THE OFFICE THE REST OF THE DAY, SO IF NATURE CALLS, TAKE A MESSAGE.

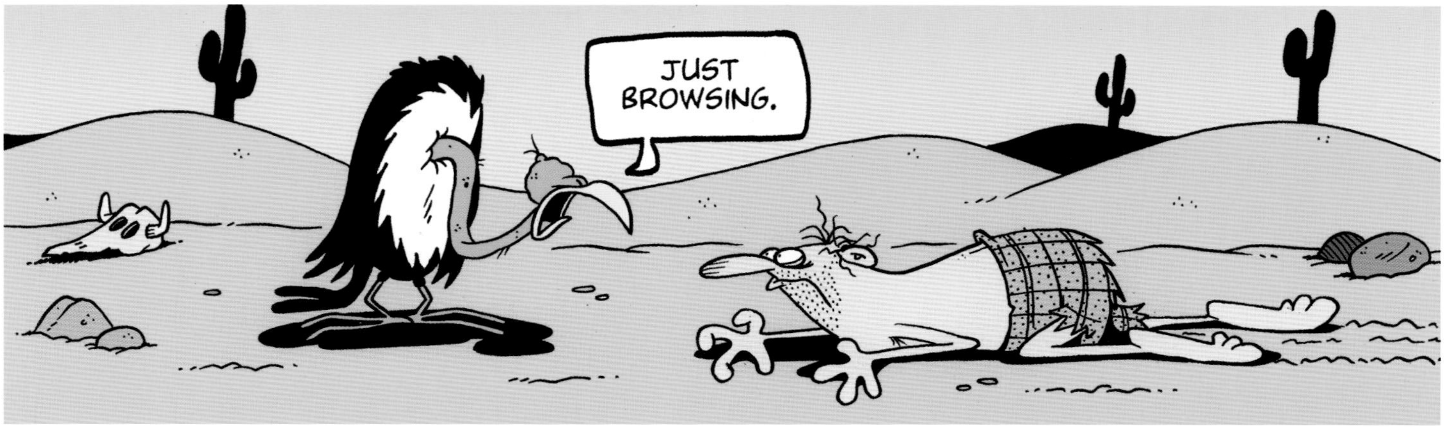
JUST BROWSING.

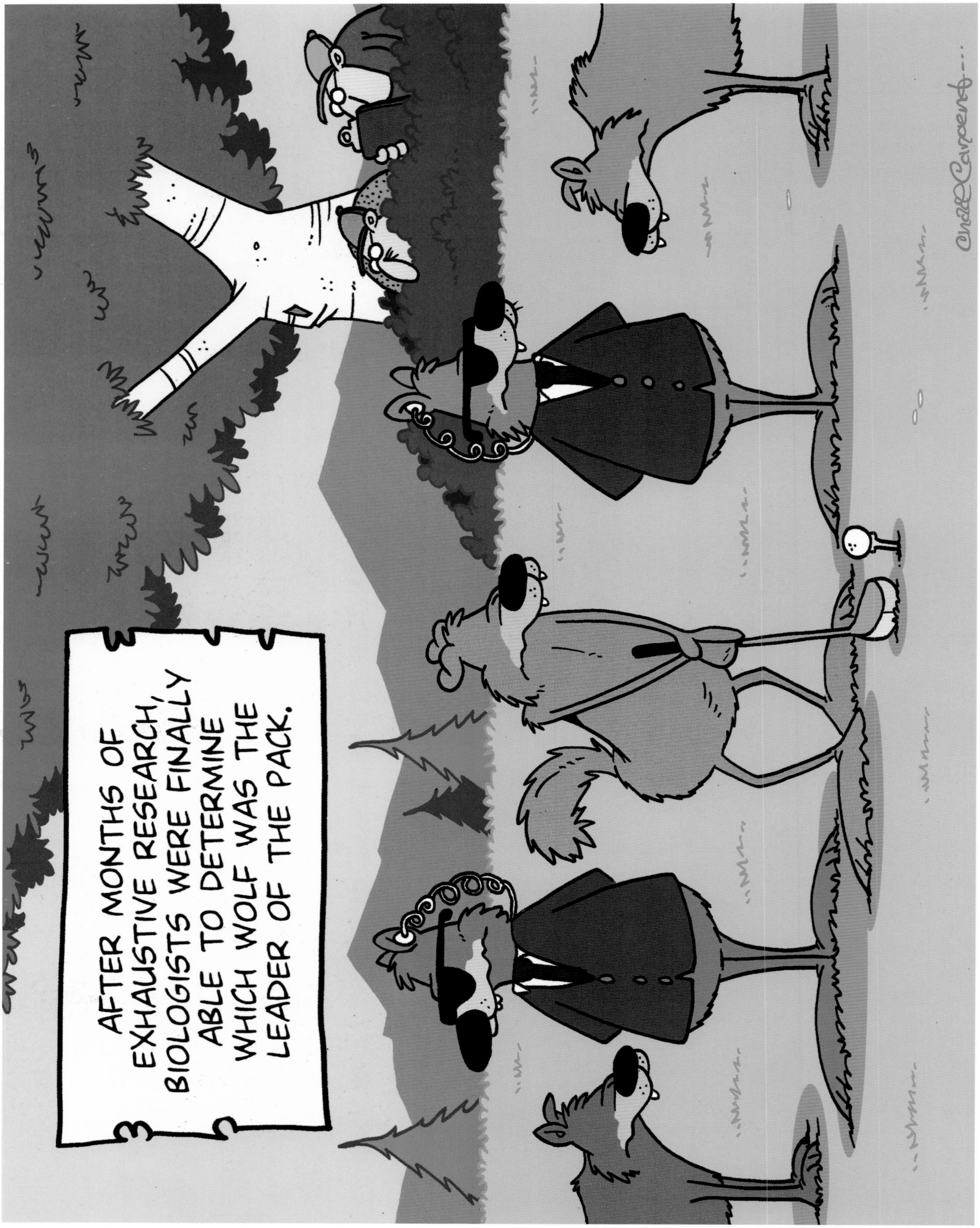
AFTER MONTHS OF
EXHAUSTIVE RESEARCH,
BIOLOGISTS WERE FINALLY
ABLE TO DETERMINE
WHICH WOLF WAS THE
LEADER OF THE PACK.

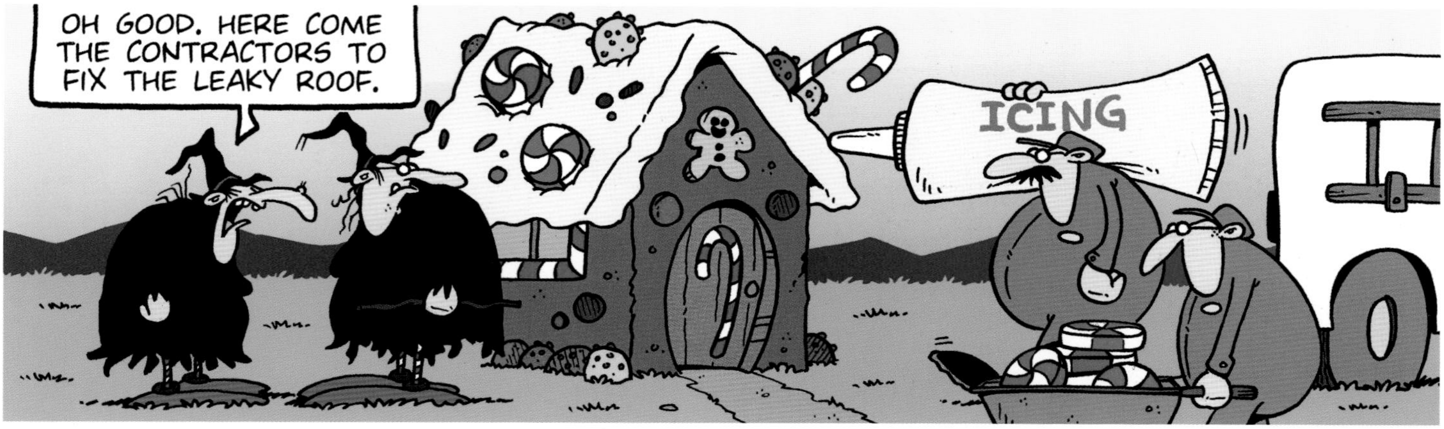
OH GOOD. HERE COME THE CONTRACTORS TO FIX THE LEAKY ROOF.
ICING

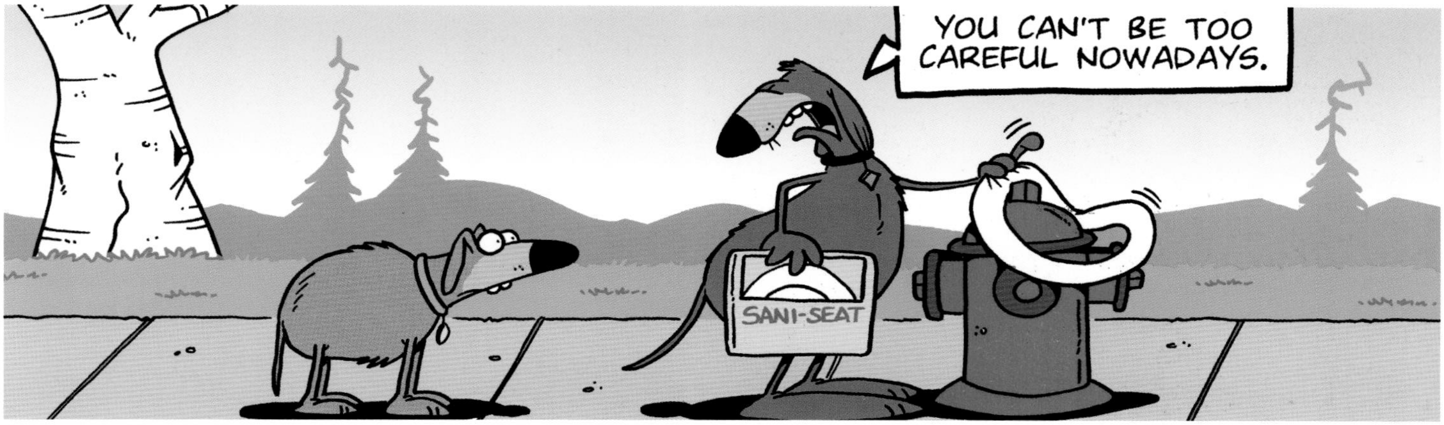
YOU CAN'T BE TOO CAREFUL NOWADAYS.
SANI-SEAT

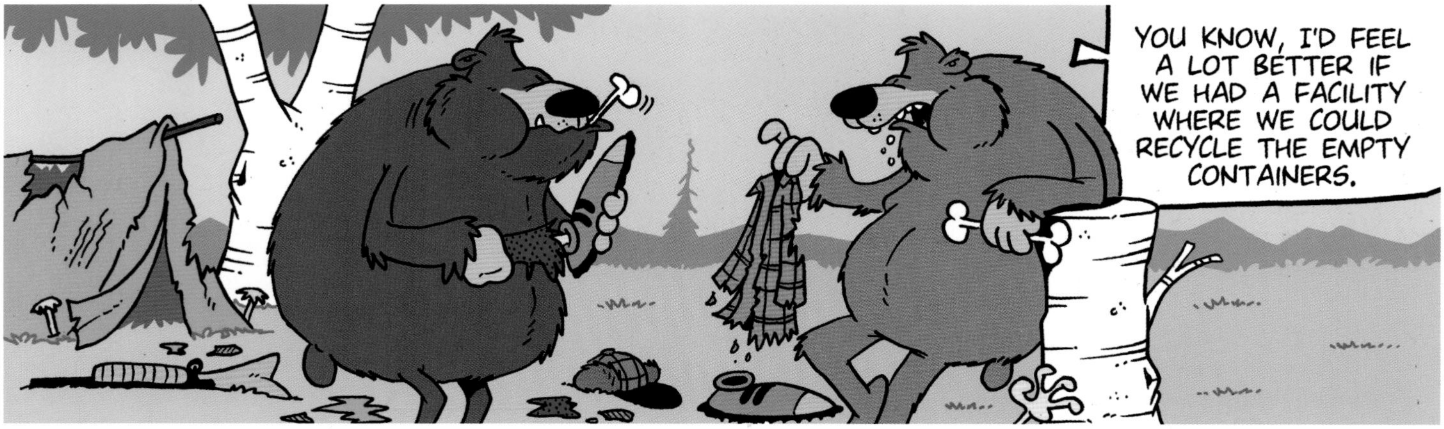
YOU KNOW, I'D FEEL A LOT BETTER IF WE HAD A FACILITY WHERE WE COULD RECYCLE THE EMPTY CONTAINERS.

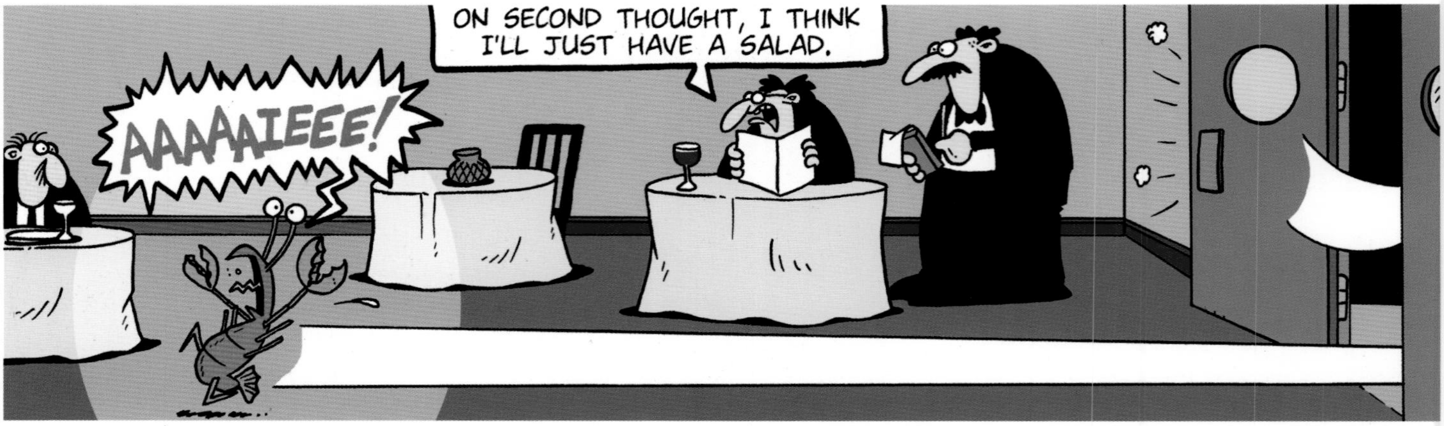
AAAAAIEEEE!
ON SECOND THOUGHT, I THINK I'LL JUST HAVE A SALAD.

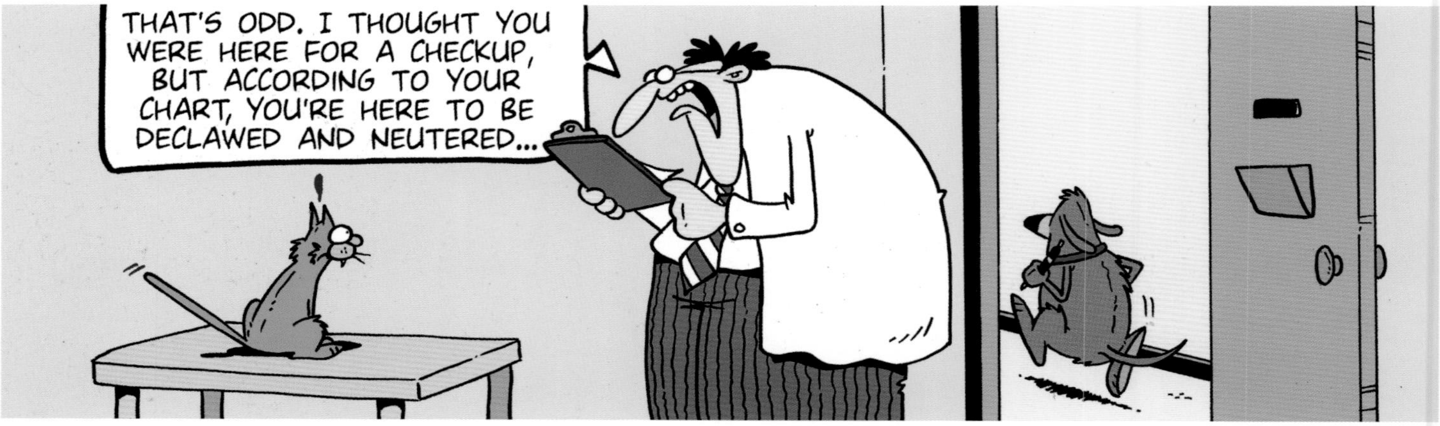
THAT'S ODD. I THOUGHT YOU WERE HERE FOR A CHECKUP, BUT ACCORDING TO YOUR CHART, YOU'RE HERE TO BE DECLAWED AND NEUTERED...

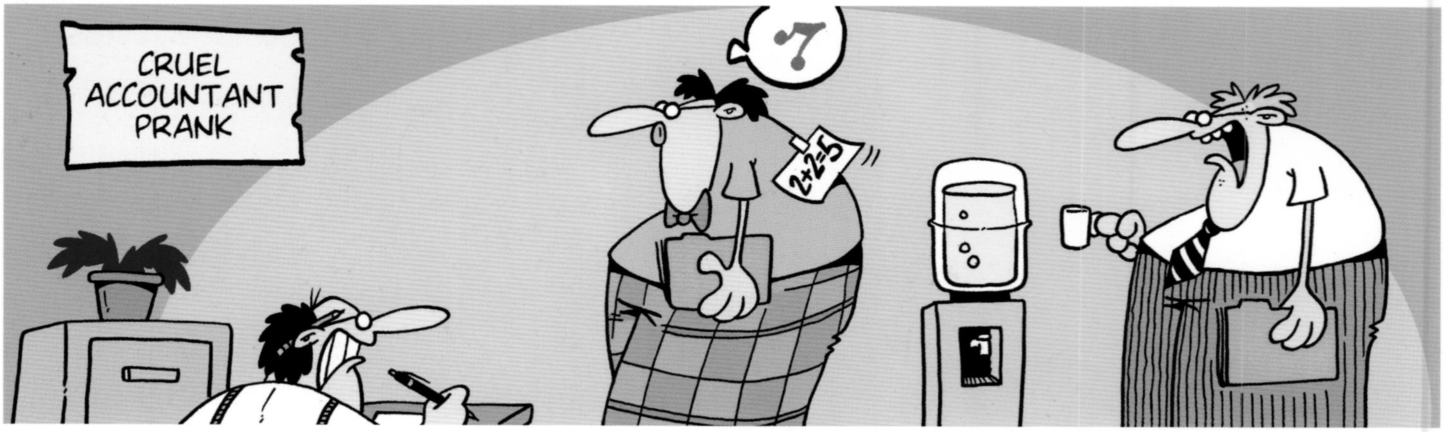
CRUEL ACCOUNTANT PRANK
2+2=5

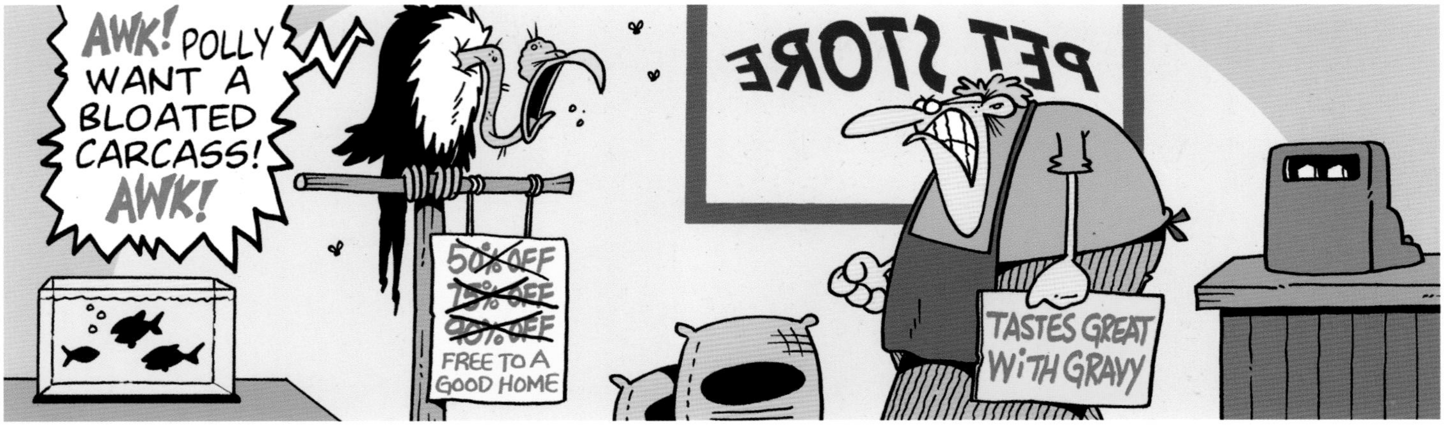
AWK! POLLY WANT A BLOATED CARCASS! AWK!
PET STORE
50% OFF
75% OFF
90% OFF
FREE TO A GOOD HOME
TASTES GREAT WITH GRAVY

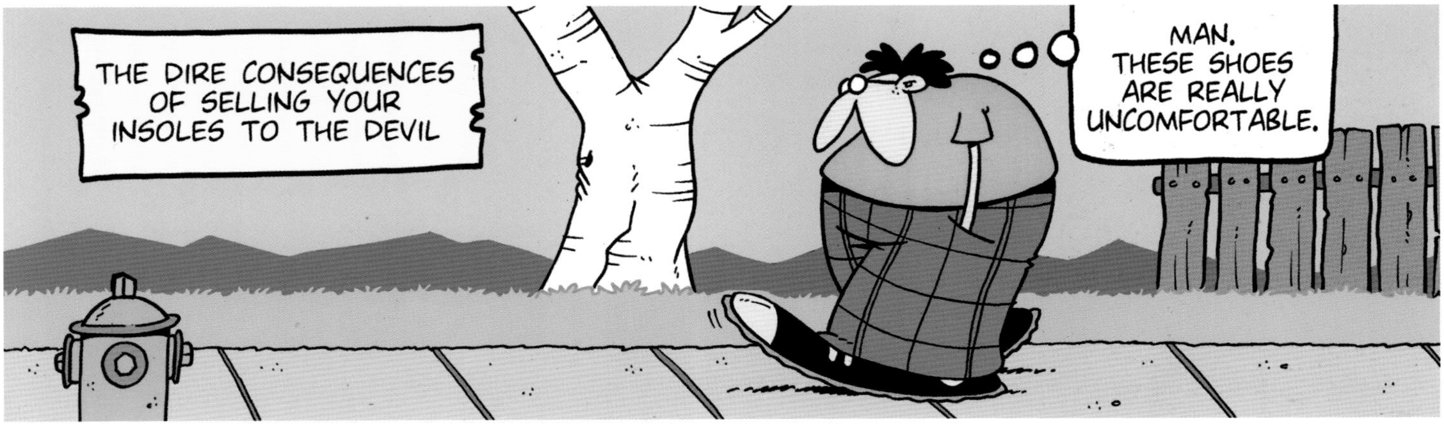
THE DIRE CONSEQUENCES OF SELLING YOUR INSOLES TO THE DEVIL
MAN. THESE SHOES ARE REALLY UNCOMFORTABLE.

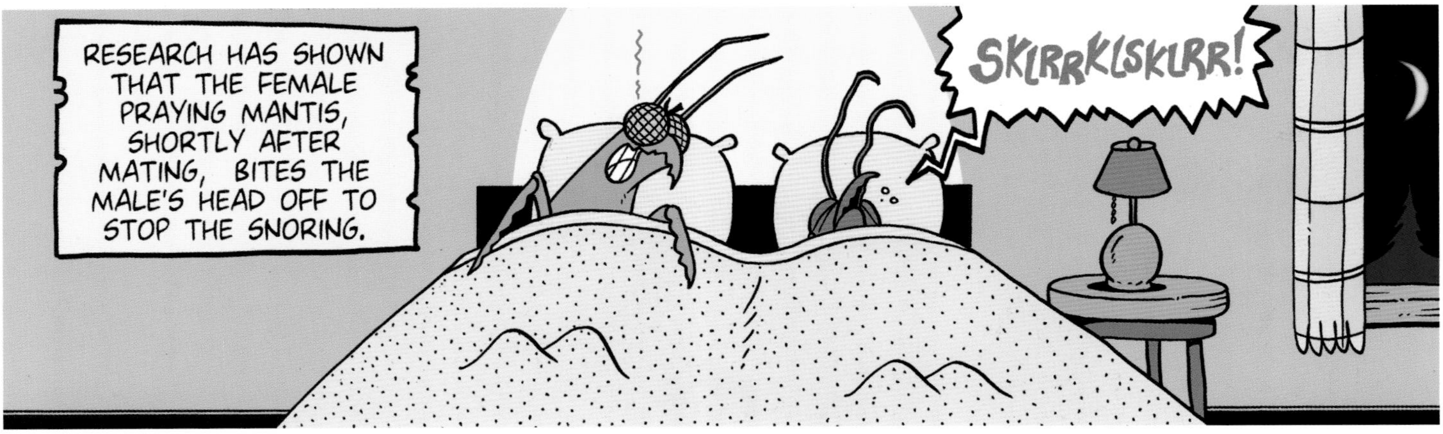
RESEARCH HAS SHOWN THAT THE FEMALE PRAYING MANTIS, SHORTLY AFTER MATING, BITES THE MALE'S HEAD OFF TO STOP THE SNORING.
SKLRRKLSKLRR!

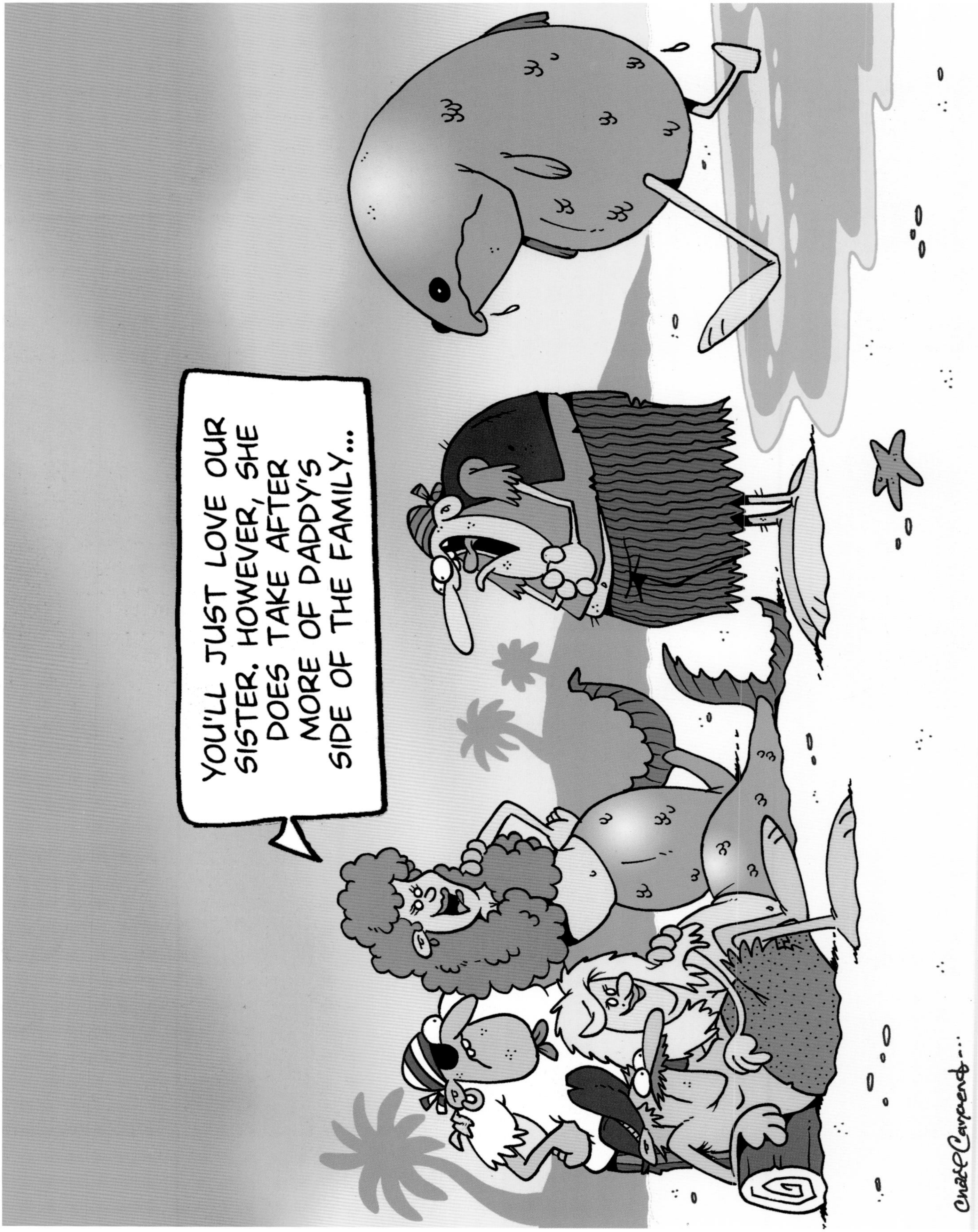
YOU'LL JUST LOVE OUR SISTER. HOWEVER, SHE DOES TAKE AFTER MORE OF DADDY'S SIDE OF THE FAMILY...
Chad Carpenter

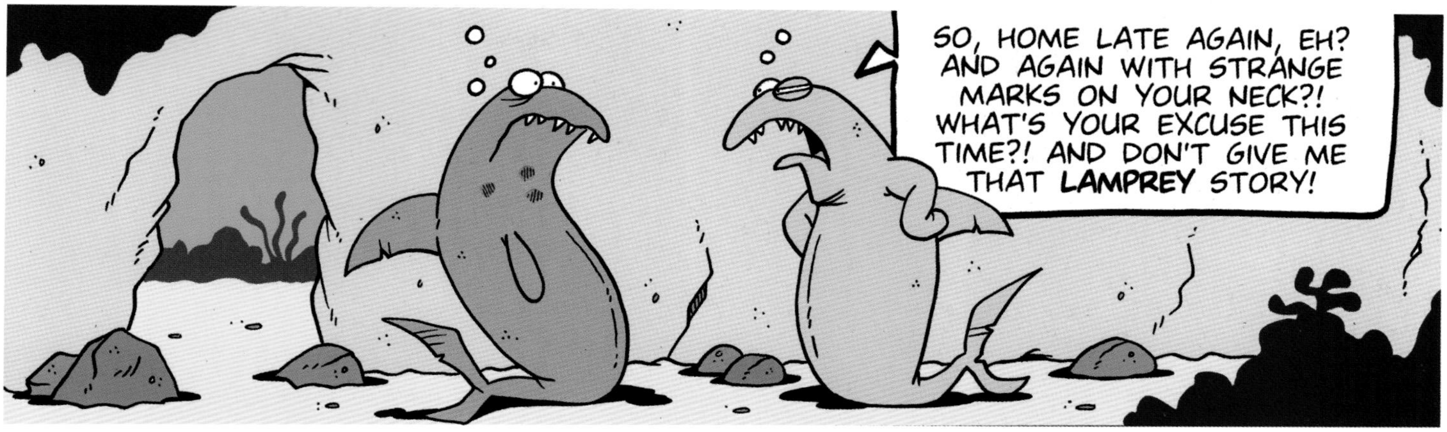
SO, HOME LATE AGAIN, EH? AND AGAIN WITH STRANGE MARKS ON YOUR NECK?! WHAT'S YOUR EXCUSE THIS TIME?! AND DON'T GIVE ME THAT **LAMPREY** STORY!

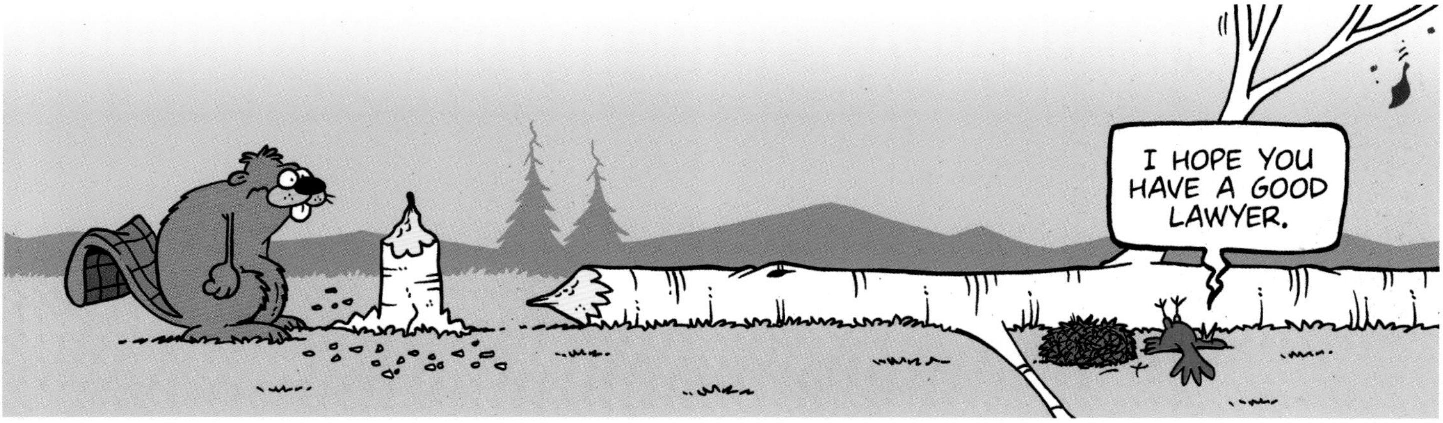
I HOPE YOU HAVE A GOOD LAWYER.

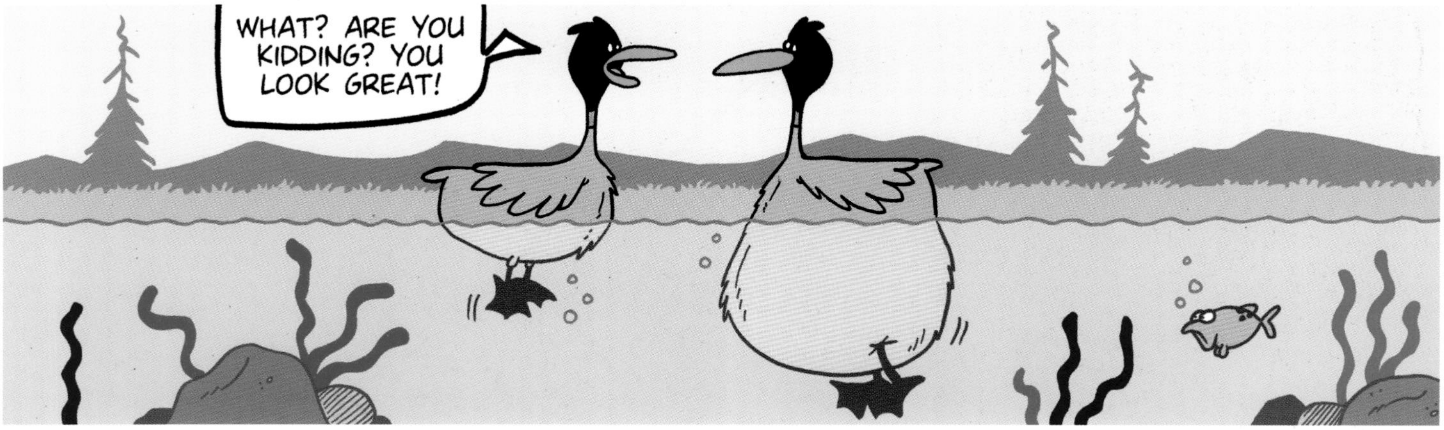
WHAT? ARE YOU KIDDING? YOU LOOK GREAT!

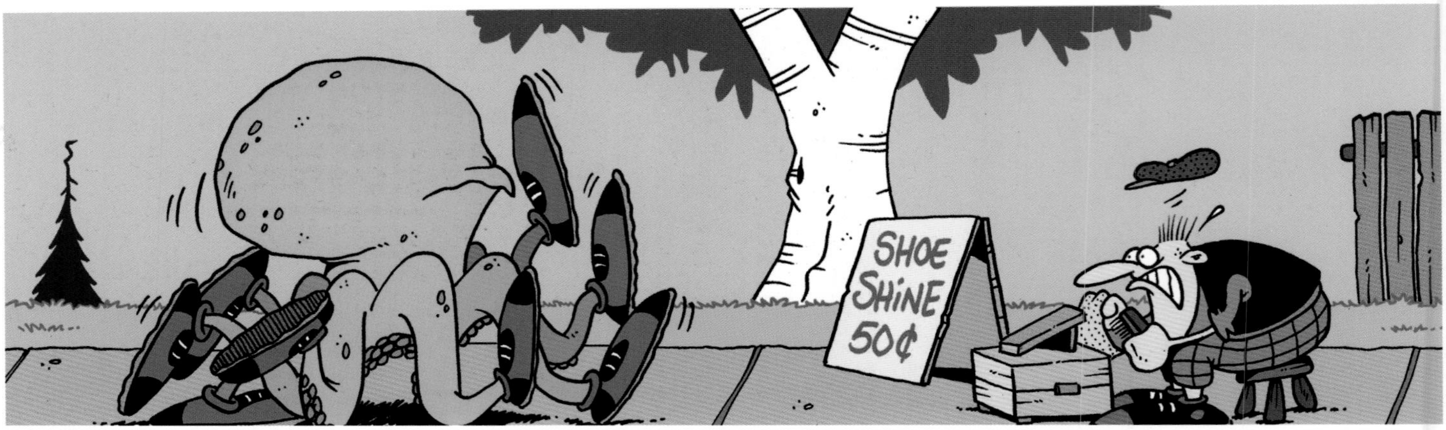
SHOE
SHINE
50¢

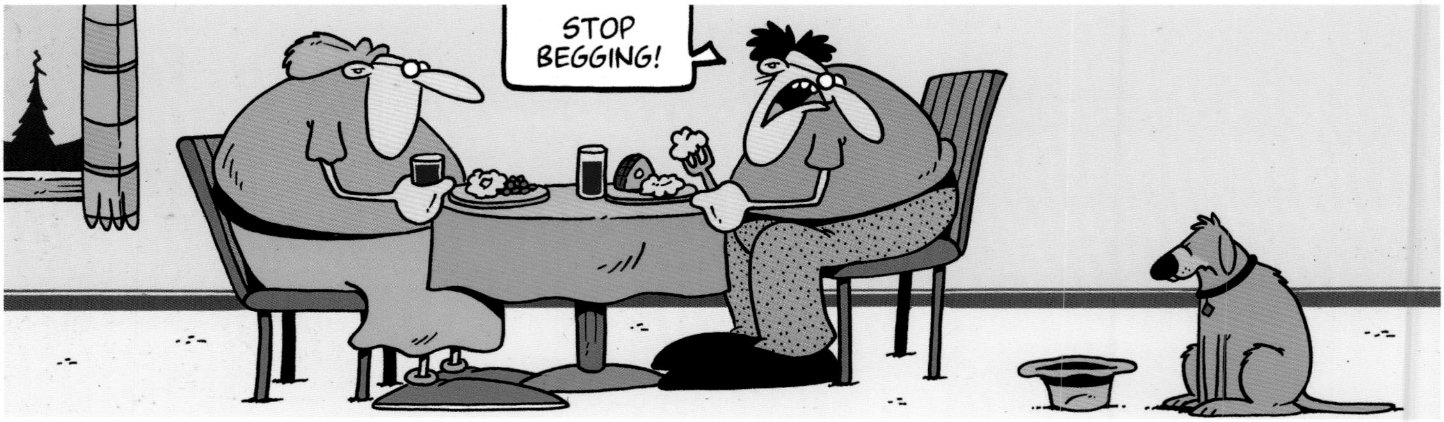
STOP BEGGING!

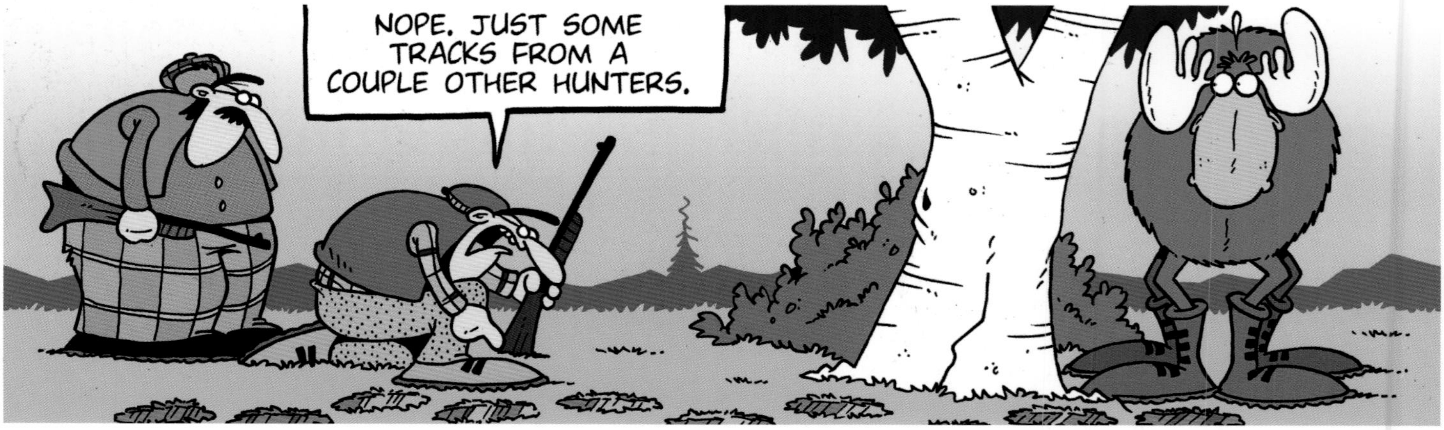
NOPE. JUST SOME TRACKS FROM A COUPLE OTHER HUNTERS.

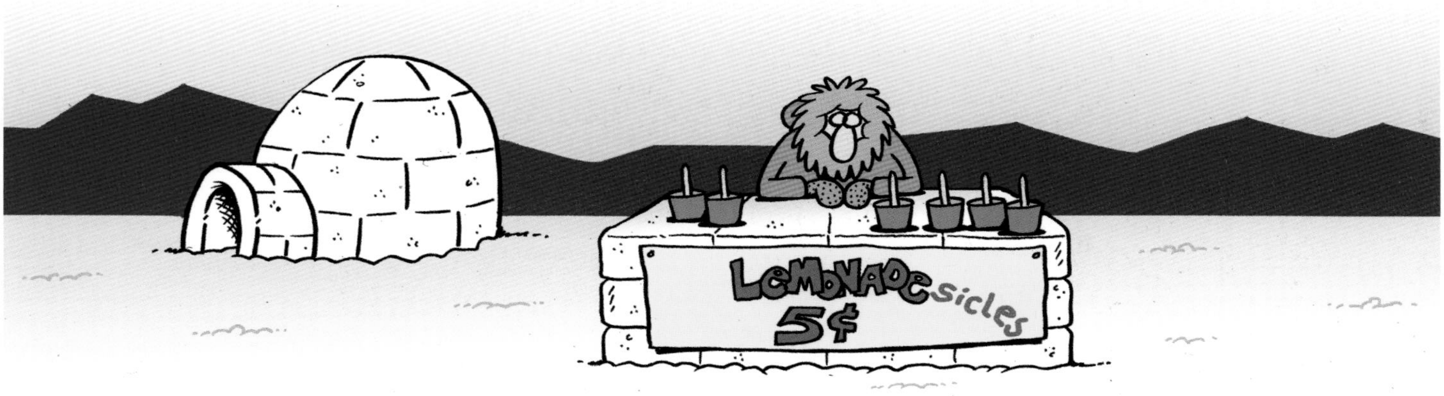
LEMONADEsicles
5¢

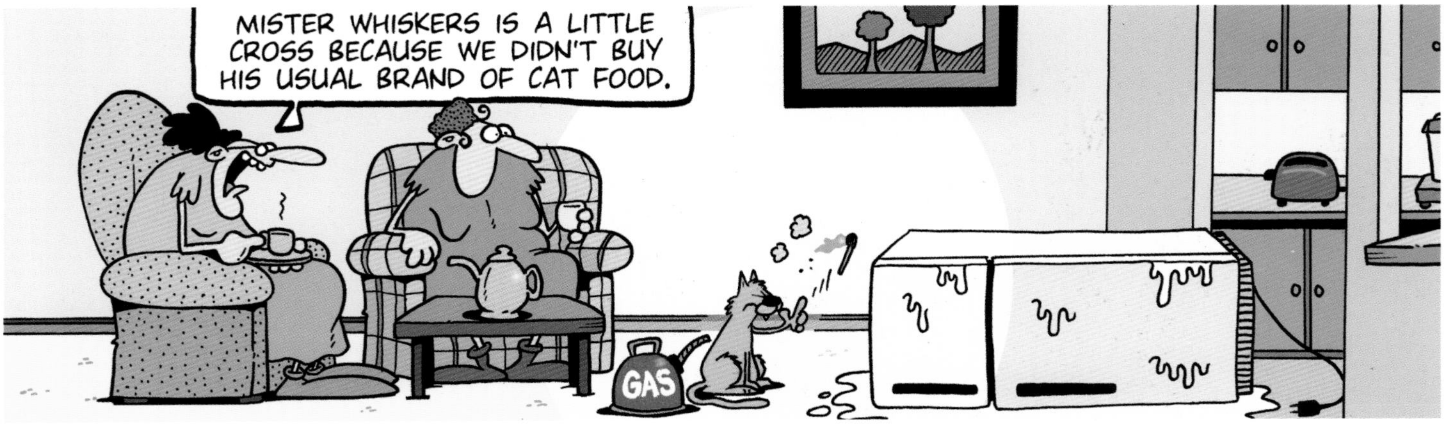
MISTER WHISKERS IS A LITTLE CROSS BECAUSE WE DIDN'T BUY HIS USUAL BRAND OF CAT FOOD.
GAS

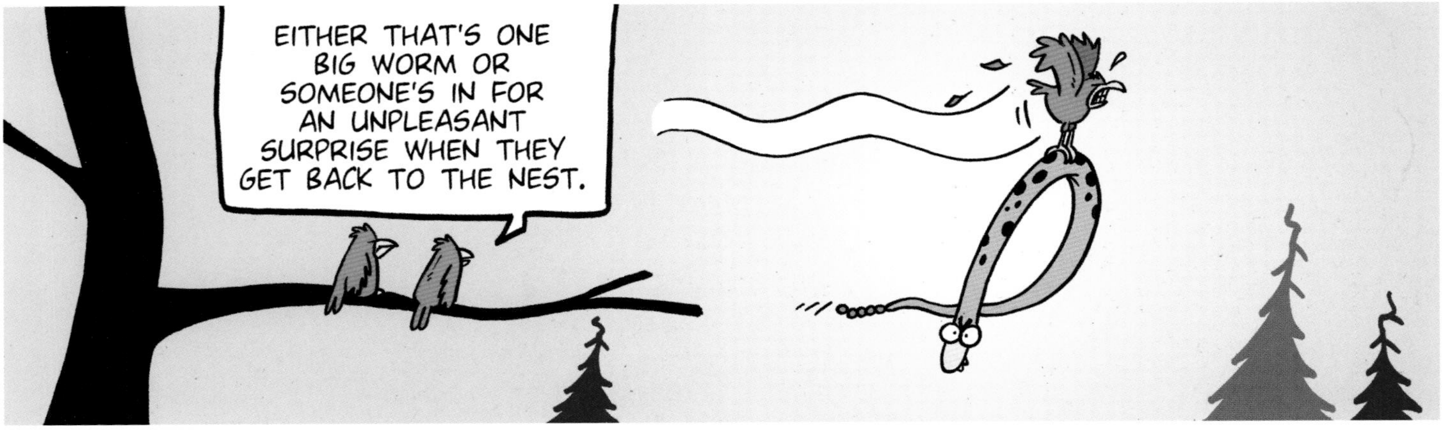
EITHER THAT'S ONE BIG WORM OR SOMEONE'S IN FOR AN UNPLEASANT SURPRISE WHEN THEY GET BACK TO THE NEST.

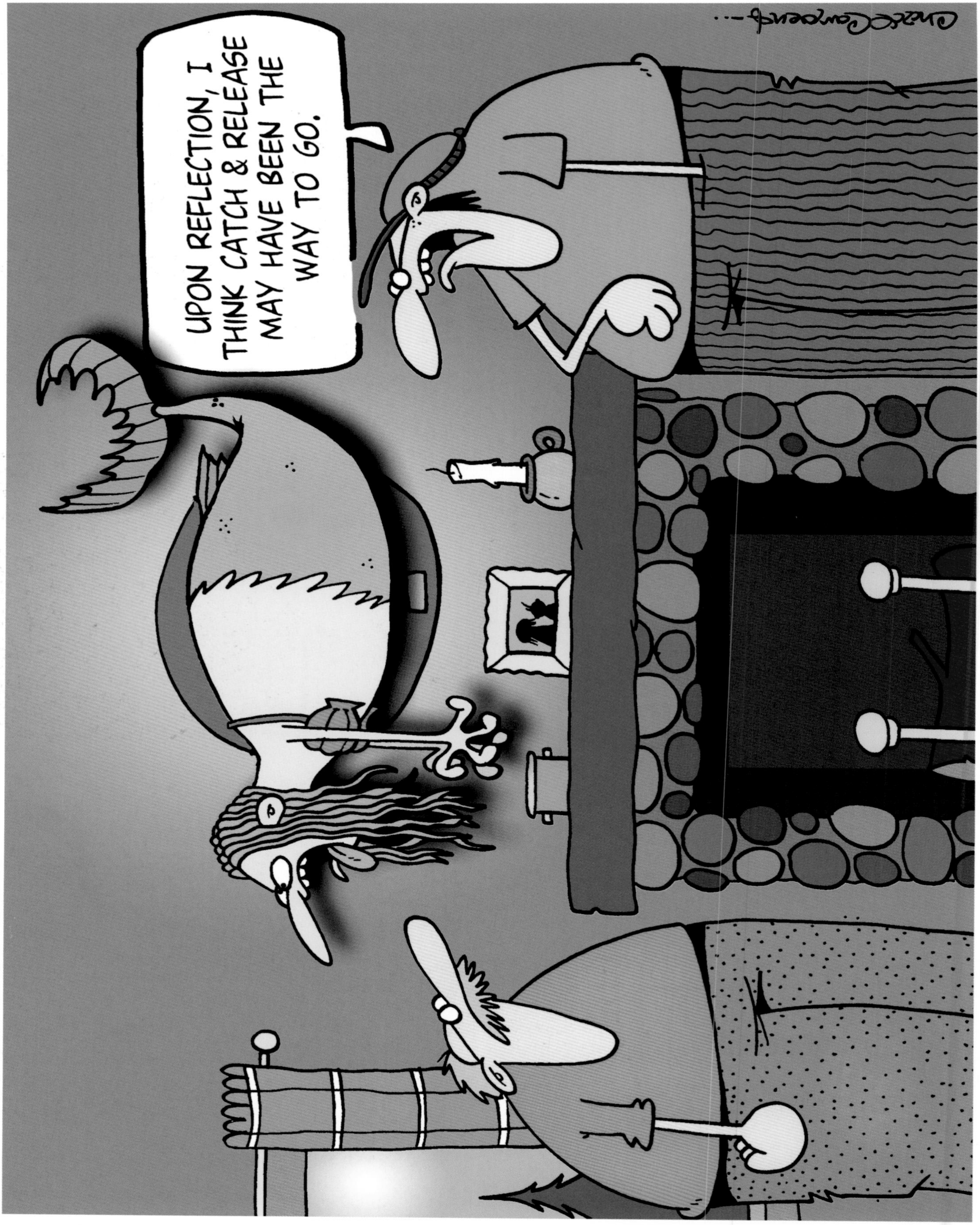
UPON REFLECTION, I THINK CATCH & RELEASE MAY HAVE BEEN THE WAY TO GO.

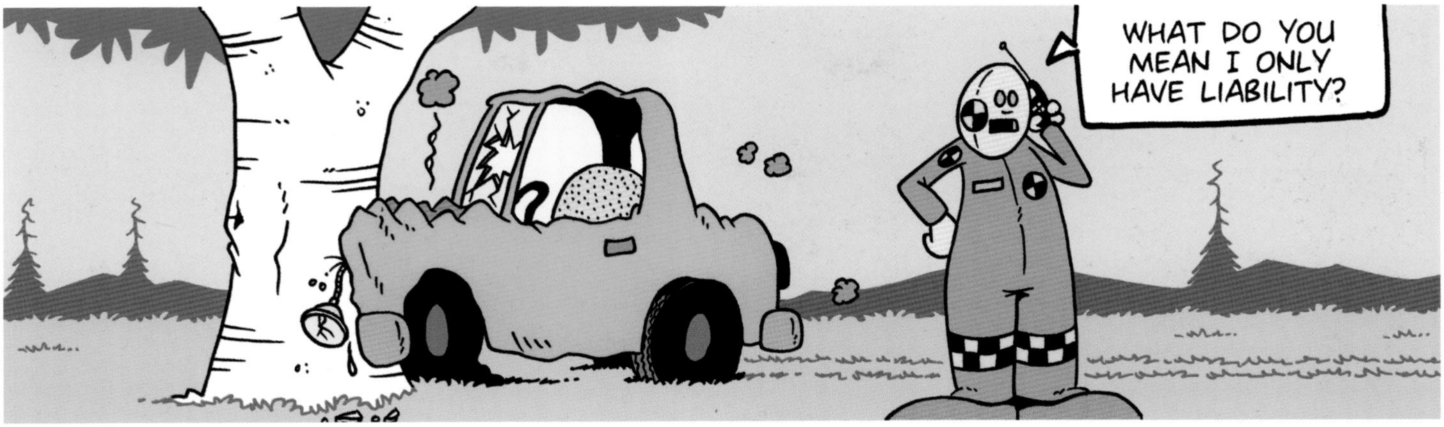
WHAT DO YOU MEAN I ONLY HAVE LIABILITY?

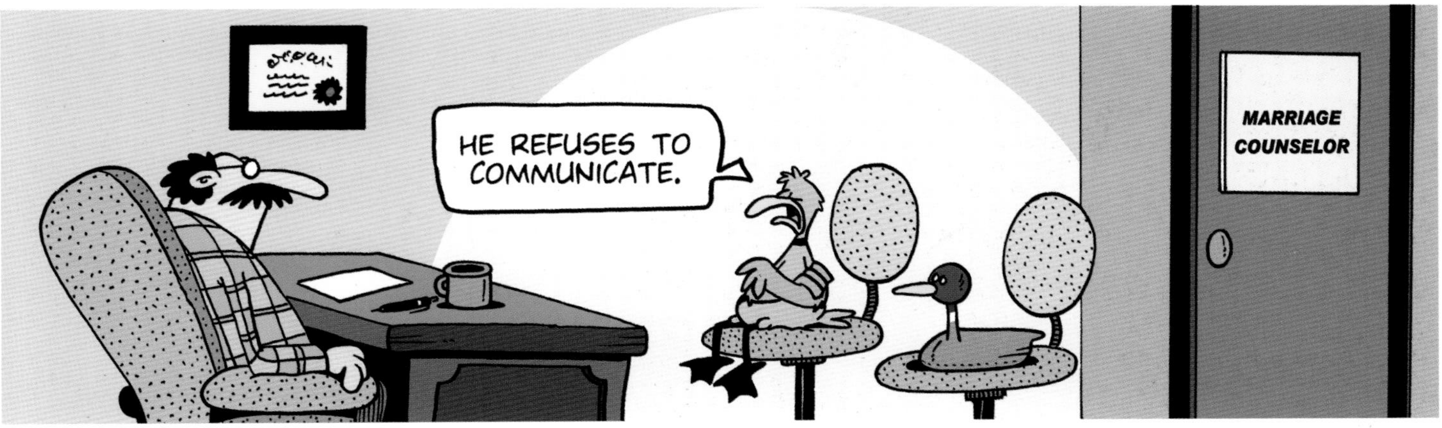
HE REFUSES TO COMMUNICATE.
MARRIAGE COUNSELOR

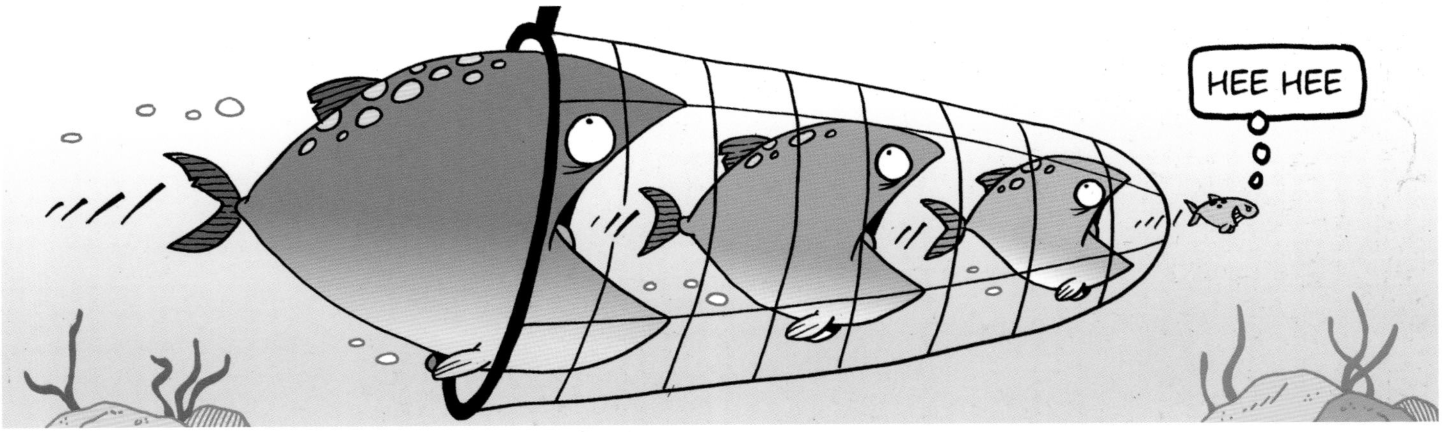
HEE HEE

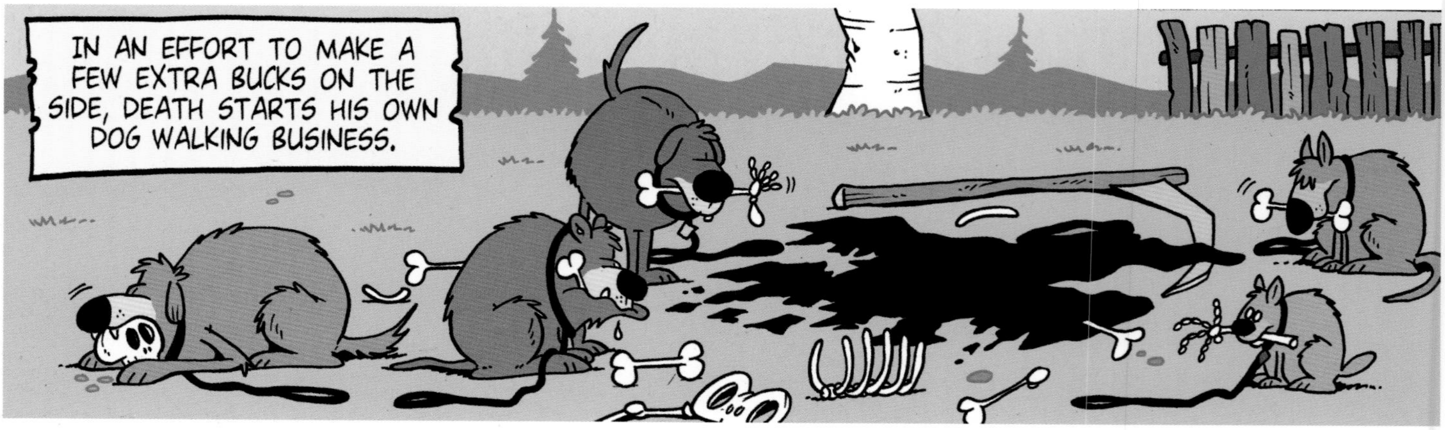
IN AN EFFORT TO MAKE A FEW EXTRA BUCKS ON THE SIDE, DEATH STARTS HIS OWN DOG WALKING BUSINESS.

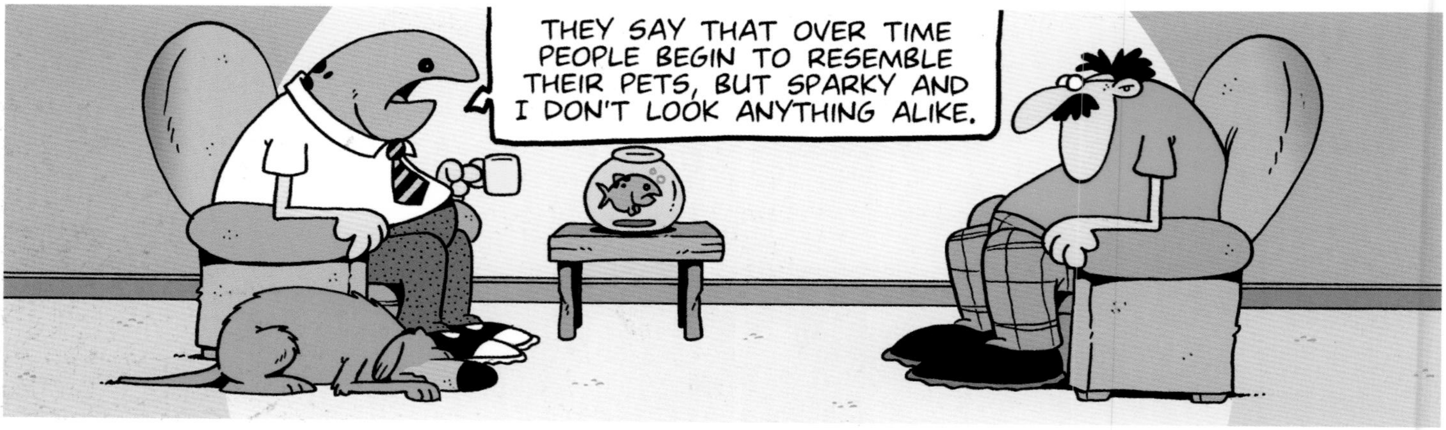
THEY SAY THAT OVER TIME PEOPLE BEGIN TO RESEMBLE THEIR PETS, BUT SPARKY AND I DON'T LOOK ANYTHING ALIKE.

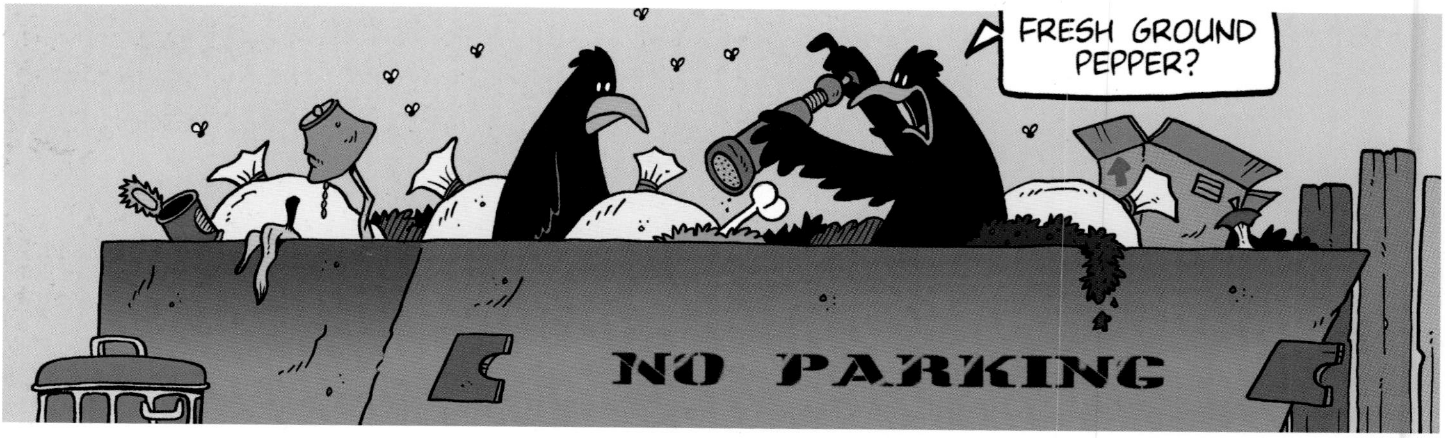
FRESH GROUND PEPPER?
NO PARKING

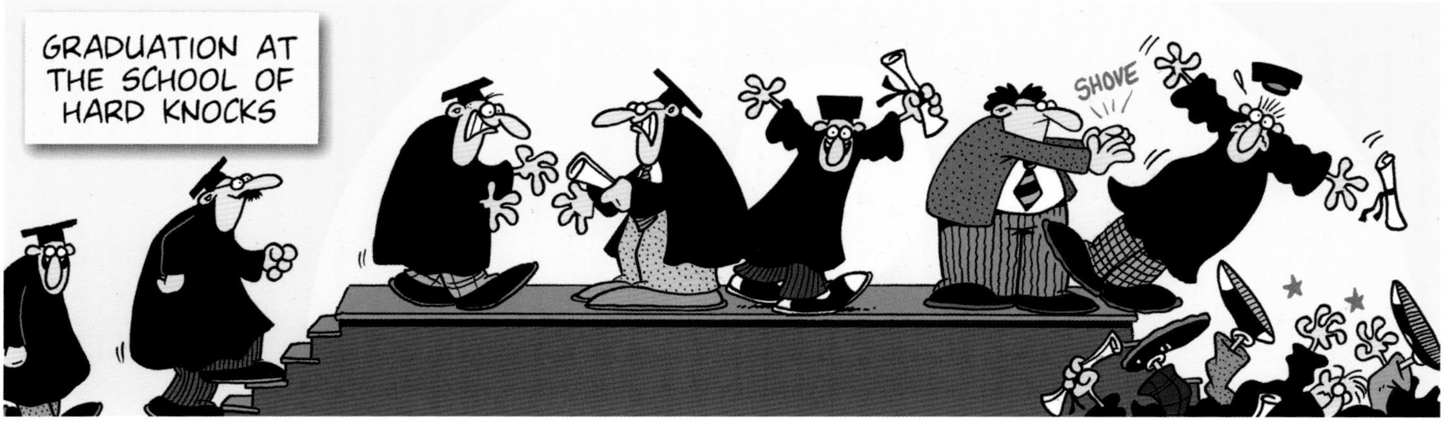
GRADUATION AT THE SCHOOL OF HARD KNOCKS
SHOVE

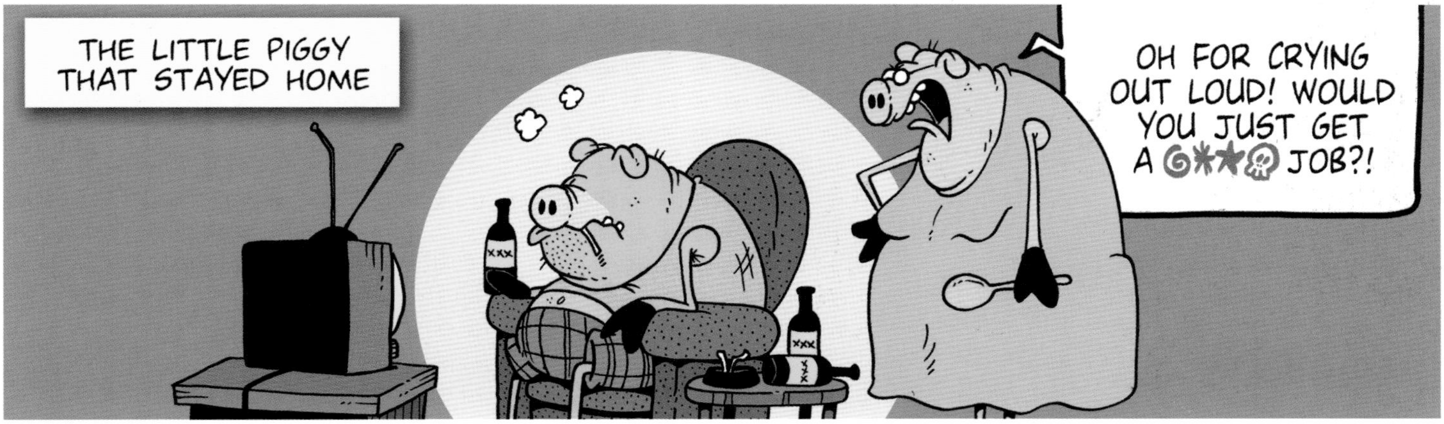
THE LITTLE PIGGY THAT STAYED HOME
OH FOR CRYING OUT LOUD! WOULD YOU JUST GET A @*★☠ JOB?!

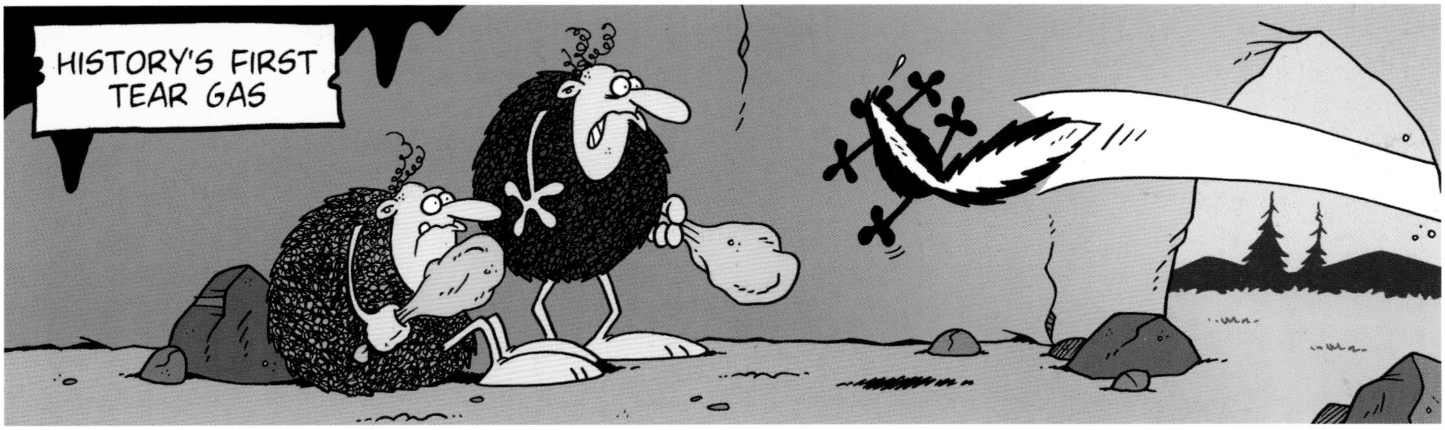
HISTORY'S FIRST TEAR GAS

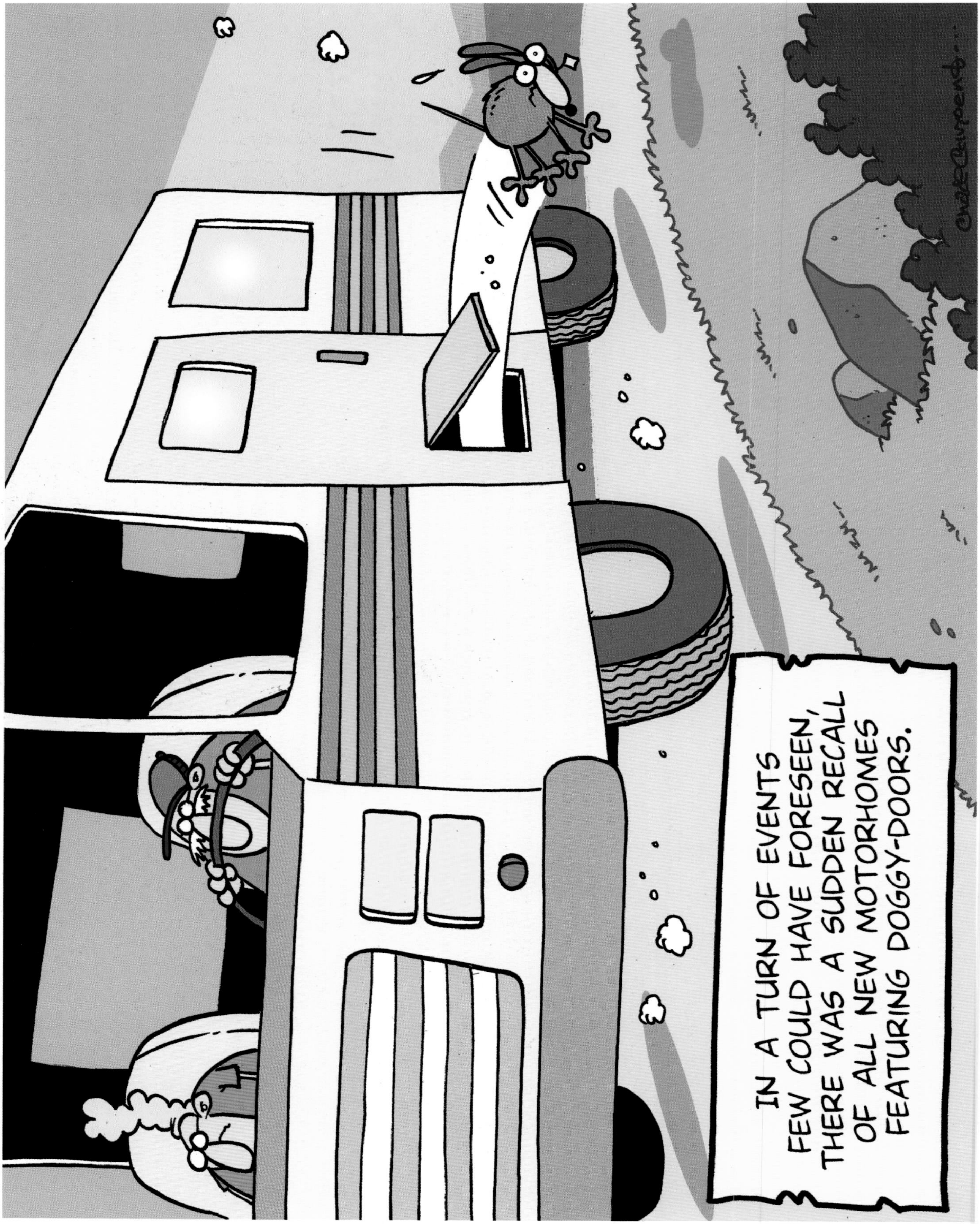
IN A TURN OF EVENTS
FEW COULD HAVE FORESEEN,
THERE WAS A SUDDEN RECALL
OF ALL NEW MOTORHOMES
FEATURING DOGGY-DOORS.

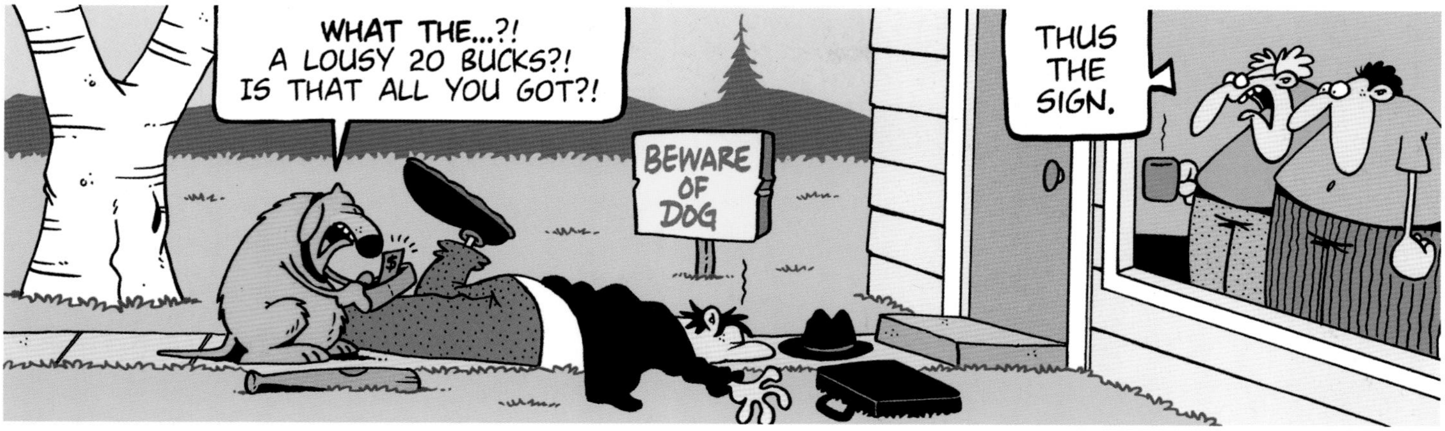
WHAT THE...?! A LOUSY 20 BUCKS?! IS THAT ALL YOU GOT?!
BEWARE OF DOG
THUS THE SIGN.

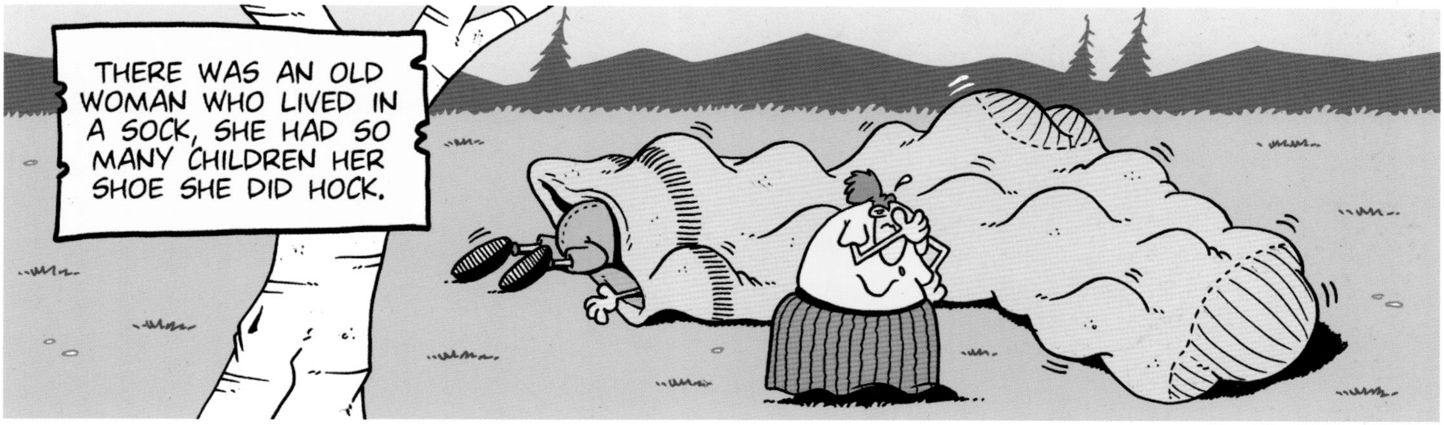
THERE WAS AN OLD WOMAN WHO LIVED IN A SOCK, SHE HAD SO MANY CHILDREN HER SHOE SHE DID HOCK.

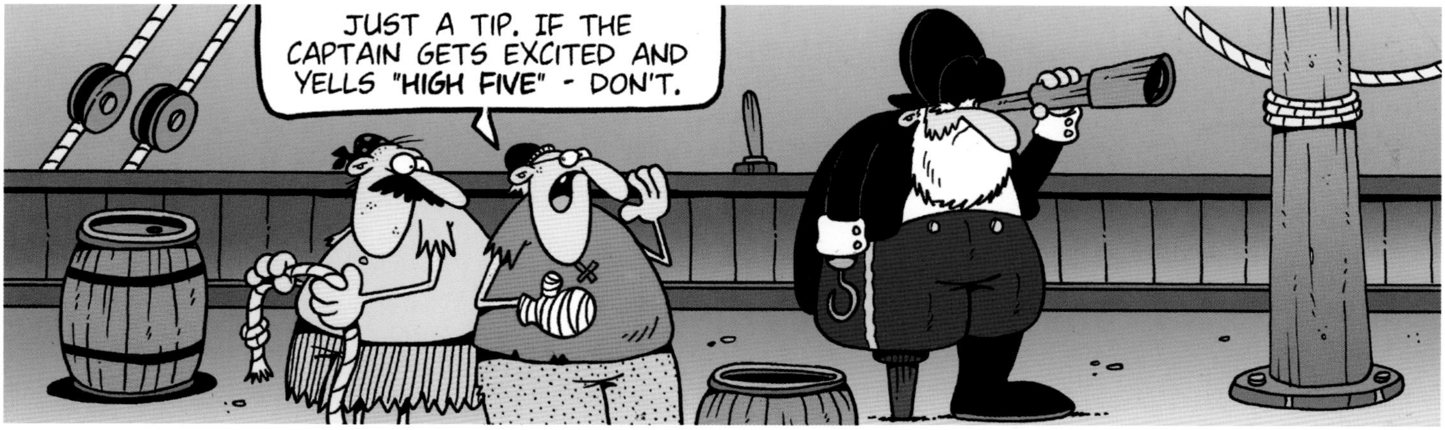
JUST A TIP. IF THE CAPTAIN GETS EXCITED AND YELLS "**HIGH FIVE**" - DON'T.

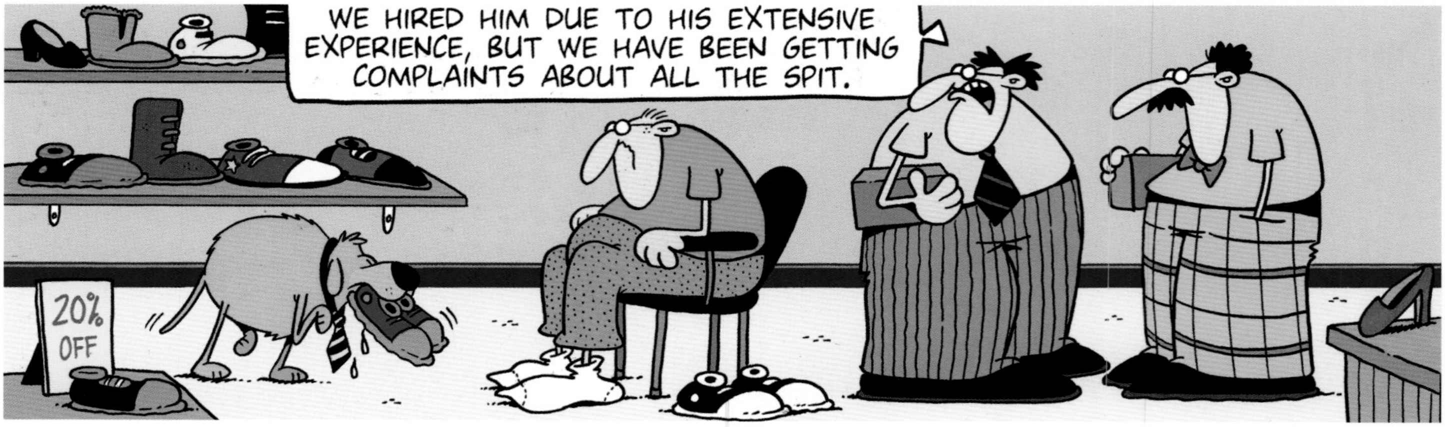
WE HIRED HIM DUE TO HIS EXTENSIVE EXPERIENCE, BUT WE HAVE BEEN GETTING COMPLAINTS ABOUT ALL THE SPIT.
20% OFF

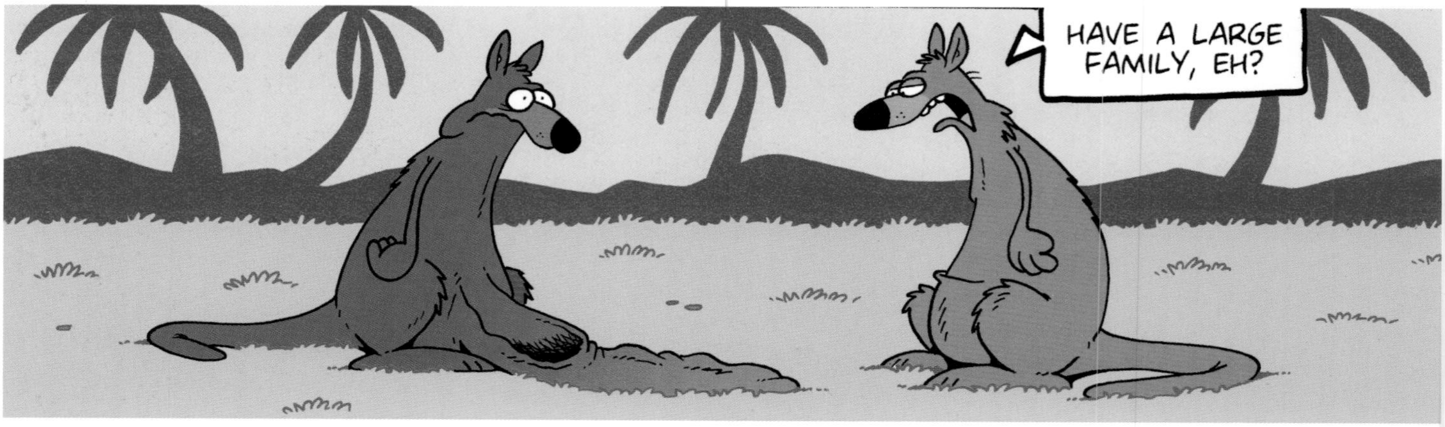
HAVE A LARGE FAMILY, EH?

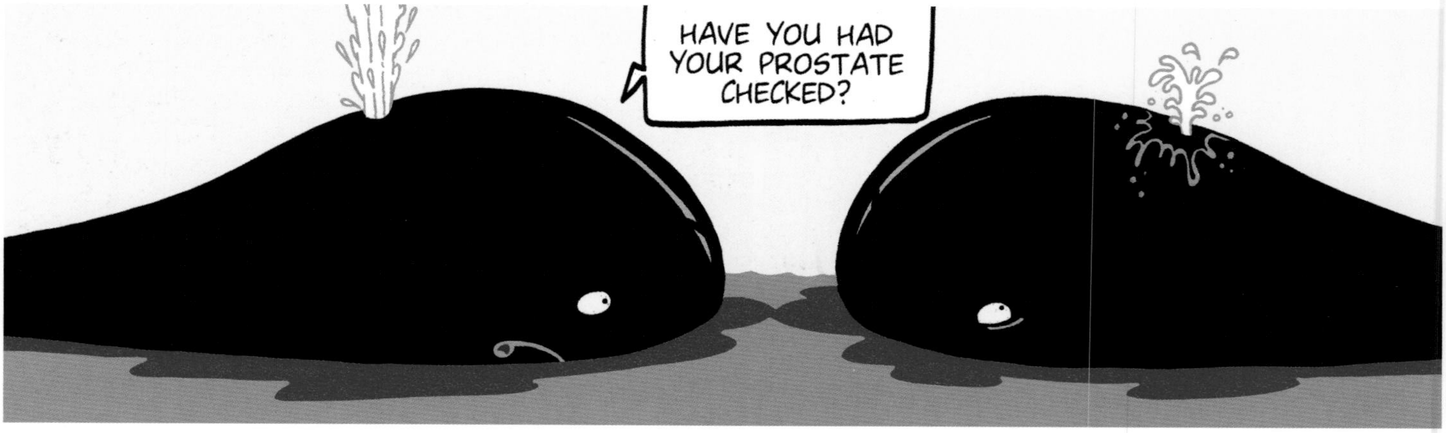
HAVE YOU HAD YOUR PROSTATE CHECKED?

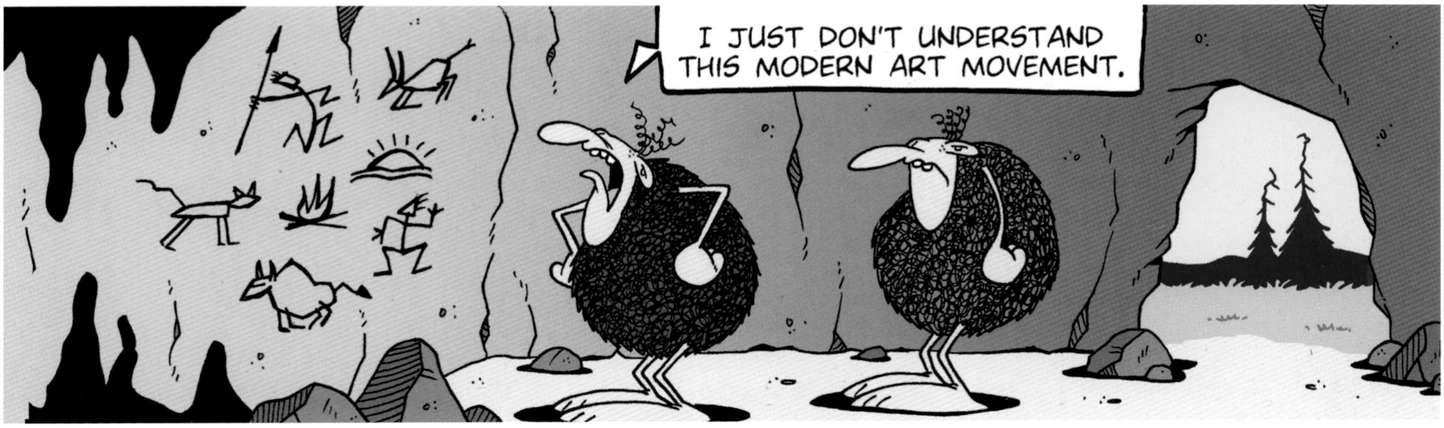
I JUST DON'T UNDERSTAND THIS MODERN ART MOVEMENT.

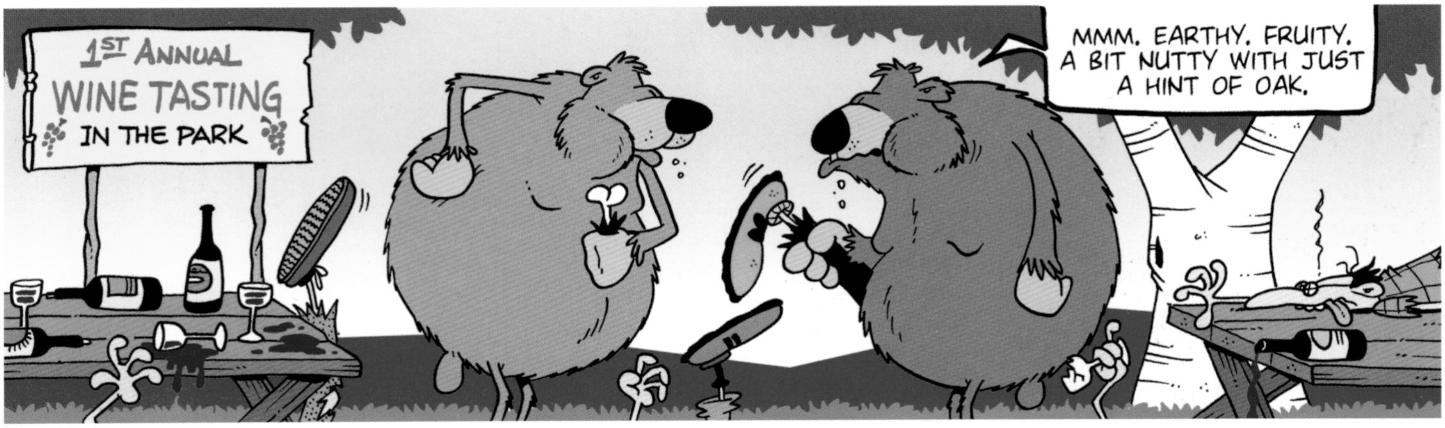
1ST ANNUAL
WINE TASTING
IN THE PARK
MMM. EARTHY. FRUITY. A BIT NUTTY WITH JUST A HINT OF OAK.

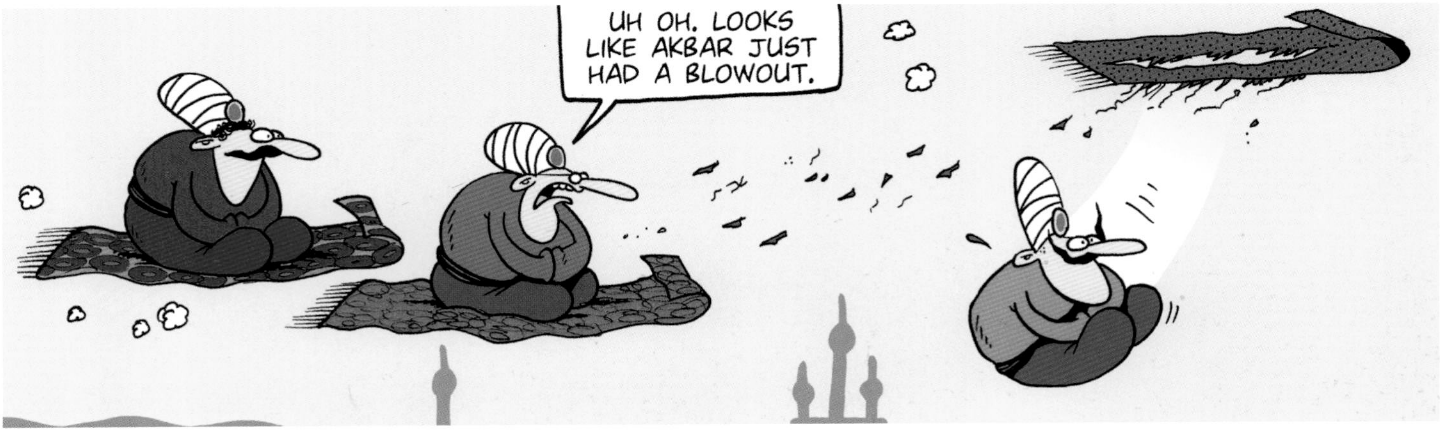
UH OH. LOOKS LIKE AKBAR JUST HAD A BLOWOUT.

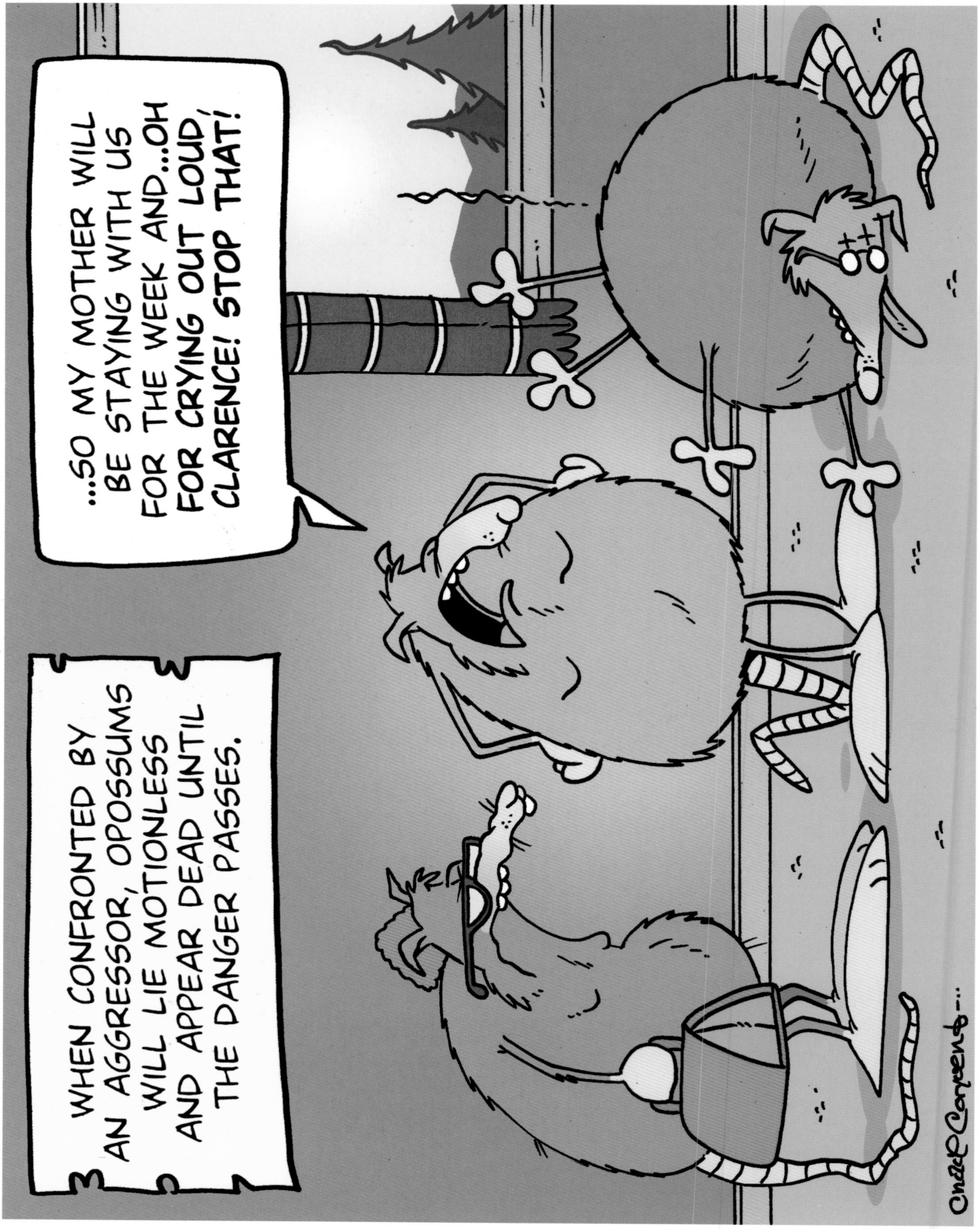
WHEN CONFRONTED BY AN AGGRESSOR, OPOSSUMS WILL LIE MOTIONLESS AND APPEAR DEAD UNTIL THE DANGER PASSES.
...SO MY MOTHER WILL BE STAYING WITH US FOR THE WEEK AND...OH FOR CRYING OUT LOUD, CLARENCE! STOP THAT!
CHAD CARPENTER

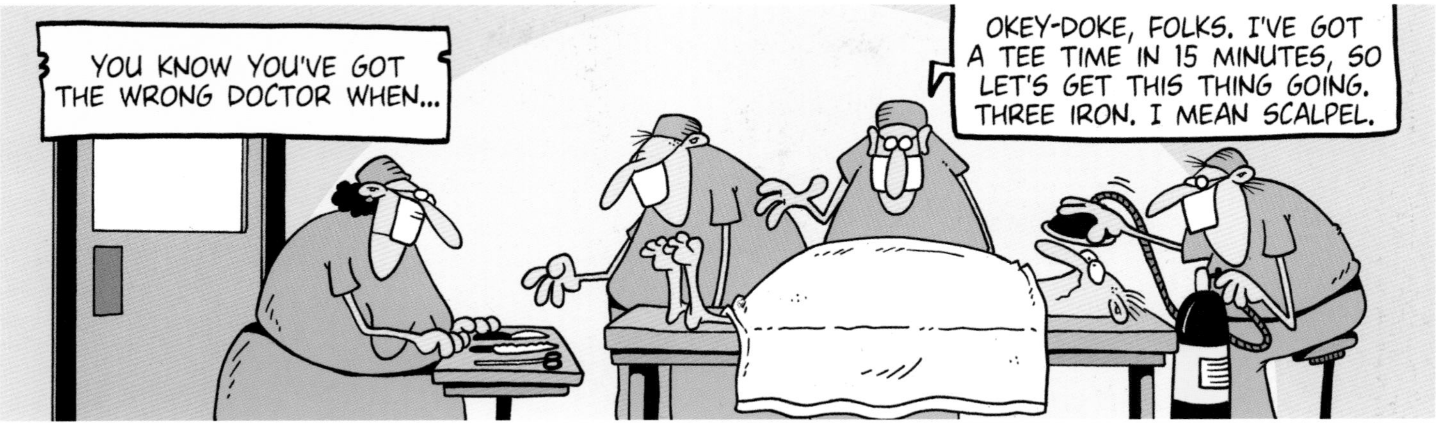
YOU KNOW YOU'VE GOT THE WRONG DOCTOR WHEN...
OKEY-DOKE, FOLKS. I'VE GOT A TEE TIME IN 15 MINUTES, SO LET'S GET THIS THING GOING. THREE IRON. I MEAN SCALPEL.

THIS STRIP IS BASED ON AN IDEA FROM:
DENNIS WITTENBERG
SPARTA, TN
DO YOU HAVE AN IDEA THAT WOULD MAKE A GREAT COMIC STRIP?
SEND IT TO:
tundracomics.com

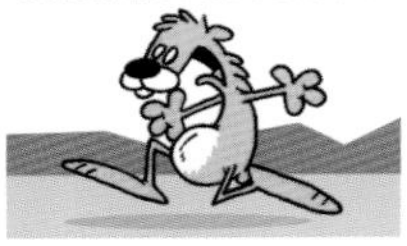

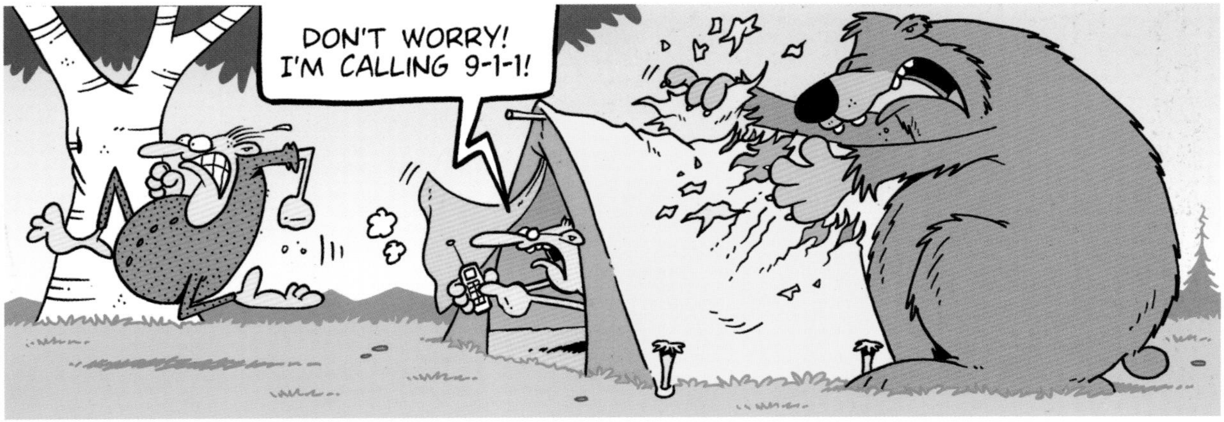
DON'T WORRY! I'M CALLING 9-1-1!

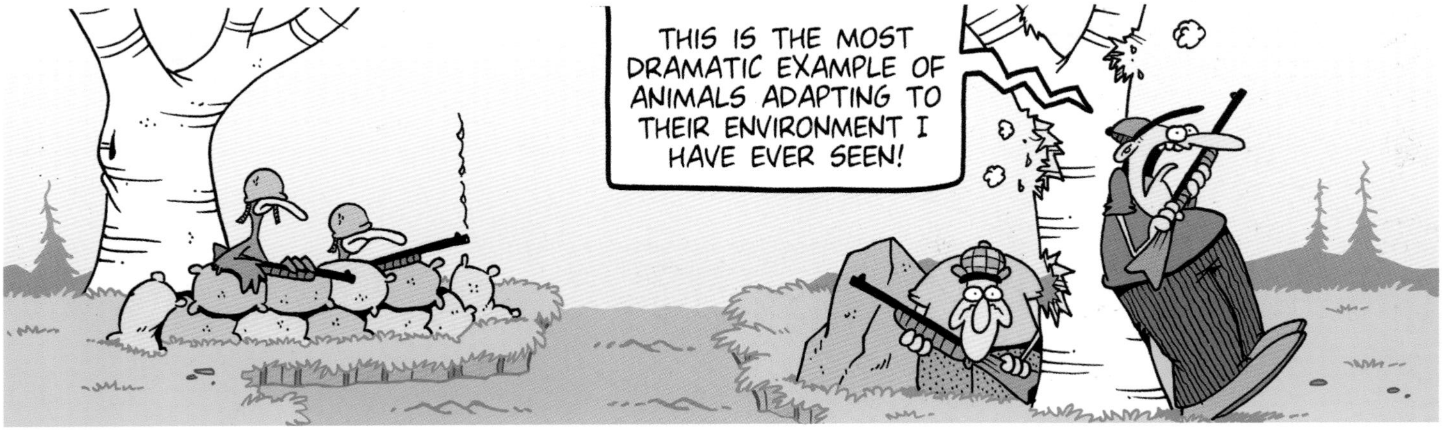
THIS IS THE MOST DRAMATIC EXAMPLE OF ANIMALS ADAPTING TO THEIR ENVIRONMENT I HAVE EVER SEEN!

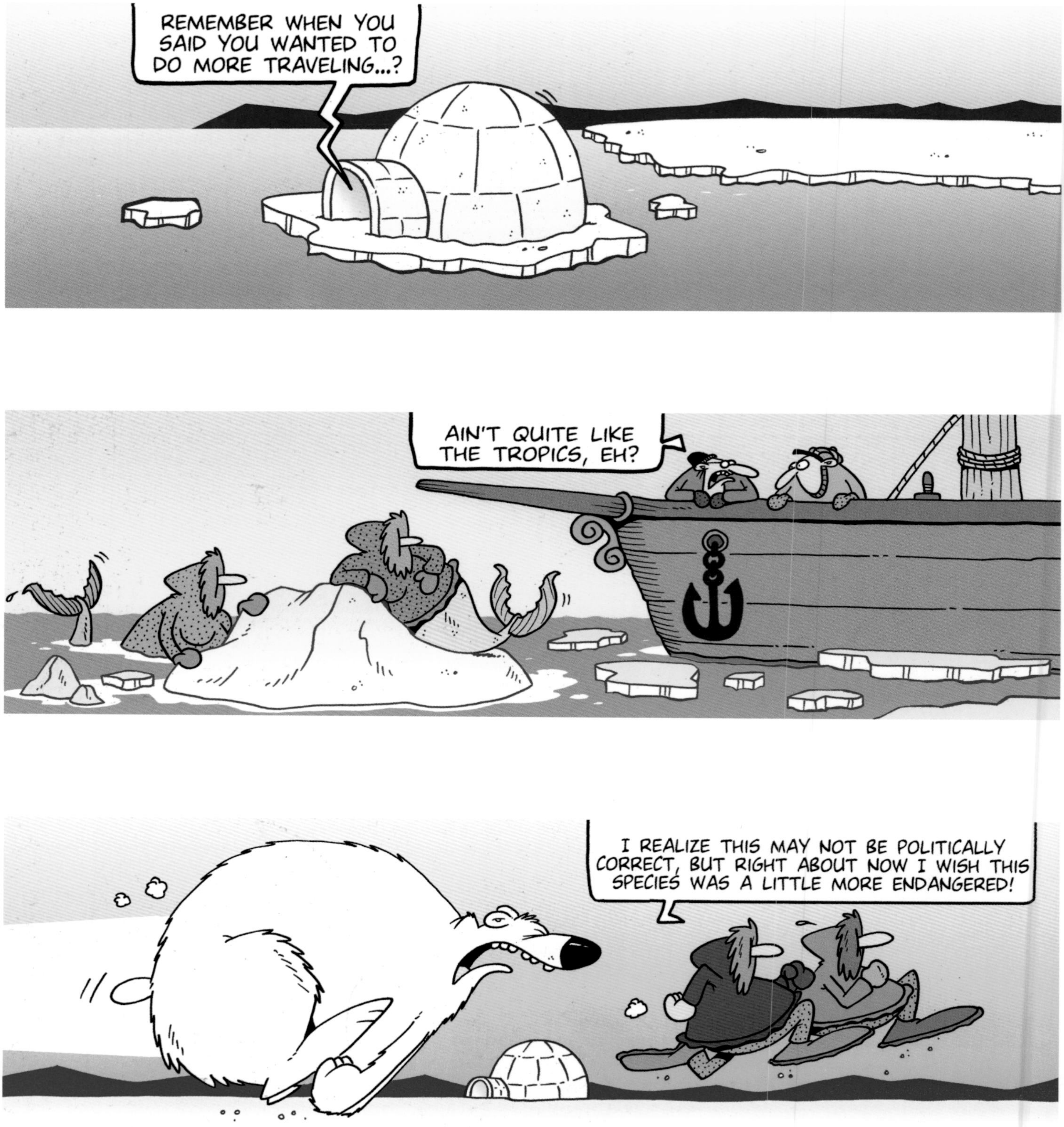
REMEMBER WHEN YOU SAID YOU WANTED TO DO MORE TRAVELING...?
AIN'T QUITE LIKE THE TROPICS, EH?
I REALIZE THIS MAY NOT BE POLITICALLY CORRECT, BUT RIGHT ABOUT NOW I WISH THIS SPECIES WAS A LITTLE MORE ENDANGERED!

THIS STRIP IS BASED ON AN IDEA FROM:

SUSAN DOUGLAS
LOS ANGELES, CA

DO YOU HAVE AN IDEA THAT WOULD MAKE A GREAT COMIC STRIP?

SEND IT TO:
tundracomics.com

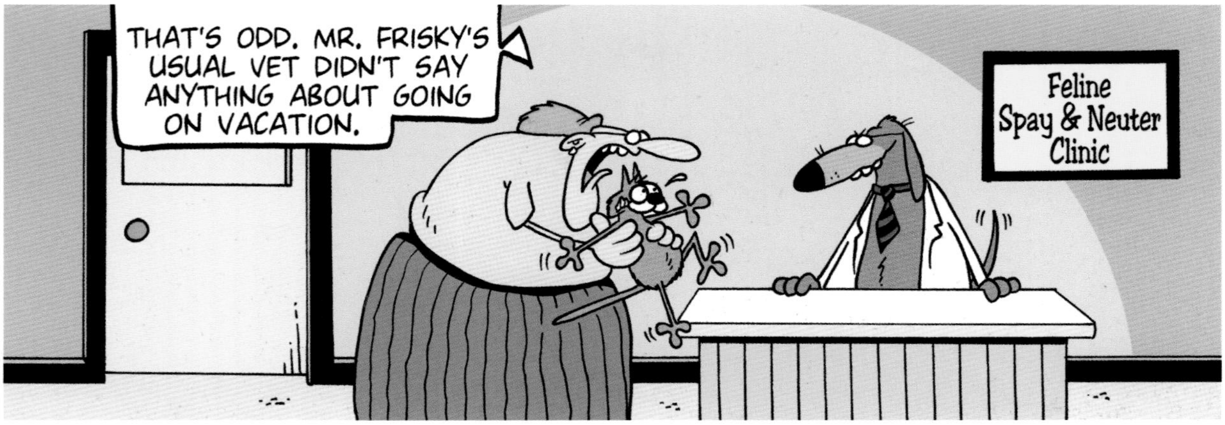
THAT'S ODD. MR. FRISKY'S USUAL VET DIDN'T SAY ANYTHING ABOUT GOING ON VACATION.
Feline Spay & Neuter Clinic

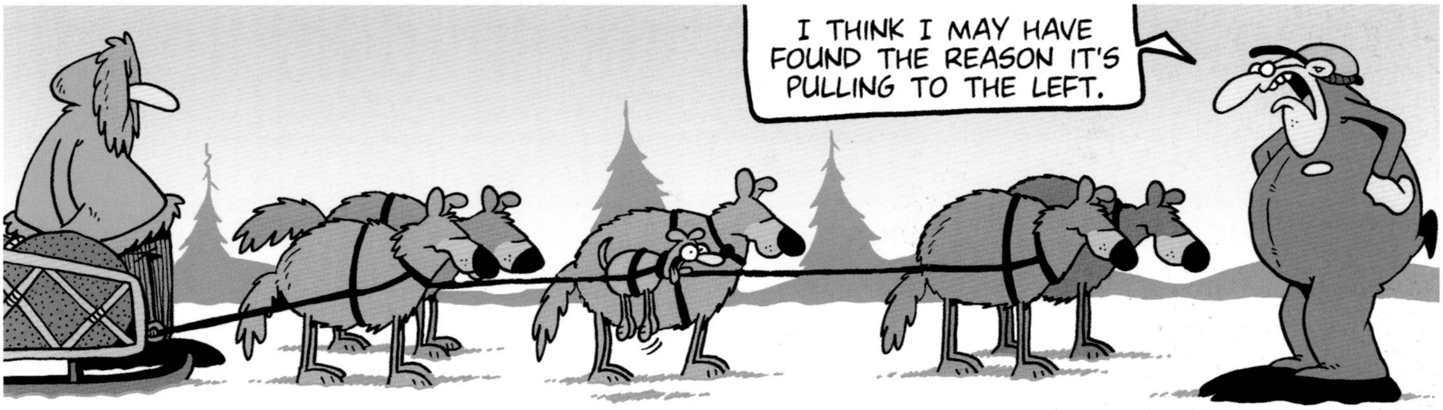
I THINK I MAY HAVE FOUND THE REASON IT'S PULLING TO THE LEFT.

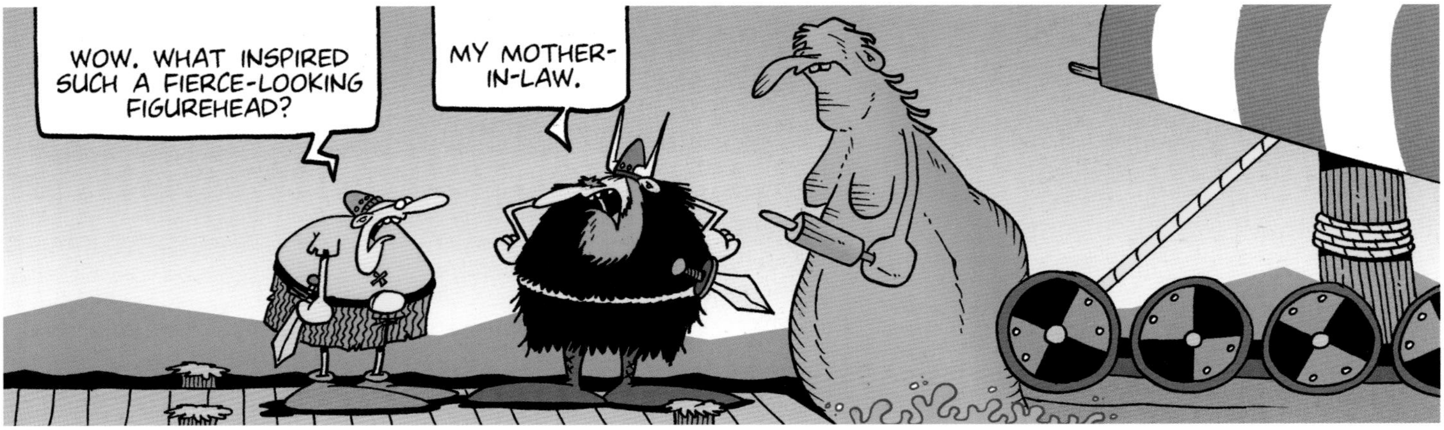
WOW. WHAT INSPIRED SUCH A FIERCE-LOOKING FIGUREHEAD?
MY MOTHER-IN-LAW.

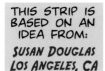

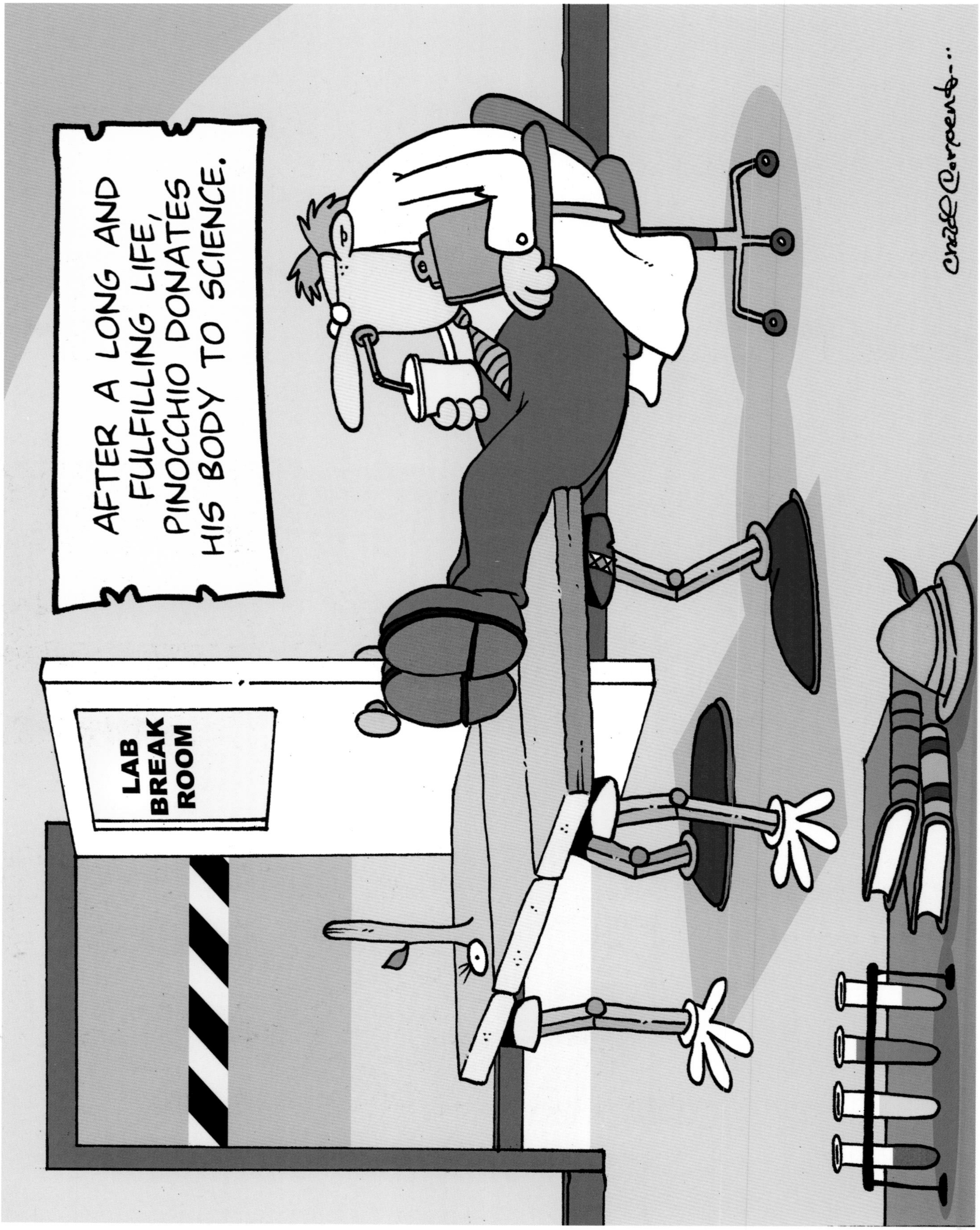
AFTER A LONG AND FULFILLING LIFE, PINOCCHIO DONATES HIS BODY TO SCIENCE.
LAB BREAK ROOM

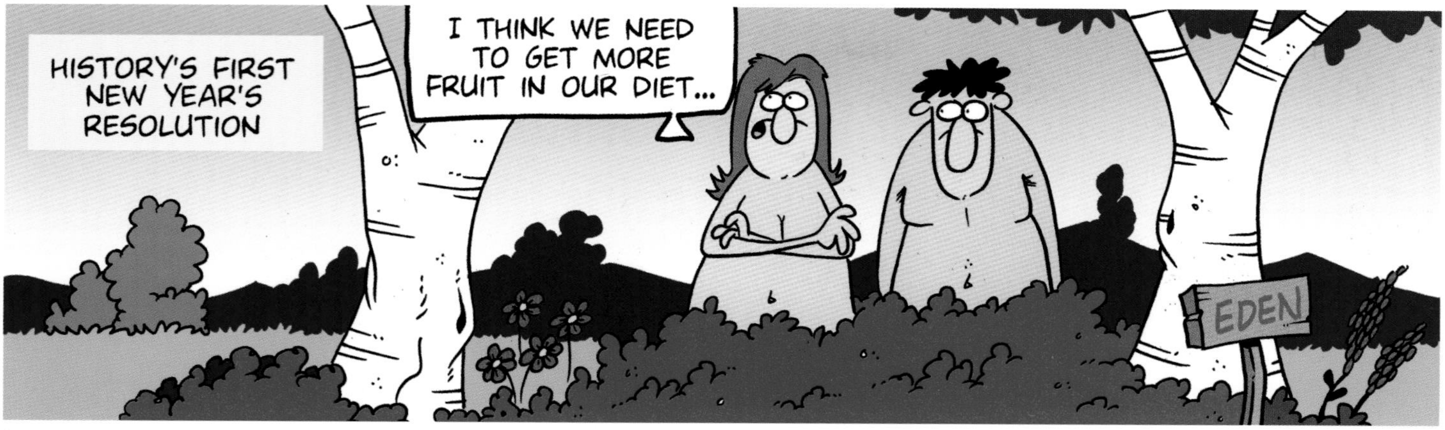
HISTORY'S FIRST NEW YEAR'S RESOLUTION
I THINK WE NEED TO GET MORE FRUIT IN OUR DIET...
EDEN

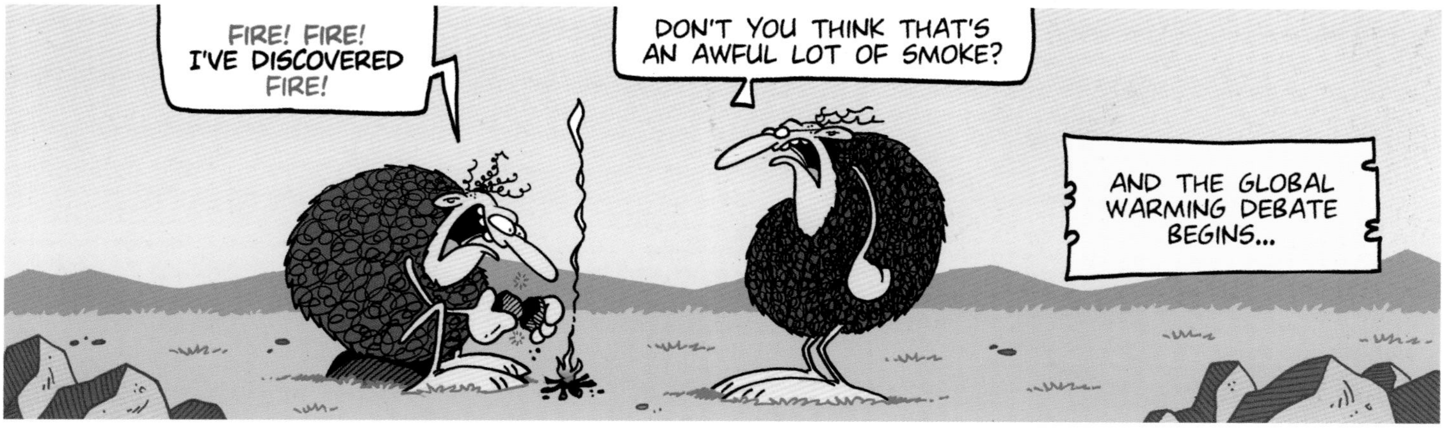
FIRE! FIRE! I'VE DISCOVERED FIRE!
DON'T YOU THINK THAT'S AN AWFUL LOT OF SMOKE?
AND THE GLOBAL WARMING DEBATE BEGINS...

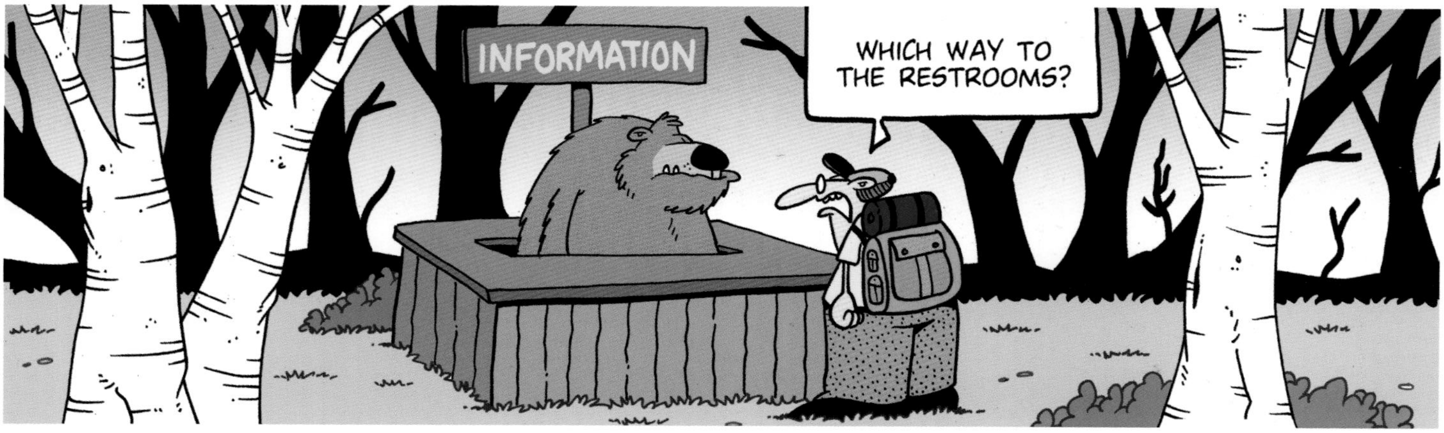
INFORMATION
WHICH WAY TO THE RESTROOMS?

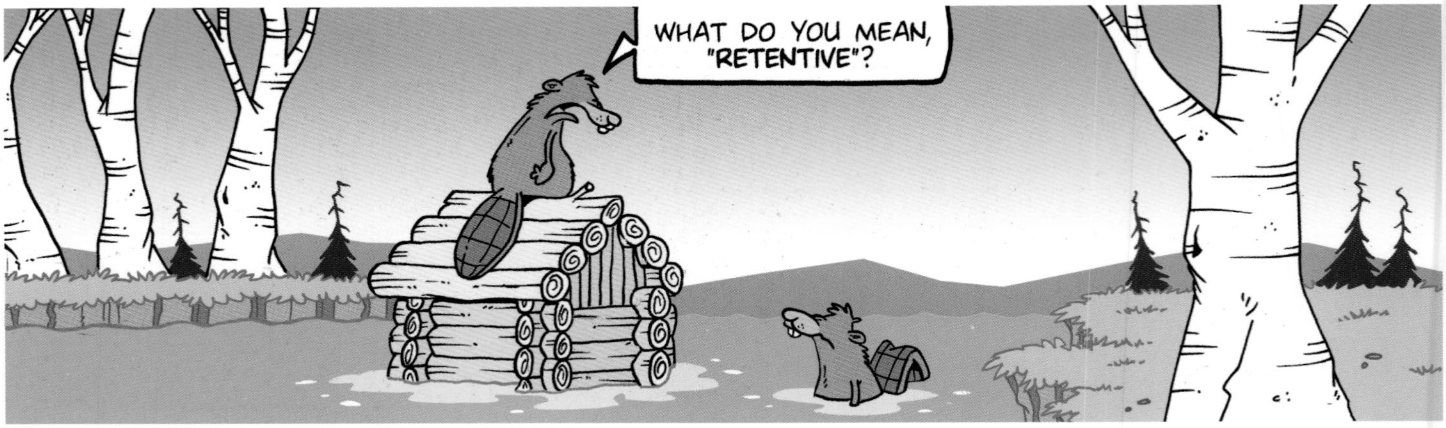
WHAT DO YOU MEAN, "RETENTIVE"?

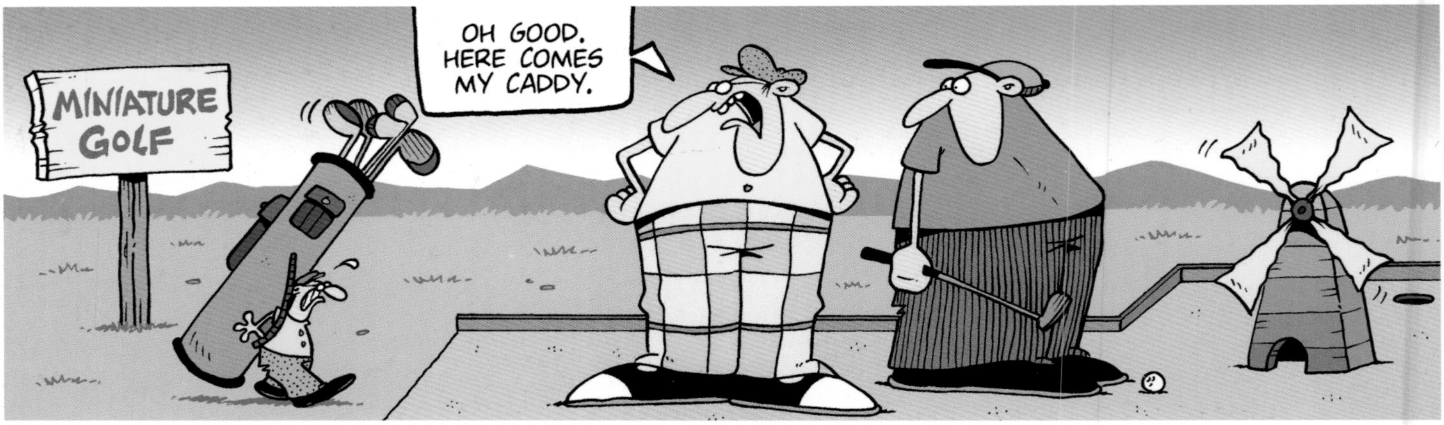
MINIATURE GOLF
OH GOOD. HERE COMES MY CADDY.

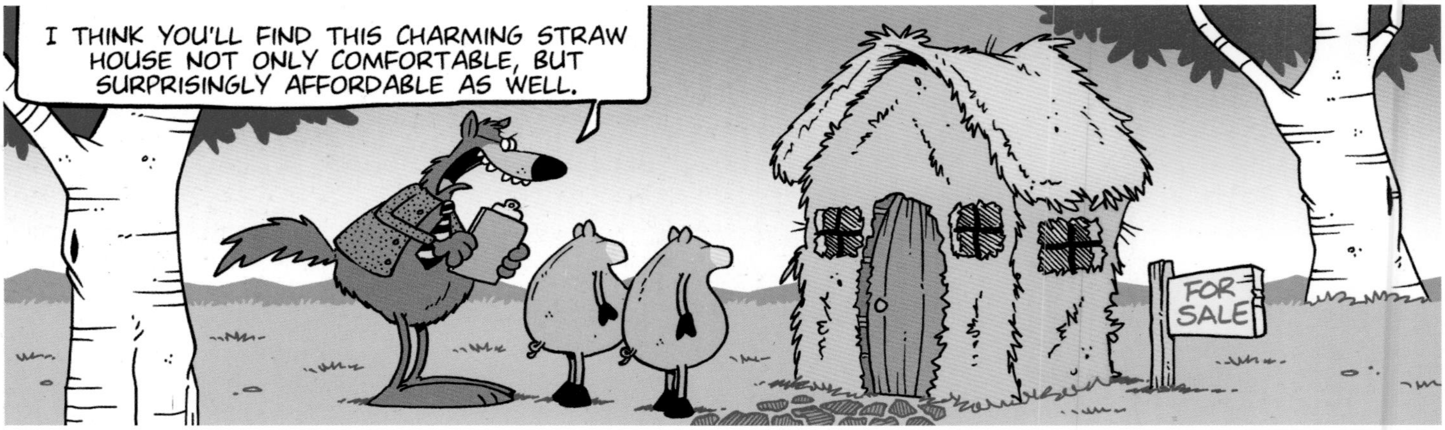
I THINK YOU'LL FIND THIS CHARMING STRAW HOUSE NOT ONLY COMFORTABLE, BUT SURPRISINGLY AFFORDABLE AS WELL.
FOR SALE

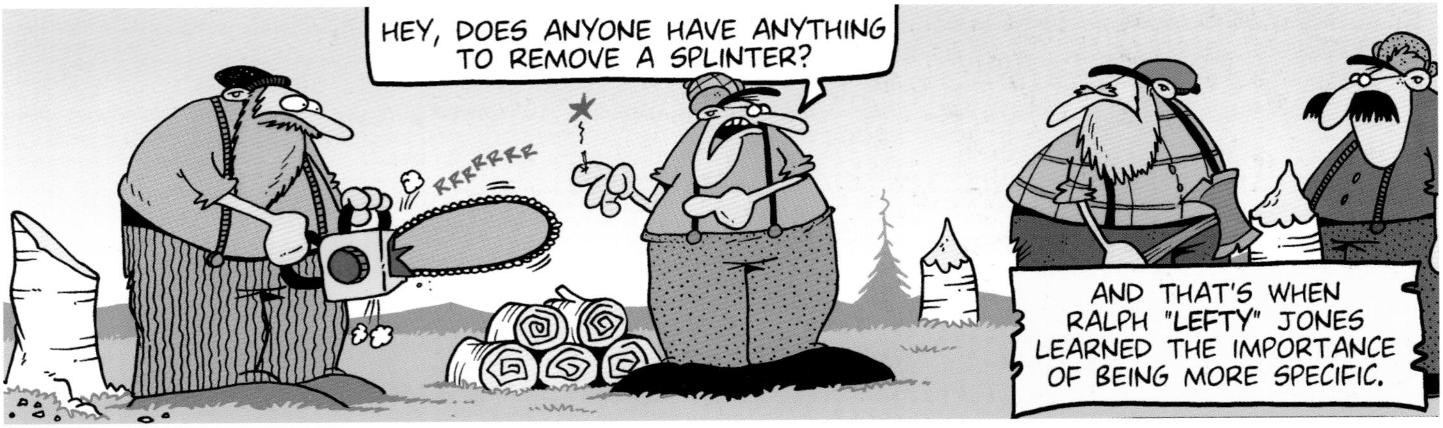
RRRRRRR
HEY, DOES ANYONE HAVE ANYTHING TO REMOVE A SPLINTER?
AND THAT'S WHEN RALPH "LEFTY" JONES LEARNED THE IMPORTANCE OF BEING MORE SPECIFIC.

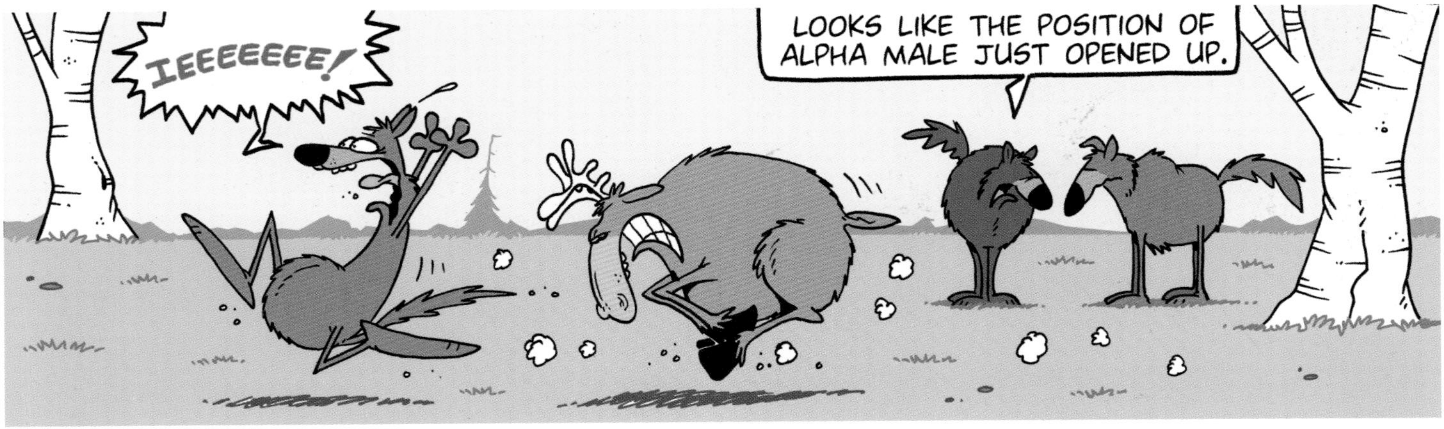
IEEEEEEE!
LOOKS LIKE THE POSITION OF ALPHA MALE JUST OPENED UP.

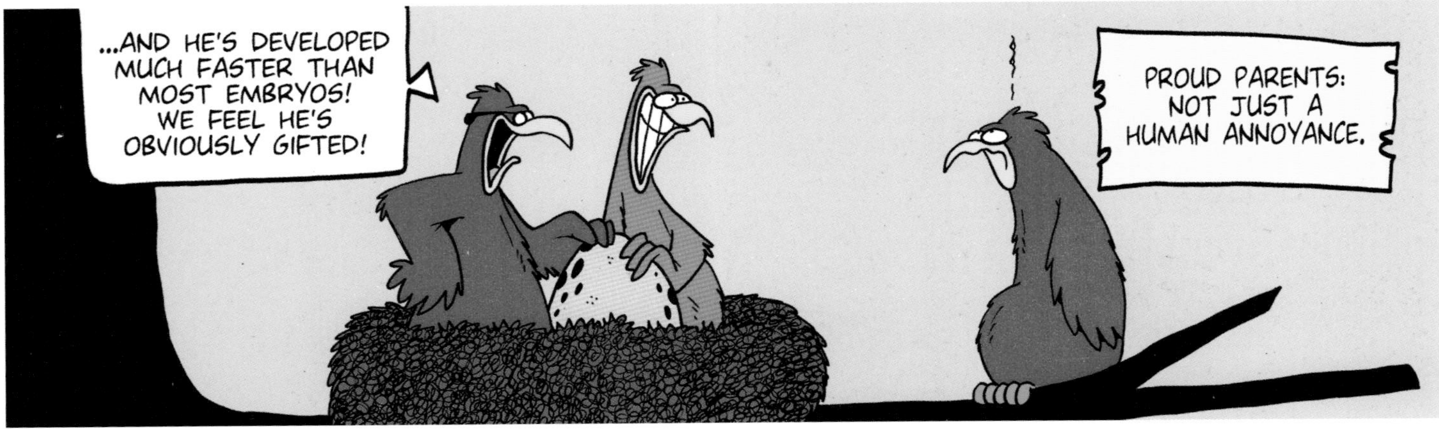
...AND HE'S DEVELOPED MUCH FASTER THAN MOST EMBRYOS! WE FEEL HE'S OBVIOUSLY GIFTED!
PROUD PARENTS: NOT JUST A HUMAN ANNOYANCE.

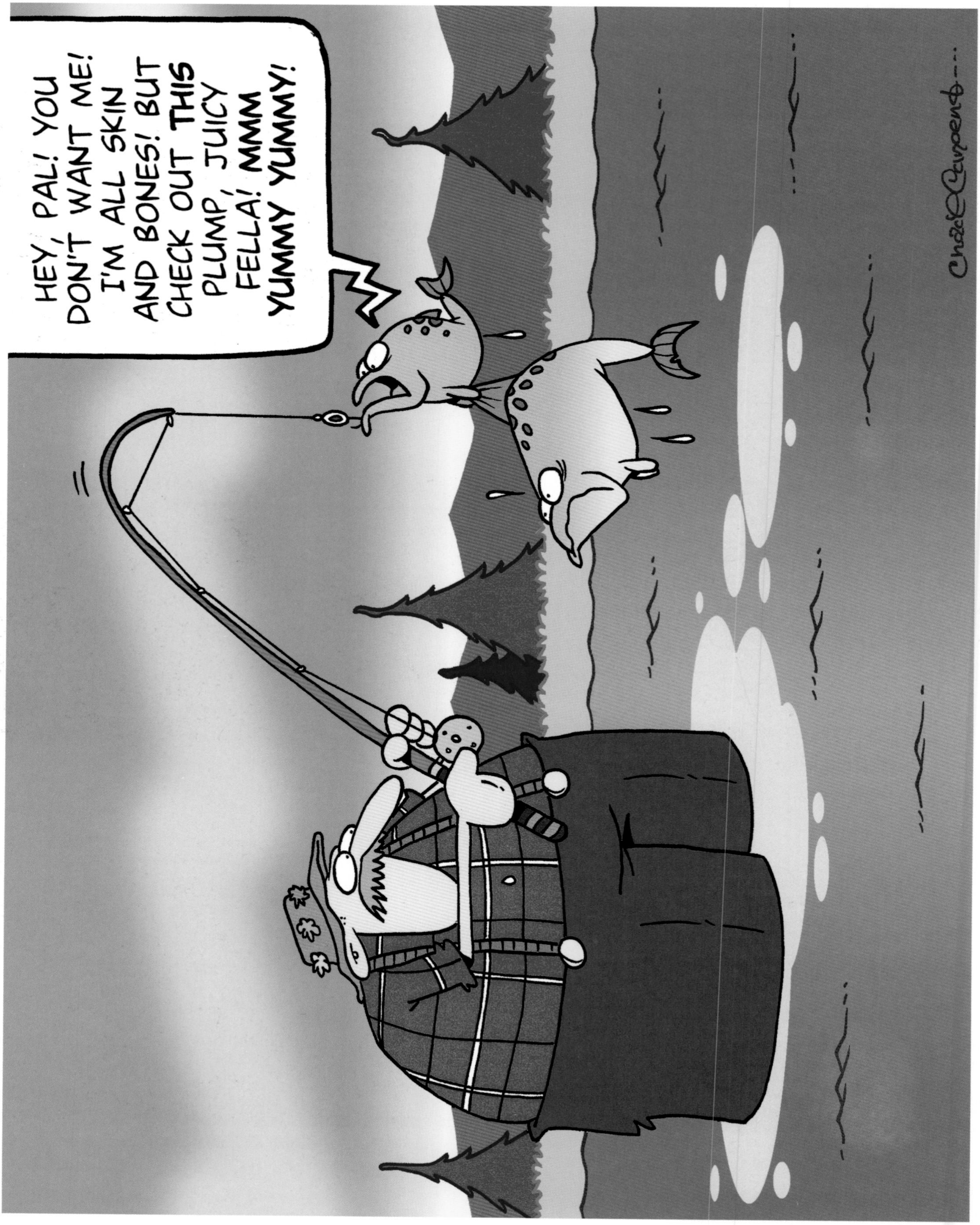
HEY, PAL! YOU DON'T WANT ME! I'M ALL SKIN AND BONES! BUT CHECK OUT THIS PLUMP, JUICY FELLA! MMM YUMMY YUMMY!

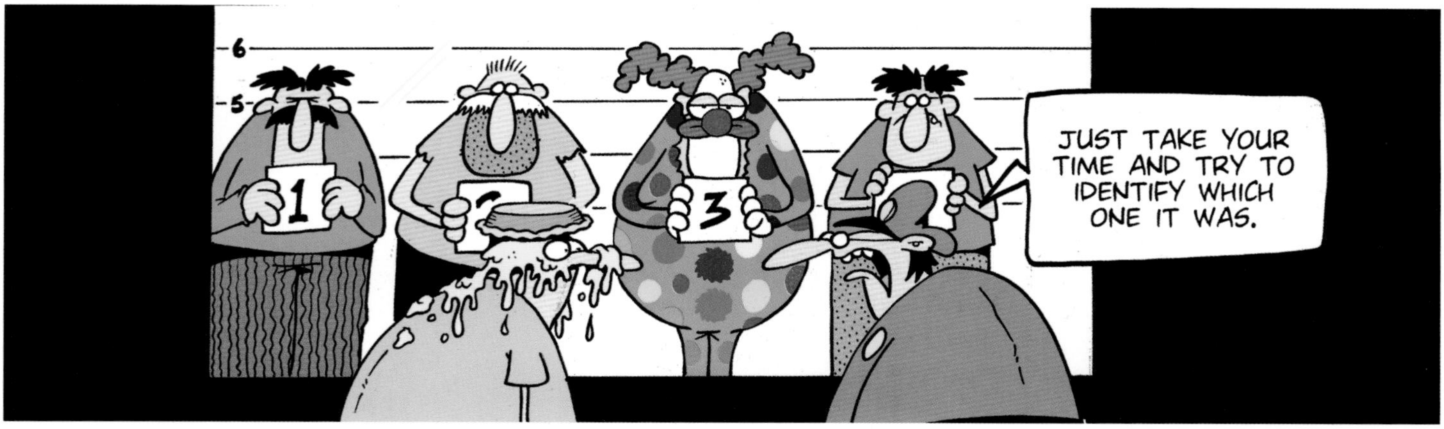
1
3
JUST TAKE YOUR TIME AND TRY TO IDENTIFY WHICH ONE IT WAS.

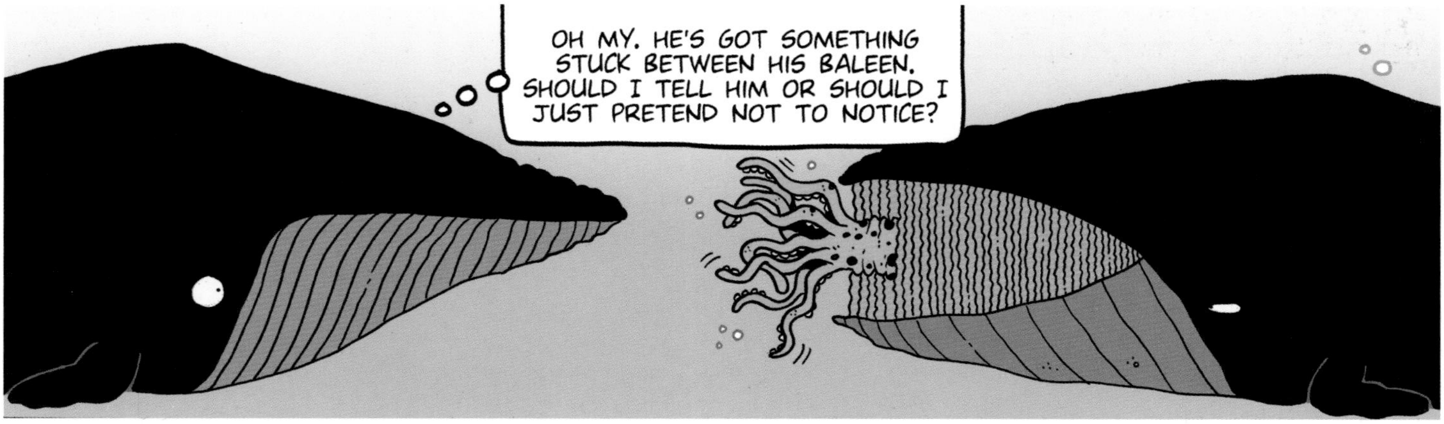
OH MY. HE'S GOT SOMETHING STUCK BETWEEN HIS BALEEN. SHOULD I TELL HIM OR SHOULD I JUST PRETEND NOT TO NOTICE?

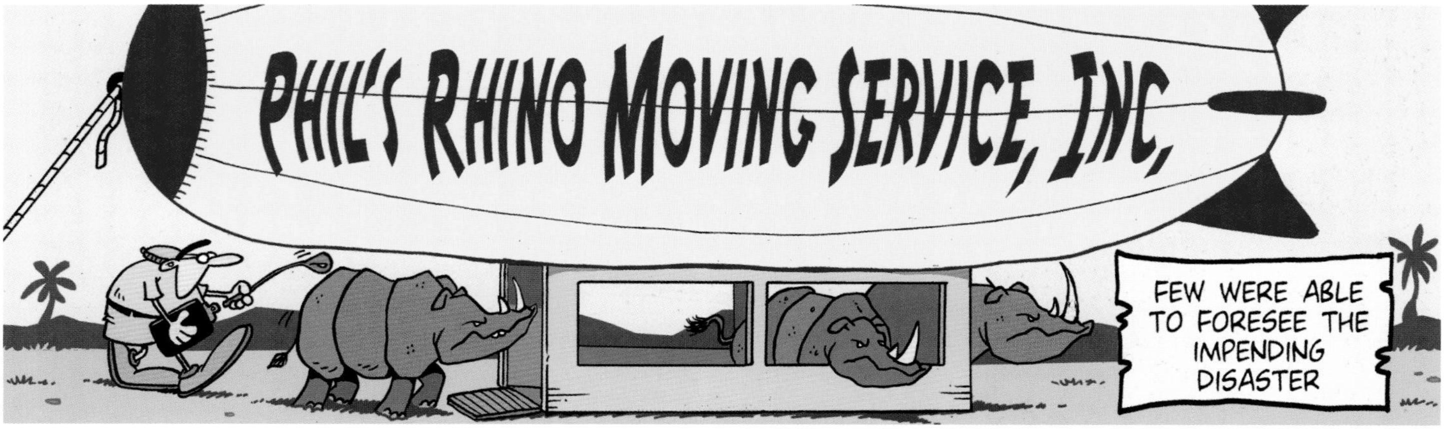
PHIL'S RHINO MOVING SERVICE, INC,
FEW WERE ABLE TO FORESEE THE IMPENDING DISASTER

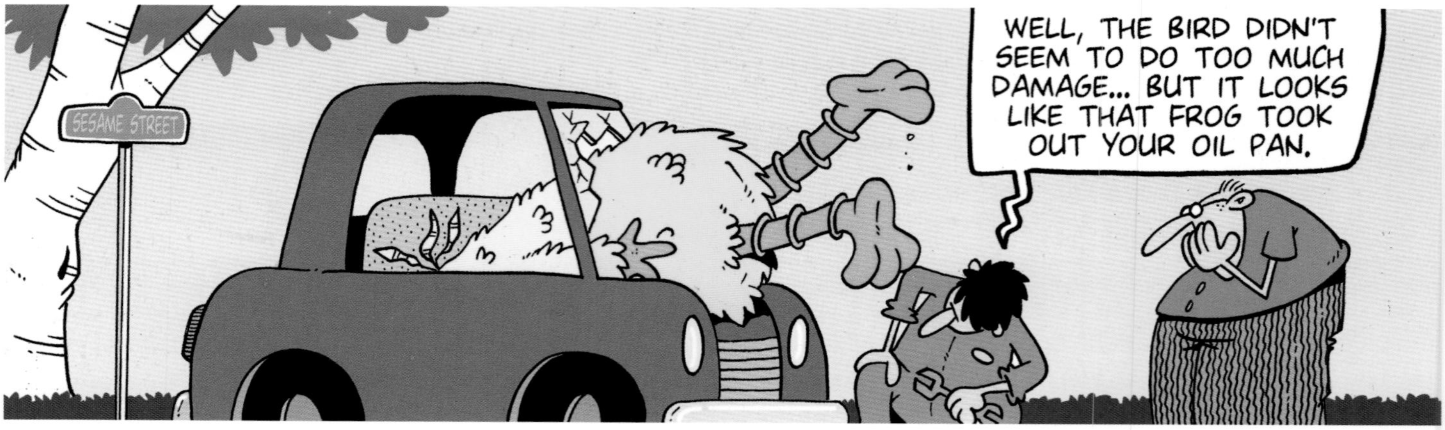
SESAME STREET
WELL, THE BIRD DIDN'T SEEM TO DO TOO MUCH DAMAGE... BUT IT LOOKS LIKE THAT FROG TOOK OUT YOUR OIL PAN.

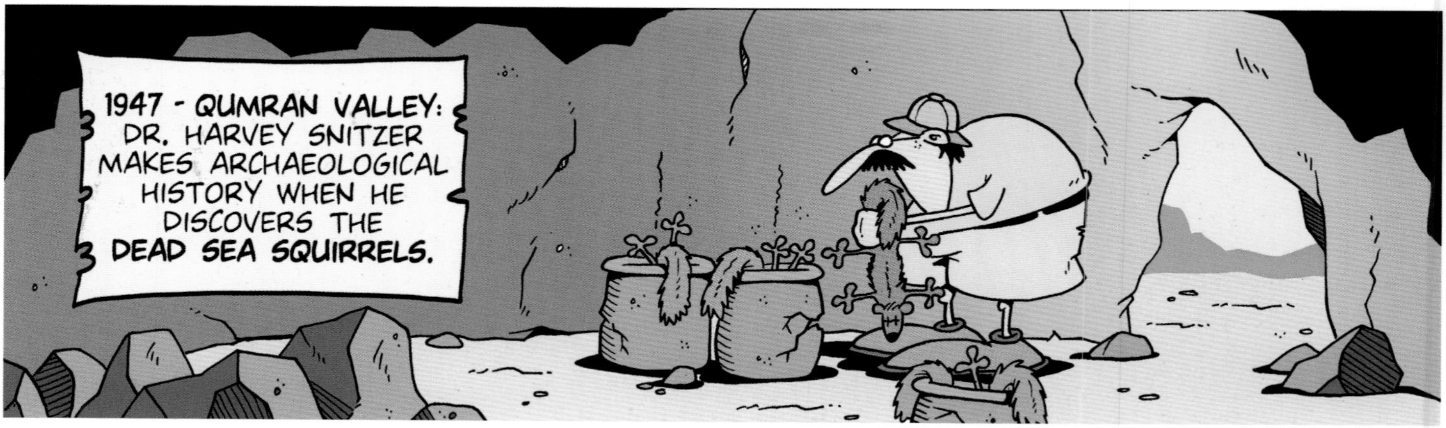
1947 - QUMRAN VALLEY: DR. HARVEY SNITZER MAKES ARCHAEOLOGICAL HISTORY WHEN HE DISCOVERS THE DEAD SEA SQUIRRELS.

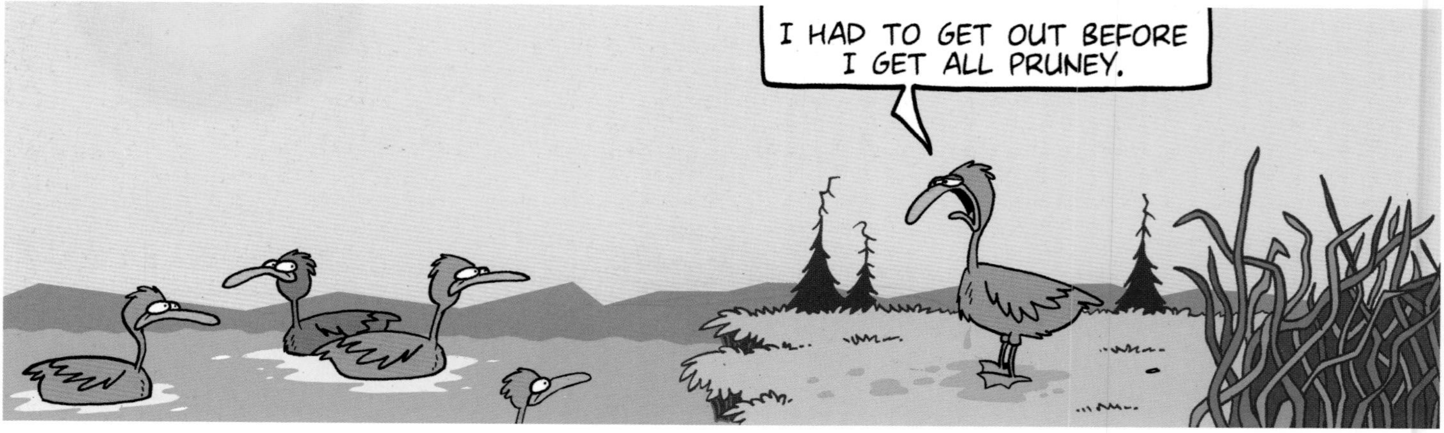
I HAD TO GET OUT BEFORE I GET ALL PRUNEY.

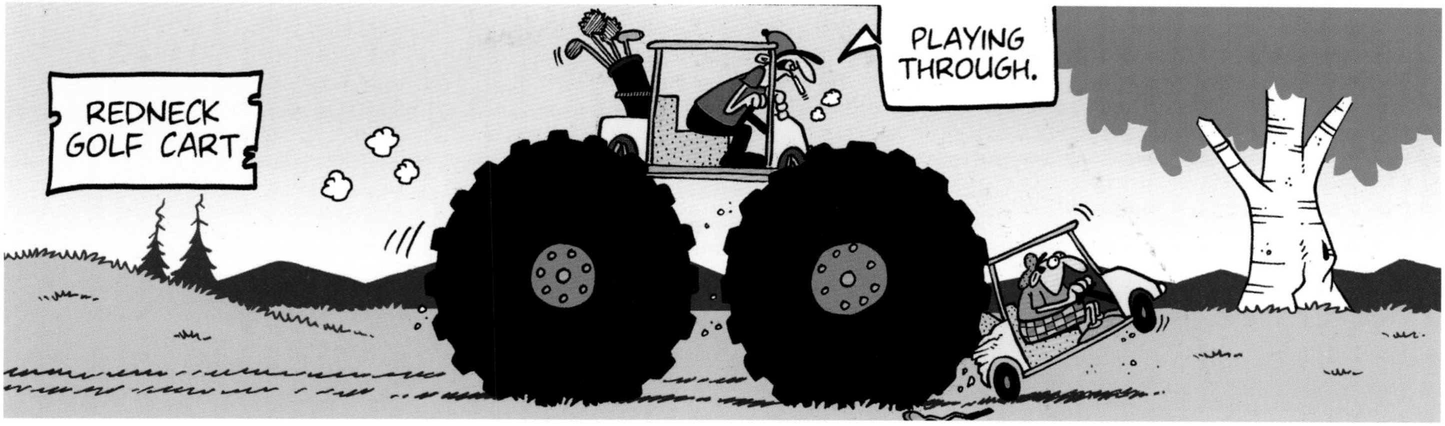

REDNECK GOLF CART
PLAYING THROUGH.

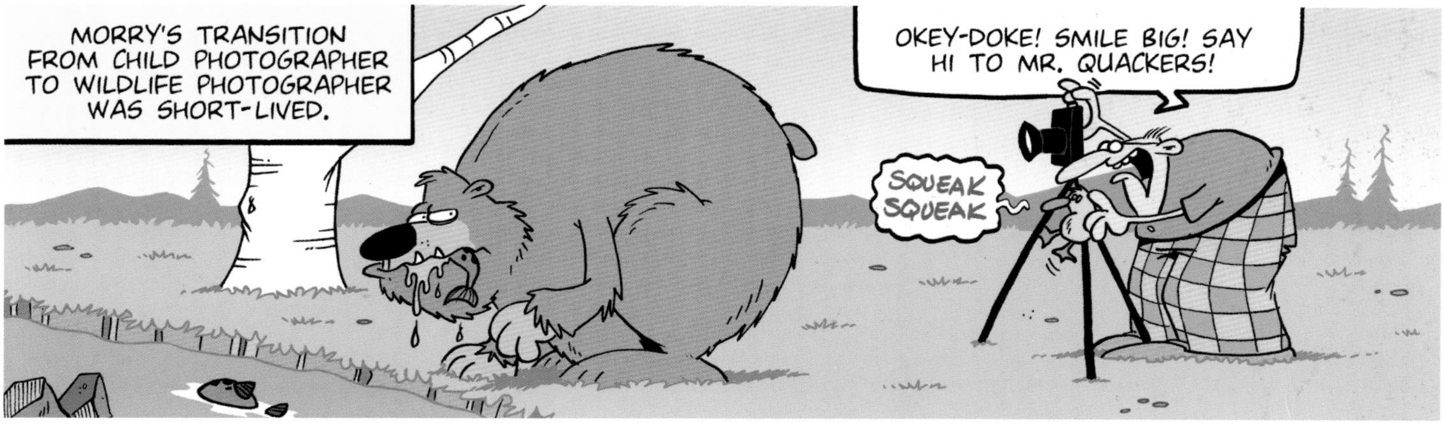

MORRY'S TRANSITION FROM CHILD PHOTOGRAPHER TO WILDLIFE PHOTOGRAPHER WAS SHORT-LIVED.
OKEY-DOKE! SMILE BIG! SAY HI TO MR. QUACKERS!
SQUEAK SQUEAK

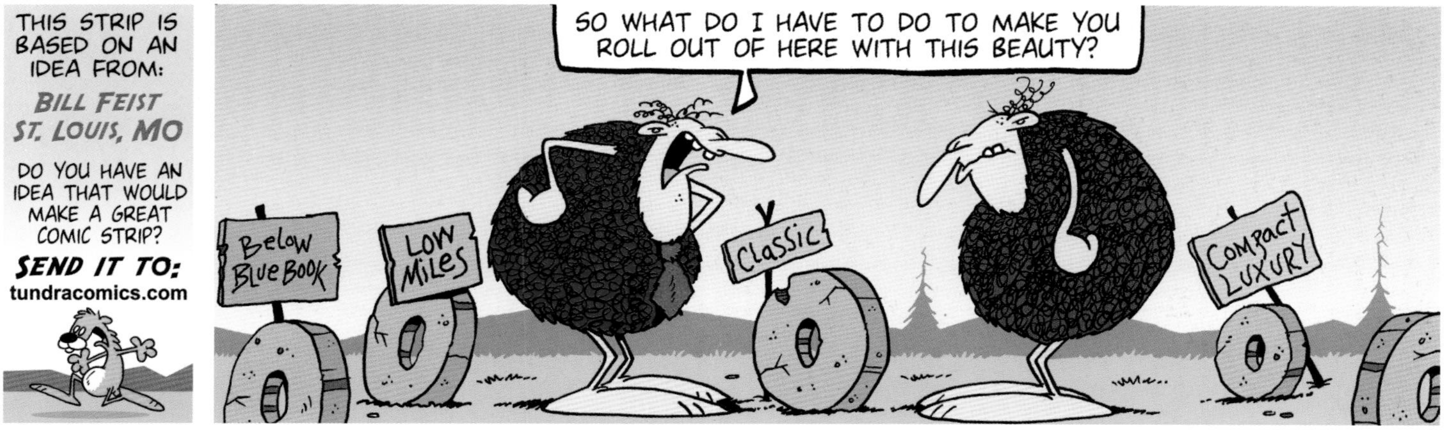

THIS STRIP IS BASED ON AN IDEA FROM:
BILL FEIST
ST. LOUIS, MO
DO YOU HAVE AN IDEA THAT WOULD MAKE A GREAT COMIC STRIP?
SEND IT TO:
tundracomics.com
SO WHAT DO I HAVE TO DO TO MAKE YOU ROLL OUT OF HERE WITH THIS BEAUTY?
Below Blue Book
Low Miles
Classic
Compact Luxury

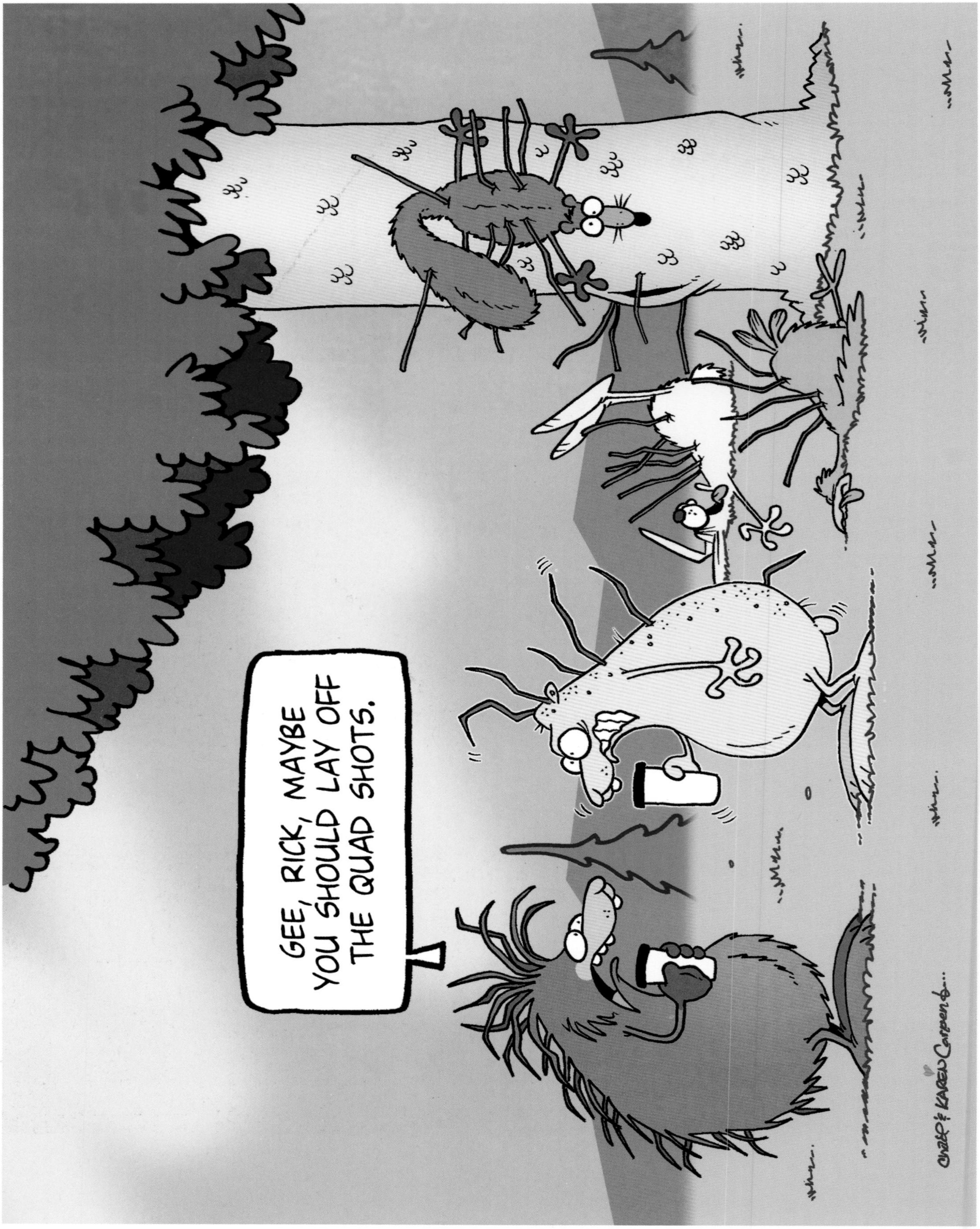
GEE, RICK, MAYBE YOU SHOULD LAY OFF THE QUAD SHOTS.

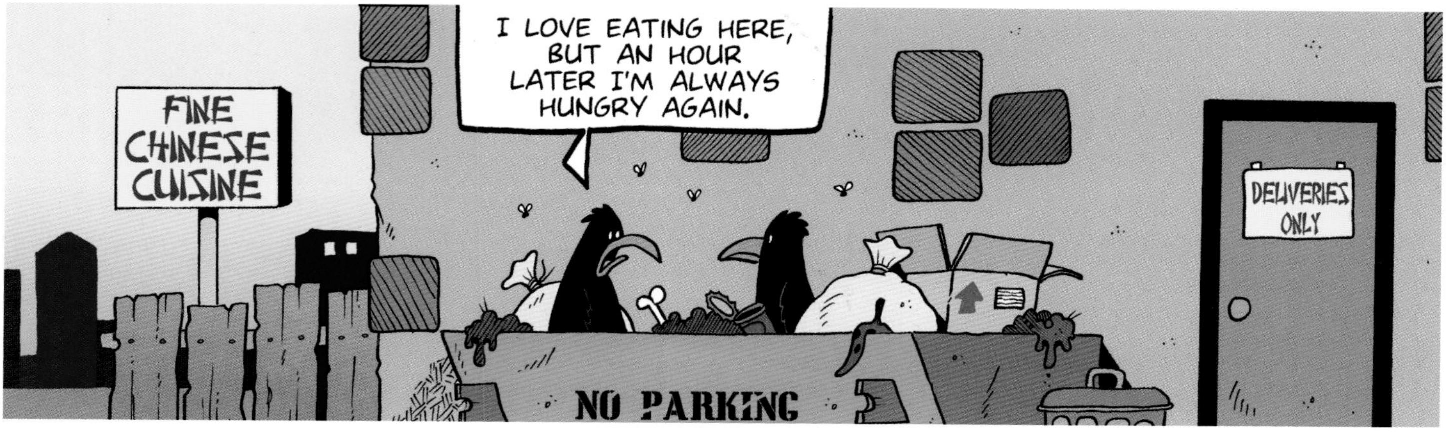
FINE CHINESE CUISINE
I LOVE EATING HERE, BUT AN HOUR LATER I'M ALWAYS HUNGRY AGAIN.
DELIVERIES ONLY
NO PARKING

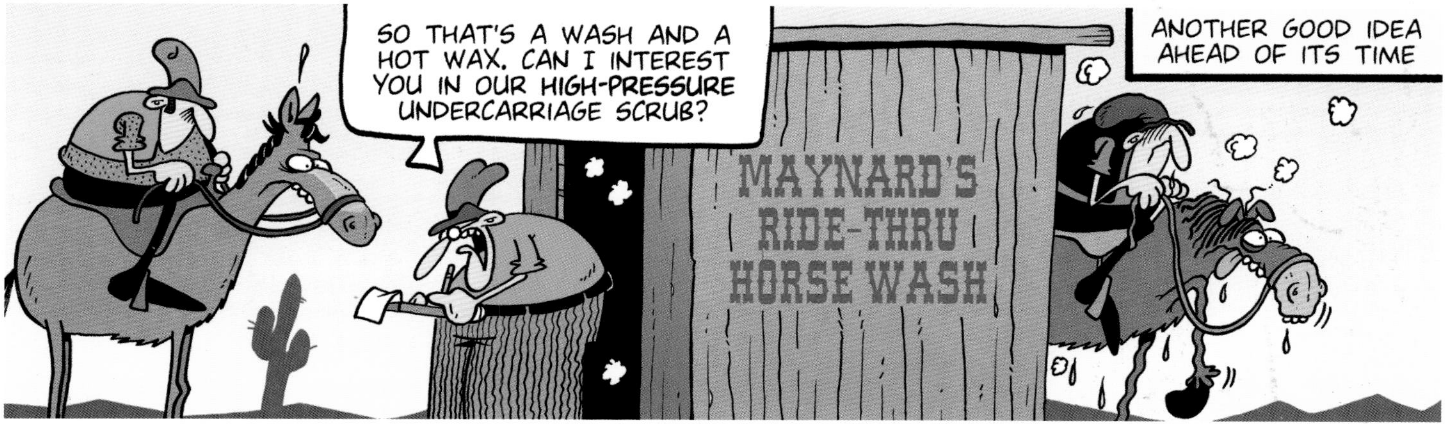
SO THAT'S A WASH AND A HOT WAX. CAN I INTEREST YOU IN OUR HIGH-PRESSURE UNDERCARRIAGE SCRUB?
MAYNARD'S RIDE-THRU HORSE WASH
ANOTHER GOOD IDEA AHEAD OF ITS TIME

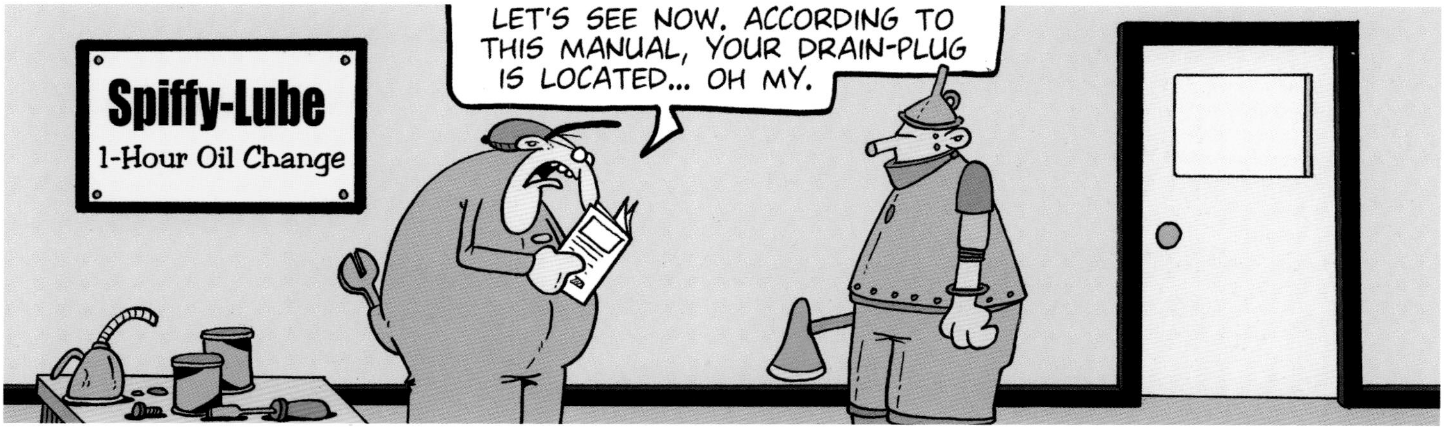
Spiffy-Lube
1-Hour Oil Change
LET'S SEE NOW. ACCORDING TO THIS MANUAL, YOUR DRAIN-PLUG IS LOCATED... OH MY.

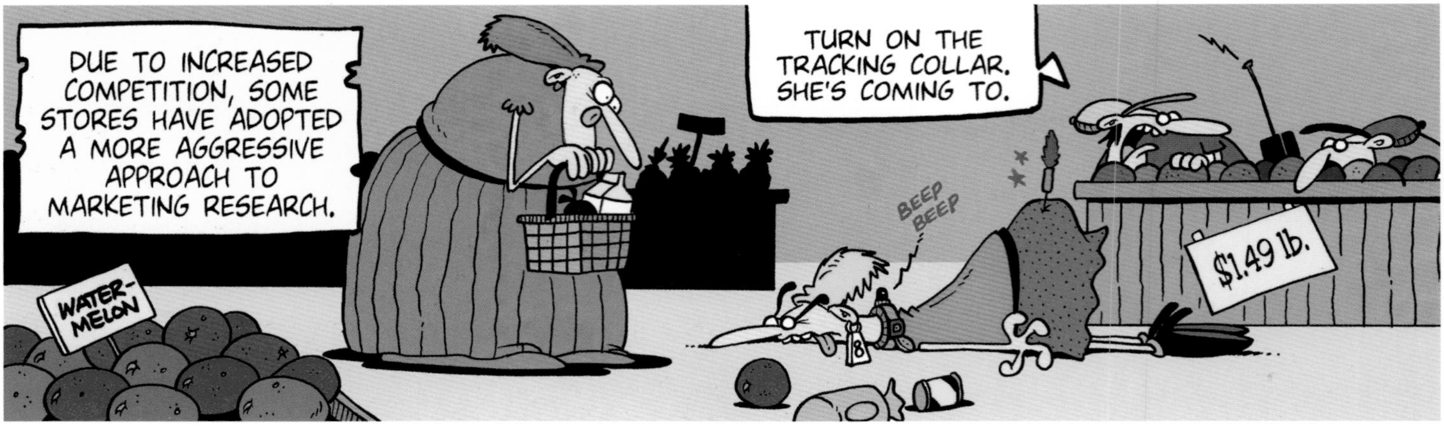
DUE TO INCREASED COMPETITION, SOME STORES HAVE ADOPTED A MORE AGGRESSIVE APPROACH TO MARKETING RESEARCH.
TURN ON THE TRACKING COLLAR. SHE'S COMING TO.
WATER-MELON
BEEP BEEP
$1.49 lb.

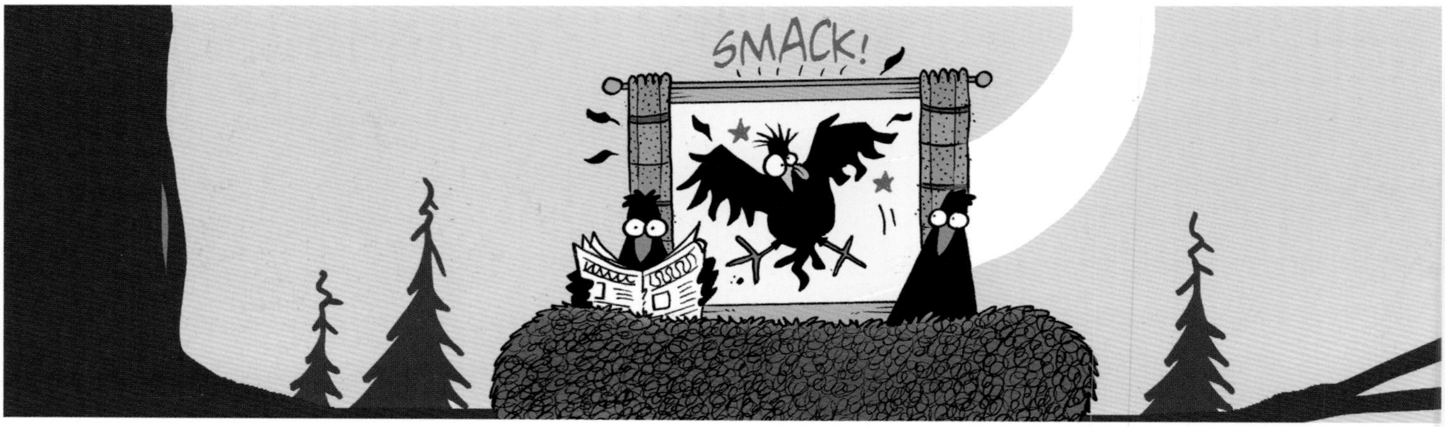
SMACK!

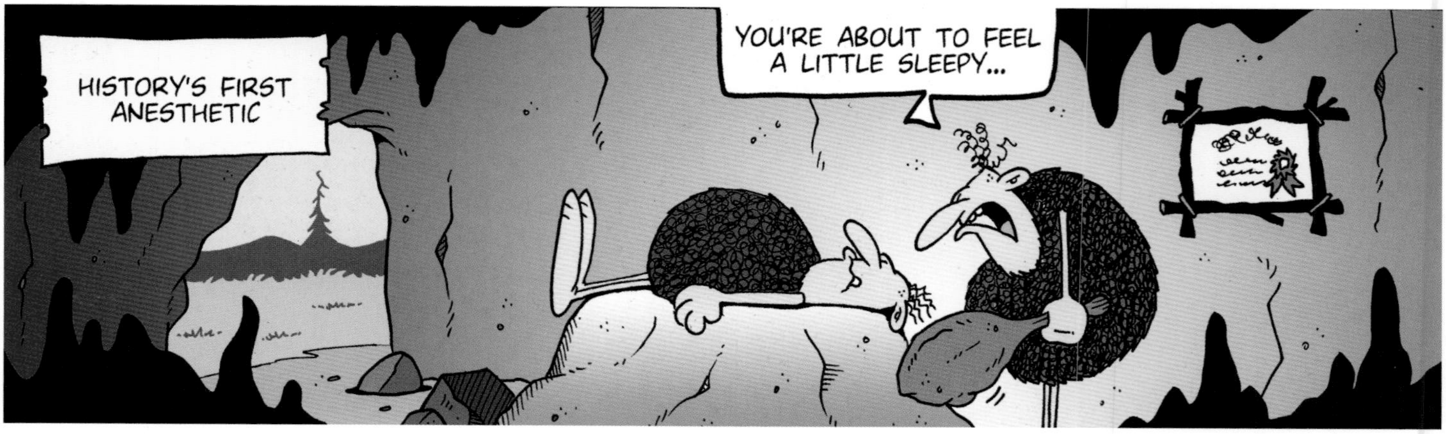
HISTORY'S FIRST ANESTHETIC
YOU'RE ABOUT TO FEEL A LITTLE SLEEPY...

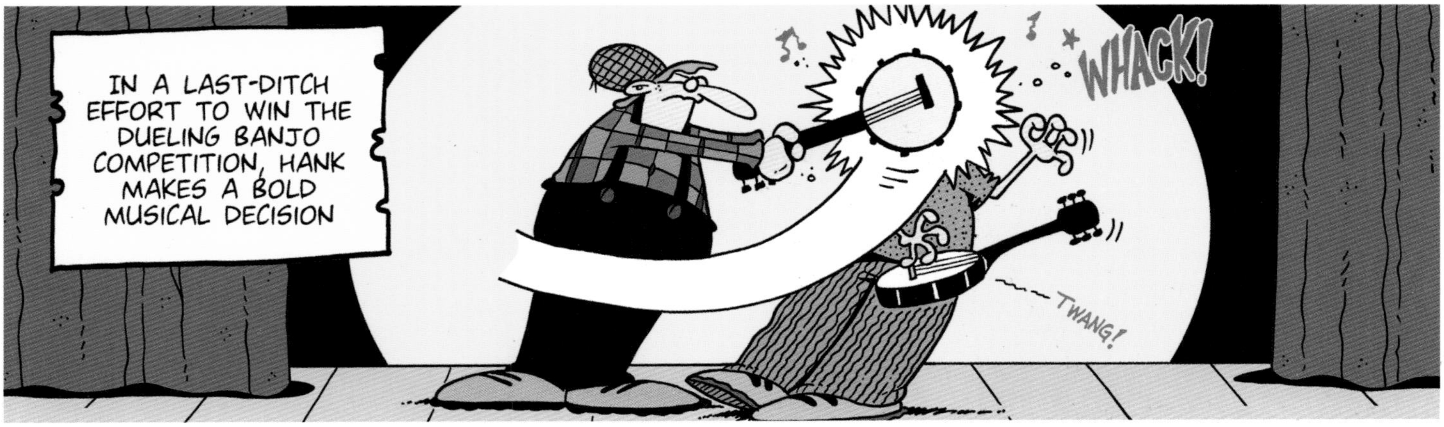
IN A LAST-DITCH EFFORT TO WIN THE DUELING BANJO COMPETITION, HANK MAKES A BOLD MUSICAL DECISION
WHACK!
TWANG!

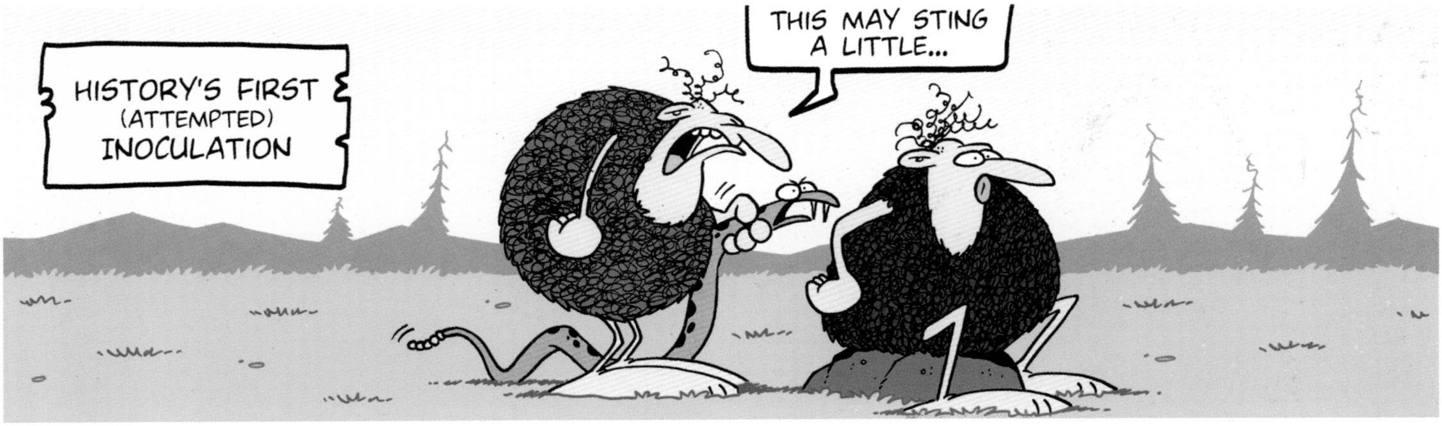
HISTORY'S FIRST (ATTEMPTED) INOCULATION
THIS MAY STING A LITTLE...

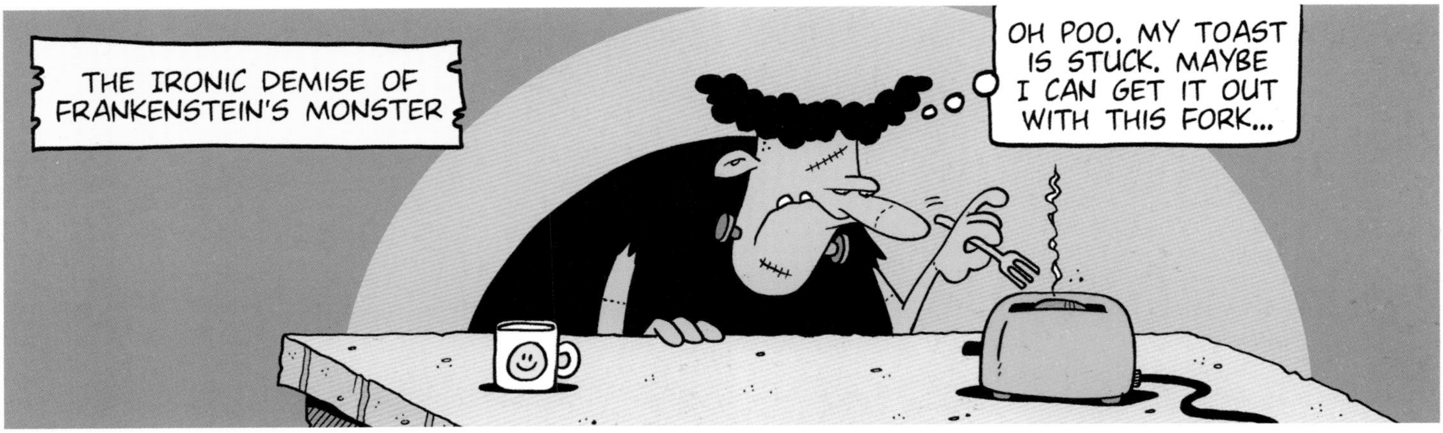
THE IRONIC DEMISE OF FRANKENSTEIN'S MONSTER
OH POO. MY TOAST IS STUCK. MAYBE I CAN GET IT OUT WITH THIS FORK...

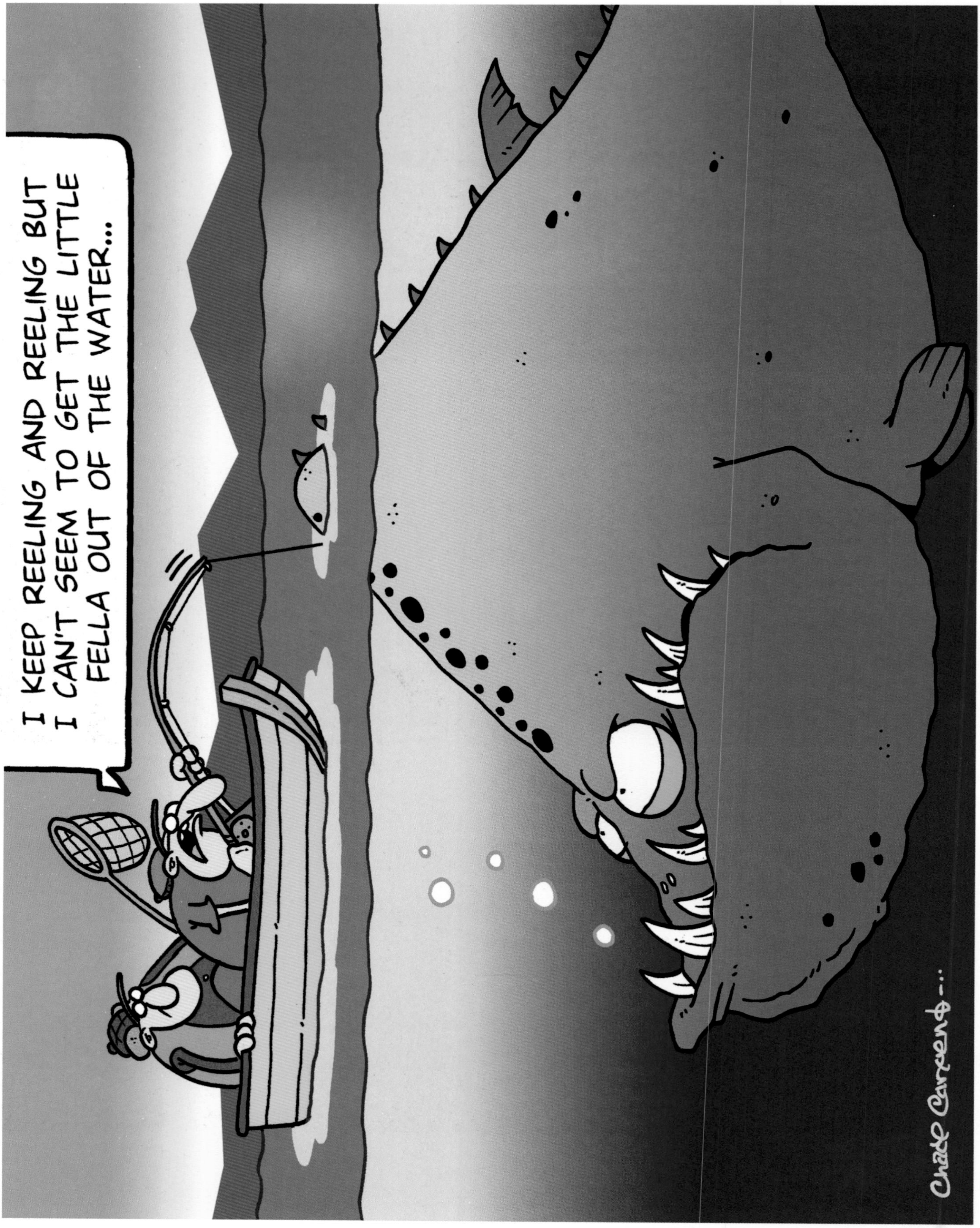
I KEEP REELING AND REELING BUT I CAN'T SEEM TO GET THE LITTLE FELLA OUT OF THE WATER...
Chad Carpenter

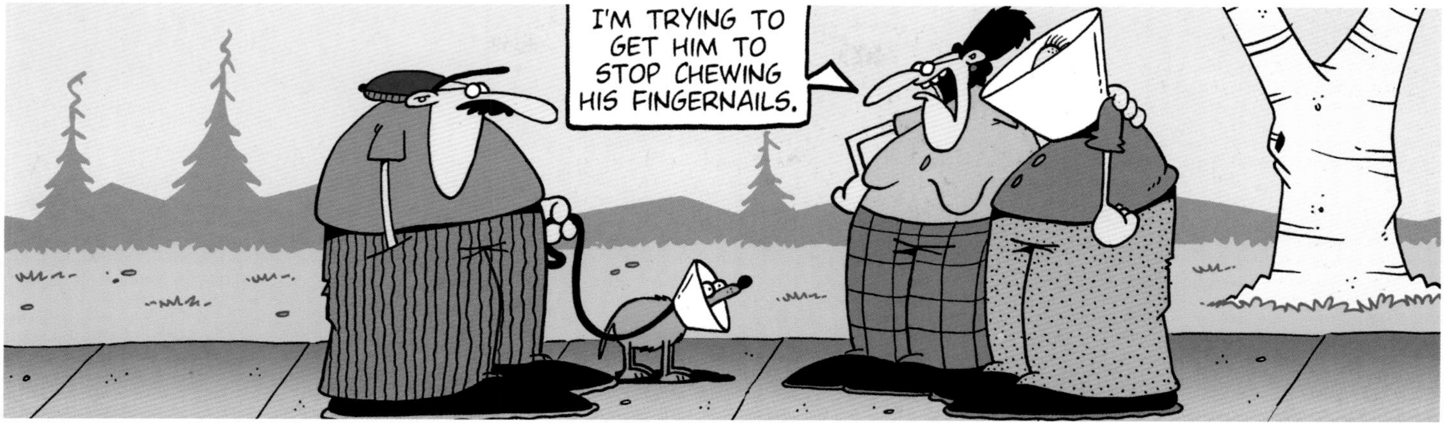
I'M TRYING TO GET HIM TO STOP CHEWING HIS FINGERNAILS.

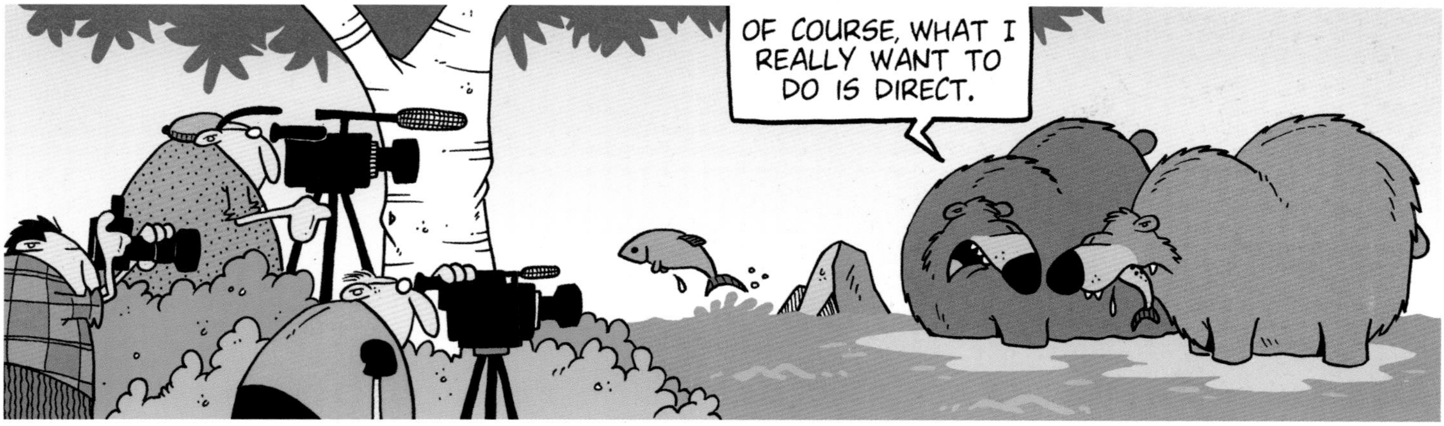
OF COURSE, WHAT I REALLY WANT TO DO IS DIRECT.

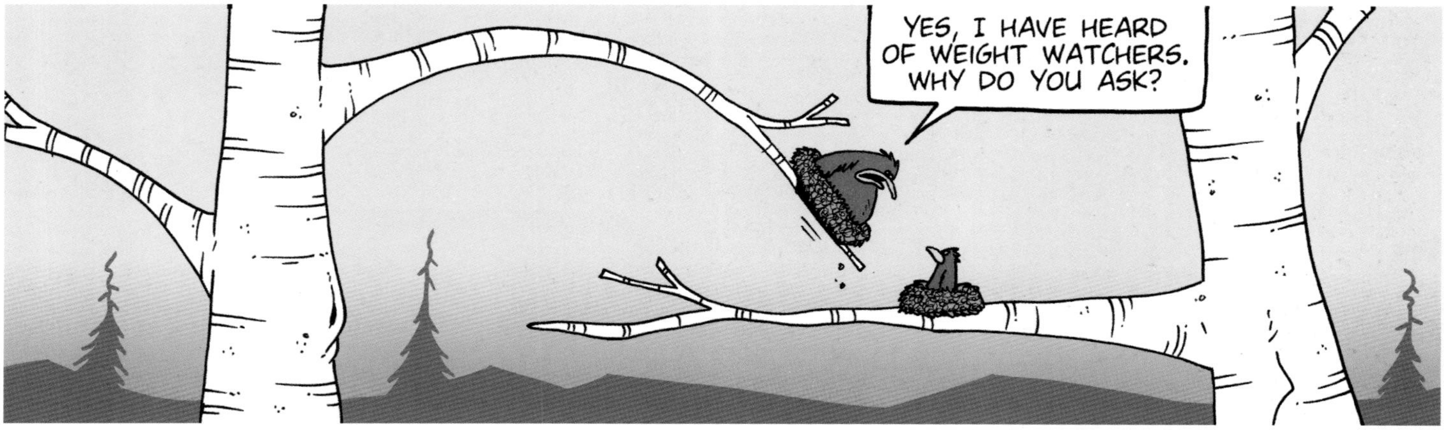
YES, I HAVE HEARD OF WEIGHT WATCHERS. WHY DO YOU ASK?

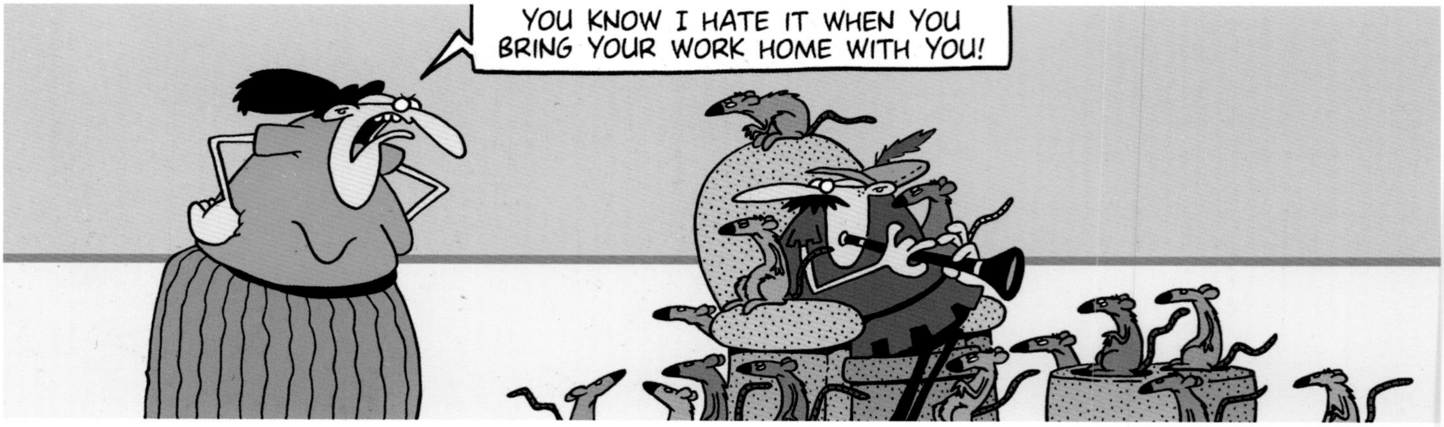
YOU KNOW I HATE IT WHEN YOU BRING YOUR WORK HOME WITH YOU!

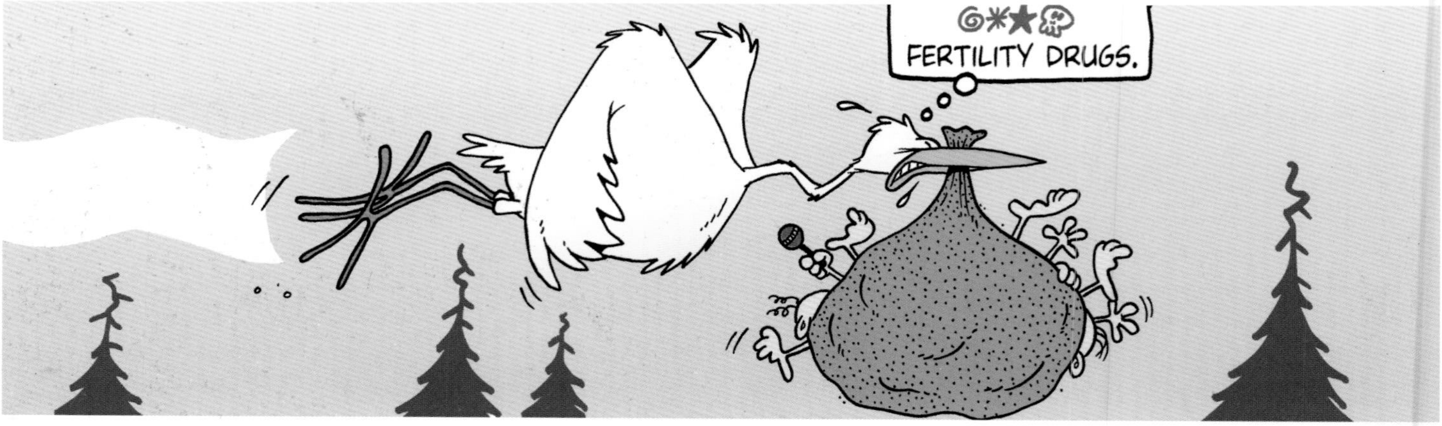
FERTILITY DRUGS.

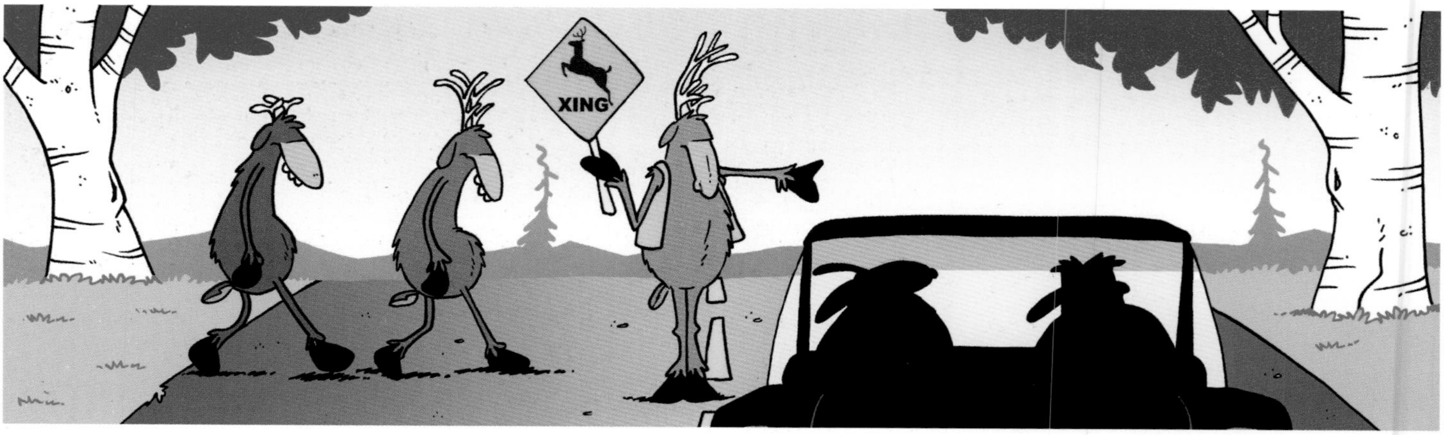
XING

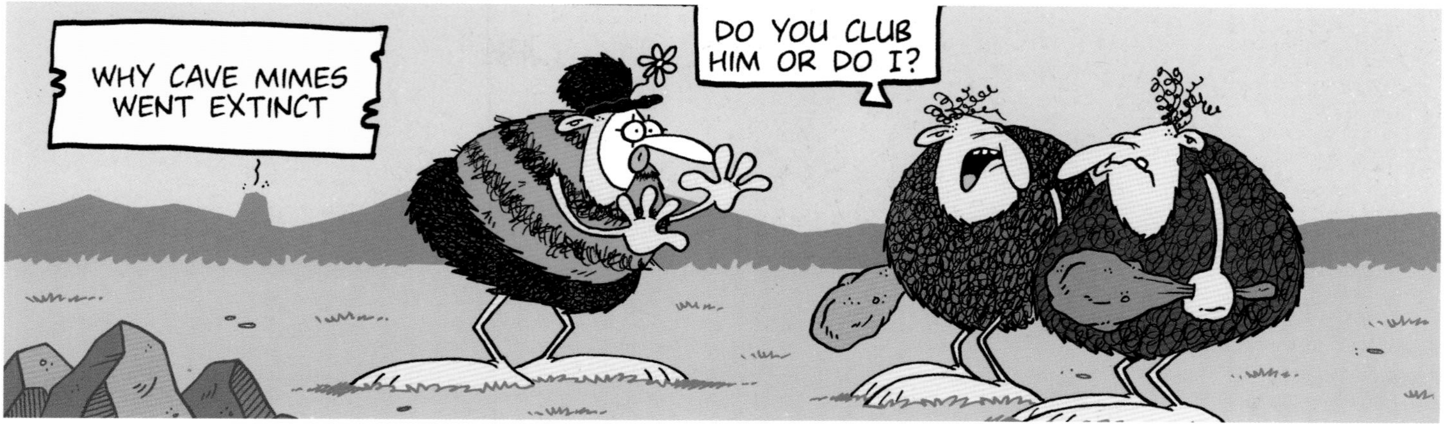
WHY CAVE MIMES WENT EXTINCT
DO YOU CLUB HIM OR DO I?

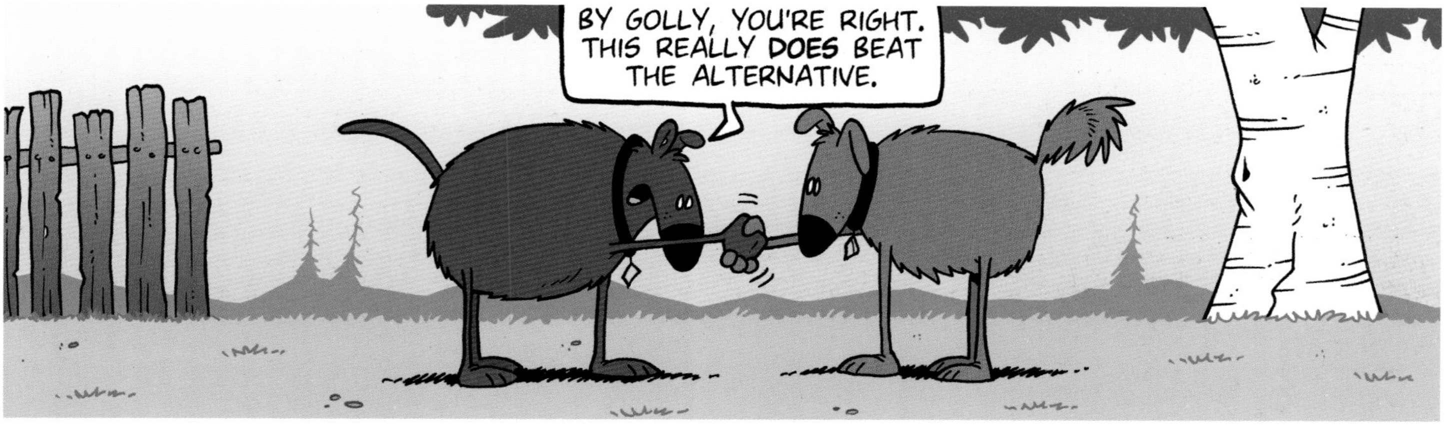
BY GOLLY, YOU'RE RIGHT. THIS REALLY DOES BEAT THE ALTERNATIVE.

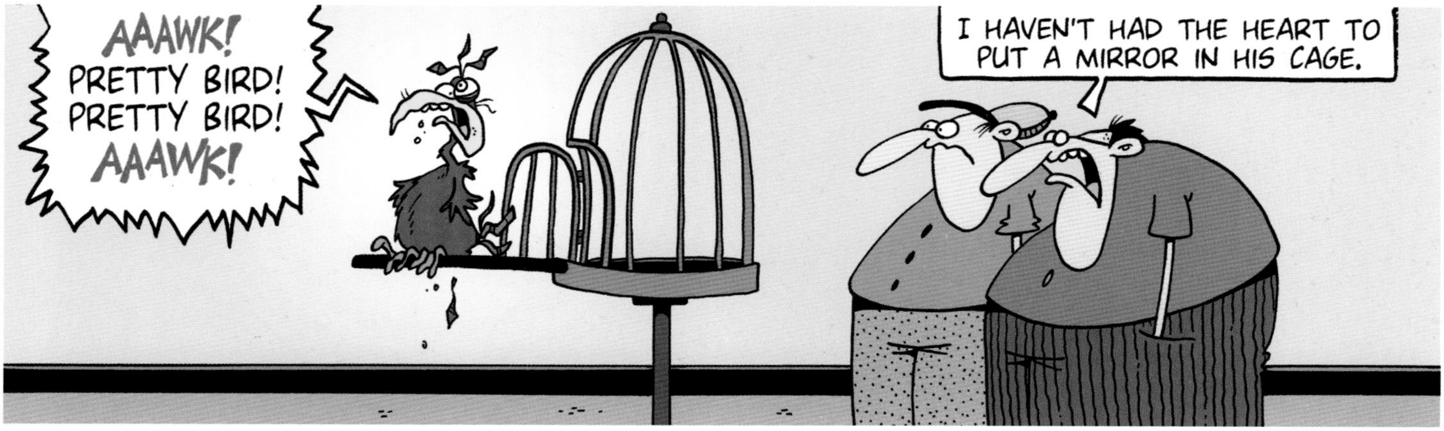
AAAWK! PRETTY BIRD! PRETTY BIRD! AAAWK!
I HAVEN'T HAD THE HEART TO PUT A MIRROR IN HIS CAGE.

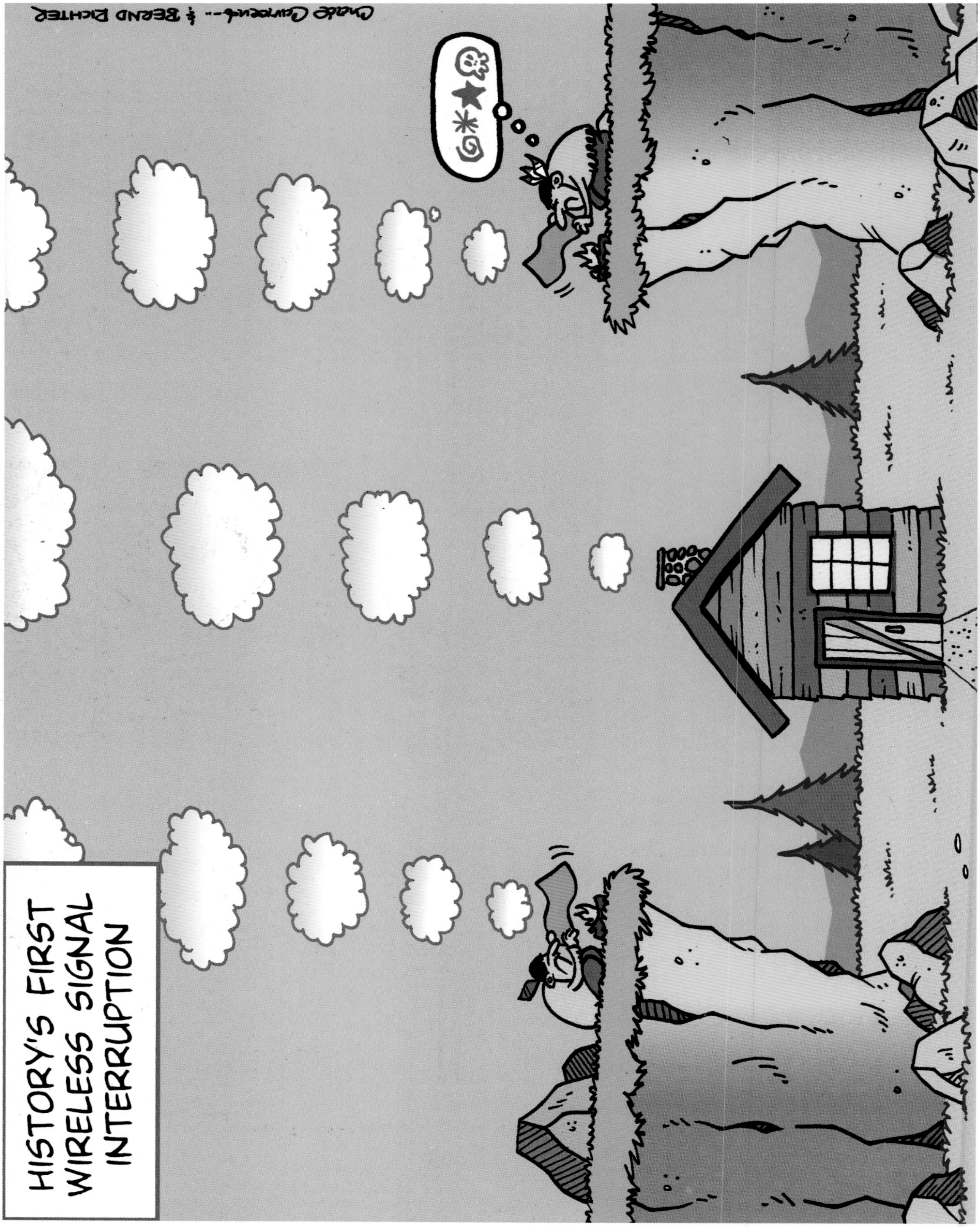
HISTORY'S FIRST
WIRELESS SIGNAL
INTERRUPTION

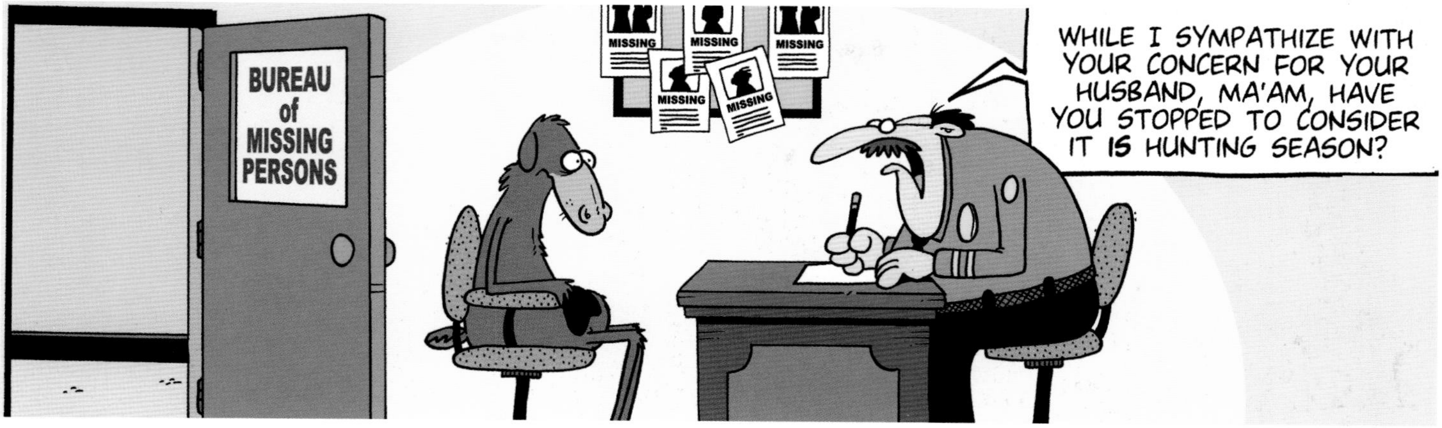
BUREAU of MISSING PERSONS
MISSING
MISSING
MISSING
MISSING
MISSING
WHILE I SYMPATHIZE WITH YOUR CONCERN FOR YOUR HUSBAND, MA'AM, HAVE YOU STOPPED TO CONSIDER IT **IS** HUNTING SEASON?

THIS STRIP IS BASED ON AN IDEA FROM:

BERND RICHTER
WASILLA, AK

DO YOU HAVE AN IDEA THAT WOULD MAKE A GREAT COMIC STRIP?

SEND IT TO:
tundracomics.com

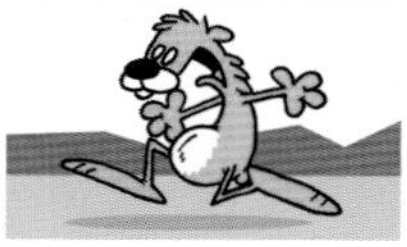

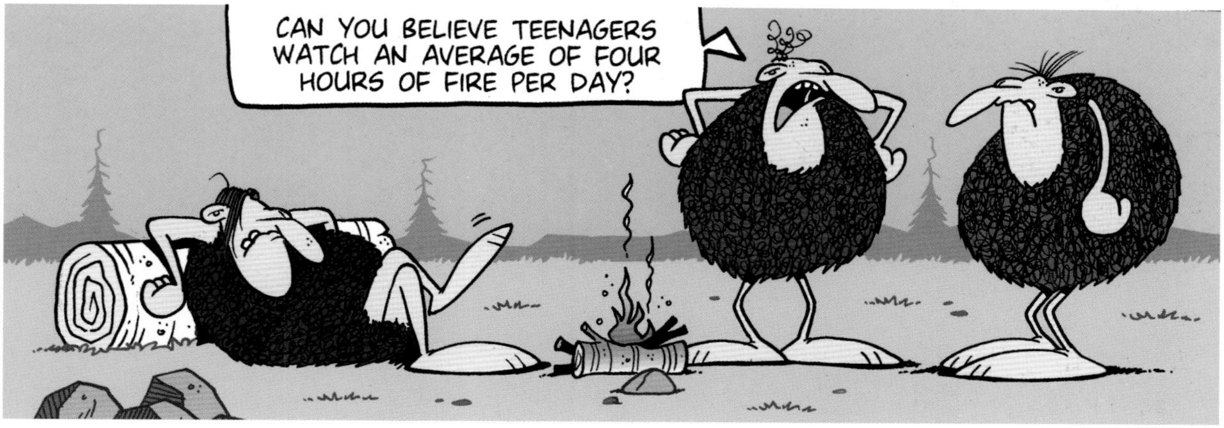
CAN YOU BELIEVE TEENAGERS WATCH AN AVERAGE OF FOUR HOURS OF FIRE PER DAY?

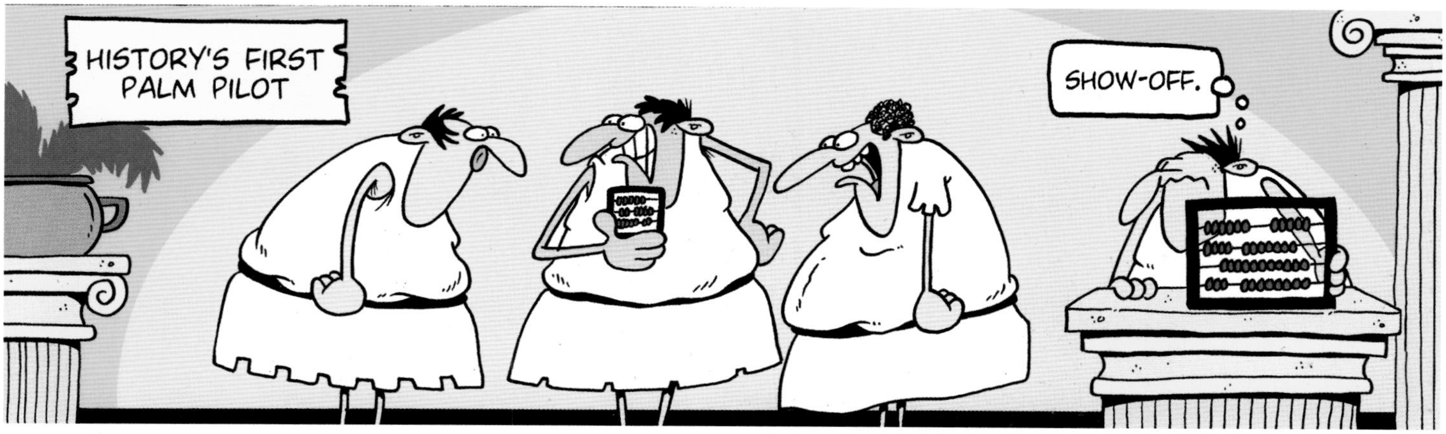
HISTORY'S FIRST PALM PILOT
SHOW-OFF.

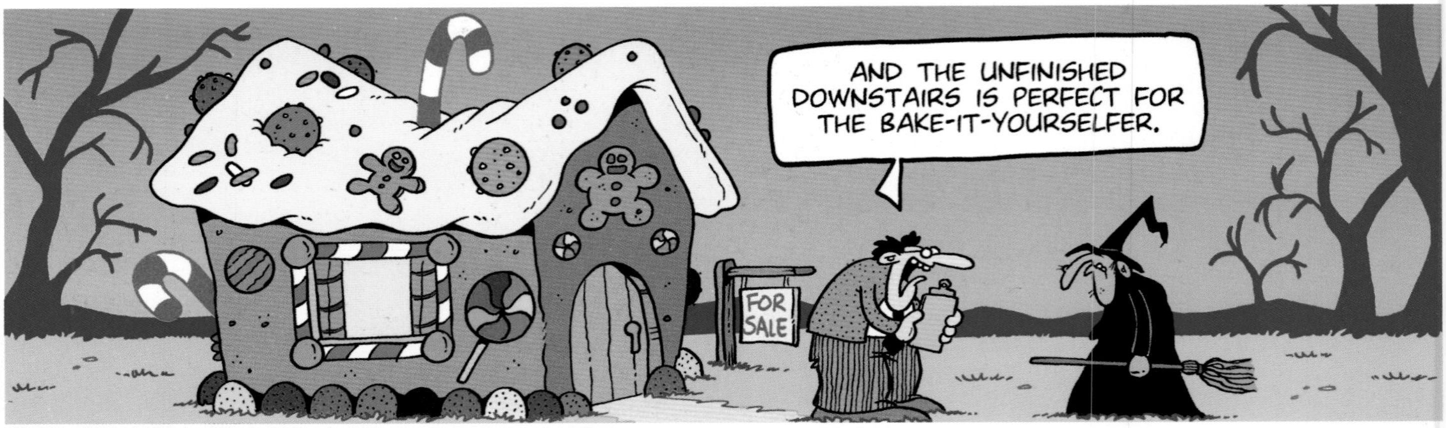
AND THE UNFINISHED DOWNSTAIRS IS PERFECT FOR THE BAKE-IT-YOURSELFER.
FOR SALE

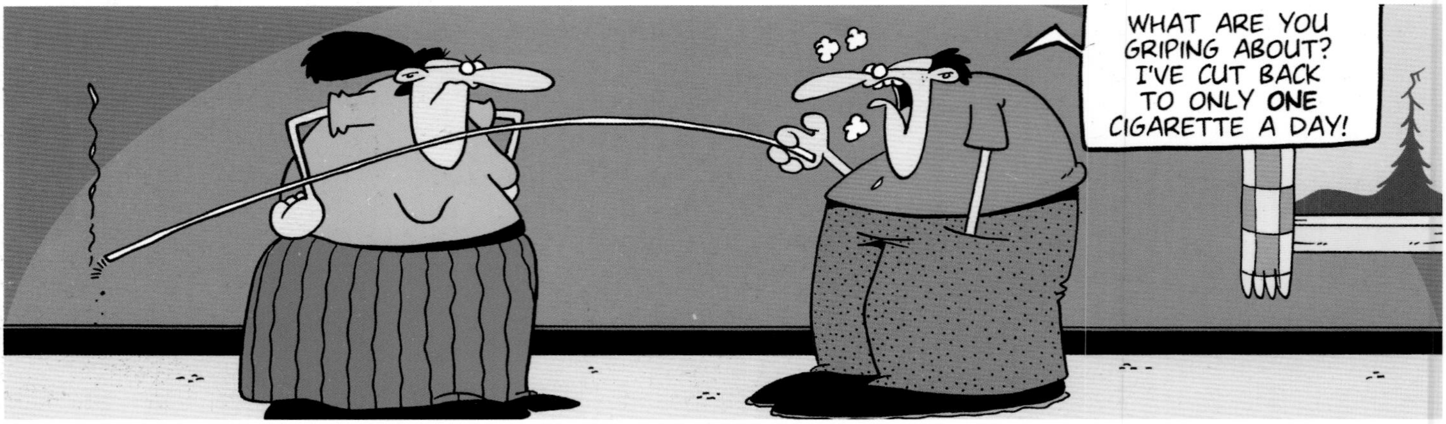
WHAT ARE YOU GRIPING ABOUT? I'VE CUT BACK TO ONLY **ONE** CIGARETTE A DAY!

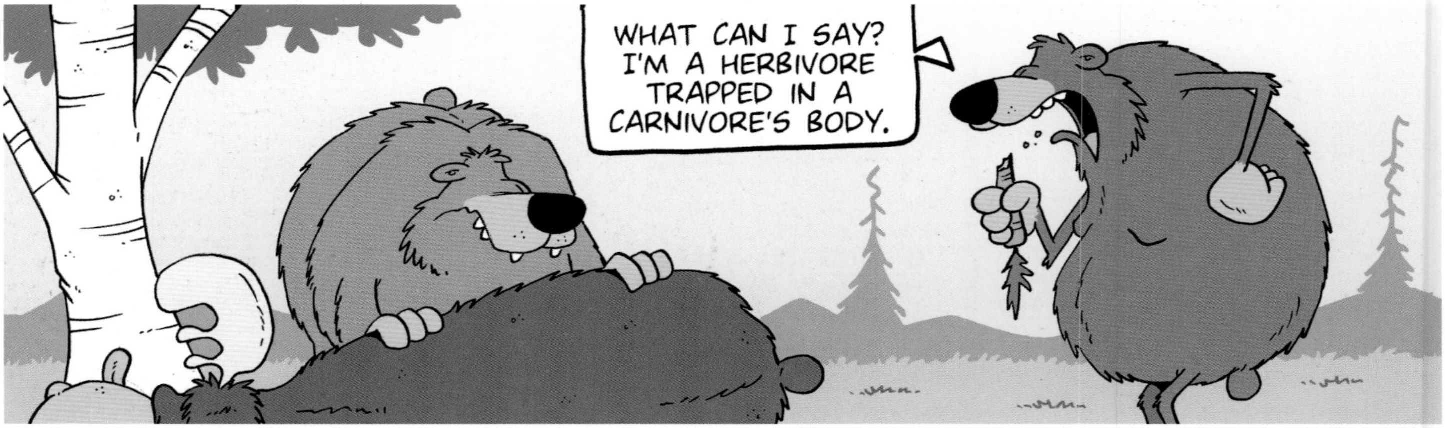
WHAT CAN I SAY? I'M A HERBIVORE TRAPPED IN A CARNIVORE'S BODY.

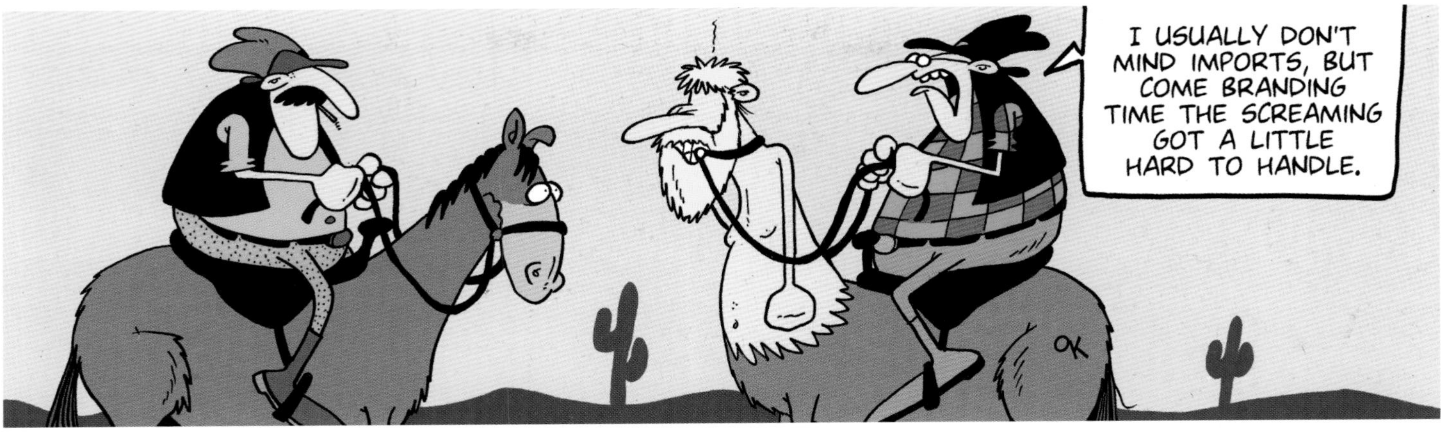
I USUALLY DON'T MIND IMPORTS, BUT COME BRANDING TIME THE SCREAMING GOT A LITTLE HARD TO HANDLE.

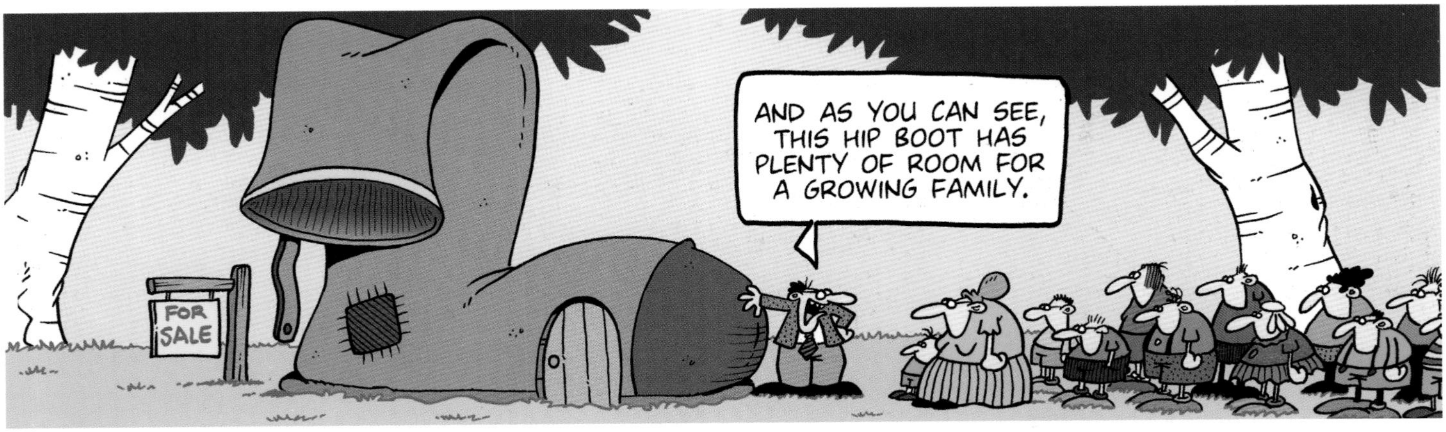
AND AS YOU CAN SEE, THIS HIP BOOT HAS PLENTY OF ROOM FOR A GROWING FAMILY.
FOR SALE

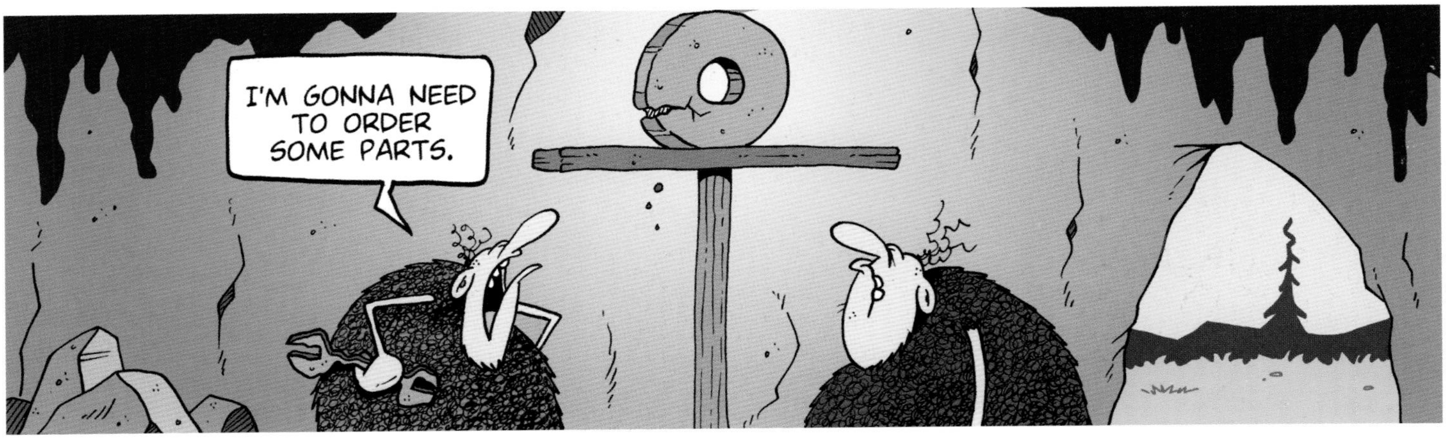
I'M GONNA NEED TO ORDER SOME PARTS.

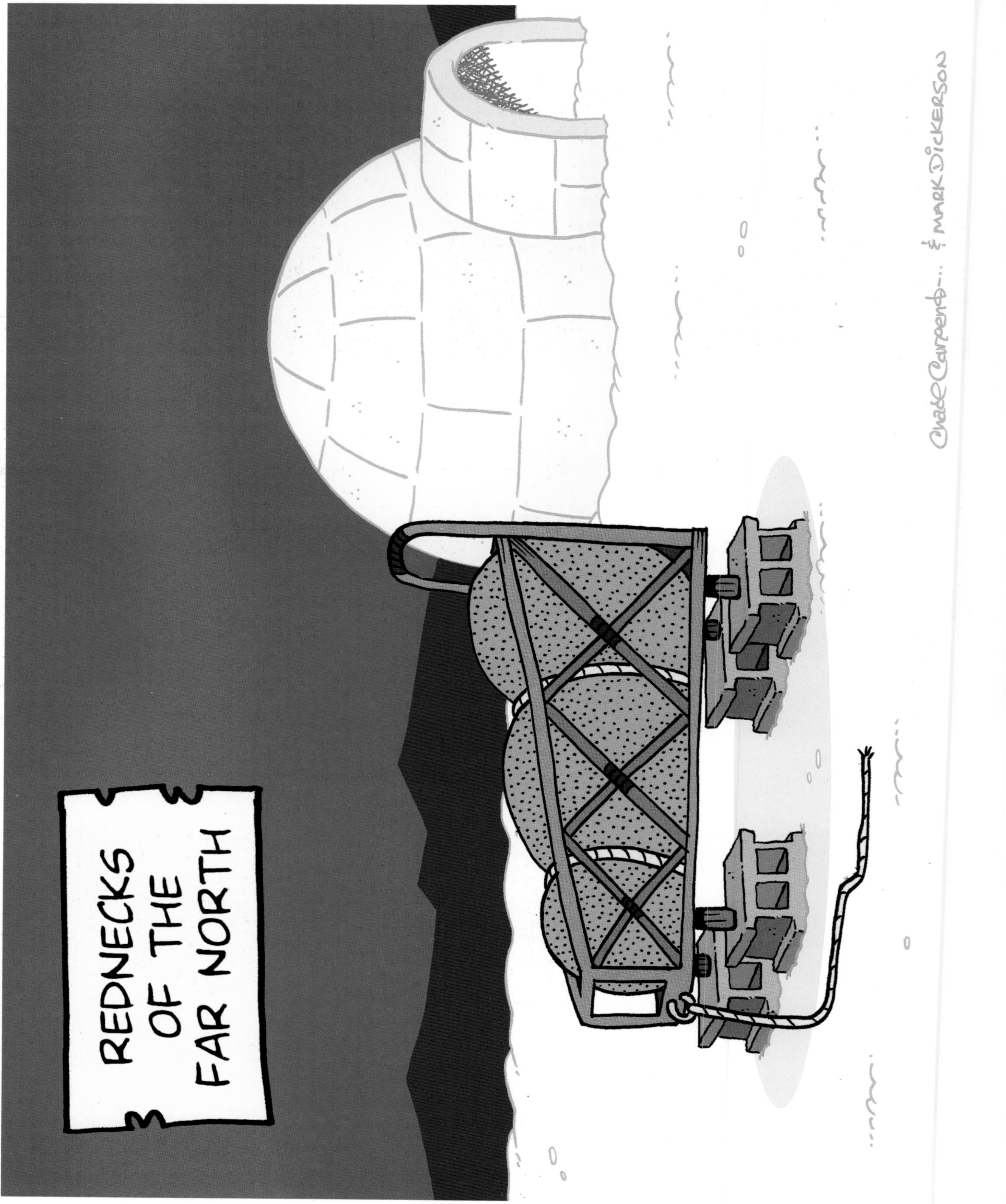
REDNECKS OF THE FAR NORTH
Chad Carpenter... & MARK DICKERSON

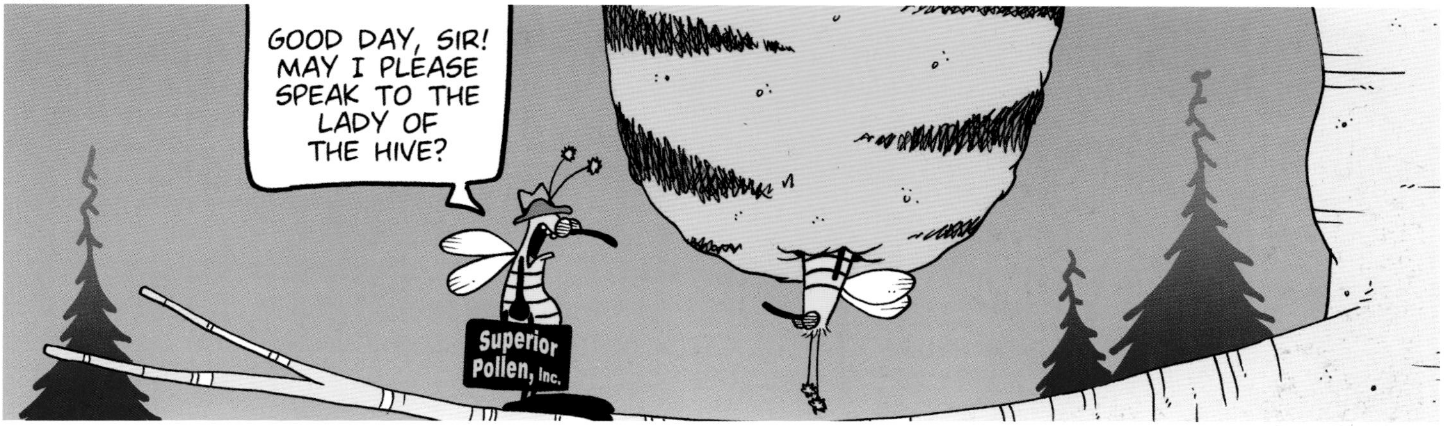
GOOD DAY, SIR! MAY I PLEASE SPEAK TO THE LADY OF THE HIVE?
Superior Pollen, Inc.

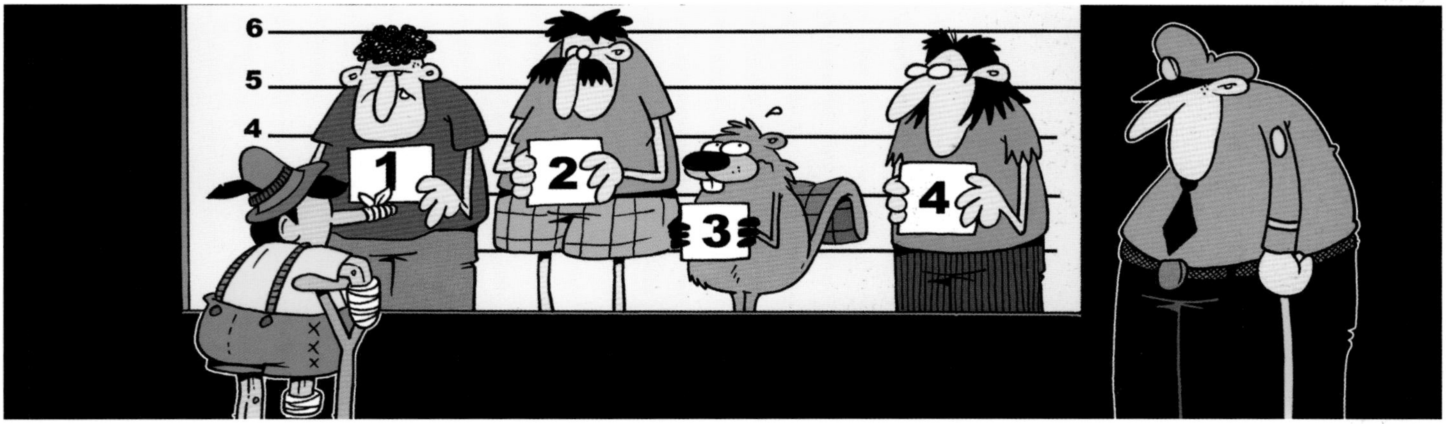
6
5
4
1
2
3
4

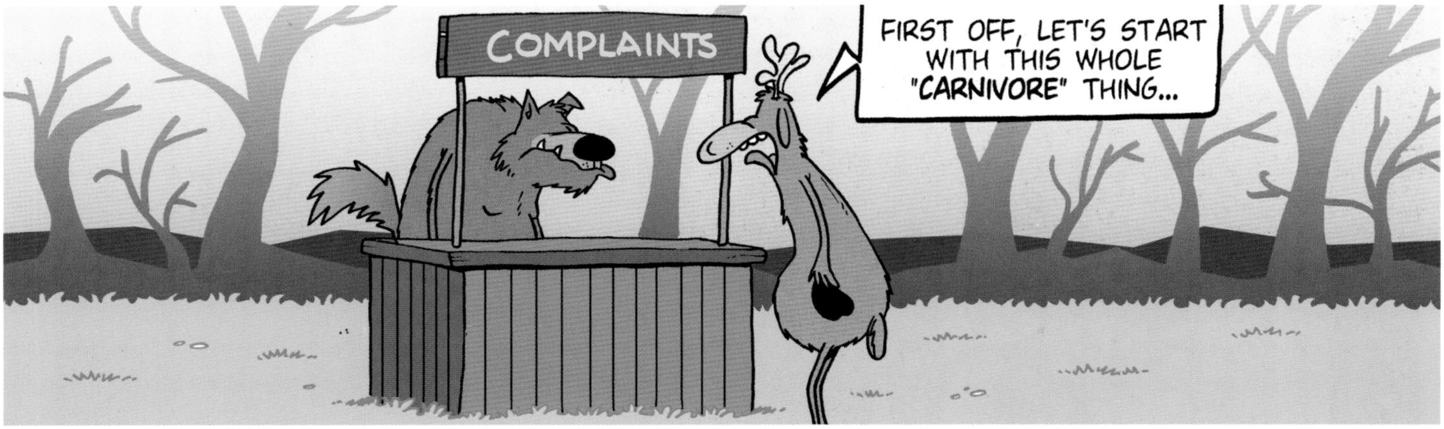
COMPLAINTS
FIRST OFF, LET'S START WITH THIS WHOLE "CARNIVORE" THING...

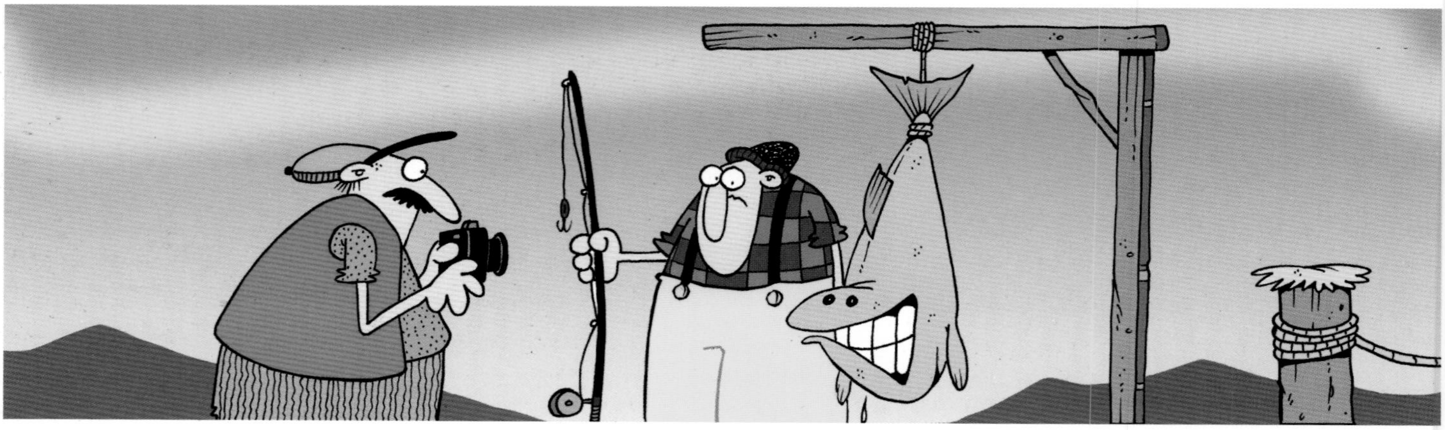

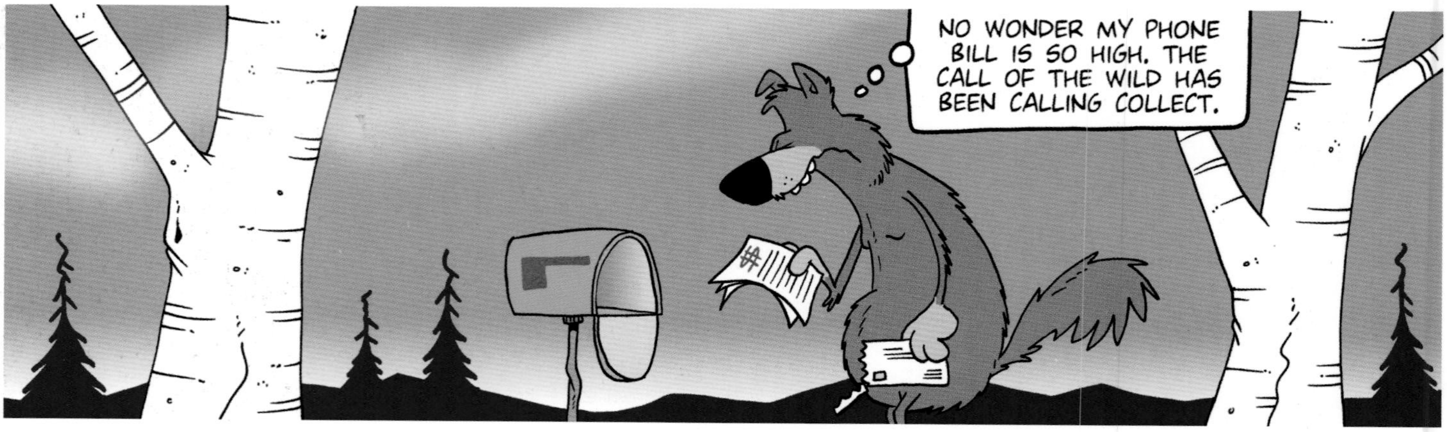
NO WONDER MY PHONE BILL IS SO HIGH. THE CALL OF THE WILD HAS BEEN CALLING COLLECT.

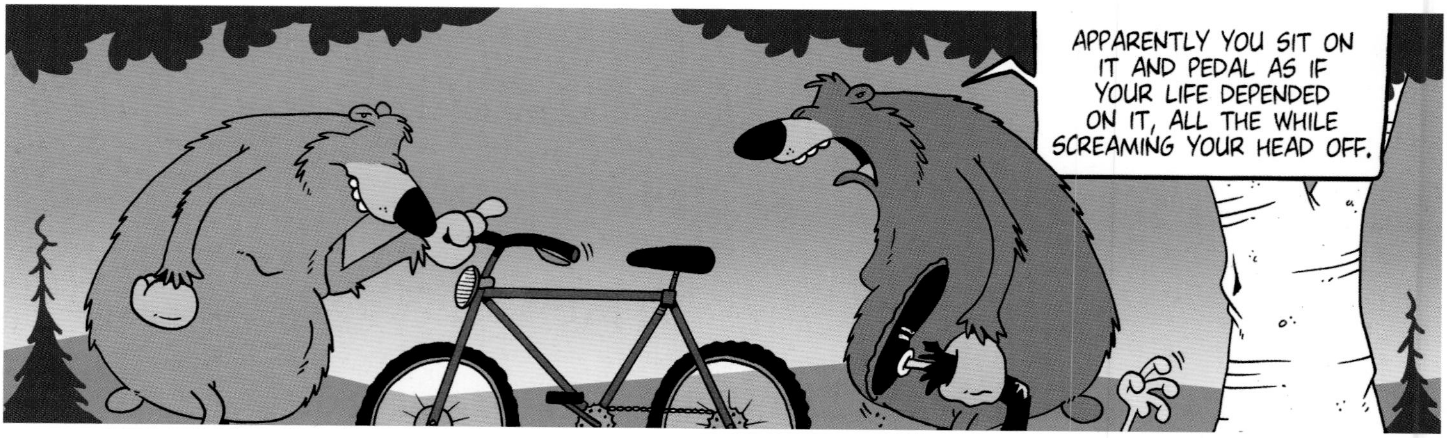
APPARENTLY YOU SIT ON IT AND PEDAL AS IF YOUR LIFE DEPENDED ON IT, ALL THE WHILE SCREAMING YOUR HEAD OFF.

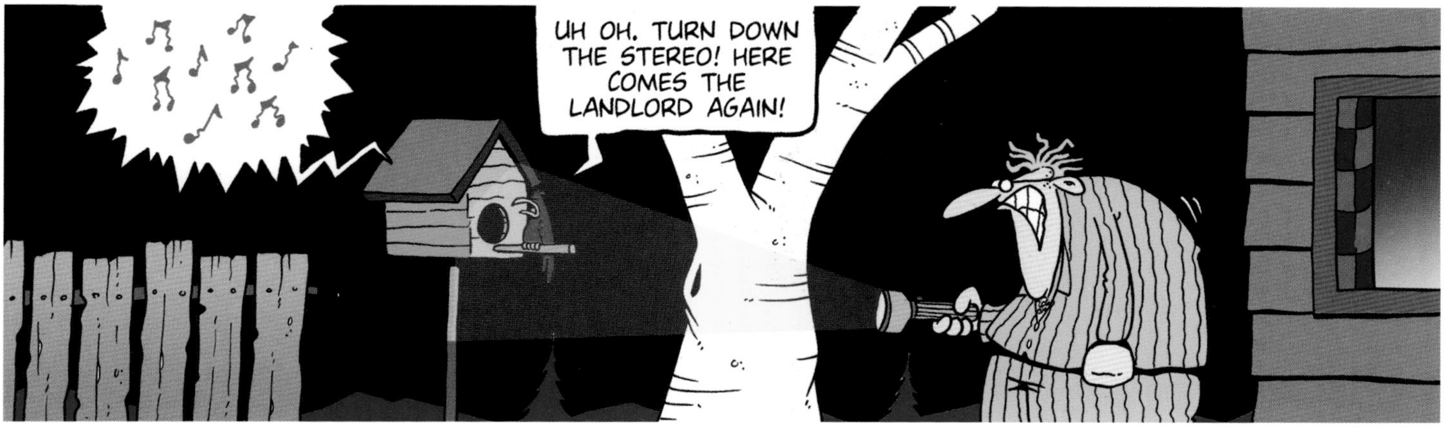
UH OH. TURN DOWN THE STEREO! HERE COMES THE LANDLORD AGAIN!

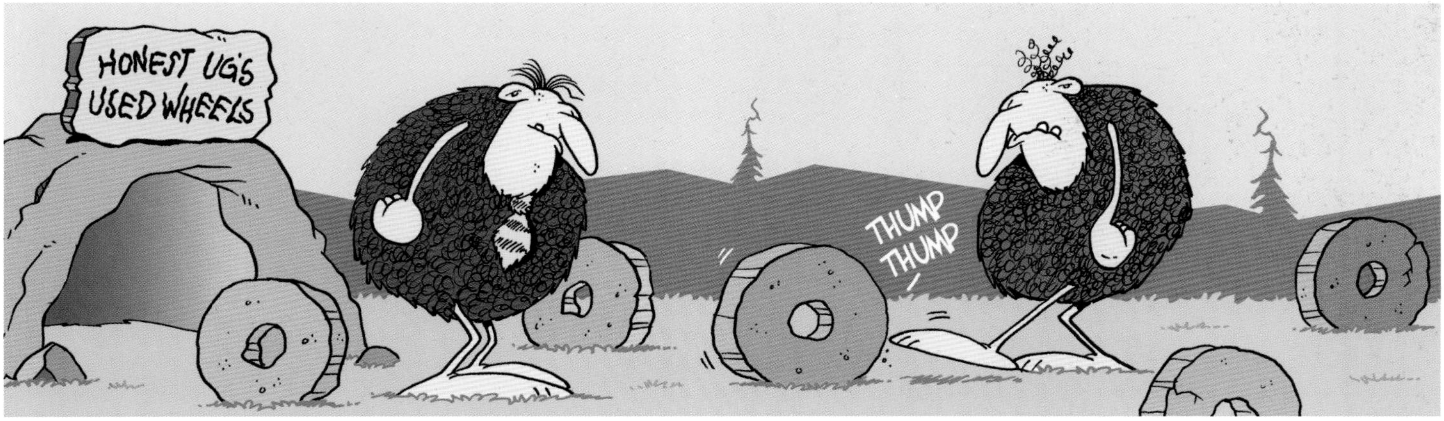
HONEST UG'S USED WHEELS
THUMP THUMP

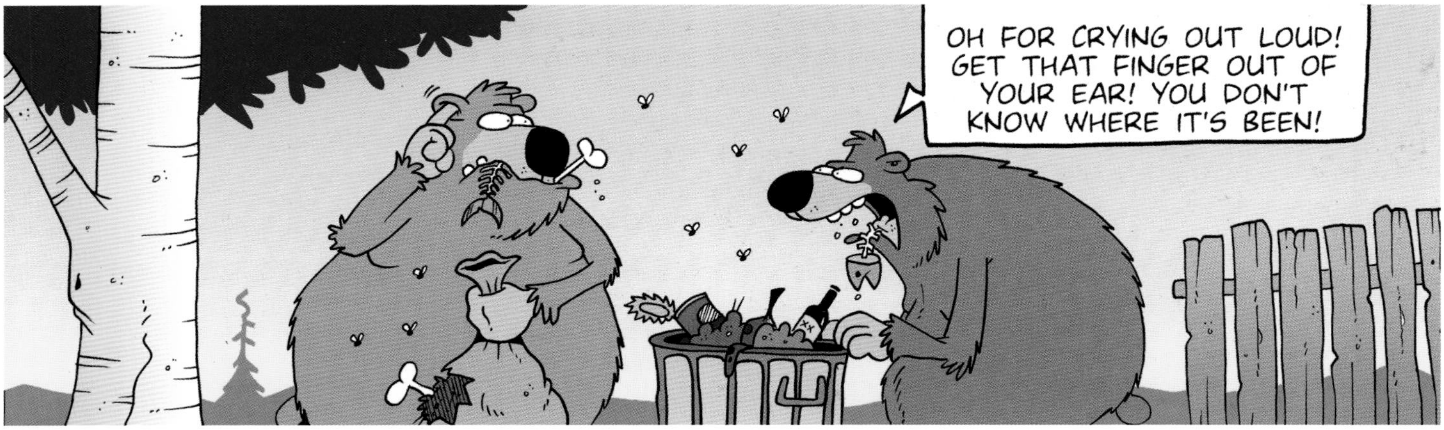
OH FOR CRYING OUT LOUD! GET THAT FINGER OUT OF YOUR EAR! YOU DON'T KNOW WHERE IT'S BEEN!

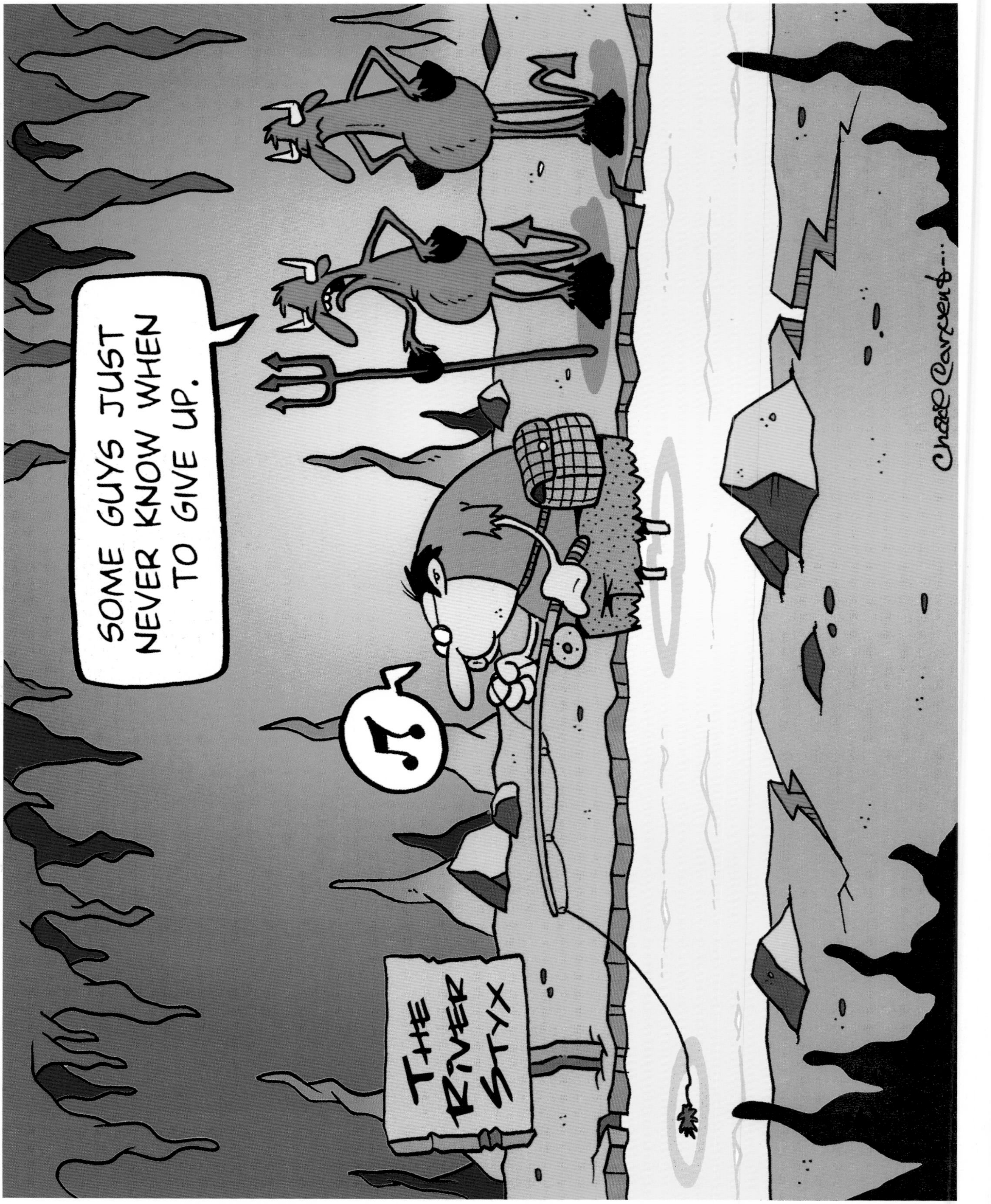
SOME GUYS JUST NEVER KNOW WHEN TO GIVE UP.
THE RIVER STYX
Chad Carpenter

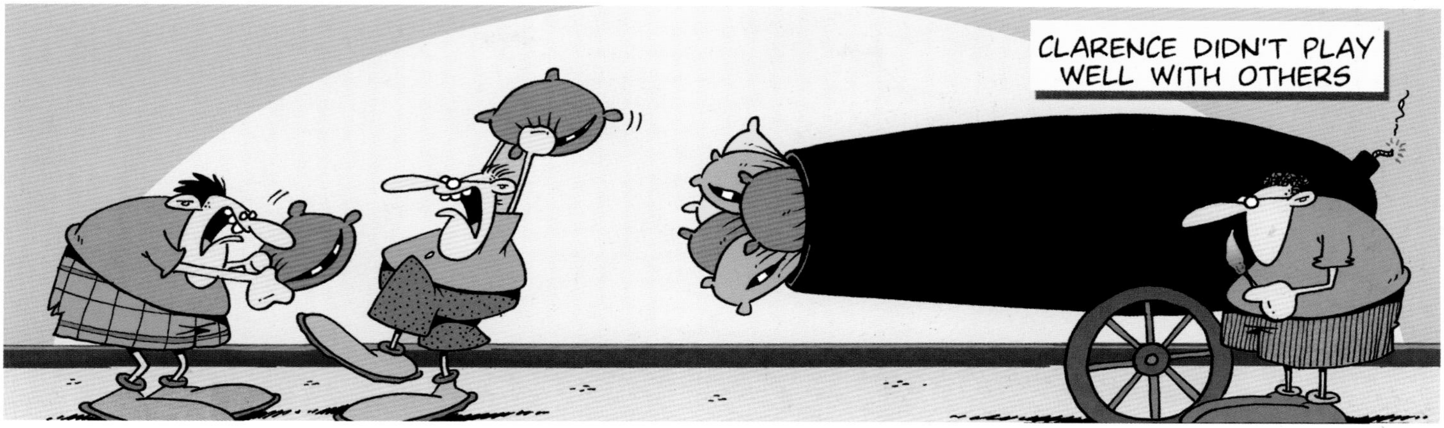
CLARENCE DIDN'T PLAY WELL WITH OTHERS

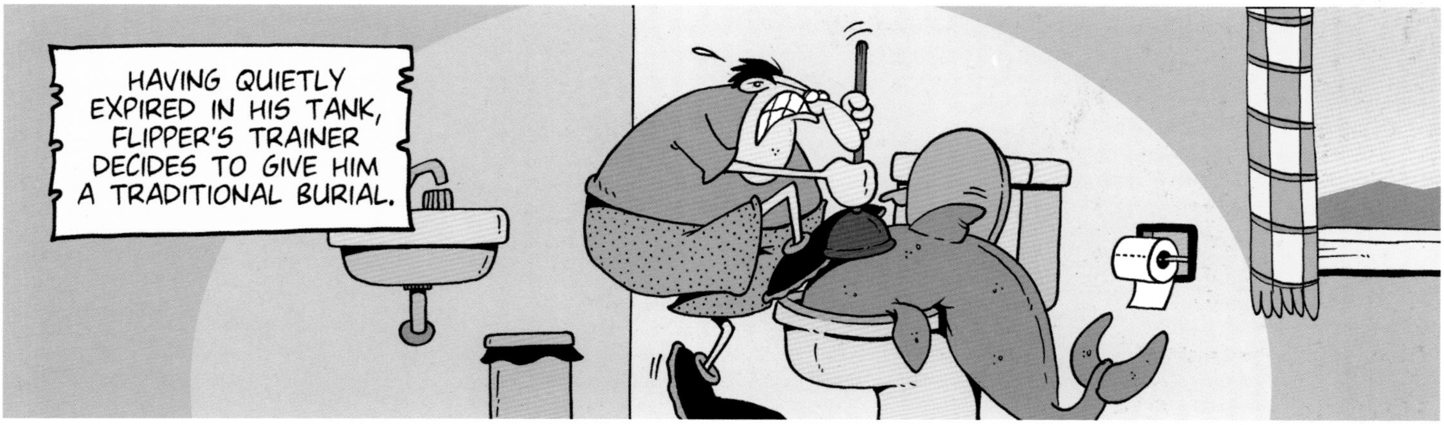
HAVING QUIETLY EXPIRED IN HIS TANK, FLIPPER'S TRAINER DECIDES TO GIVE HIM A TRADITIONAL BURIAL.

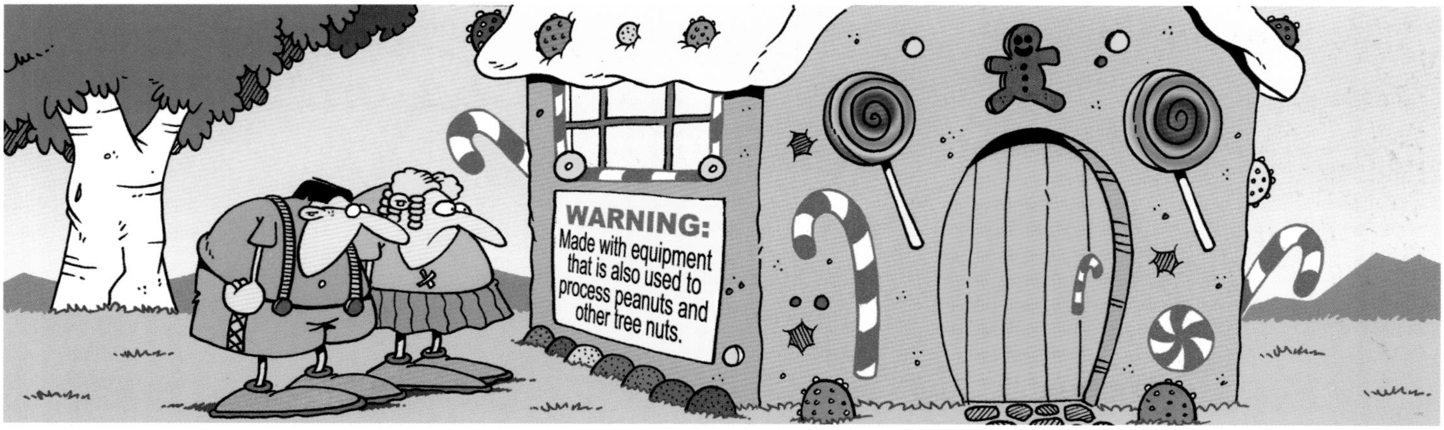
WARNING:
Made with equipment that is also used to process peanuts and other tree nuts.

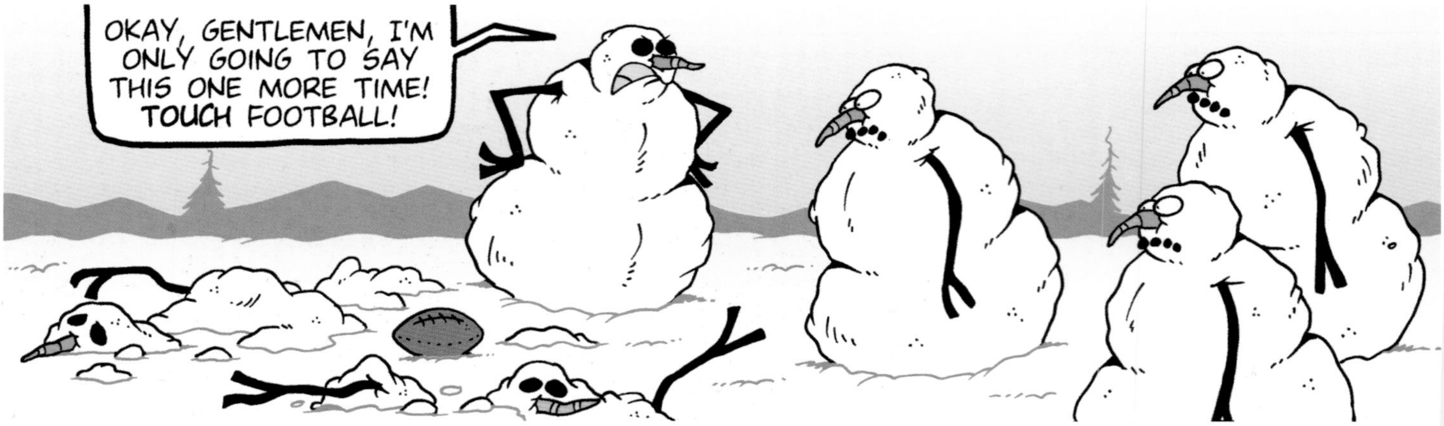
OKAY, GENTLEMEN, I'M ONLY GOING TO SAY THIS ONE MORE TIME! TOUCH FOOTBALL!

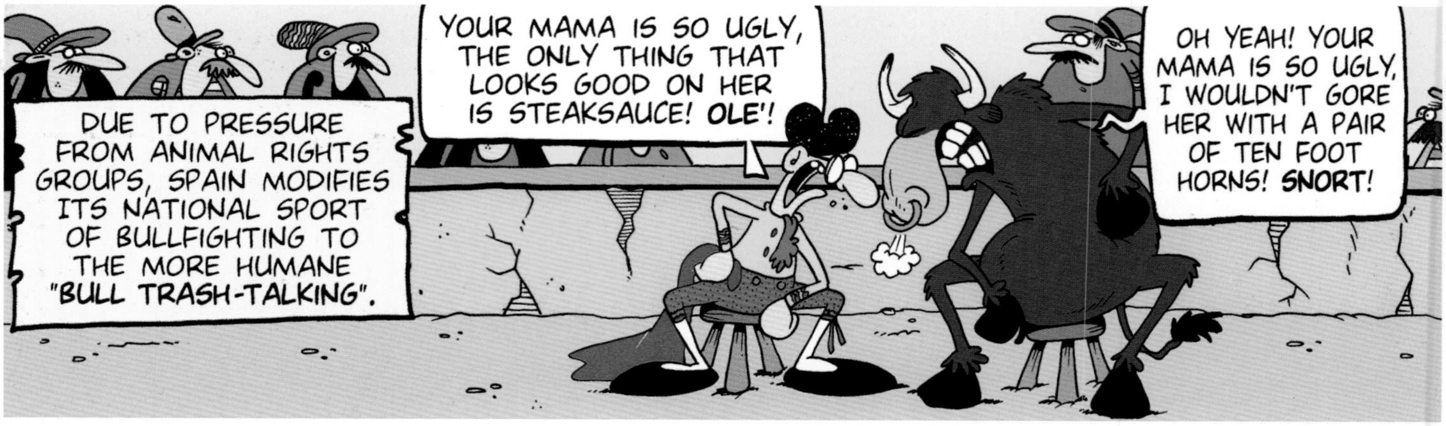
DUE TO PRESSURE FROM ANIMAL RIGHTS GROUPS, SPAIN MODIFIES ITS NATIONAL SPORT OF BULLFIGHTING TO THE MORE HUMANE "BULL TRASH-TALKING".
YOUR MAMA IS SO UGLY, THE ONLY THING THAT LOOKS GOOD ON HER IS STEAKSAUCE! OLE'!
OH YEAH! YOUR MAMA IS SO UGLY, I WOULDN'T GORE HER WITH A PAIR OF TEN FOOT HORNS! SNORT!

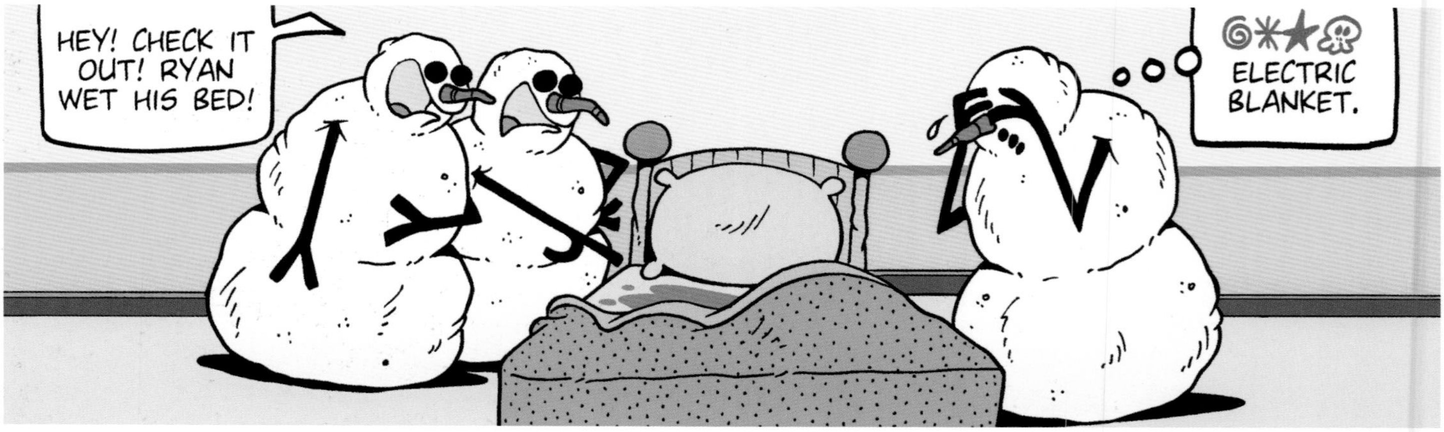
HEY! CHECK IT OUT! RYAN WET HIS BED!
ELECTRIC BLANKET.

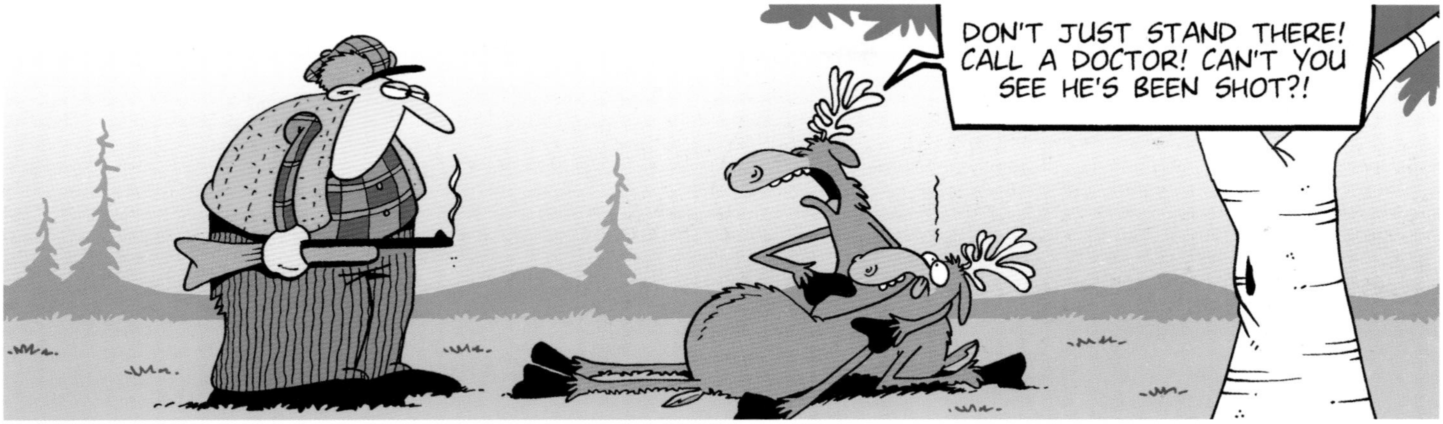
DON'T JUST STAND THERE! CALL A DOCTOR! CAN'T YOU SEE HE'S BEEN SHOT?!

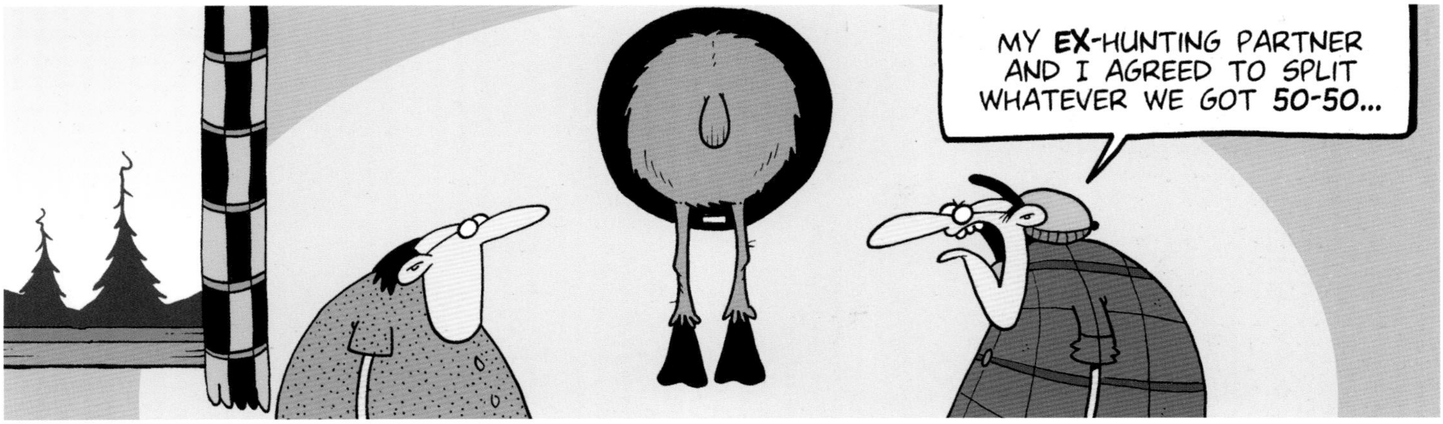
MY **EX**-HUNTING PARTNER AND I AGREED TO SPLIT WHATEVER WE GOT **50-50...**

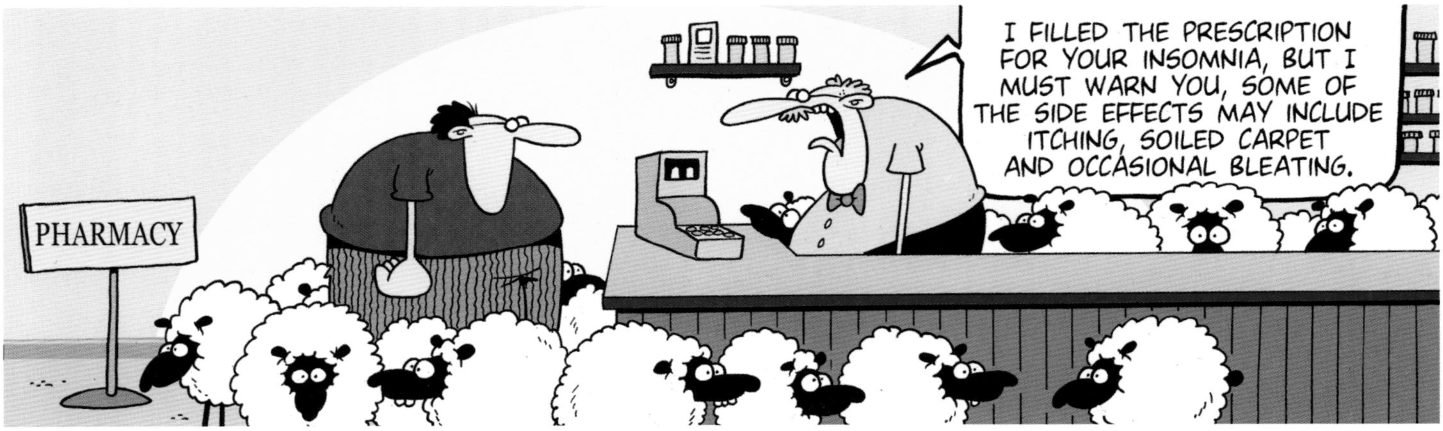
I FILLED THE PRESCRIPTION FOR YOUR INSOMNIA, BUT I MUST WARN YOU, SOME OF THE SIDE EFFECTS MAY INCLUDE ITCHING, SOILED CARPET AND OCCASIONAL BLEATING.
PHARMACY

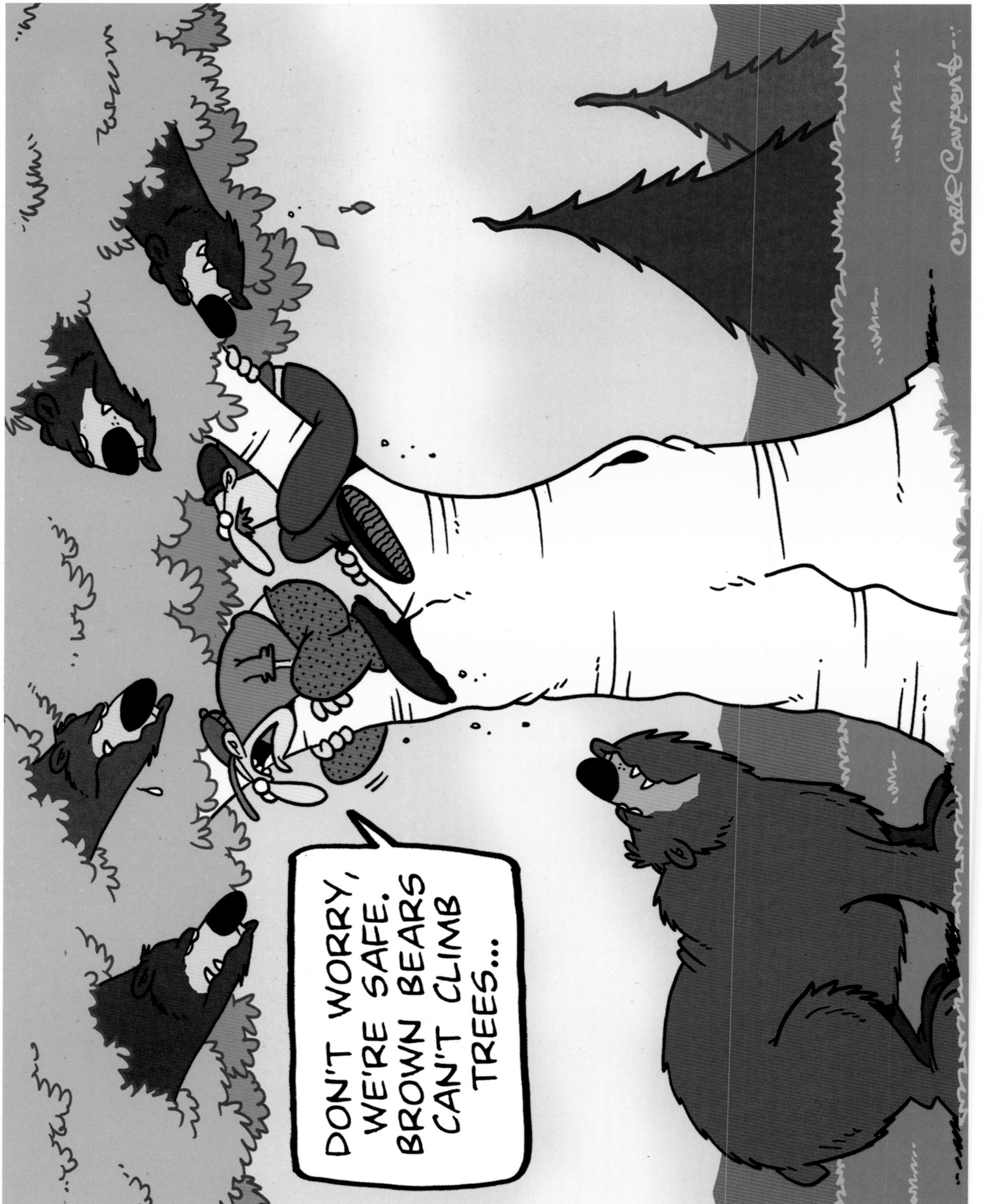
DON'T WORRY, WE'RE SAFE. BROWN BEARS CAN'T CLIMB TREES...

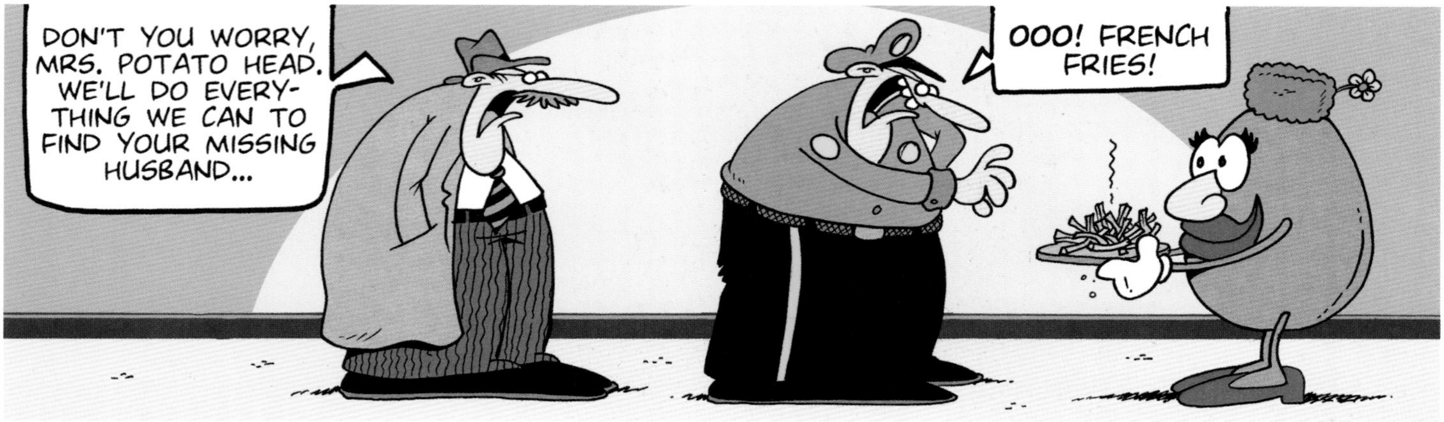
DON'T YOU WORRY, MRS. POTATO HEAD. WE'LL DO EVERY-THING WE CAN TO FIND YOUR MISSING HUSBAND...
OOO! FRENCH FRIES!

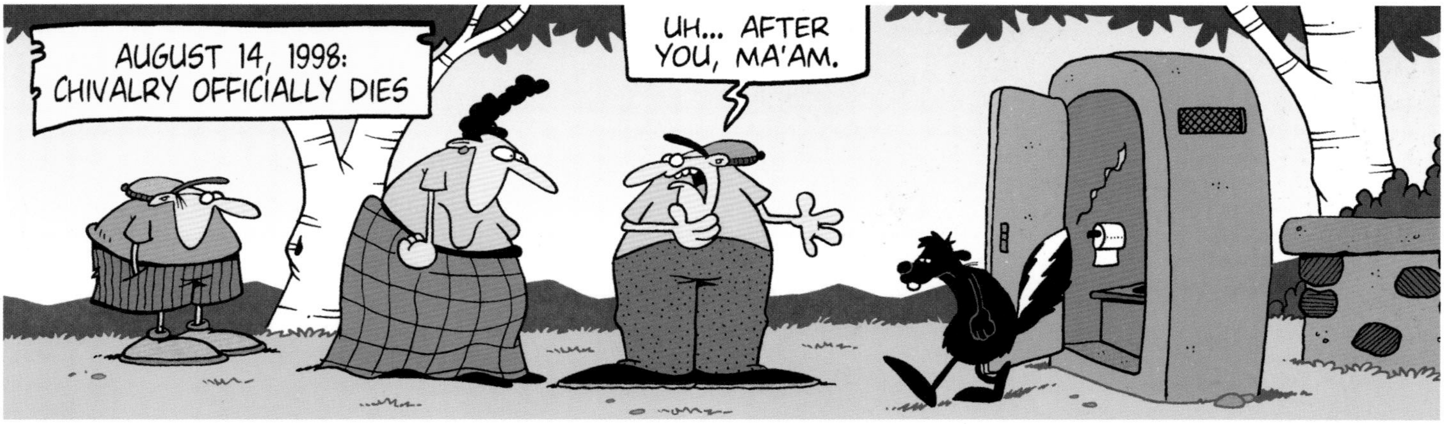
AUGUST 14, 1998: CHIVALRY OFFICIALLY DIES
UH... AFTER YOU, MA'AM.

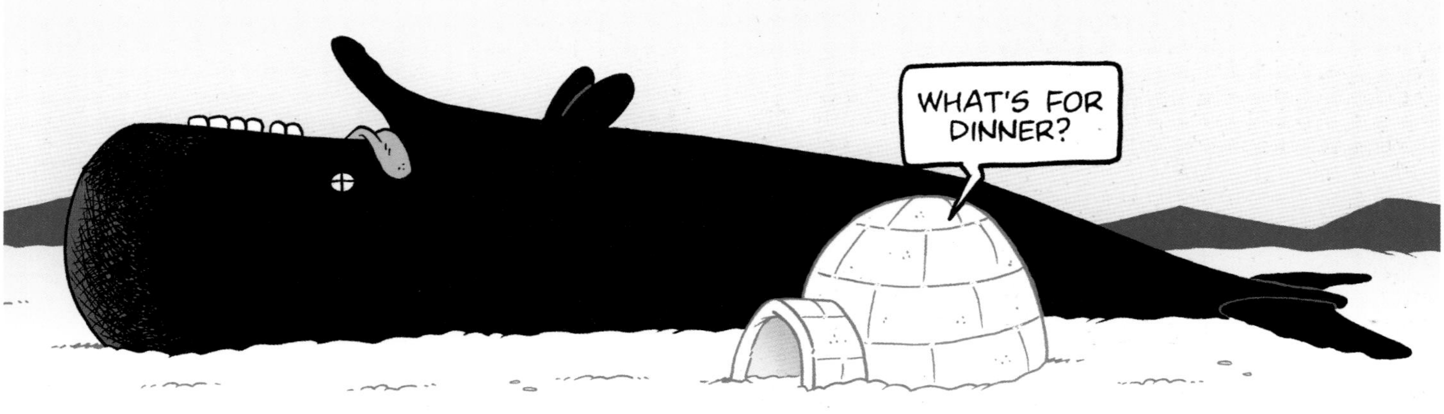
WHAT'S FOR DINNER?

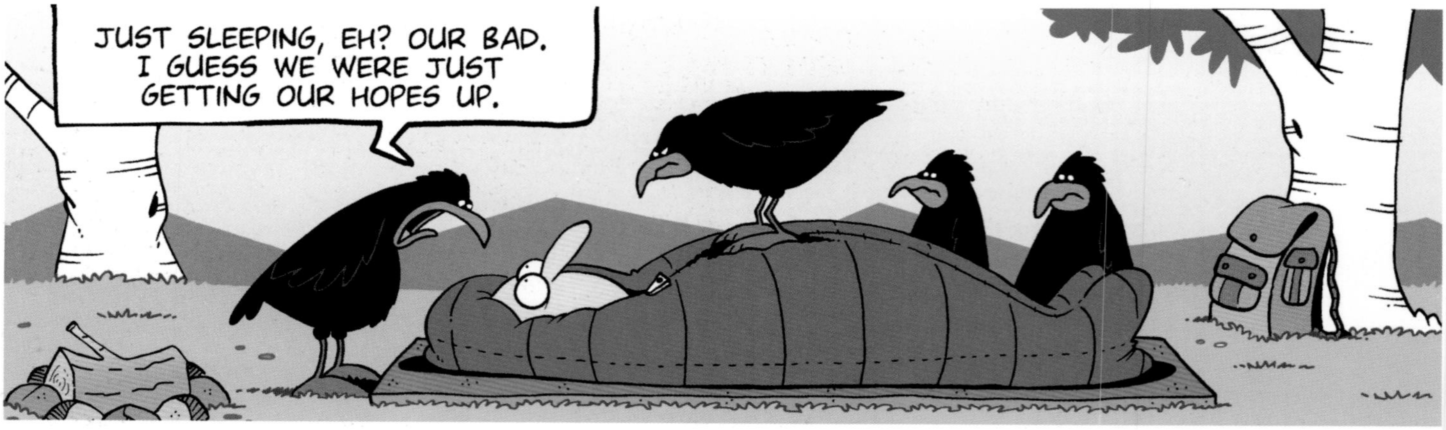
JUST SLEEPING, EH? OUR BAD. I GUESS WE WERE JUST GETTING OUR HOPES UP.

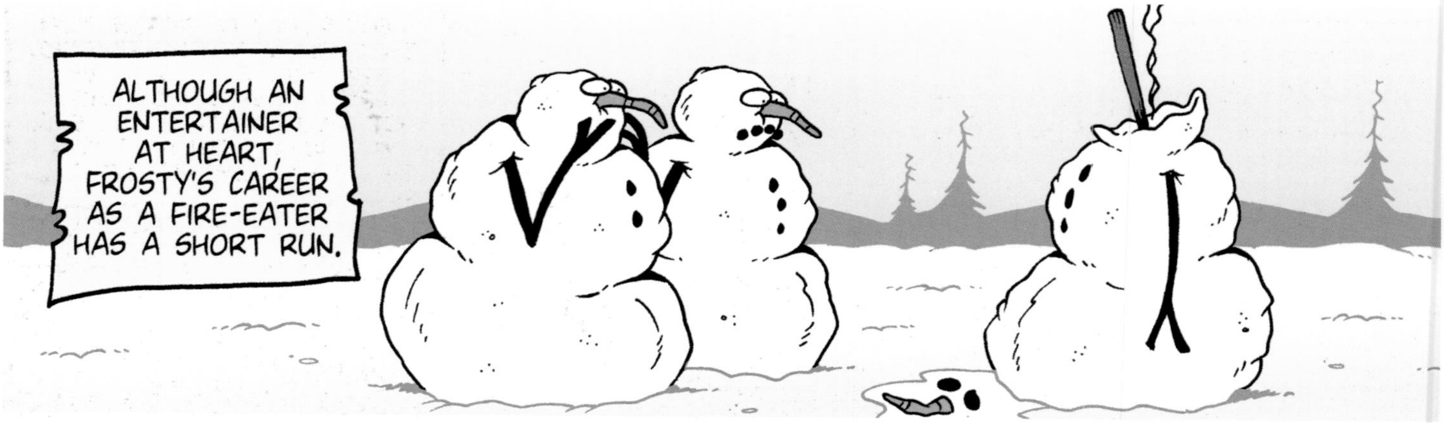
ALTHOUGH AN ENTERTAINER AT HEART, FROSTY'S CAREER AS A FIRE-EATER HAS A SHORT RUN.

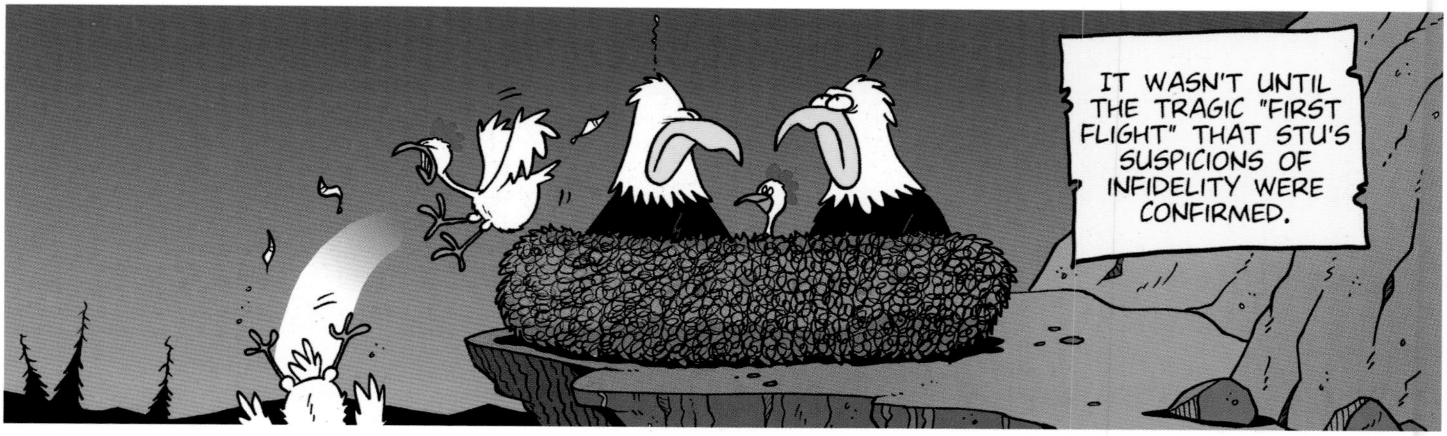
IT WASN'T UNTIL THE TRAGIC "FIRST FLIGHT" THAT STU'S SUSPICIONS OF INFIDELITY WERE CONFIRMED.

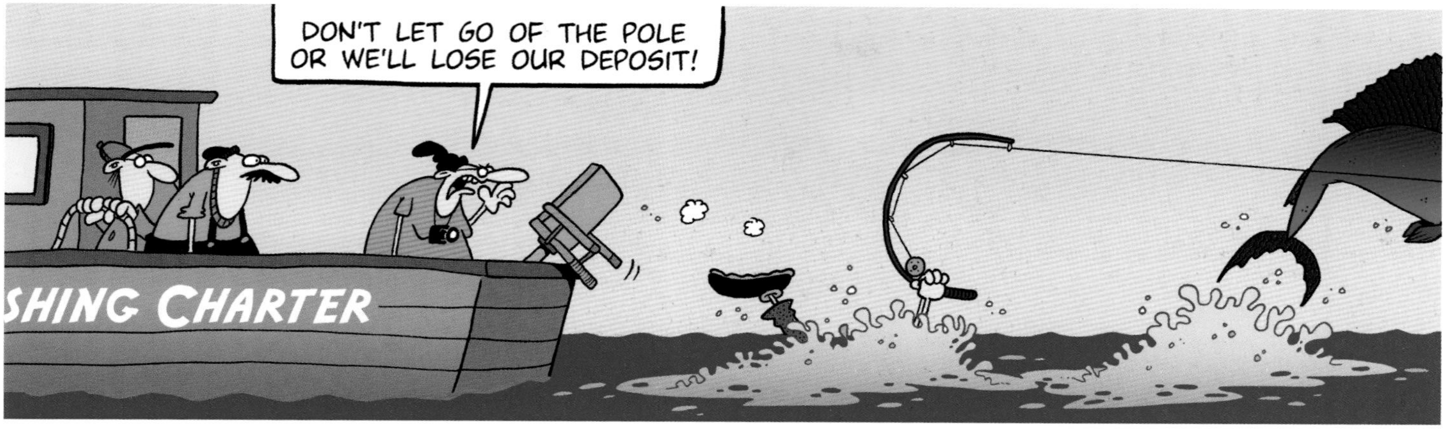
DON'T LET GO OF THE POLE OR WE'LL LOSE OUR DEPOSIT!
SHING CHARTER

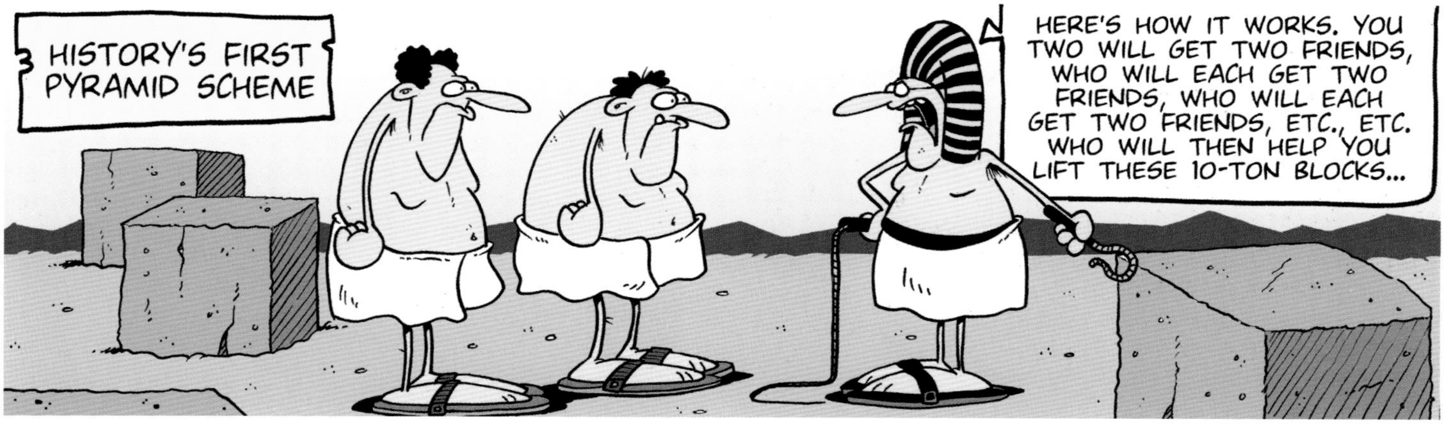
HISTORY'S FIRST PYRAMID SCHEME
HERE'S HOW IT WORKS. YOU TWO WILL GET TWO FRIENDS, WHO WILL EACH GET TWO FRIENDS, WHO WILL EACH GET TWO FRIENDS, ETC., ETC. WHO WILL THEN HELP YOU LIFT THESE 10-TON BLOCKS...

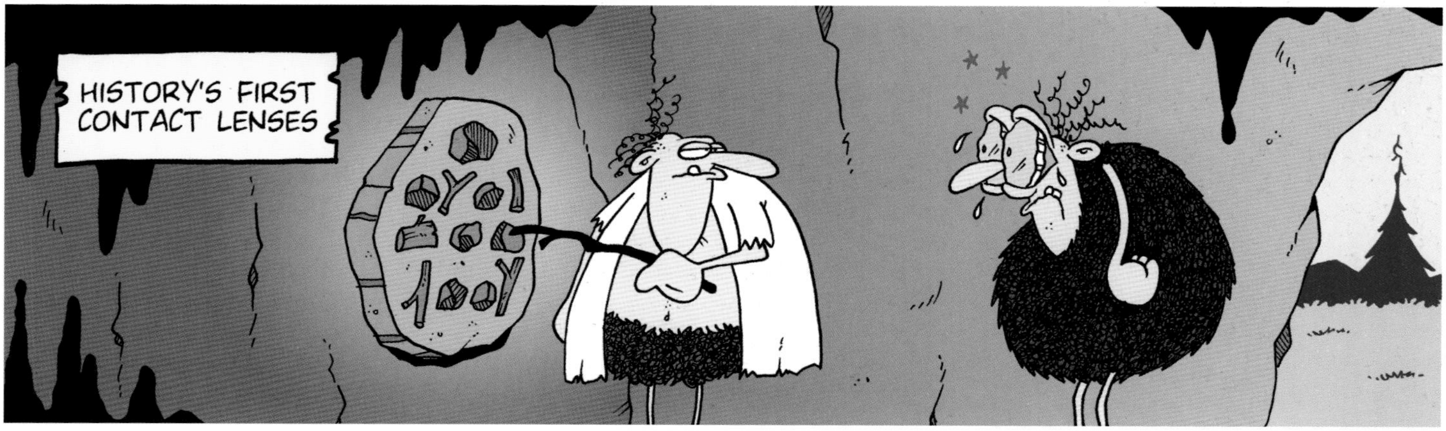
HISTORY'S FIRST CONTACT LENSES

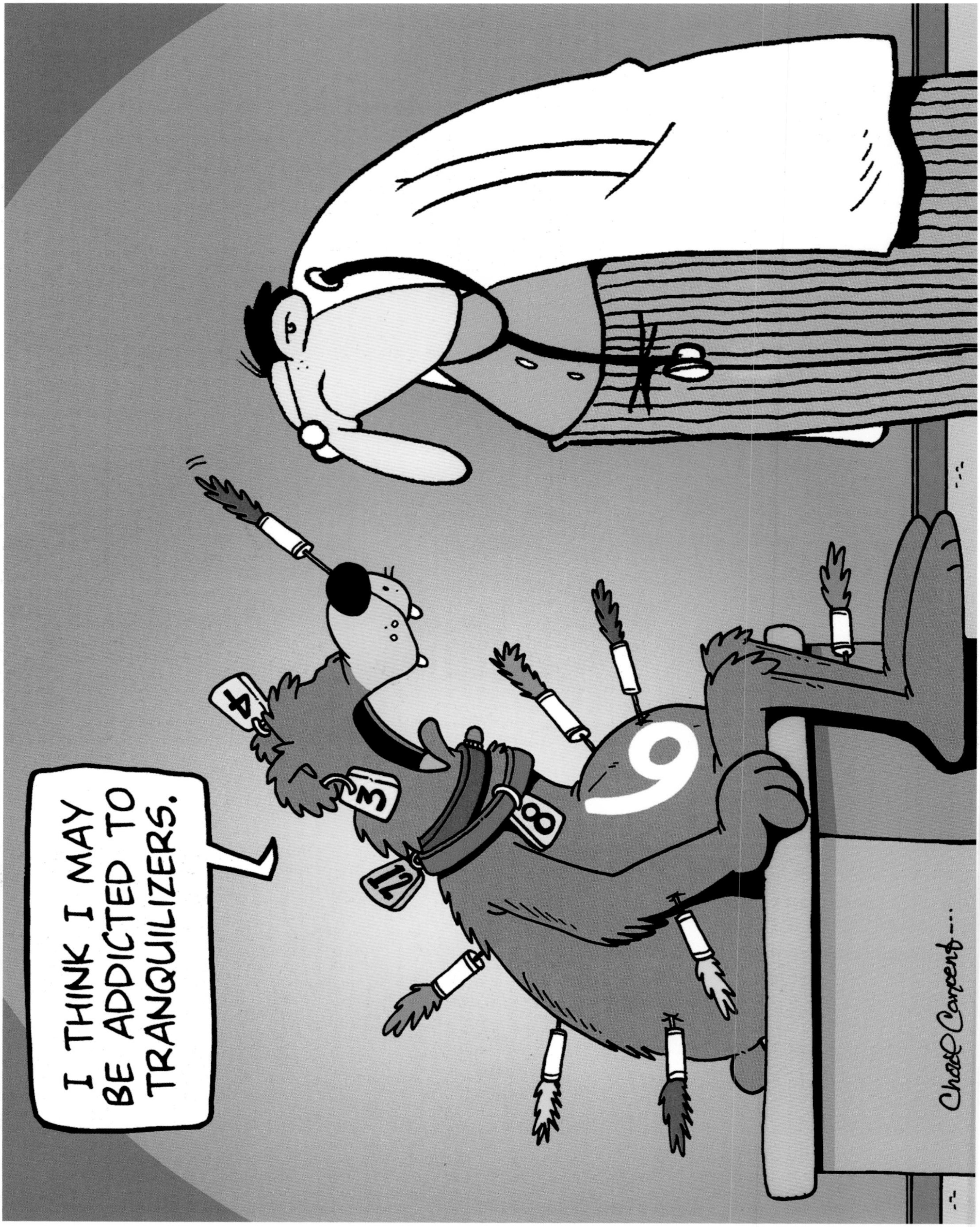
I THINK I MAY BE ADDICTED TO TRANQUILIZERS.

THIS STRIP IS BASED ON AN IDEA FROM:

KRISTI CARPENTER
NORTH POLE, AK

DO YOU HAVE AN IDEA THAT WOULD MAKE A GREAT COMIC STRIP?

SEND IT TO:
tundracomics.com

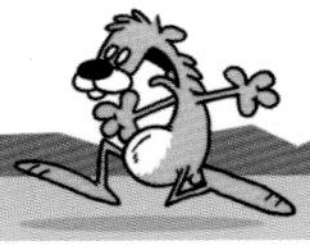

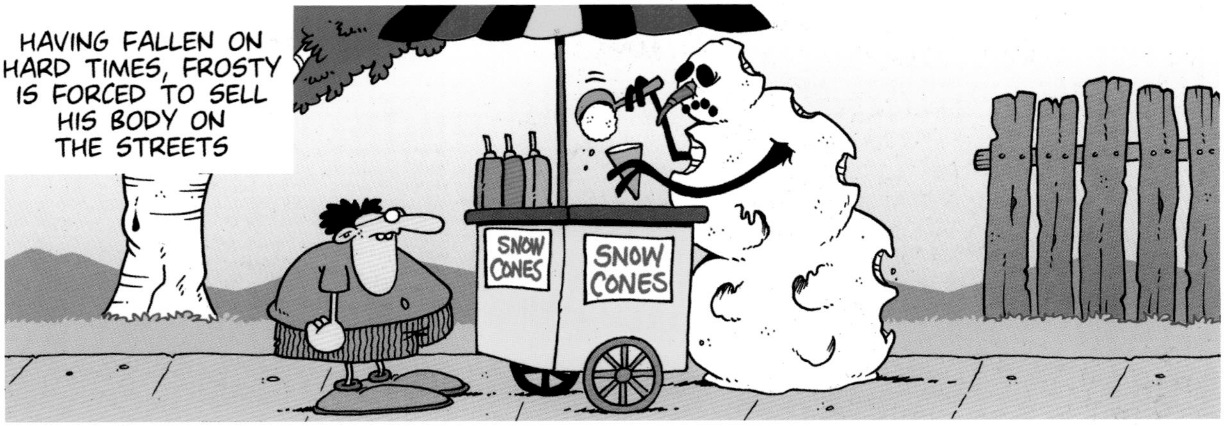
HAVING FALLEN ON HARD TIMES, FROSTY IS FORCED TO SELL HIS BODY ON THE STREETS
SNOW CONES
SNOW CONES

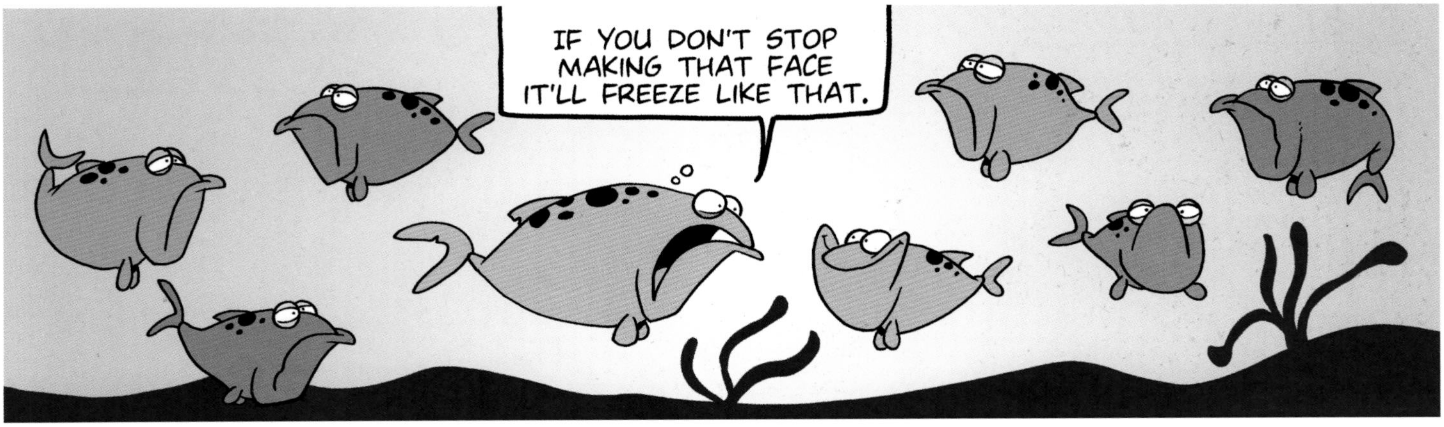
IF YOU DON'T STOP MAKING THAT FACE IT'LL FREEZE LIKE THAT.

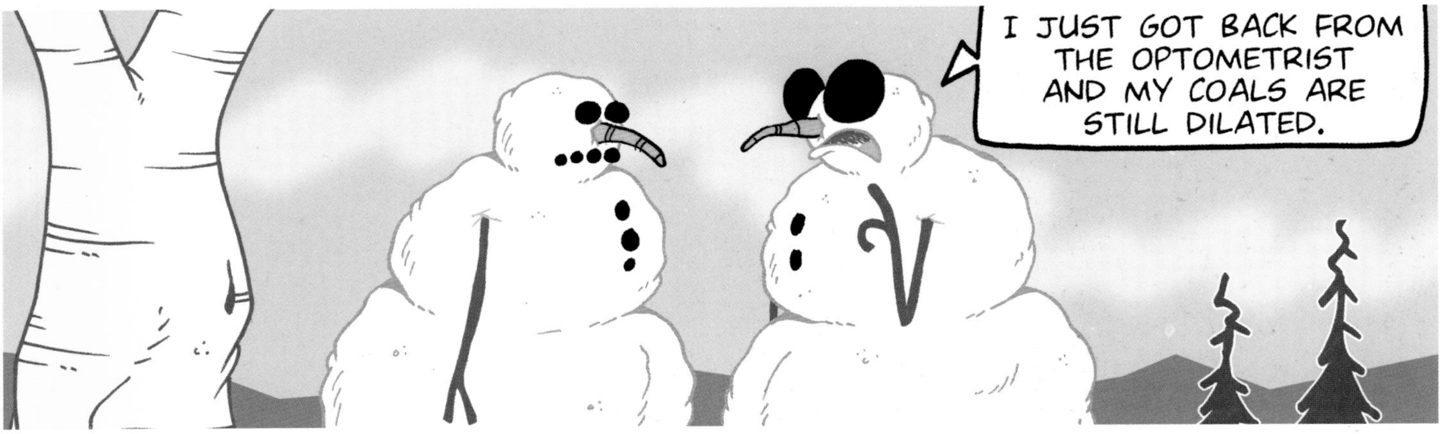
I JUST GOT BACK FROM THE OPTOMETRIST AND MY COALS ARE STILL DILATED.

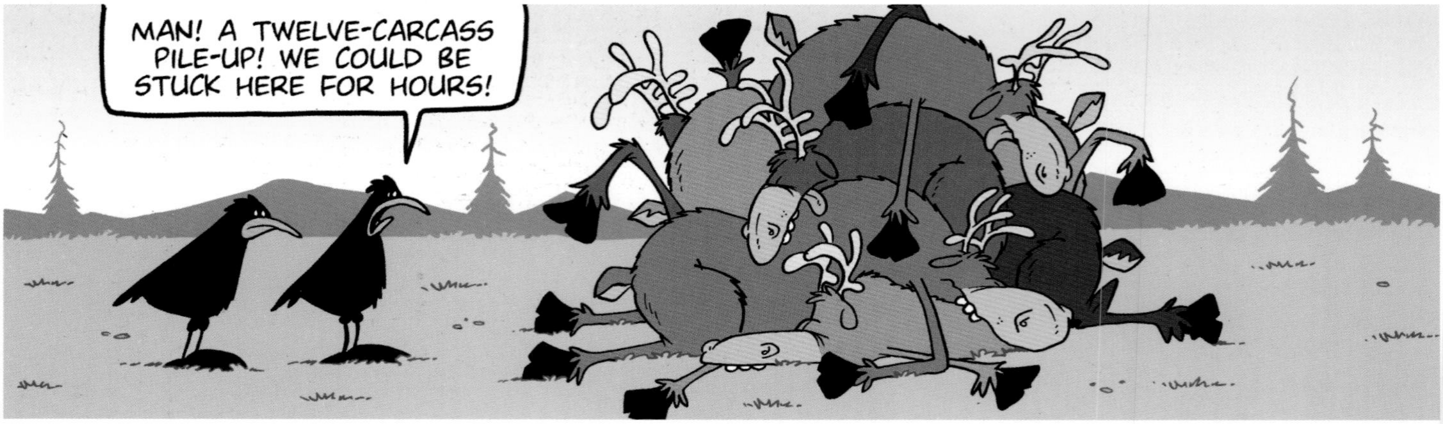
MAN! A TWELVE-CARCASS PILE-UP! WE COULD BE STUCK HERE FOR HOURS!

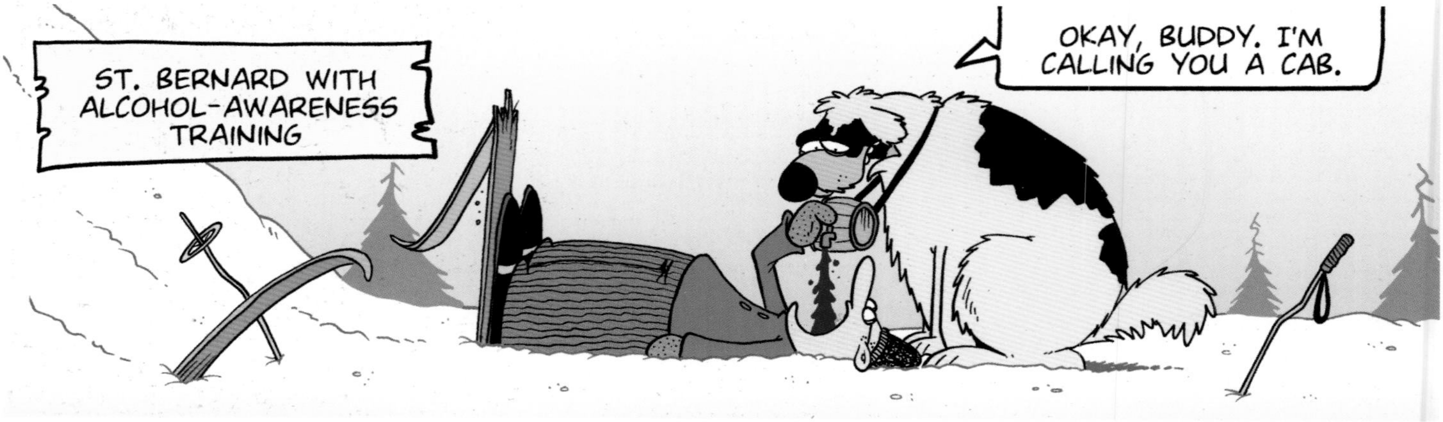
ST. BERNARD WITH ALCOHOL-AWARENESS TRAINING
OKAY, BUDDY. I'M CALLING YOU A CAB.

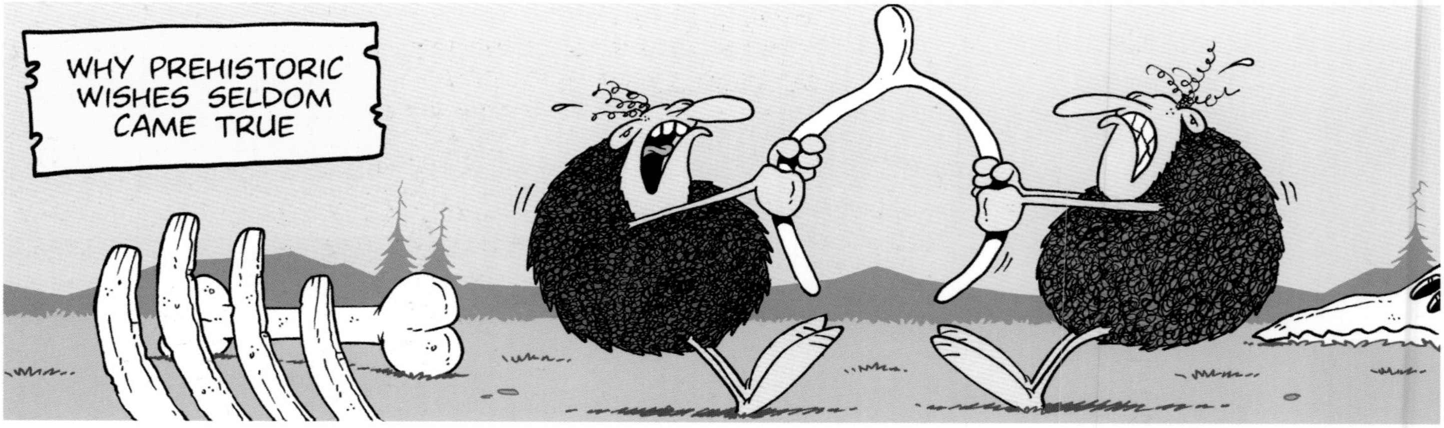
WHY PREHISTORIC WISHES SELDOM CAME TRUE

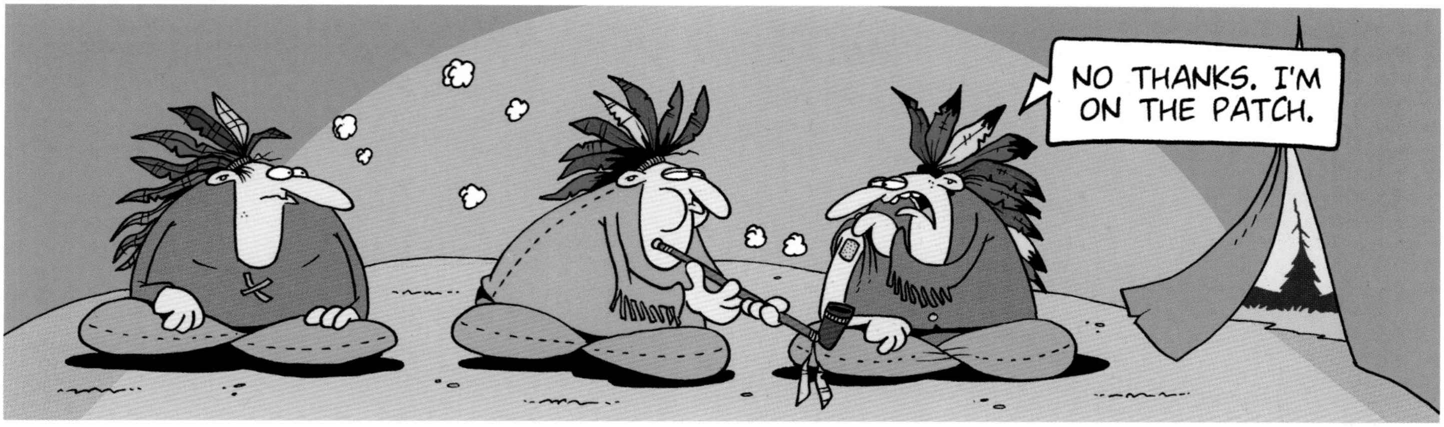
NO THANKS. I'M ON THE PATCH.

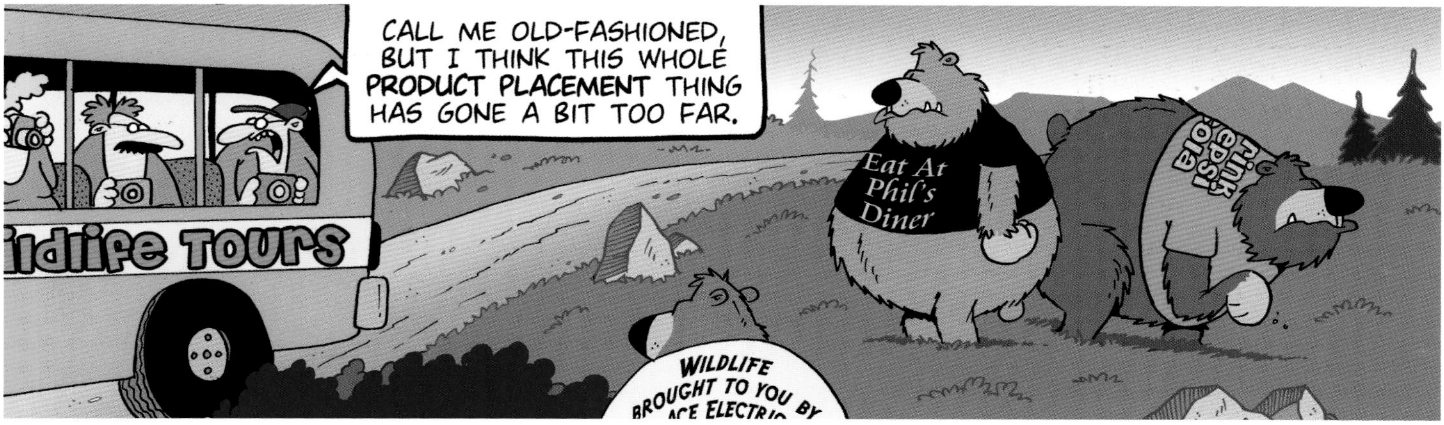
CALL ME OLD-FASHIONED, BUT I THINK THIS WHOLE **PRODUCT PLACEMENT** THING HAS GONE A BIT TOO FAR.
Eat At Phil's Diner
WILDLIFE BROUGHT TO YOU BY

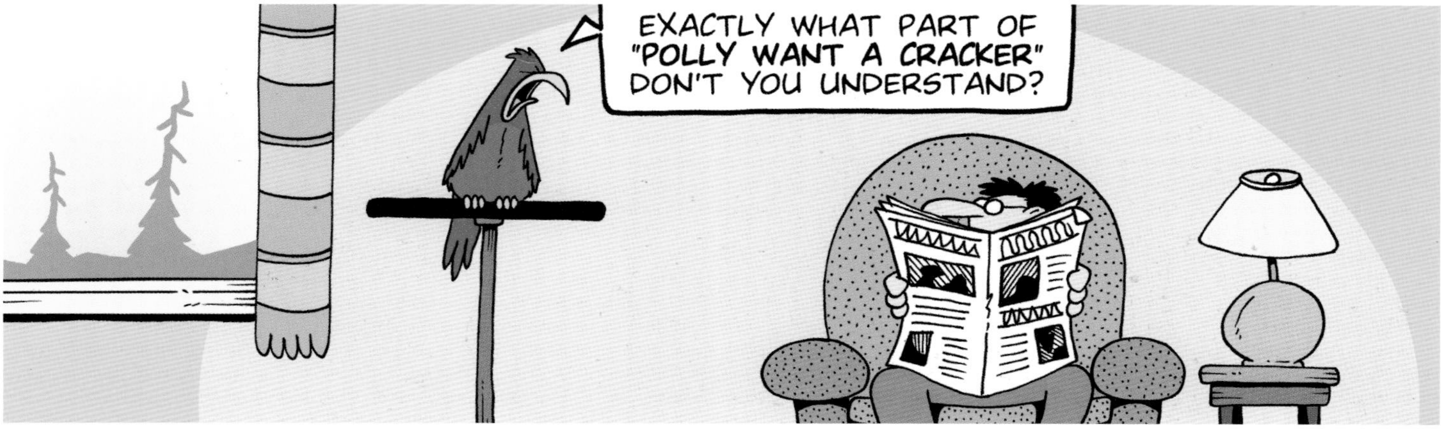
EXACTLY WHAT PART OF **"POLLY WANT A CRACKER"** DON'T YOU UNDERSTAND?

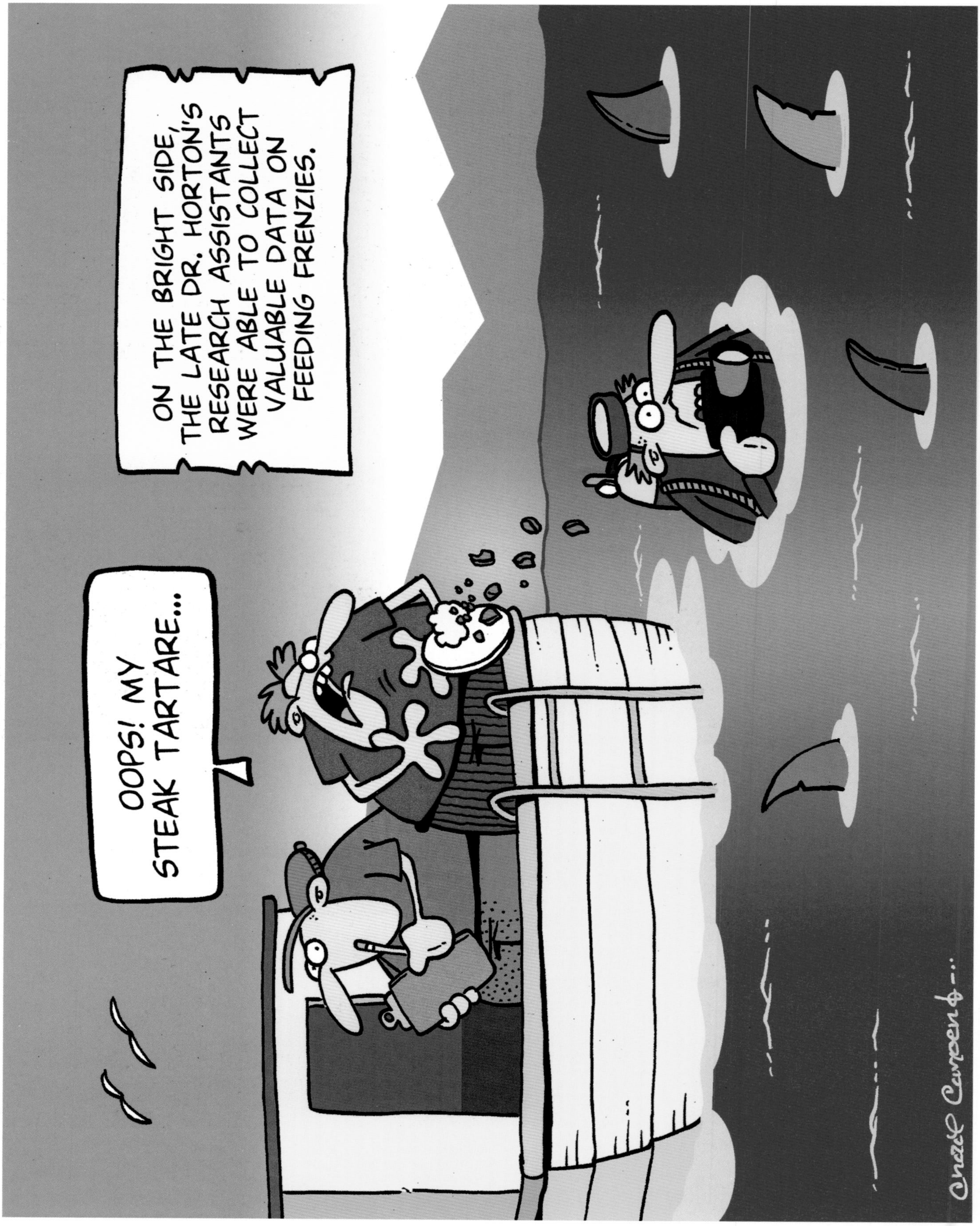
ON THE BRIGHT SIDE, THE LATE DR. HORTON'S RESEARCH ASSISTANTS WERE ABLE TO COLLECT VALUABLE DATA ON FEEDING FRENZIES.
OOPS! MY STEAK TARTARE...
Chad Carpenter

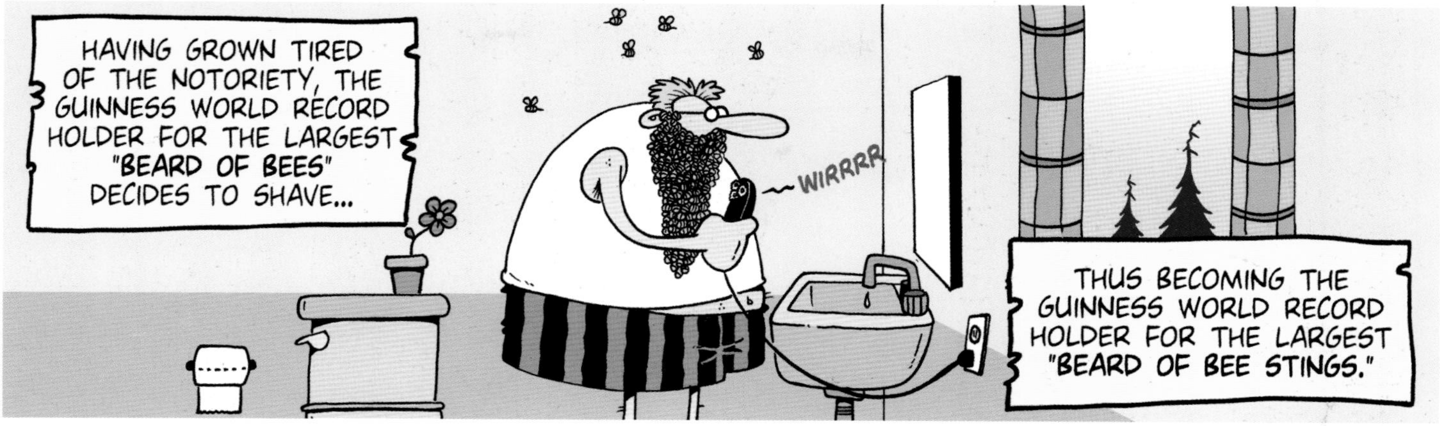
HAVING GROWN TIRED OF THE NOTORIETY, THE GUINNESS WORLD RECORD HOLDER FOR THE LARGEST "BEARD OF BEES" DECIDES TO SHAVE...
WIRRRR
THUS BECOMING THE GUINNESS WORLD RECORD HOLDER FOR THE LARGEST "BEARD OF BEE STINGS."

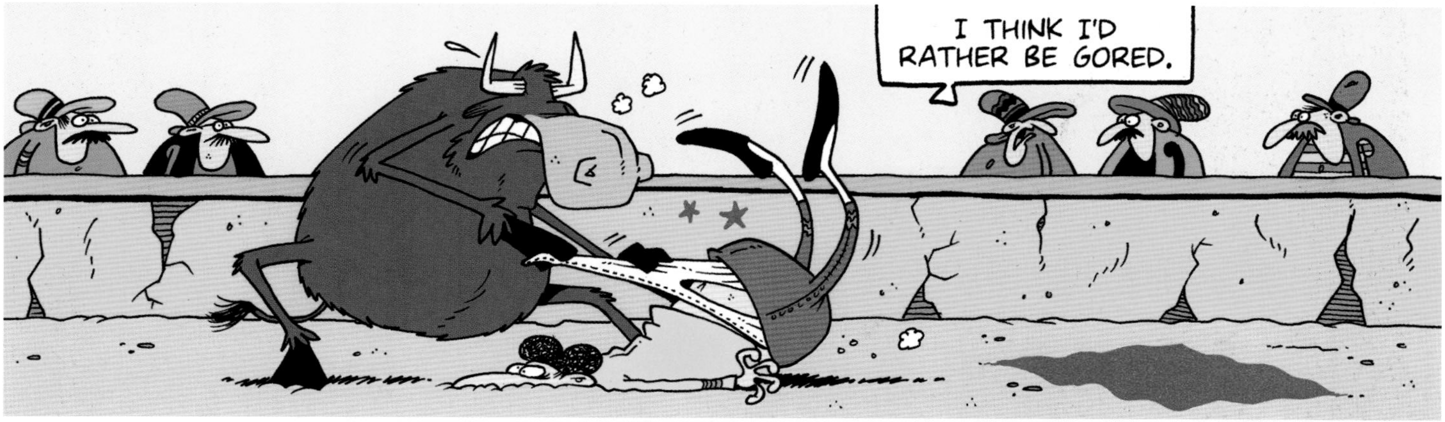
I THINK I'D RATHER BE GORED.

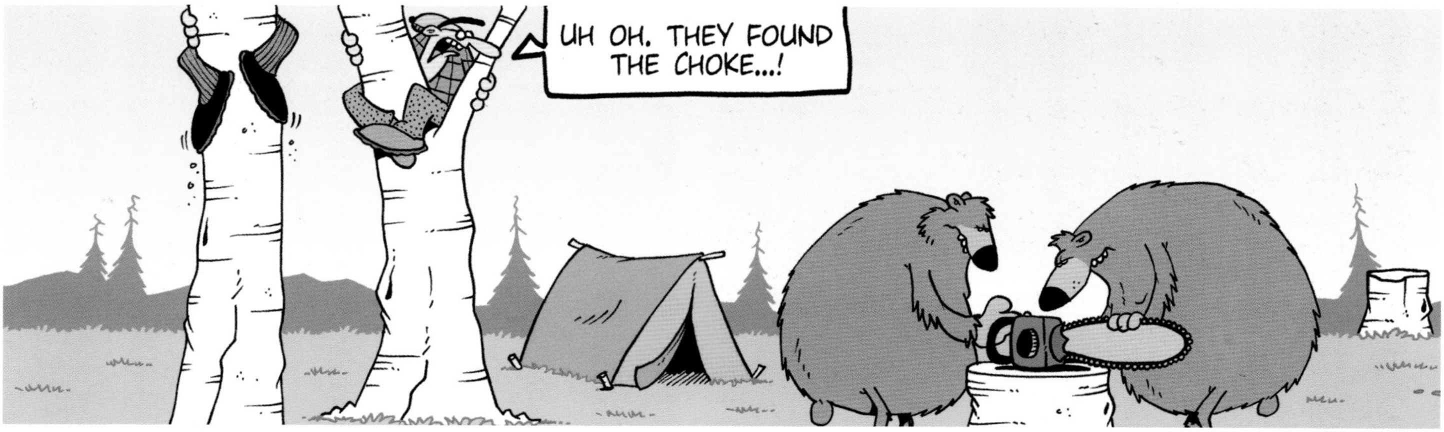
UH OH. THEY FOUND THE CHOKE...!

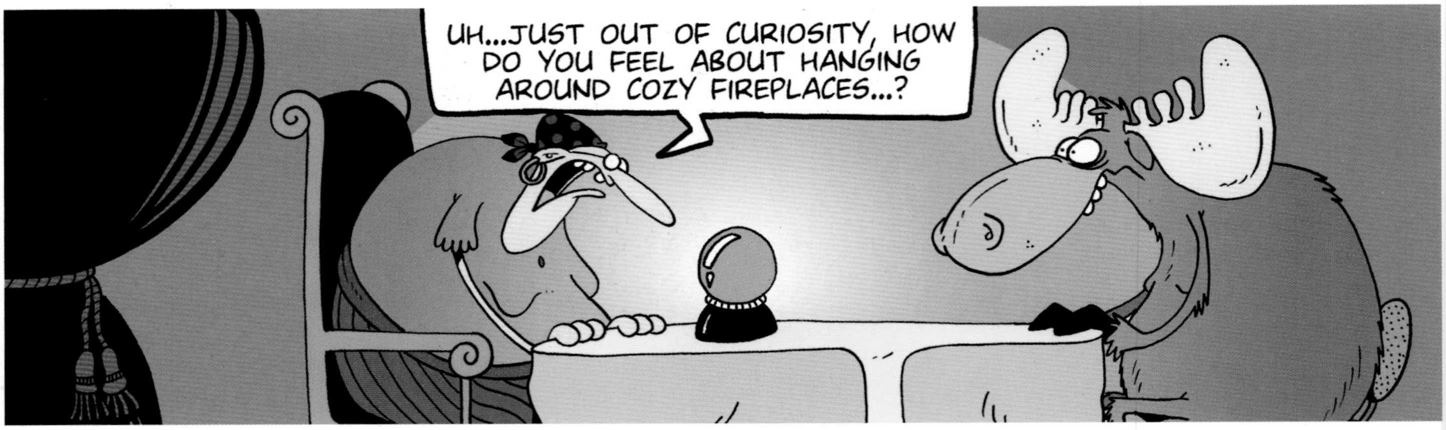
UH...JUST OUT OF CURIOSITY, HOW DO YOU FEEL ABOUT HANGING AROUND COZY FIREPLACES...?

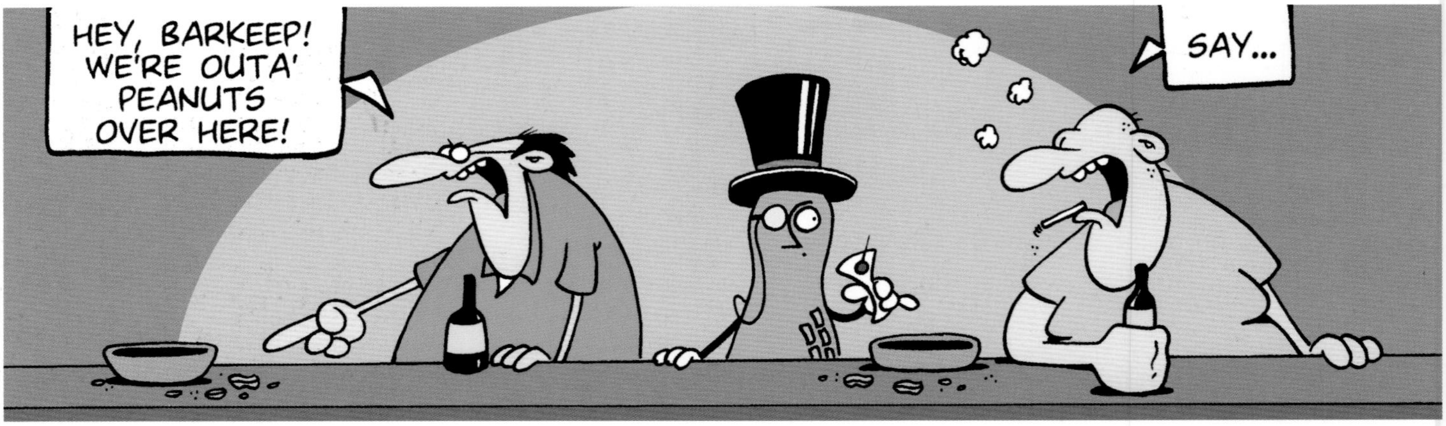
HEY, BARKEEP! WE'RE OUTA' PEANUTS OVER HERE!
SAY...

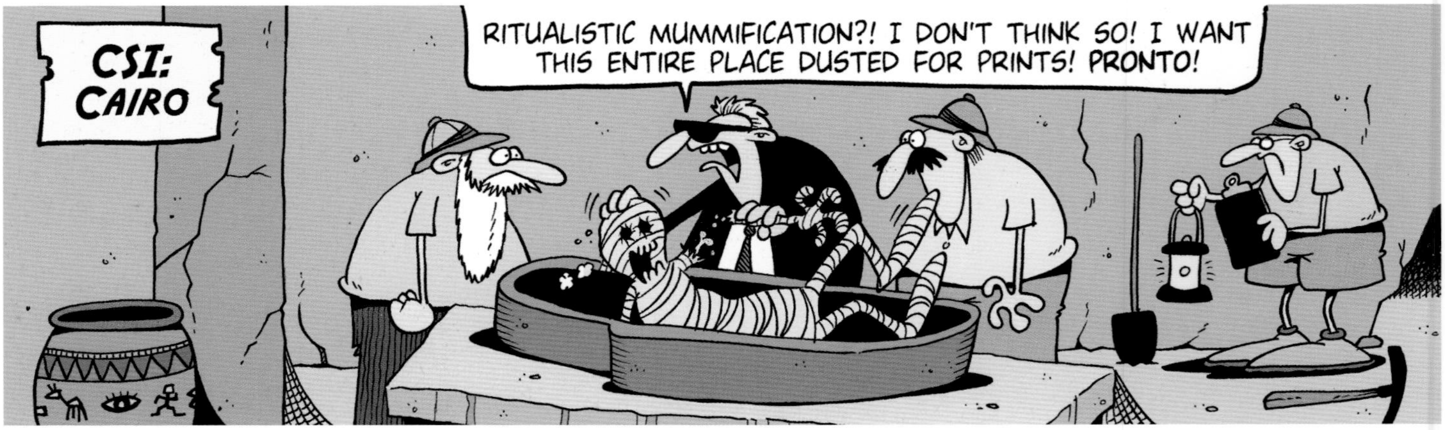
CSI: CAIRO
RITUALISTIC MUMMIFICATION?! I DON'T THINK SO! I WANT THIS ENTIRE PLACE DUSTED FOR PRINTS! PRONTO!

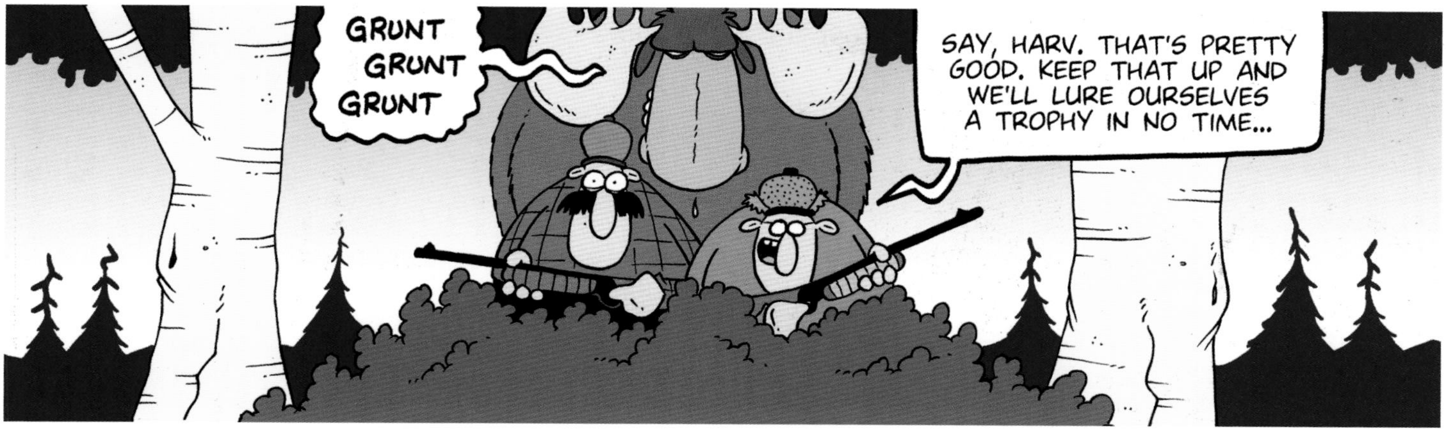
GRUNT GRUNT GRUNT
SAY, HARV. THAT'S PRETTY GOOD. KEEP THAT UP AND WE'LL LURE OURSELVES A TROPHY IN NO TIME...

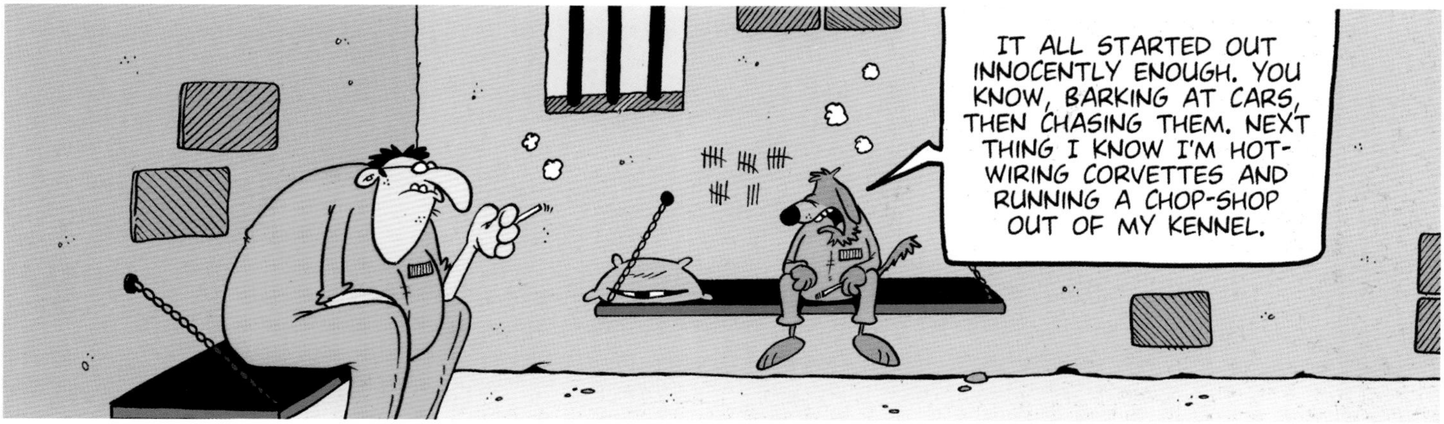
IT ALL STARTED OUT INNOCENTLY ENOUGH. YOU KNOW, BARKING AT CARS, THEN CHASING THEM. NEXT THING I KNOW I'M HOT-WIRING CORVETTES AND RUNNING A CHOP-SHOP OUT OF MY KENNEL.

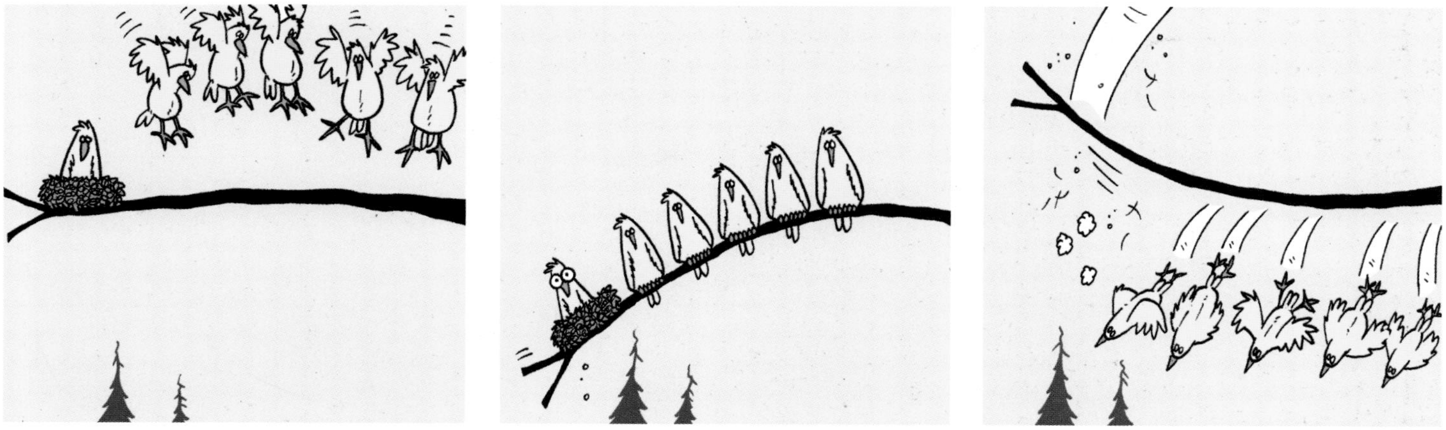

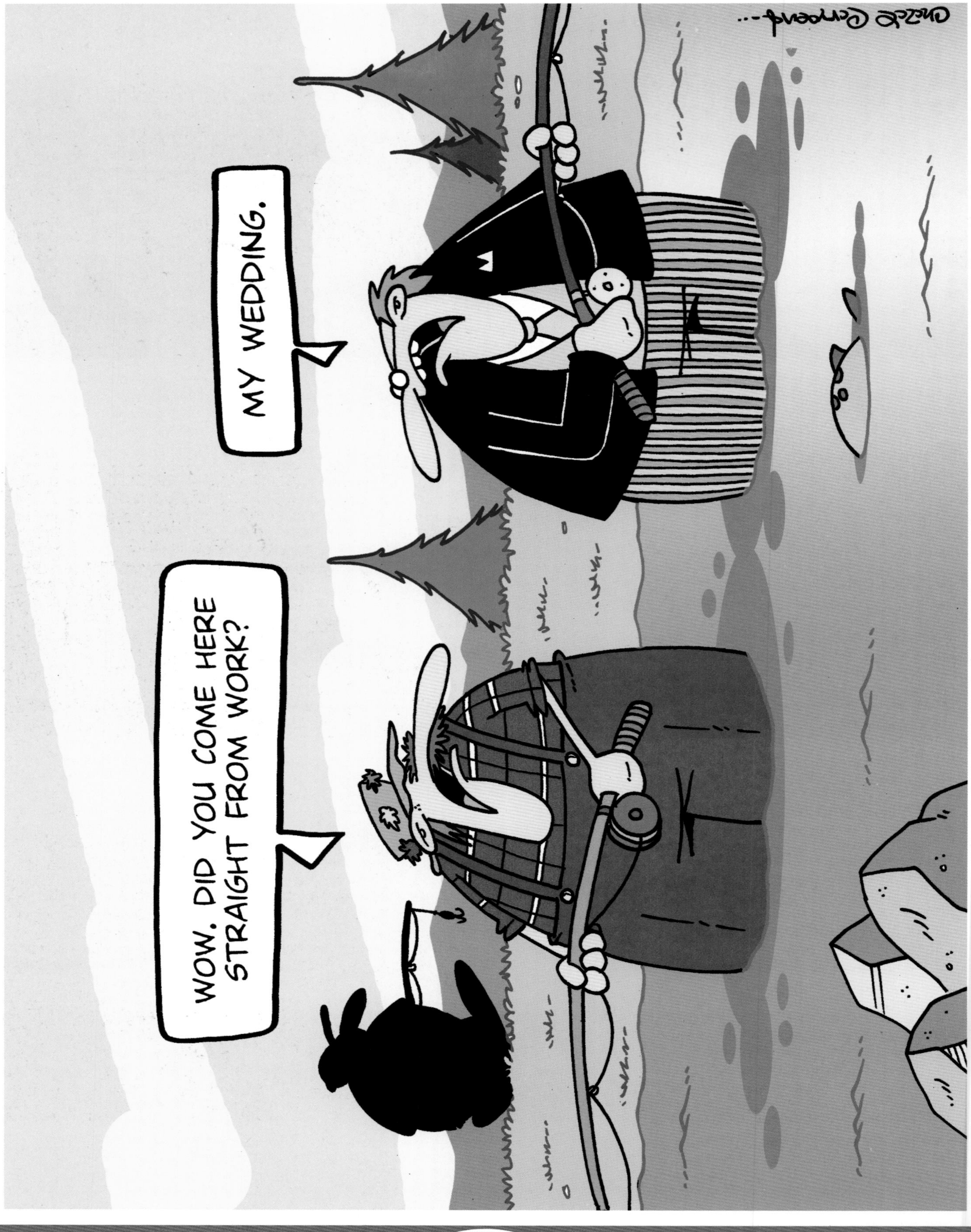
WOW. DID YOU COME HERE STRAIGHT FROM WORK?
MY WEDDING.

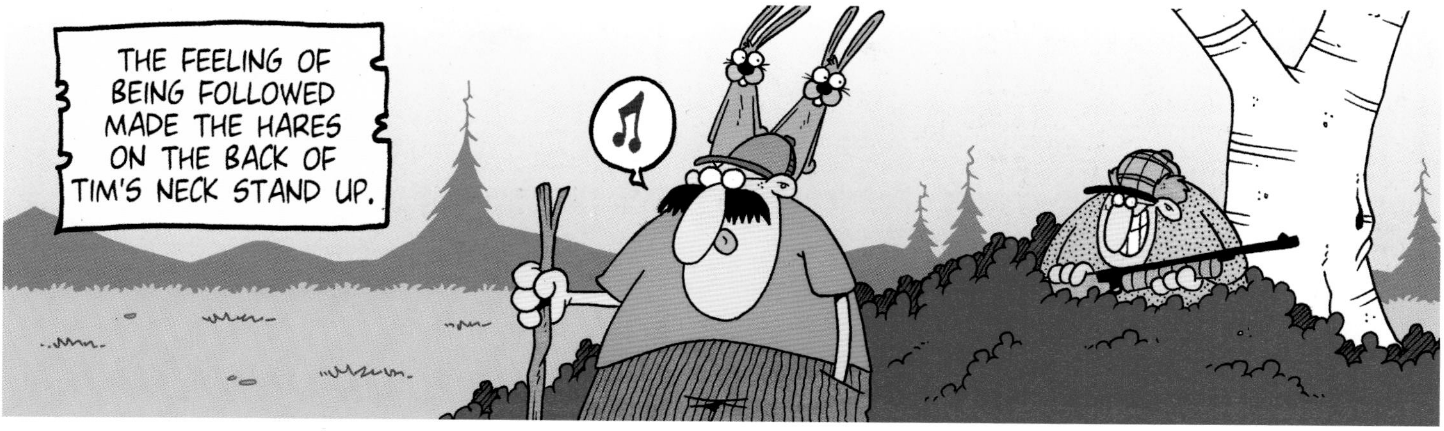
THE FEELING OF BEING FOLLOWED MADE THE HARES ON THE BACK OF TIM'S NECK STAND UP.

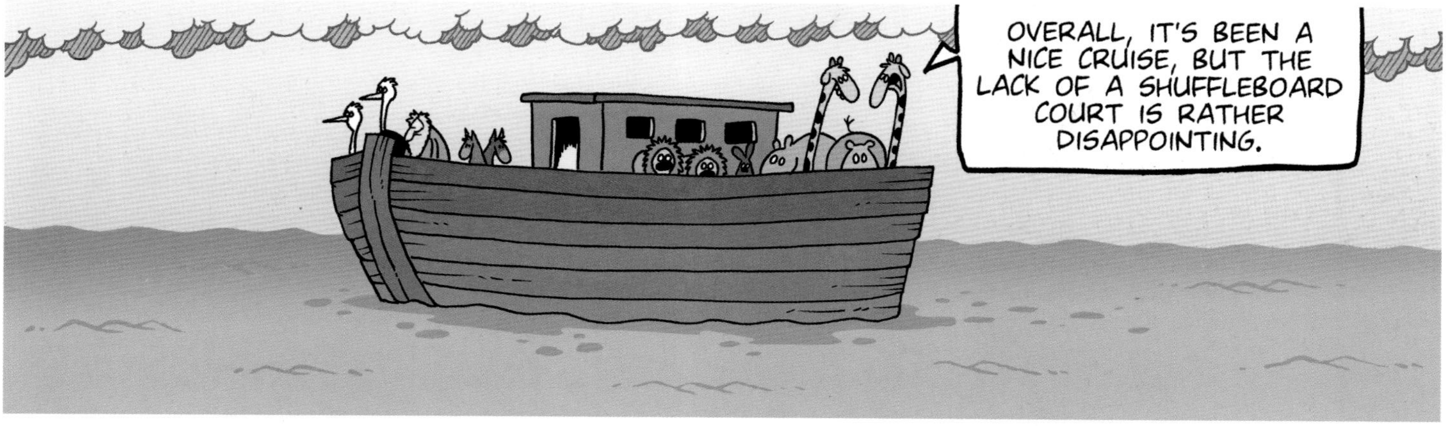
OVERALL, IT'S BEEN A NICE CRUISE, BUT THE LACK OF A SHUFFLEBOARD COURT IS RATHER DISAPPOINTING.

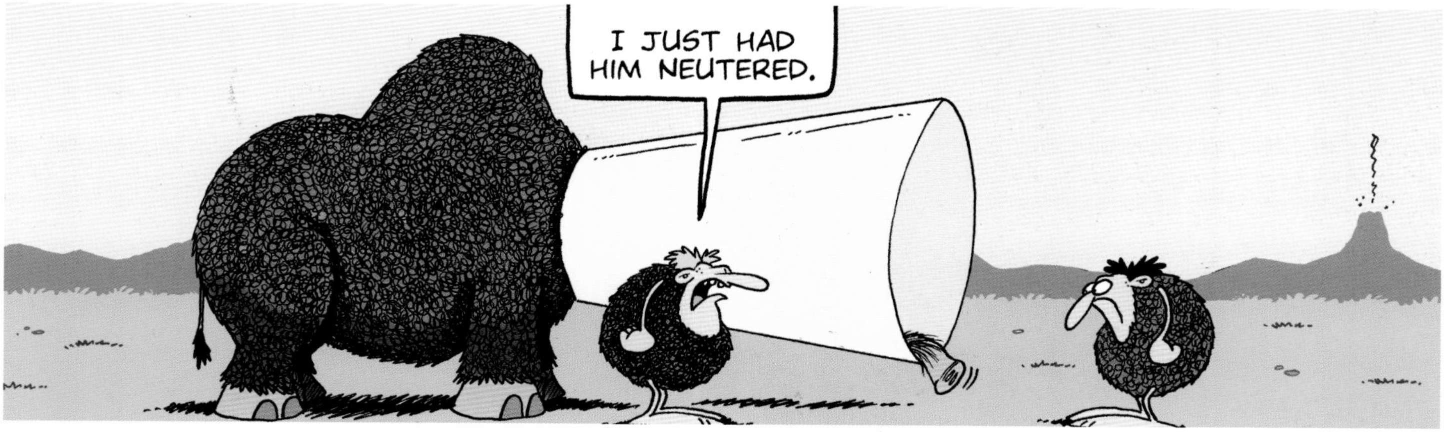
I JUST HAD HIM NEUTERED.

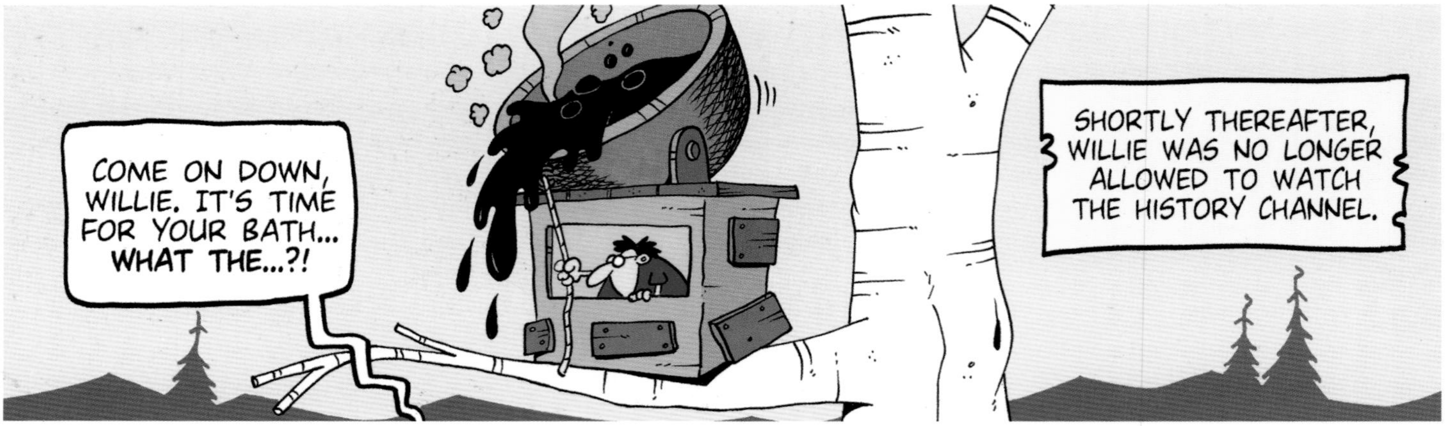
COME ON DOWN, WILLIE. IT'S TIME FOR YOUR BATH... WHAT THE...?!
SHORTLY THEREAFTER, WILLIE WAS NO LONGER ALLOWED TO WATCH THE HISTORY CHANNEL.

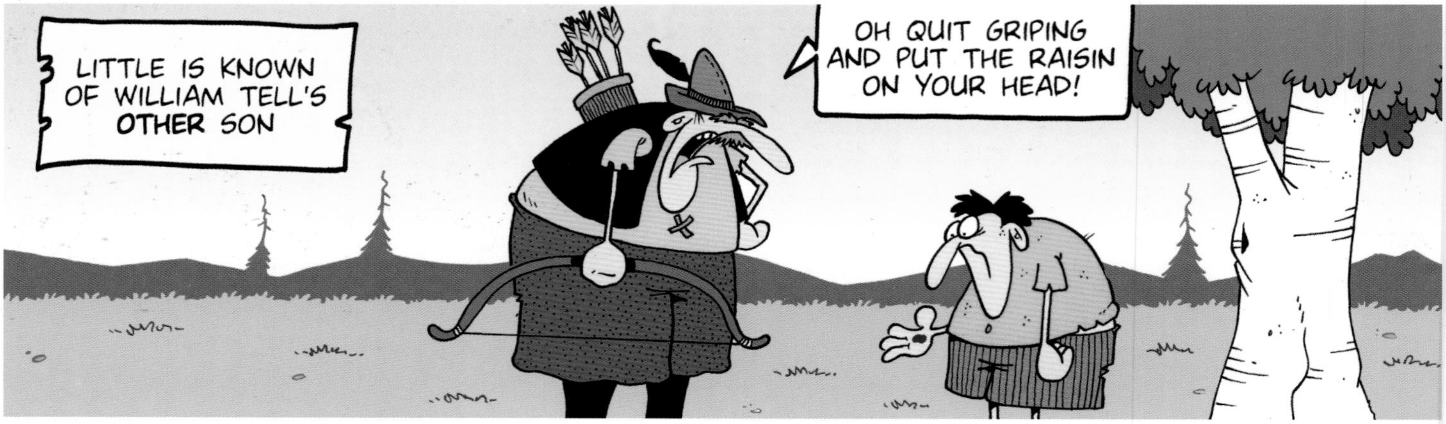
LITTLE IS KNOWN OF WILLIAM TELL'S OTHER SON
OH QUIT GRIPING AND PUT THE RAISIN ON YOUR HEAD!

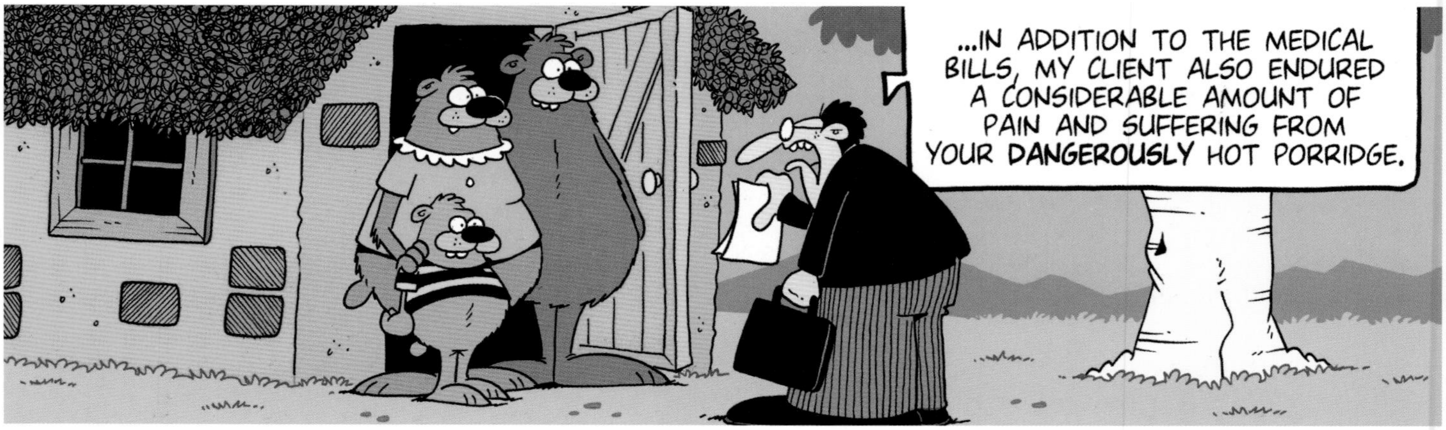
...IN ADDITION TO THE MEDICAL BILLS, MY CLIENT ALSO ENDURED A CONSIDERABLE AMOUNT OF PAIN AND SUFFERING FROM YOUR DANGEROUSLY HOT PORRIDGE.

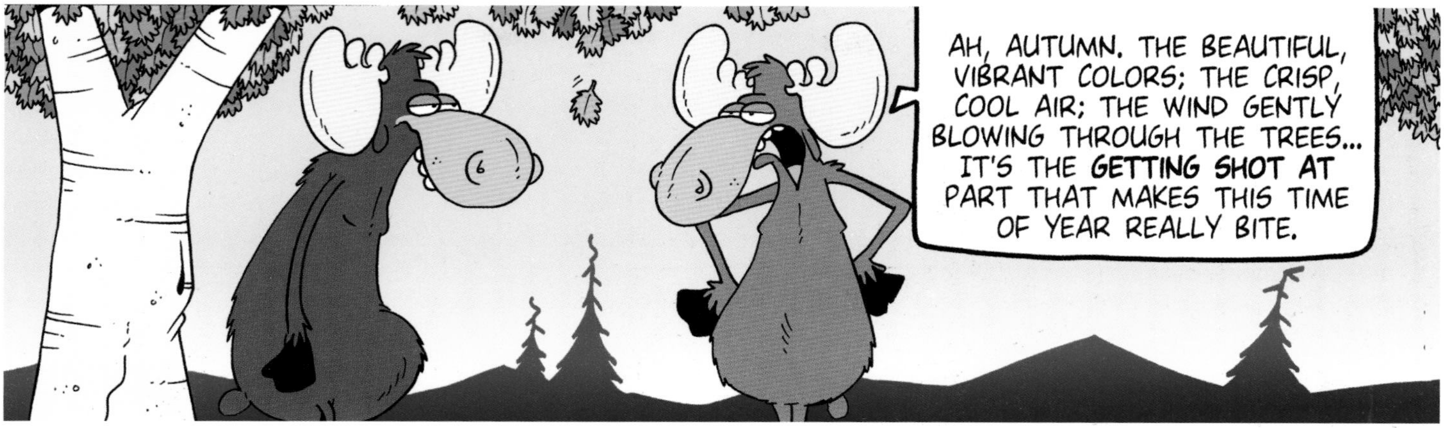
AH, AUTUMN. THE BEAUTIFUL, VIBRANT COLORS; THE CRISP, COOL AIR; THE WIND GENTLY BLOWING THROUGH THE TREES... IT'S THE GETTING SHOT AT PART THAT MAKES THIS TIME OF YEAR REALLY BITE.

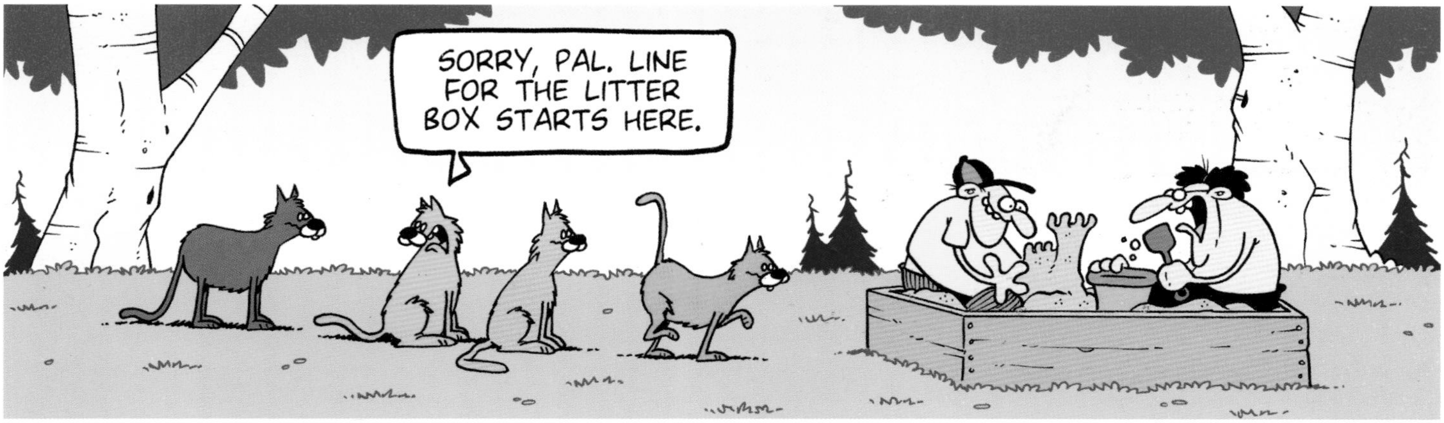
SORRY, PAL. LINE FOR THE LITTER BOX STARTS HERE.

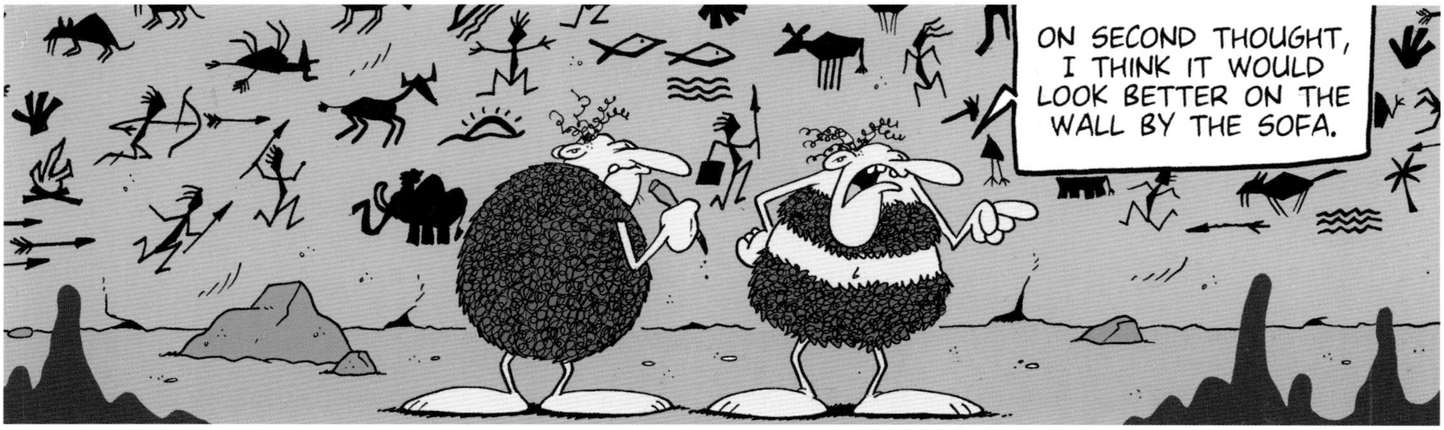
ON SECOND THOUGHT, I THINK IT WOULD LOOK BETTER ON THE WALL BY THE SOFA.

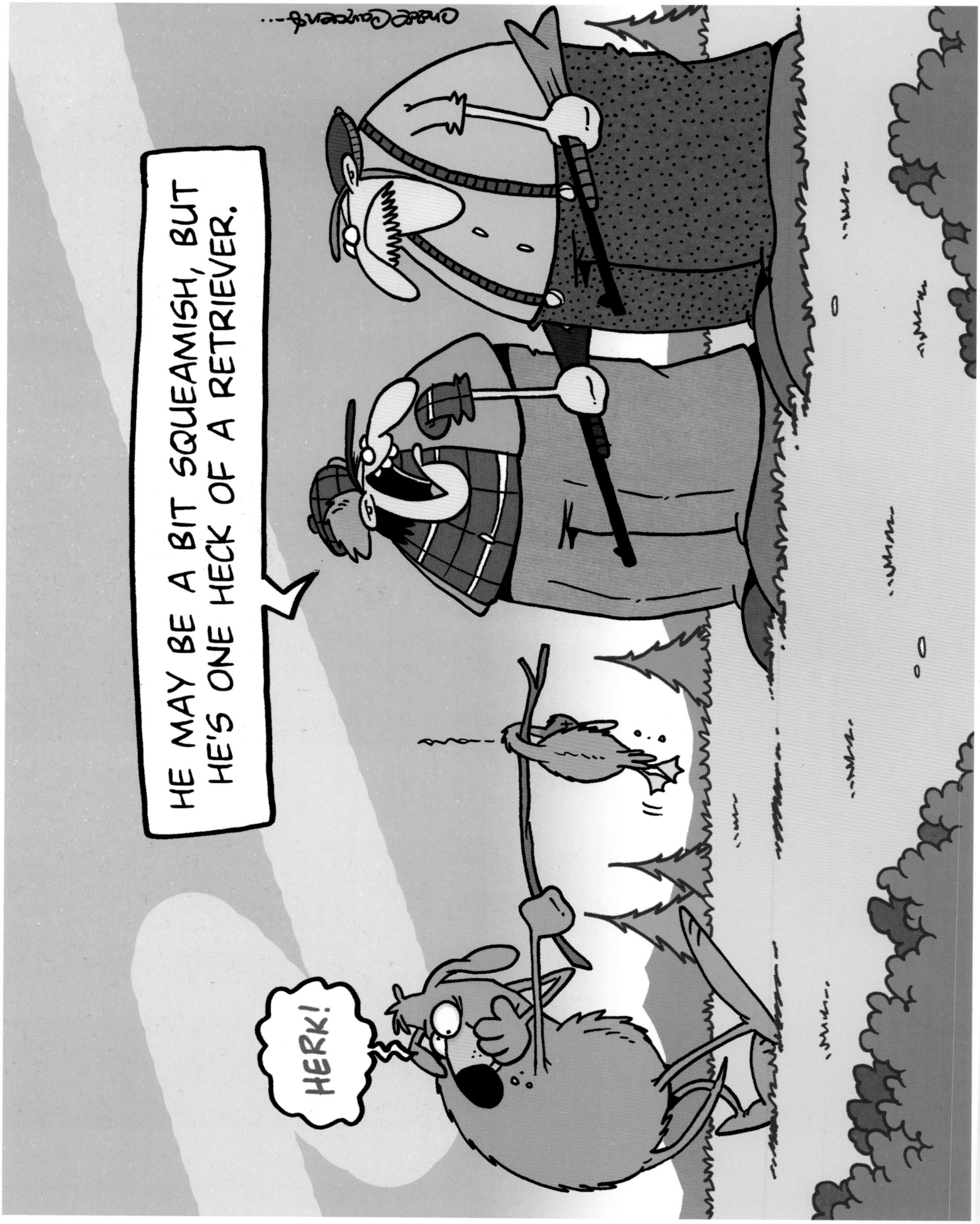
HE MAY BE A BIT SQUEAMISH, BUT HE'S ONE HECK OF A RETRIEVER.
HERK!

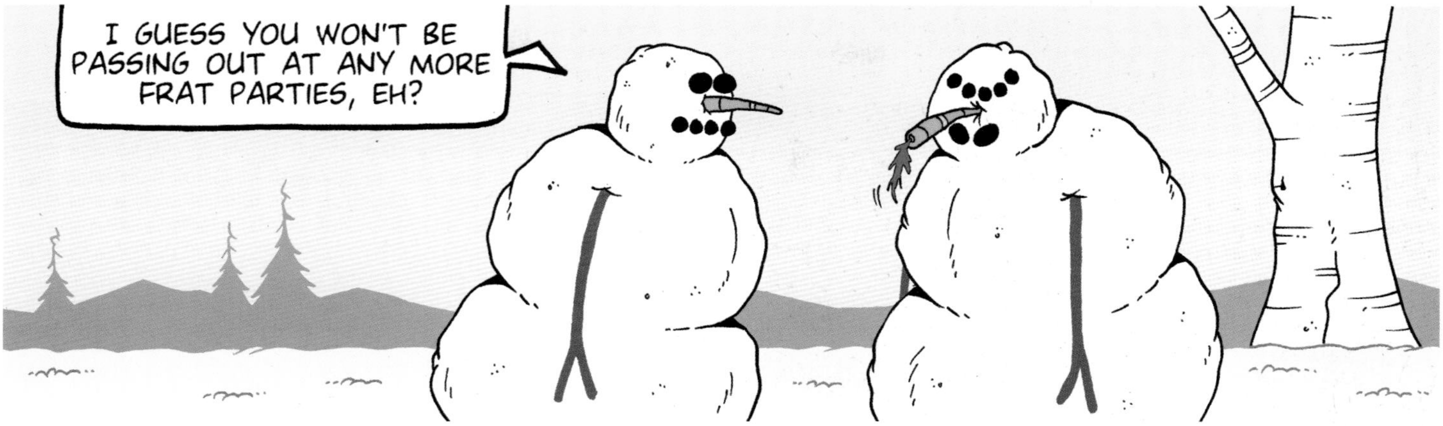
I GUESS YOU WON'T BE PASSING OUT AT ANY MORE FRAT PARTIES, EH?

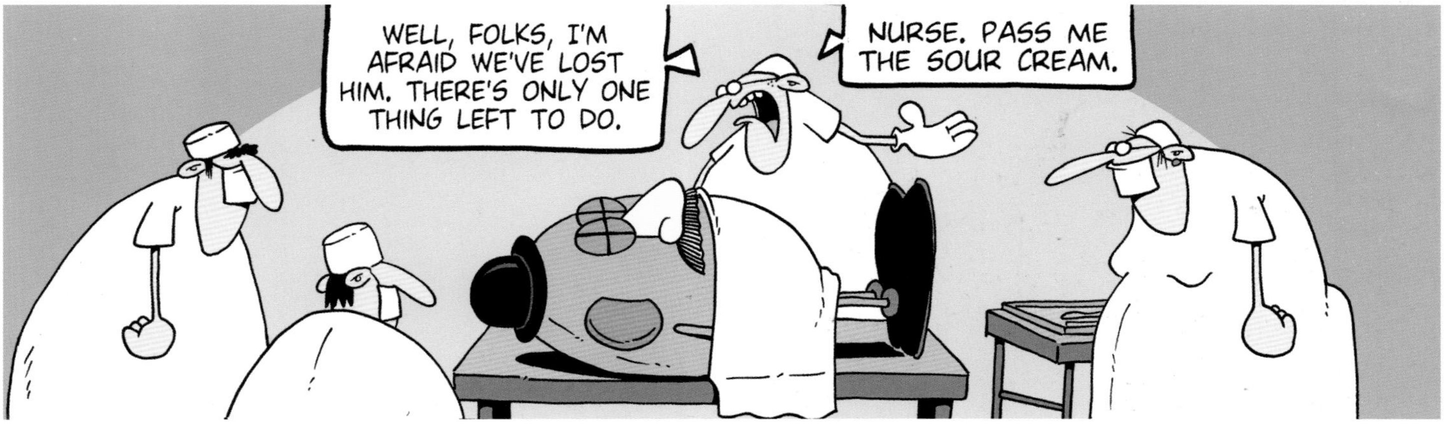
WELL, FOLKS, I'M AFRAID WE'VE LOST HIM. THERE'S ONLY ONE THING LEFT TO DO.
NURSE. PASS ME THE SOUR CREAM.

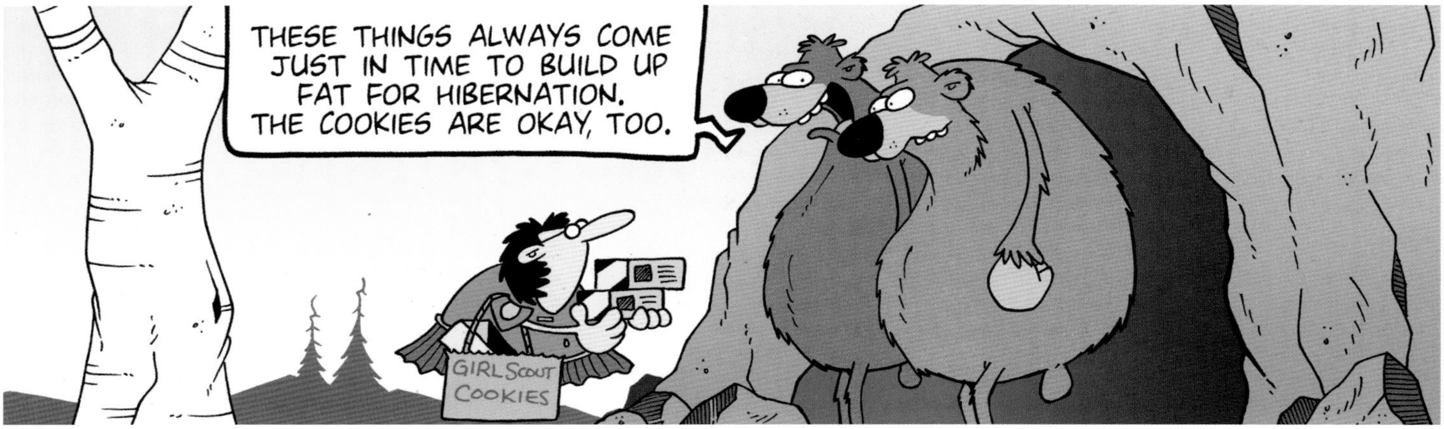
THESE THINGS ALWAYS COME JUST IN TIME TO BUILD UP FAT FOR HIBERNATION. THE COOKIES ARE OKAY, TOO.
GIRL SCOUT COOKIES

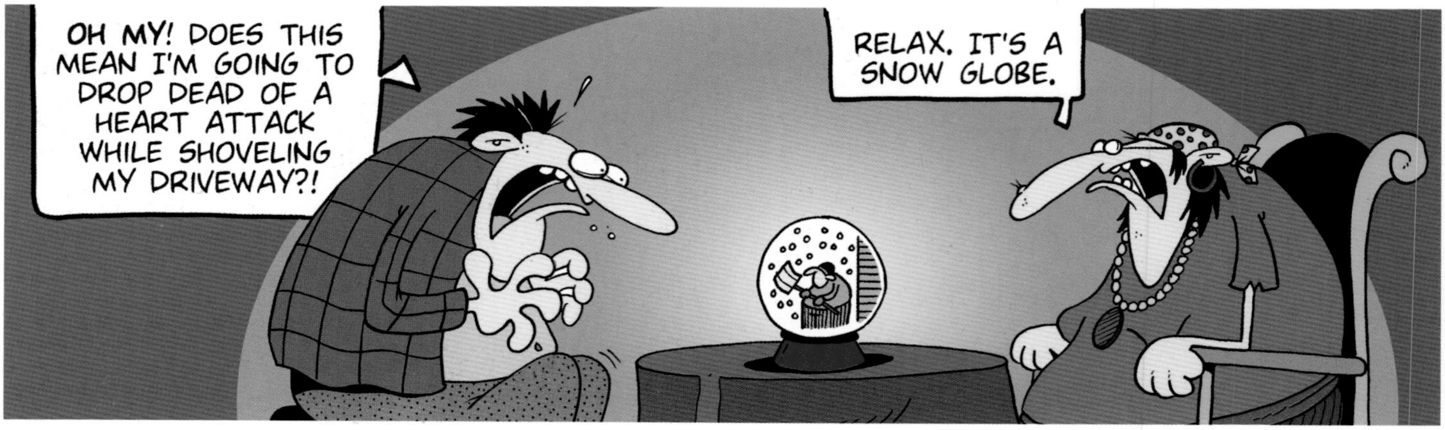
OH MY! DOES THIS MEAN I'M GOING TO DROP DEAD OF A HEART ATTACK WHILE SHOVELING MY DRIVEWAY?!
RELAX. IT'S A SNOW GLOBE.

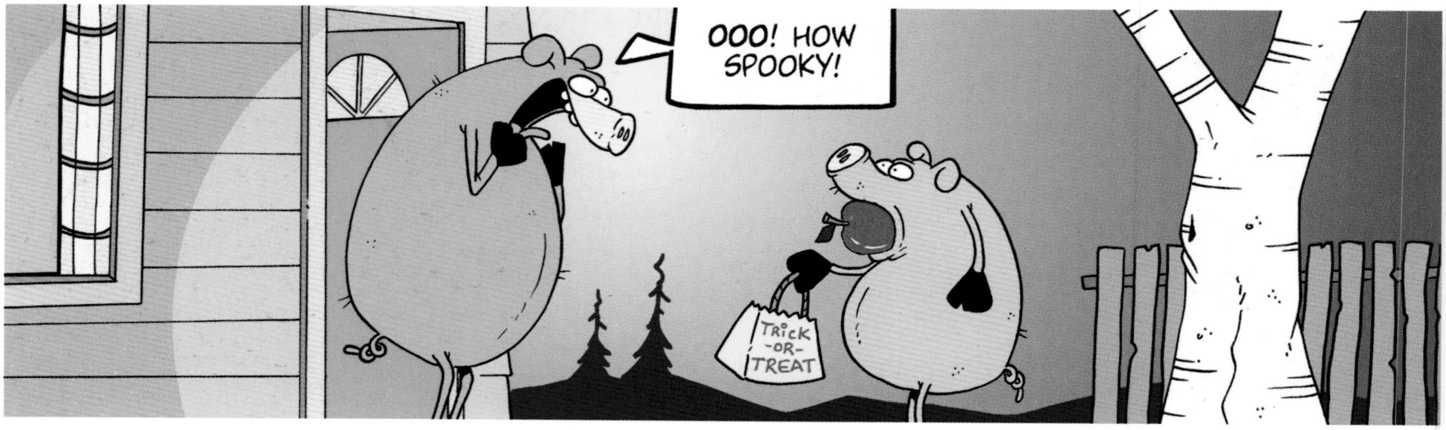
OOO! HOW SPOOKY!
TRICK -OR- TREAT

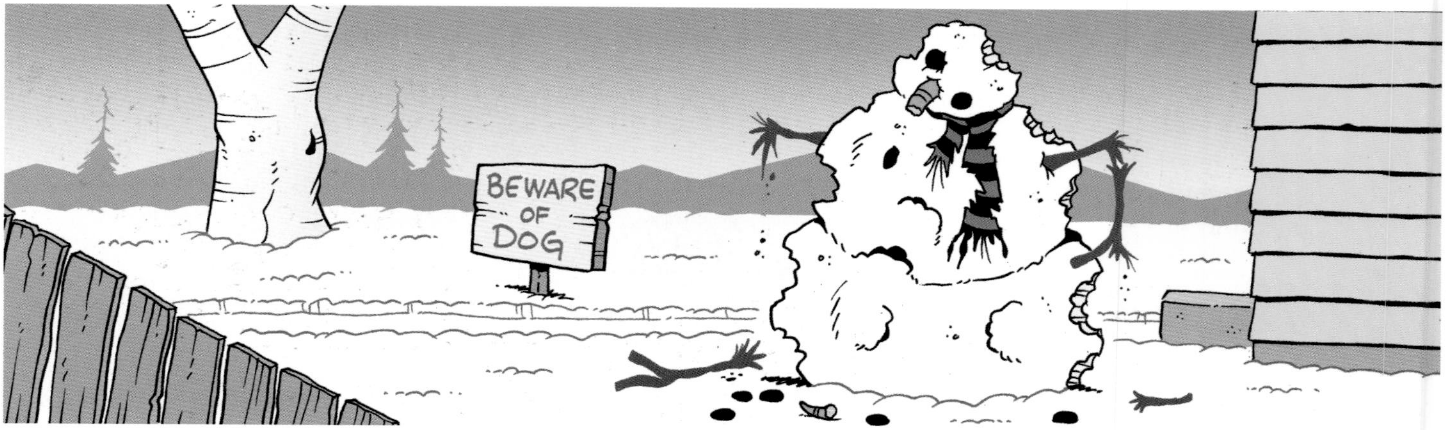
BEWARE OF DOG

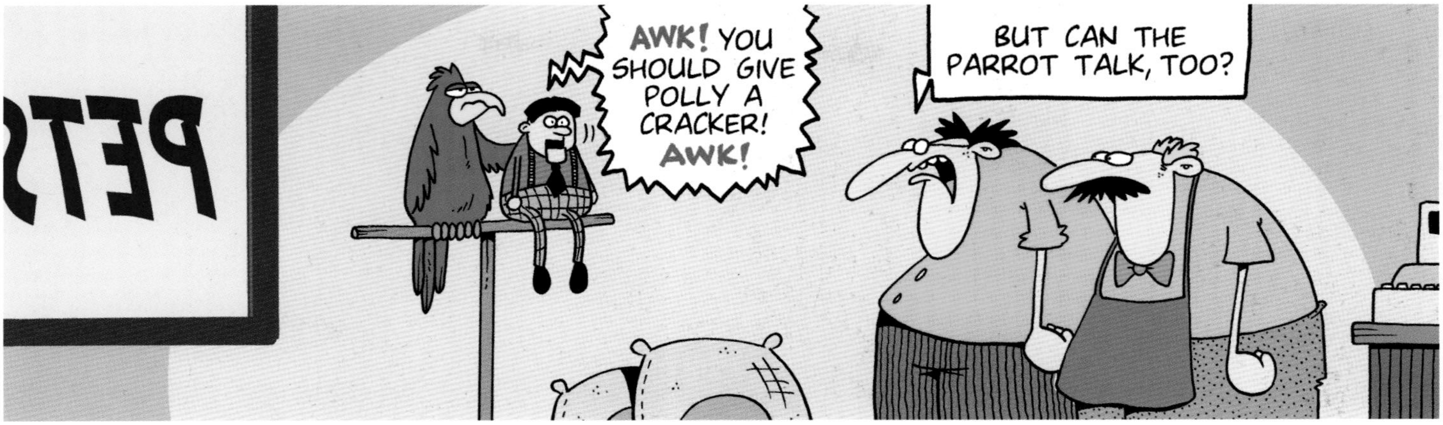
AWK! YOU SHOULD GIVE POLLY A CRACKER! AWK!
BUT CAN THE PARROT TALK, TOO?

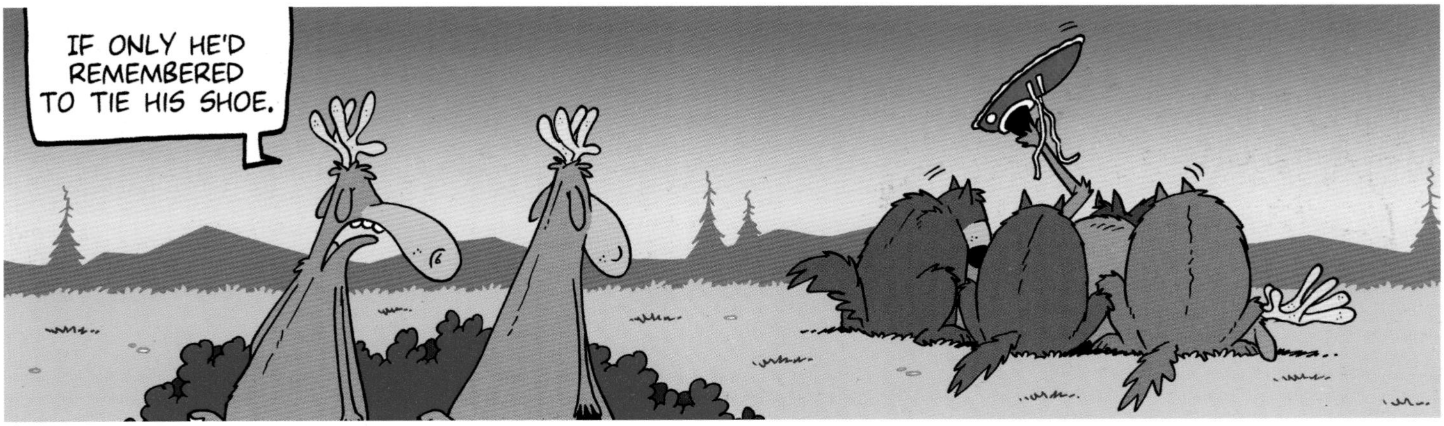
IF ONLY HE'D REMEMBERED TO TIE HIS SHOE.

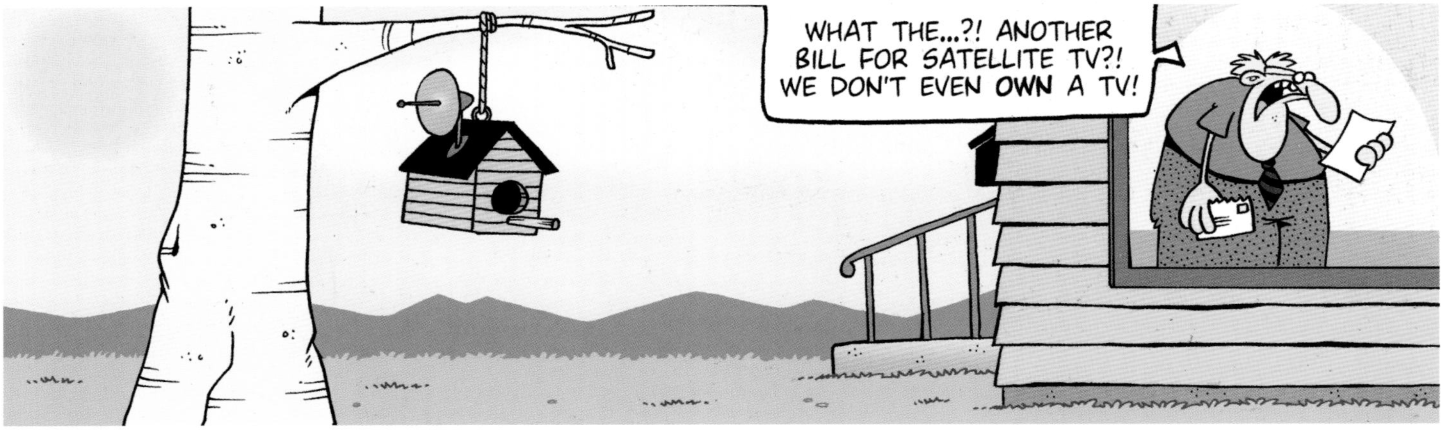
WHAT THE...?! ANOTHER BILL FOR SATELLITE TV?! WE DON'T EVEN OWN A TV!

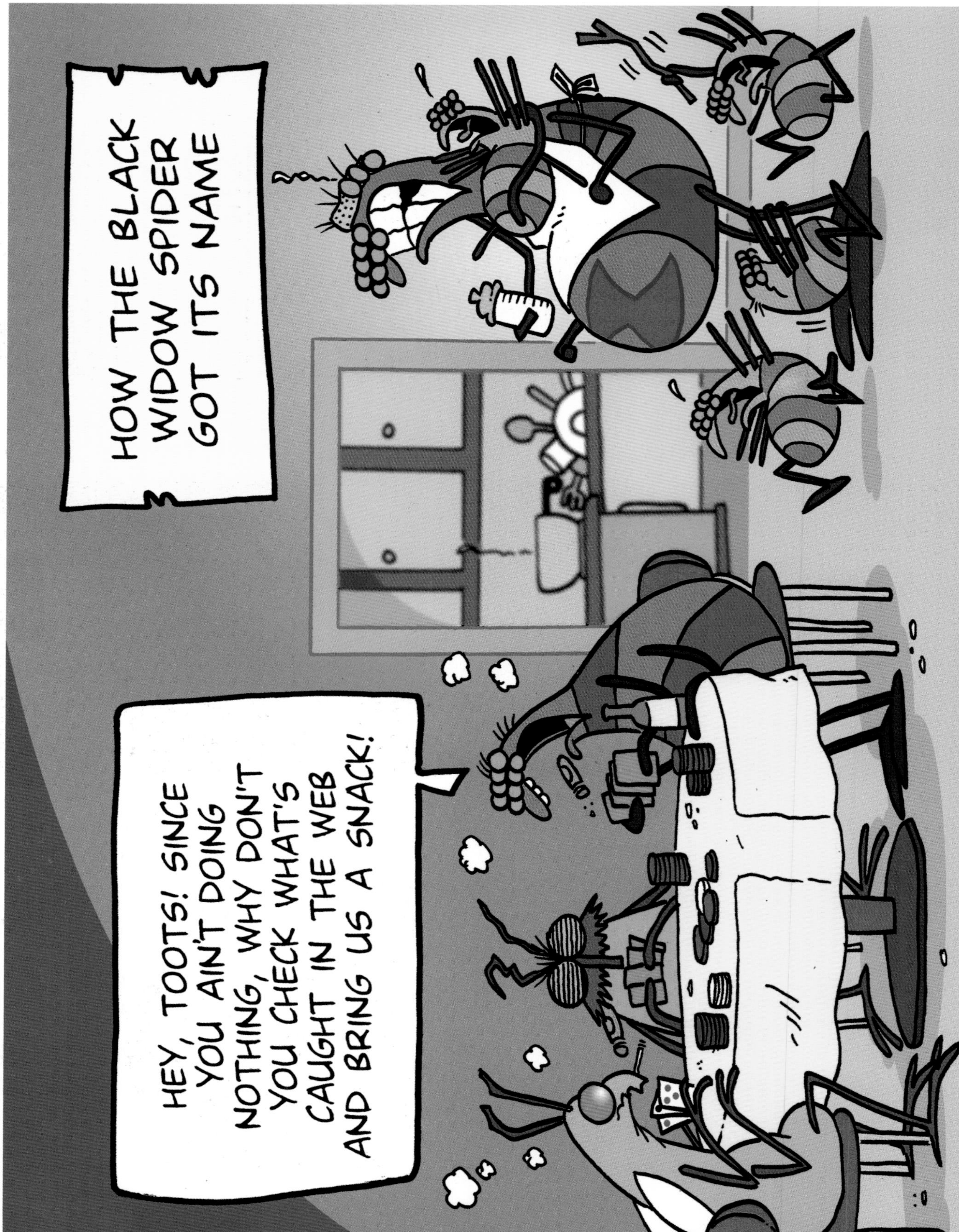
HOW THE BLACK WIDOW SPIDER GOT ITS NAME
HEY, TOOTS! SINCE YOU AIN'T DOING NOTHING, WHY DON'T YOU CHECK WHAT'S CAUGHT IN THE WEB AND BRING US A SNACK!

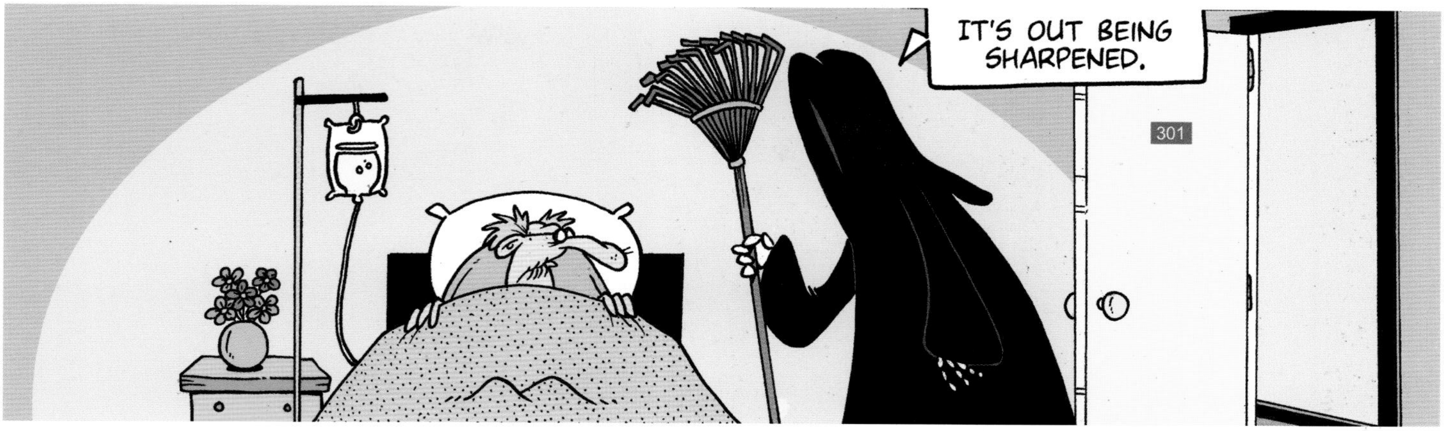
IT'S OUT BEING SHARPENED.
301

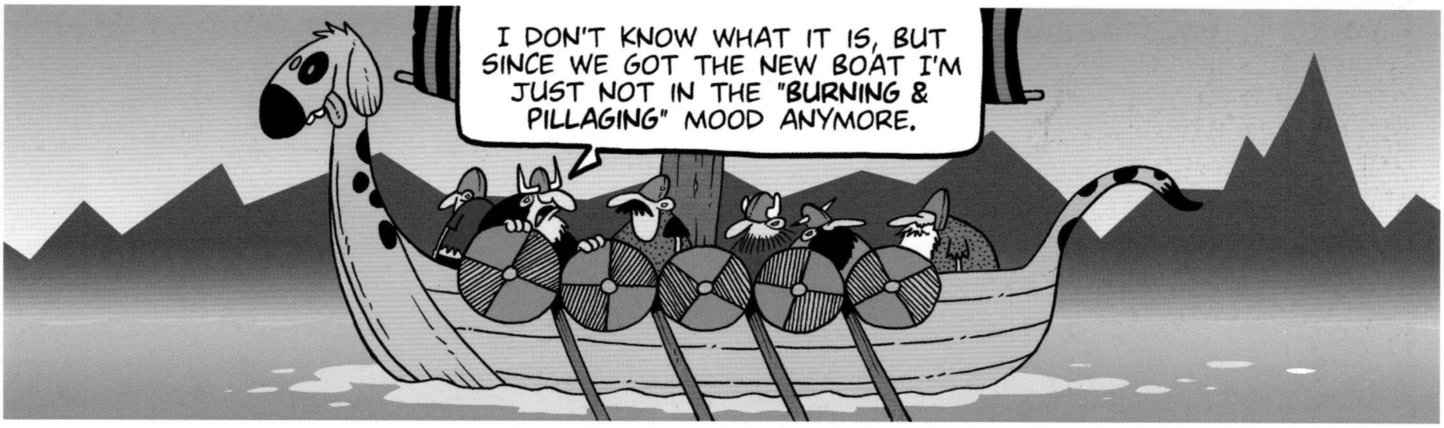
I DON'T KNOW WHAT IT IS, BUT SINCE WE GOT THE NEW BOAT I'M JUST NOT IN THE "BURNING & PILLAGING" MOOD ANYMORE.

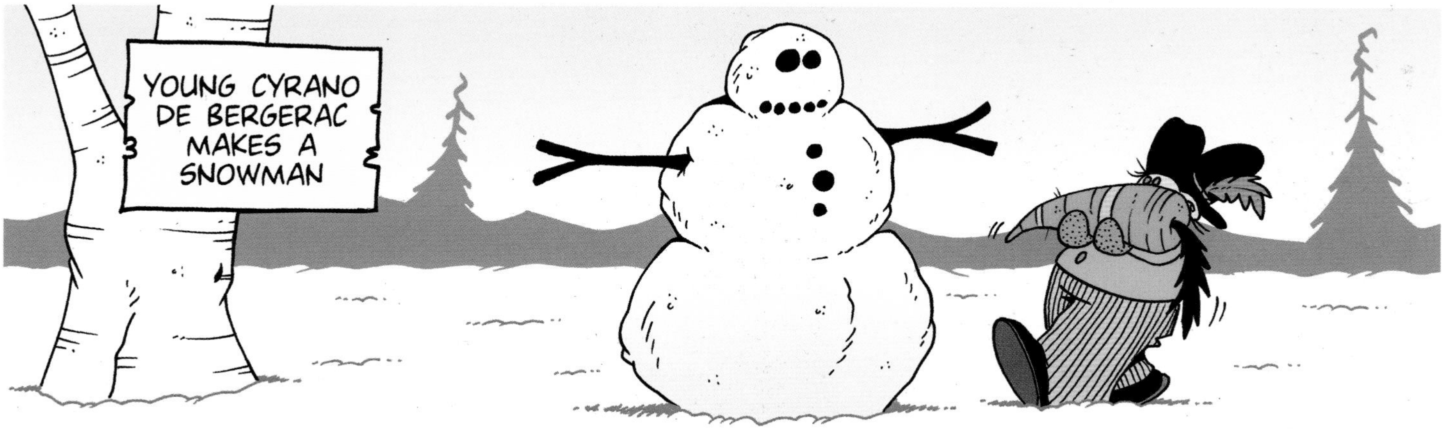
YOUNG CYRANO DE BERGERAC MAKES A SNOWMAN

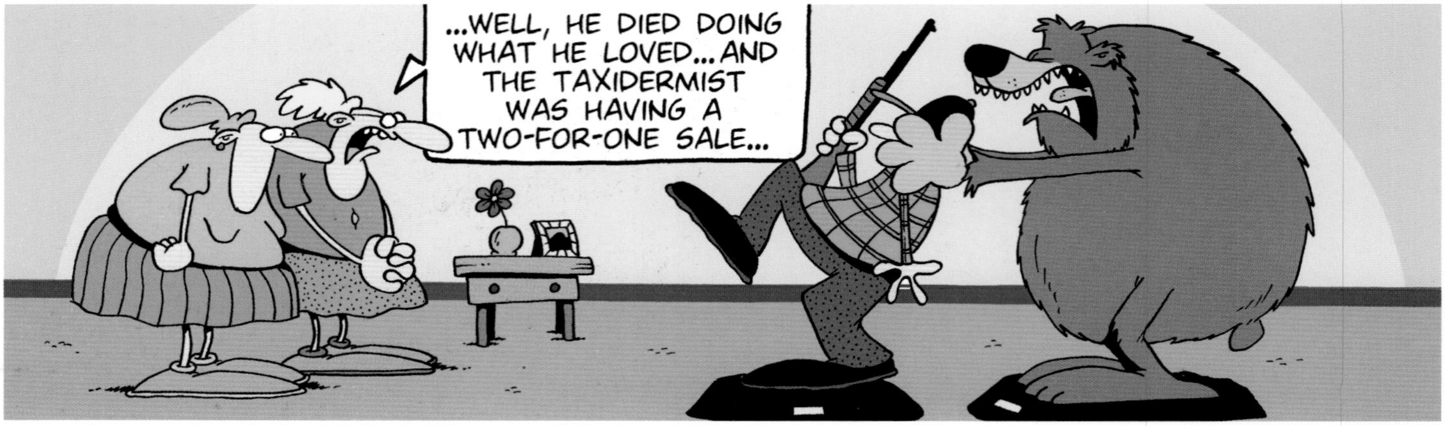
...WELL, HE DIED DOING WHAT HE LOVED...AND THE TAXIDERMIST WAS HAVING A TWO-FOR-ONE SALE...

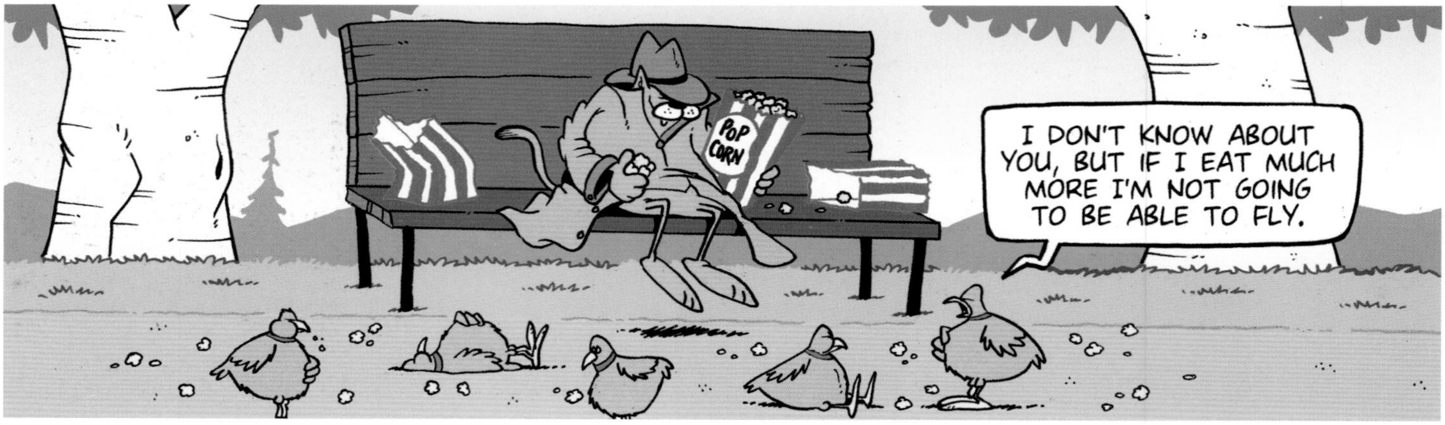
POP CORN
I DON'T KNOW ABOUT YOU, BUT IF I EAT MUCH MORE I'M NOT GOING TO BE ABLE TO FLY.

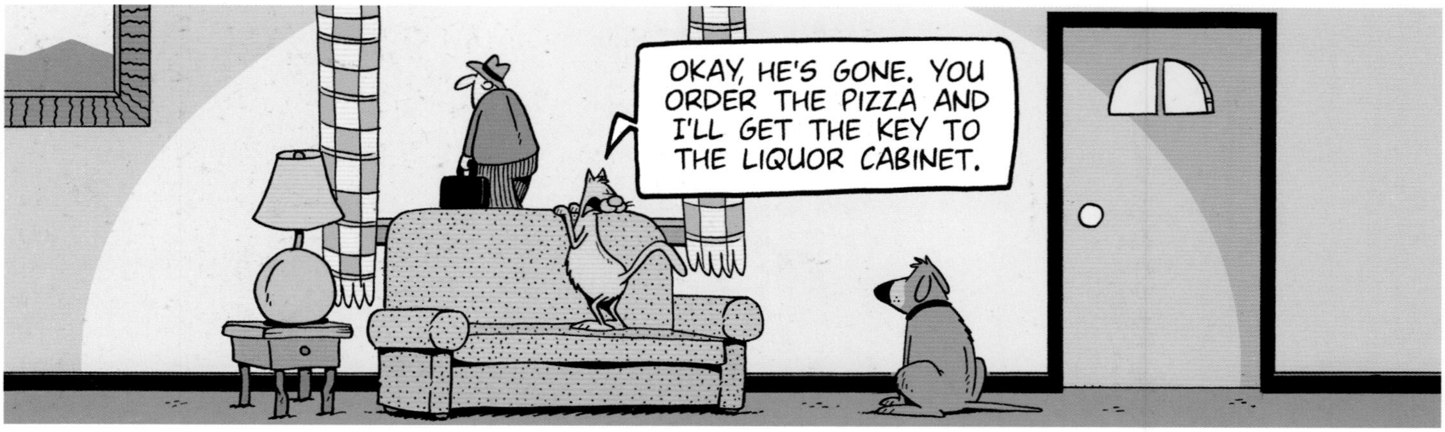
OKAY, HE'S GONE. YOU ORDER THE PIZZA AND I'LL GET THE KEY TO THE LIQUOR CABINET.

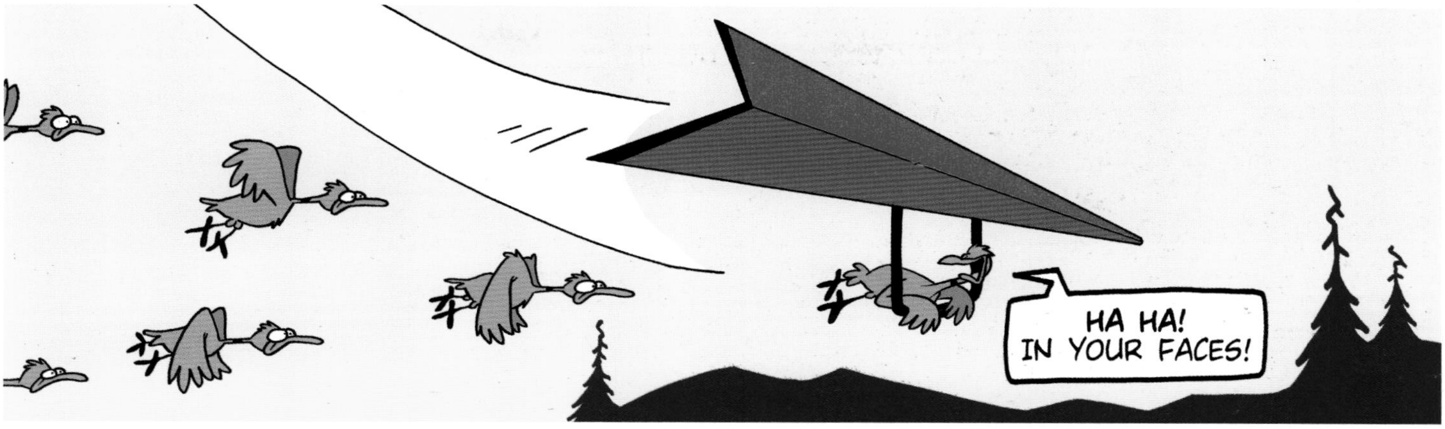
HA HA!
IN YOUR FACES!

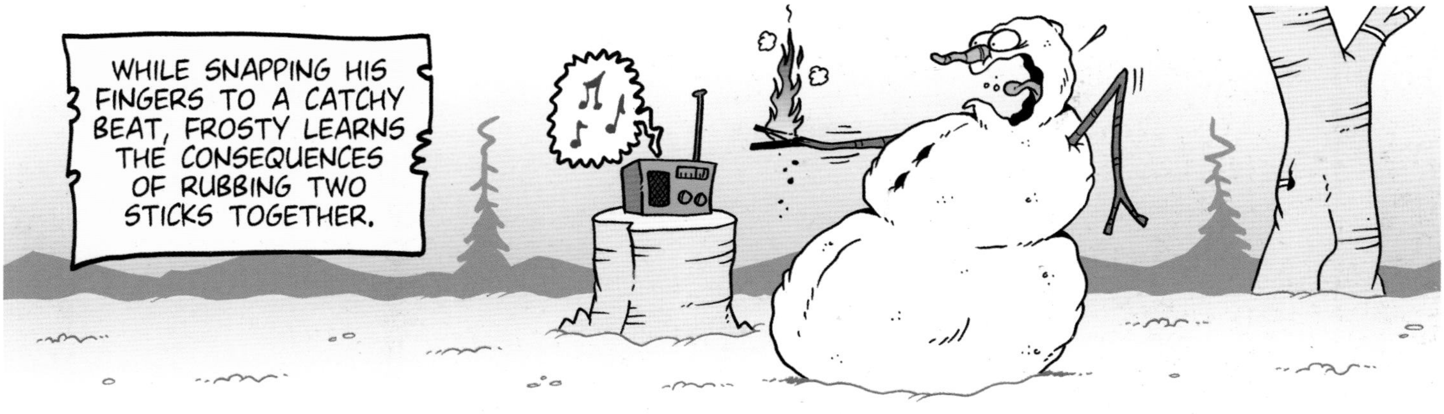
WHILE SNAPPING HIS FINGERS TO A CATCHY BEAT, FROSTY LEARNS THE CONSEQUENCES OF RUBBING TWO STICKS TOGETHER.

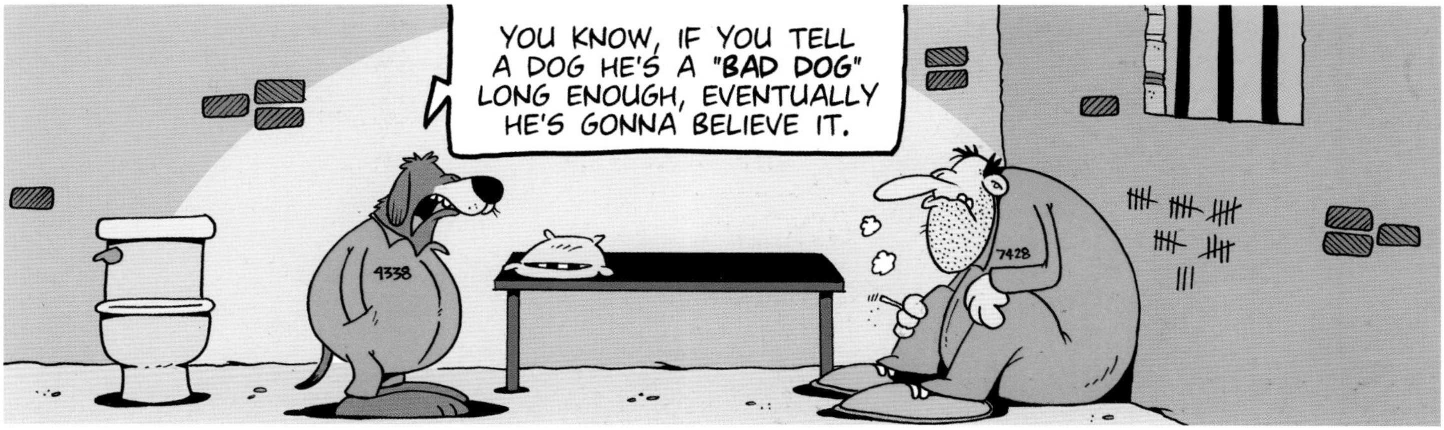
YOU KNOW, IF YOU TELL A DOG HE'S A "BAD DOG" LONG ENOUGH, EVENTUALLY HE'S GONNA BELIEVE IT.
4338
7428

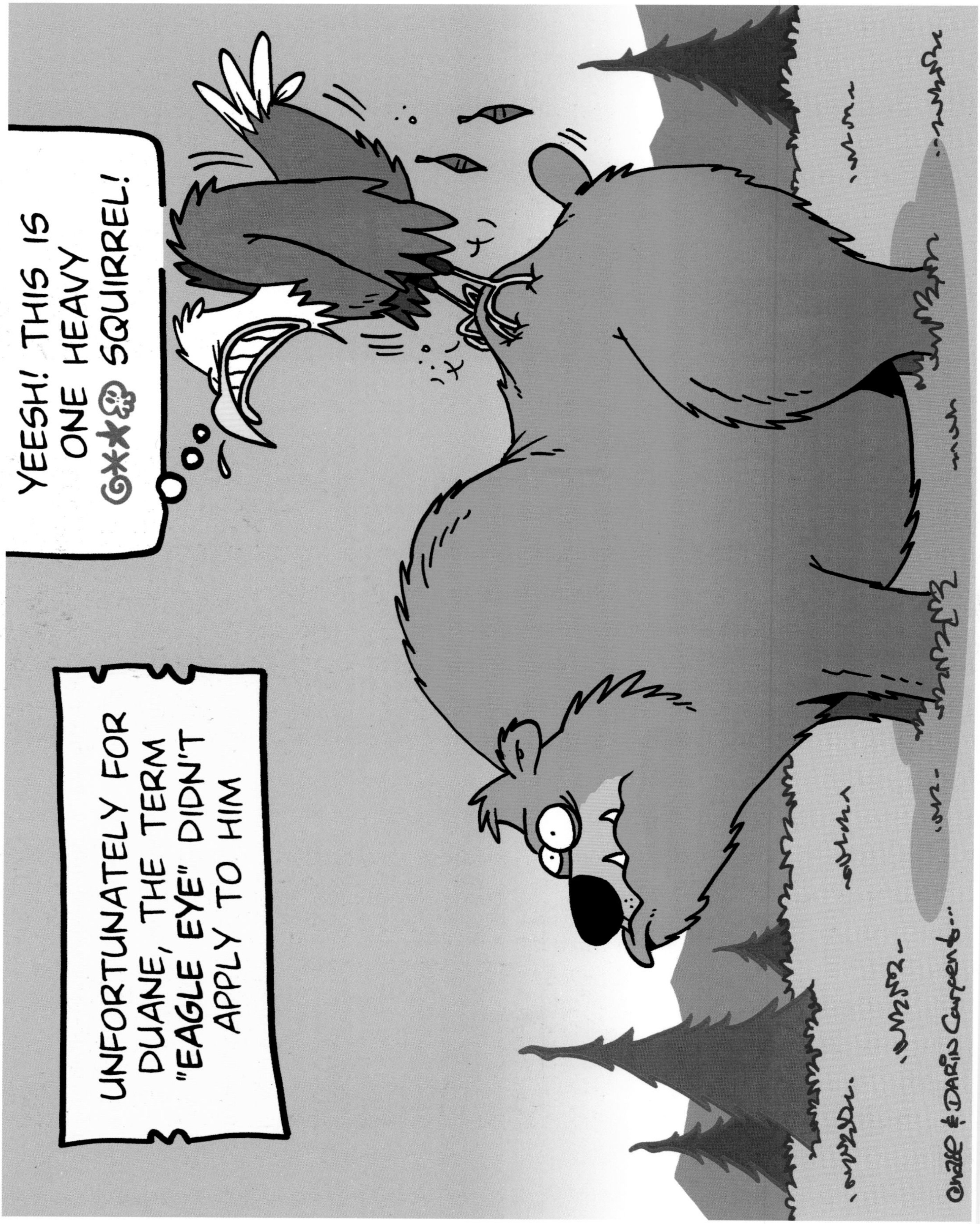
UNFORTUNATELY FOR DUANE, THE TERM "EAGLE EYE" DIDN'T APPLY TO HIM
YEESH! THIS IS ONE HEAVY @*★☠ SQUIRREL!

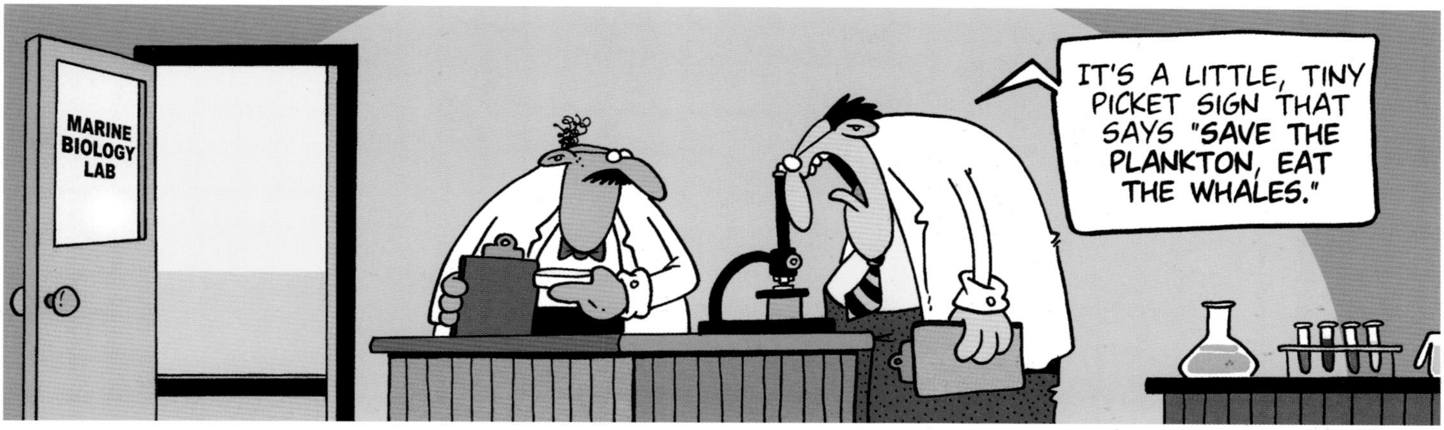
MARINE BIOLOGY LAB
IT'S A LITTLE, TINY PICKET SIGN THAT SAYS "SAVE THE PLANKTON, EAT THE WHALES."

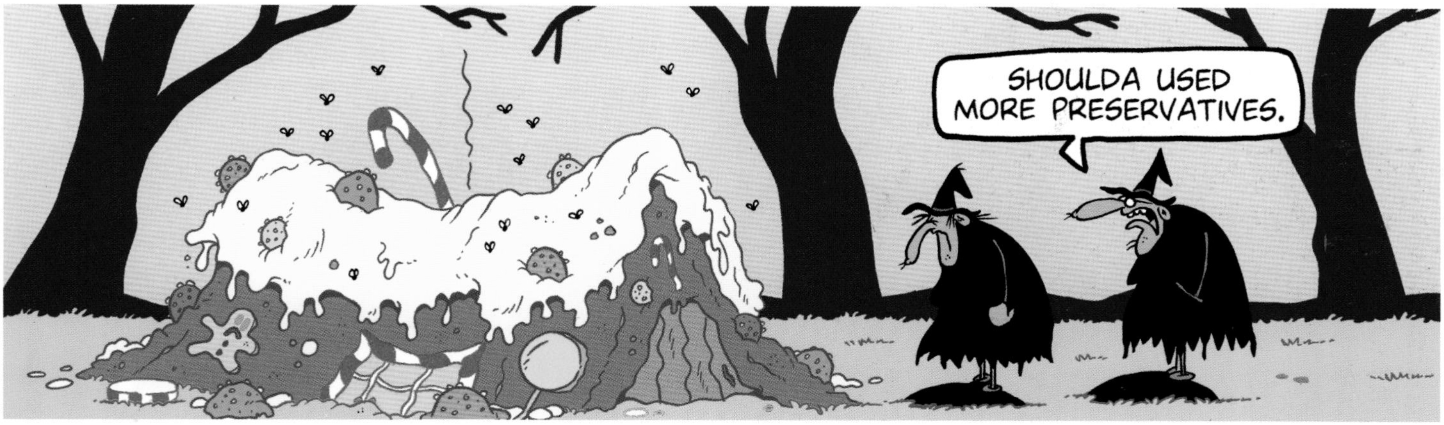
SHOULDA USED MORE PRESERVATIVES.

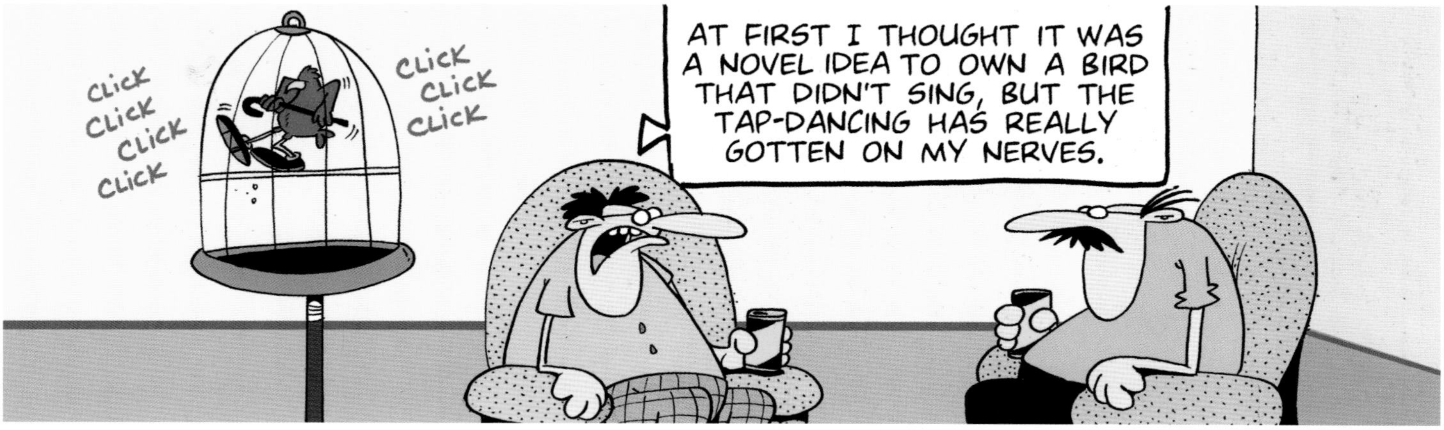
CLICK CLICK CLICK CLICK CLICK
CLICK CLICK CLICK
AT FIRST I THOUGHT IT WAS A NOVEL IDEA TO OWN A BIRD THAT DIDN'T SING, BUT THE TAP-DANCING HAS REALLY GOTTEN ON MY NERVES.

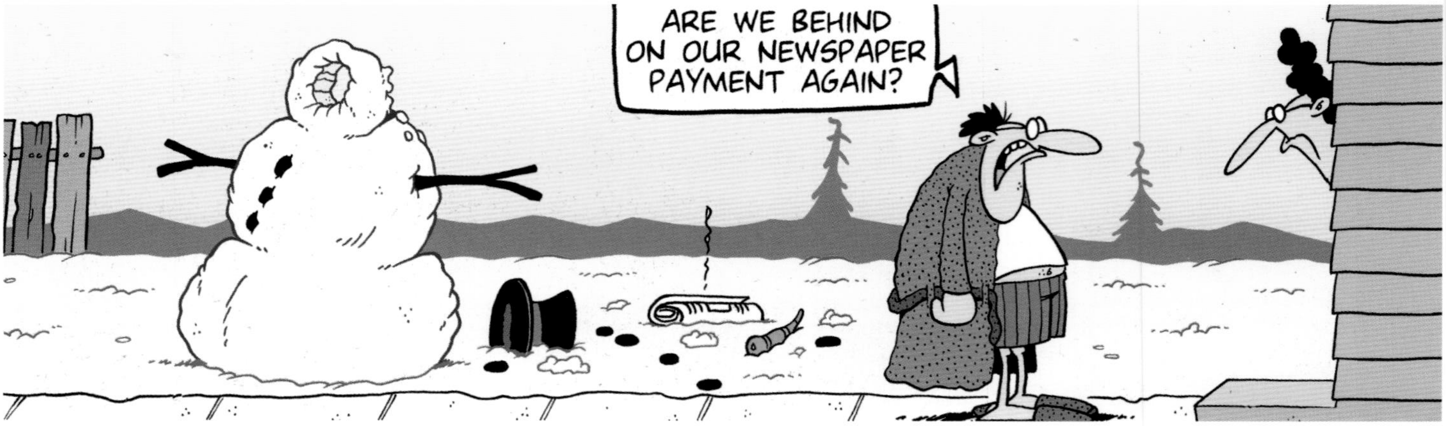
ARE WE BEHIND ON OUR NEWSPAPER PAYMENT AGAIN?

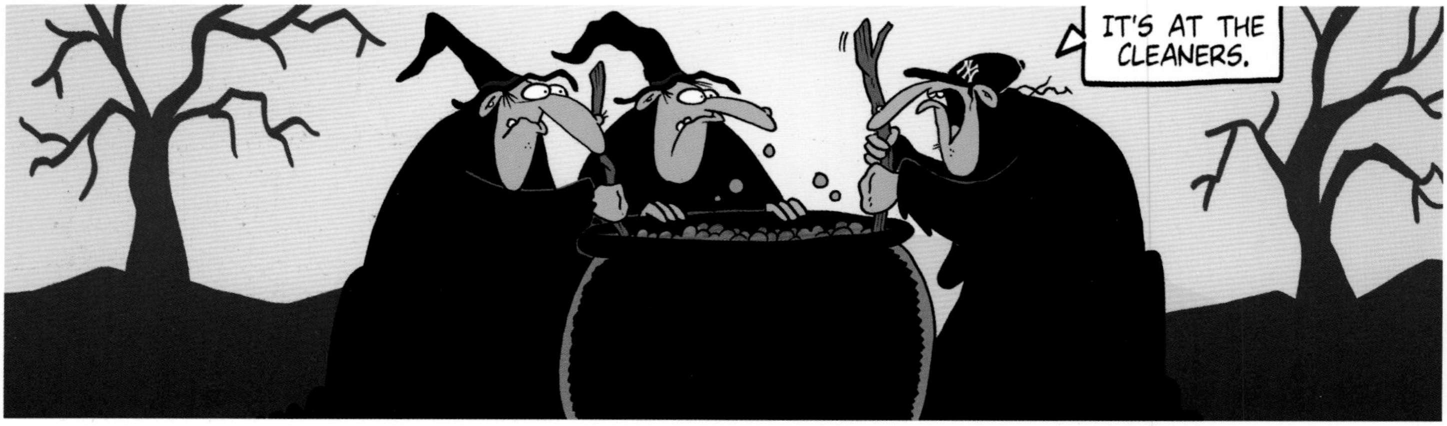
IT'S AT THE CLEANERS.

THIS STRIP IS BASED ON AN IDEA FROM:

ROBERT DUCKETT ANCHORAGE, AK

DO YOU HAVE AN IDEA THAT WOULD MAKE A GREAT COMIC STRIP?

SEND IT TO:
tundracomics.com

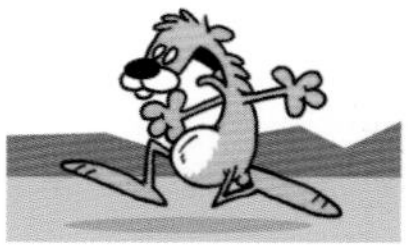

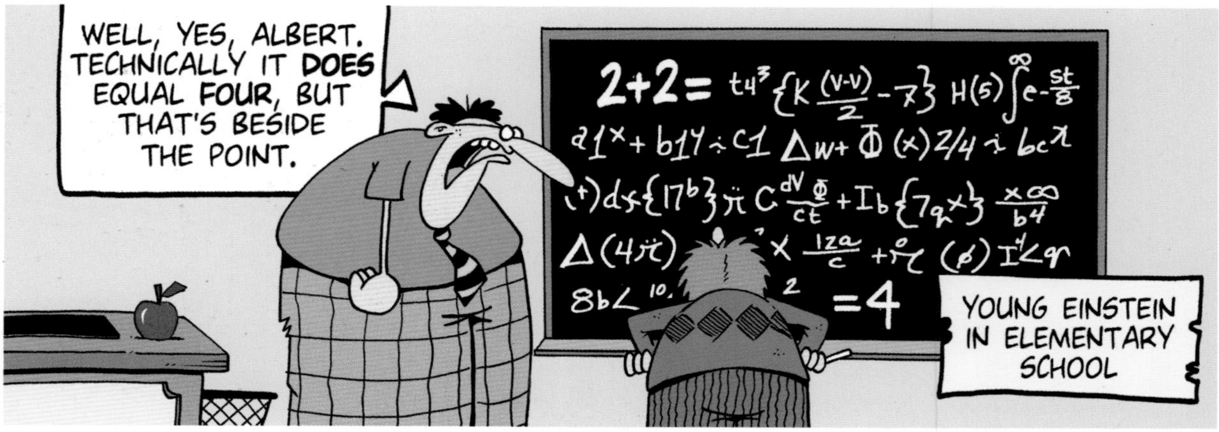
WELL, YES, ALBERT. TECHNICALLY IT **DOES** EQUAL **FOUR**, BUT THAT'S BESIDE THE POINT.
2+2=
=4
YOUNG EINSTEIN IN ELEMENTARY SCHOOL

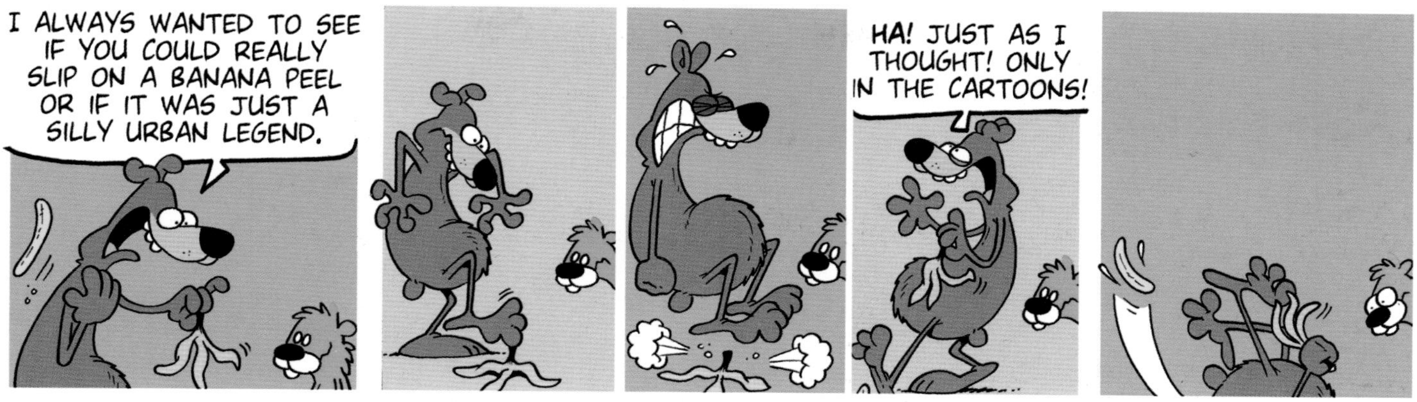
I ALWAYS WANTED TO SEE IF YOU COULD REALLY SLIP ON A BANANA PEEL OR IF IT WAS JUST A SILLY URBAN LEGEND.
HA! JUST AS I THOUGHT! ONLY IN THE CARTOONS!

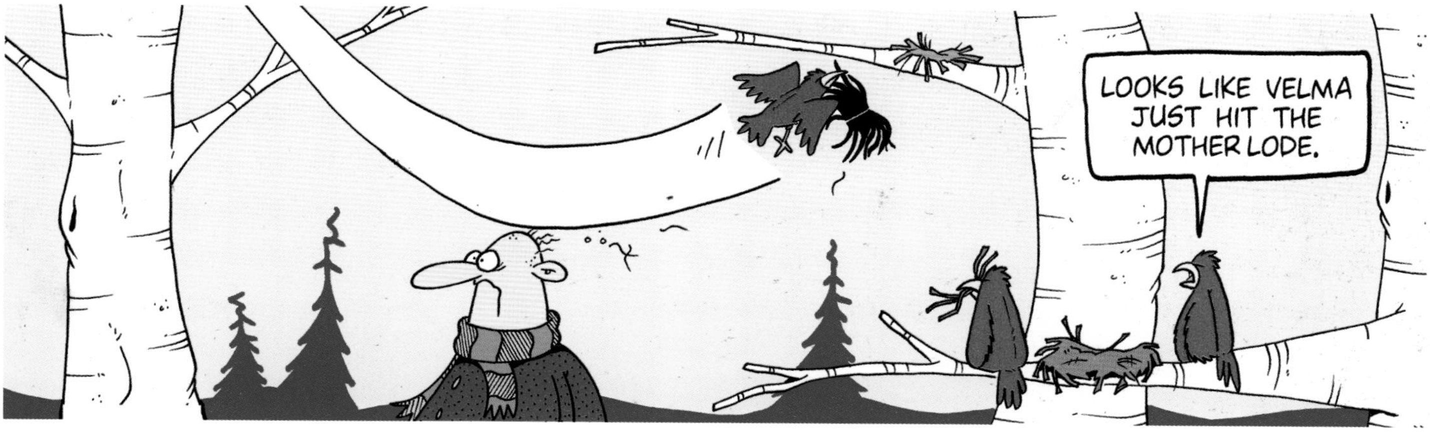
LOOKS LIKE VELMA JUST HIT THE MOTHER LODE.

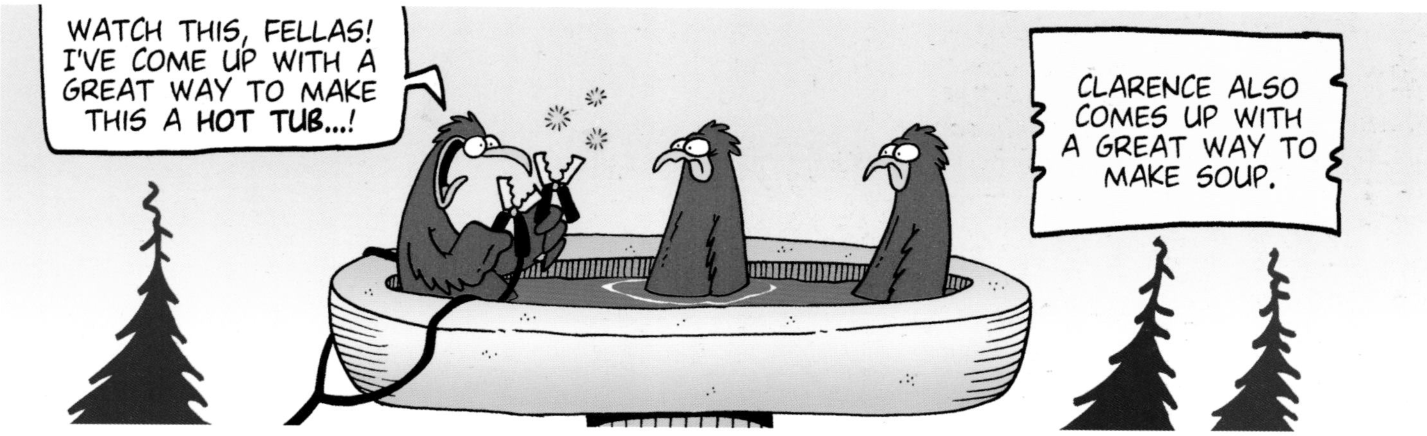
WATCH THIS, FELLAS! I'VE COME UP WITH A GREAT WAY TO MAKE THIS A **HOT TUB...!**
CLARENCE ALSO COMES UP WITH A GREAT WAY TO MAKE SOUP.

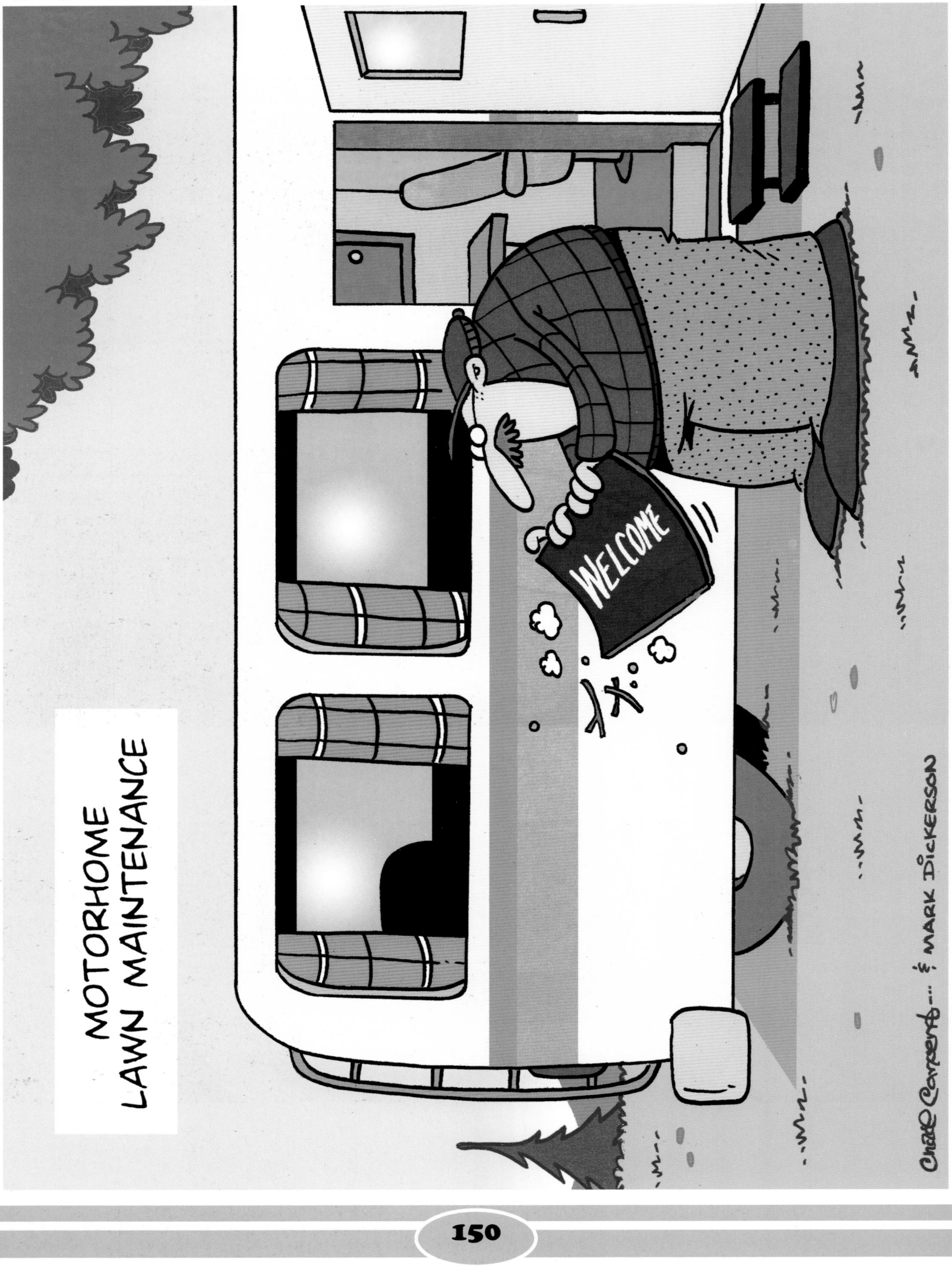
MOTORHOME
LAWN MAINTENANCE
WELCOME
Chad Carpenter... & MARK DICKERSON

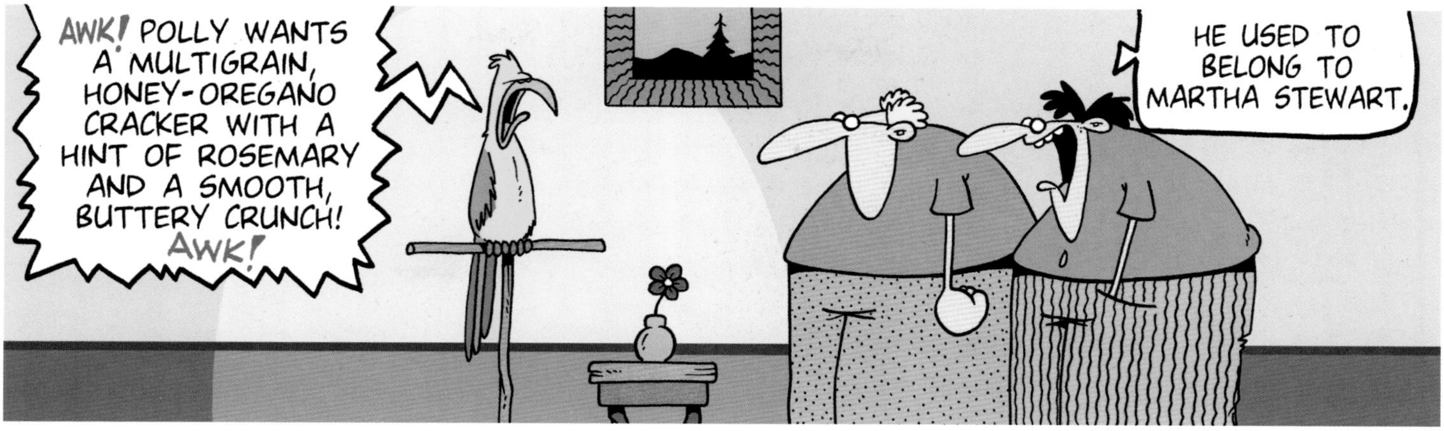
AWK! POLLY WANTS A MULTIGRAIN, HONEY-OREGANO CRACKER WITH A HINT OF ROSEMARY AND A SMOOTH, BUTTERY CRUNCH! AWK!
HE USED TO BELONG TO MARTHA STEWART.

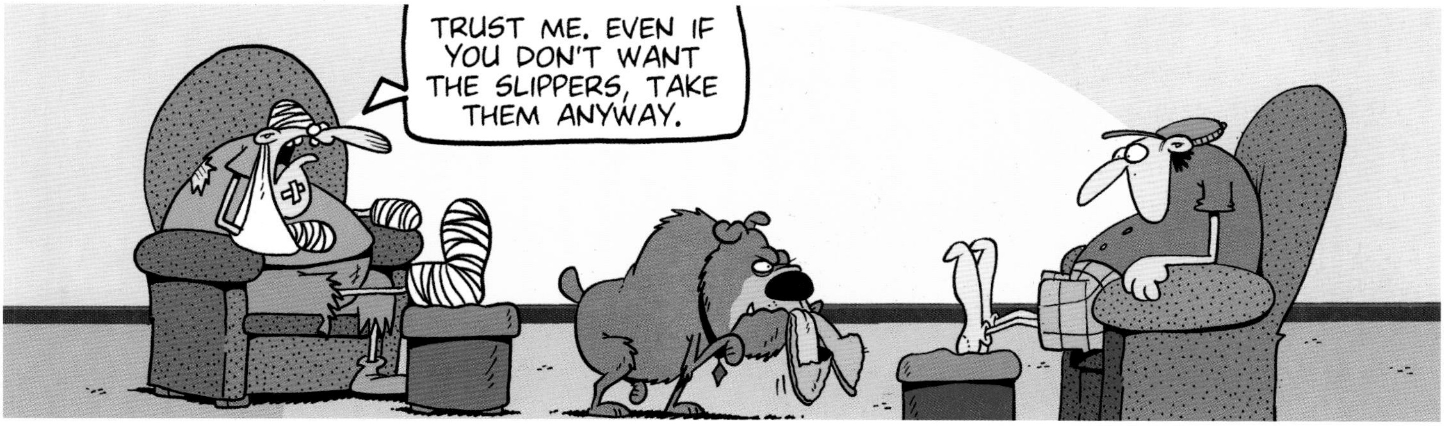
TRUST ME. EVEN IF YOU DON'T WANT THE SLIPPERS, TAKE THEM ANYWAY.

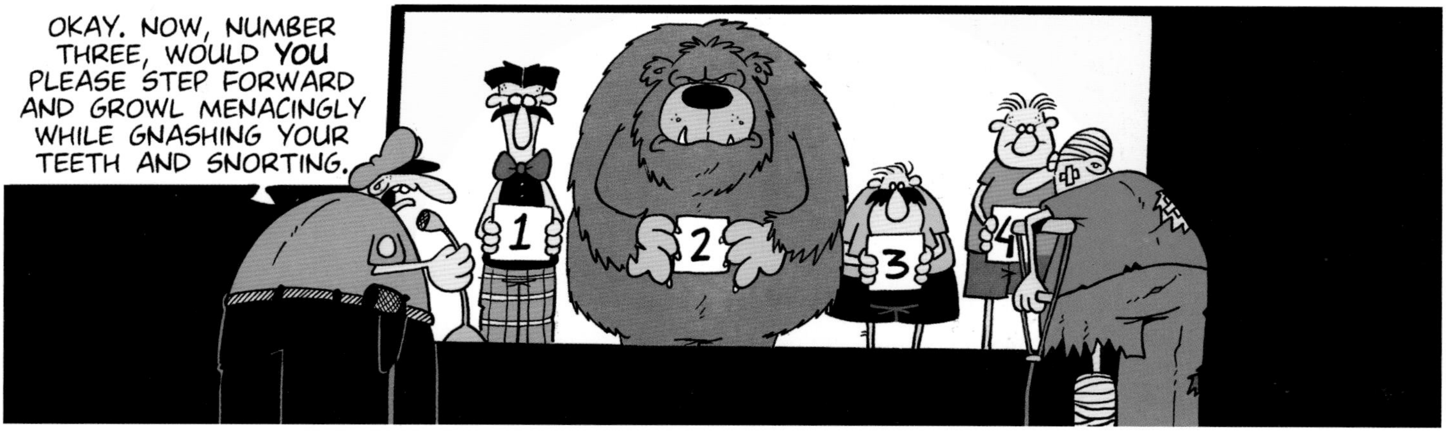
OKAY. NOW, NUMBER THREE, WOULD **YOU** PLEASE STEP FORWARD AND GROWL MENACINGLY WHILE GNASHING YOUR TEETH AND SNORTING.
1
2
3
4

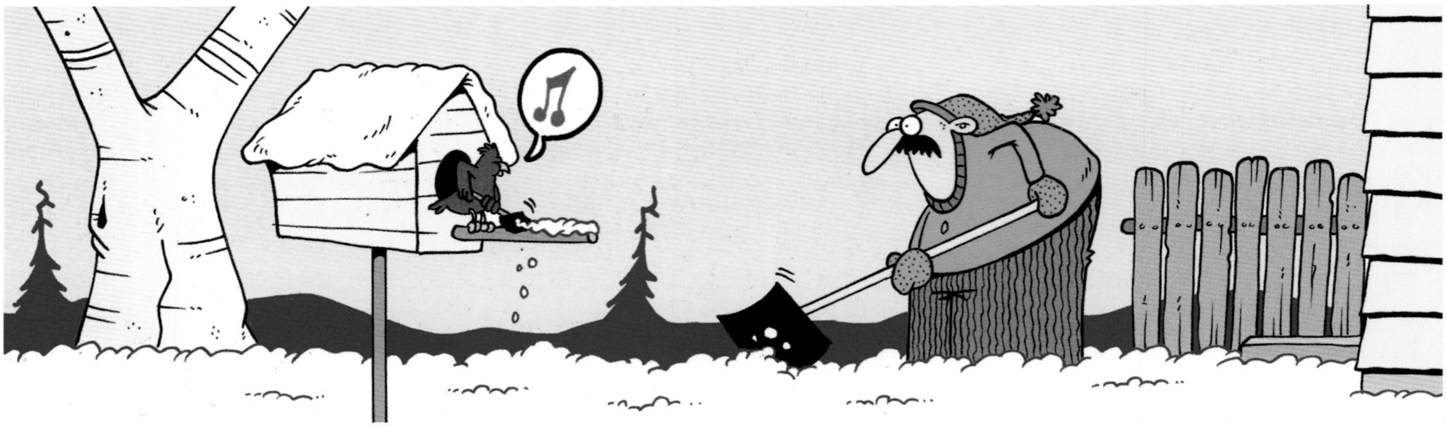

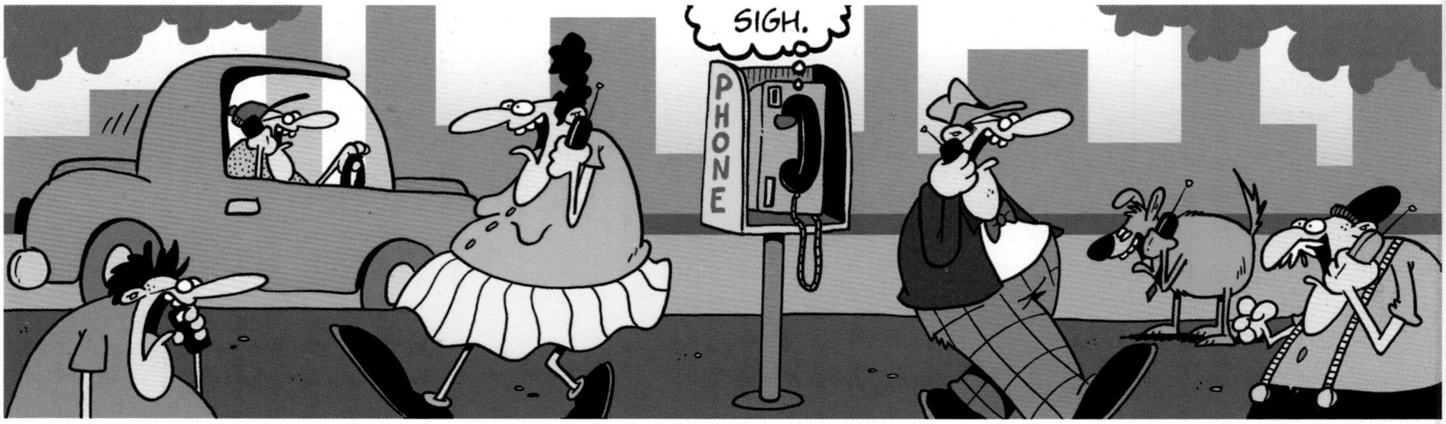
SIGH.
PHONE

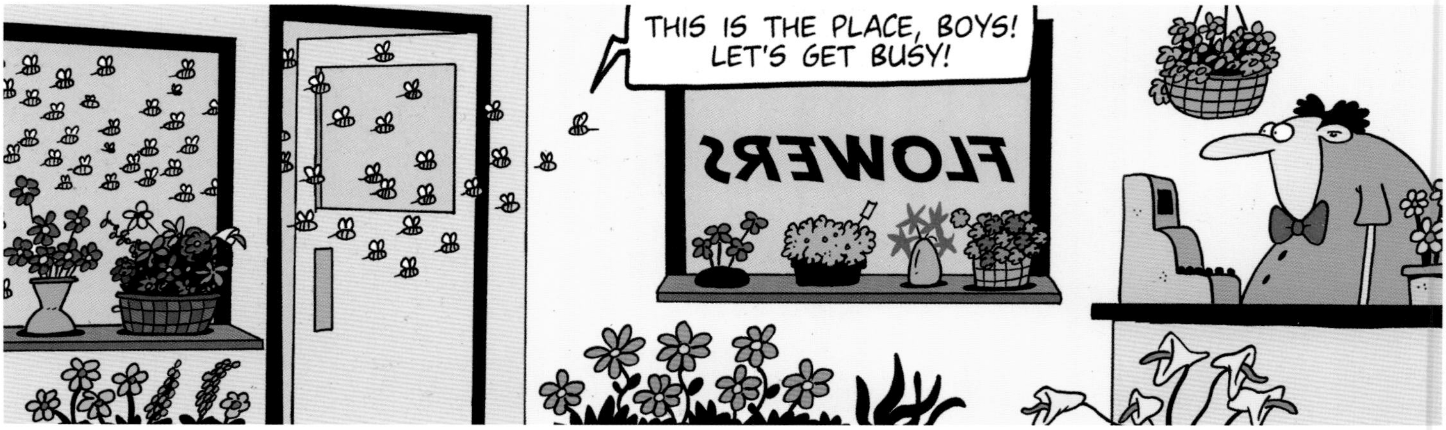
THIS IS THE PLACE, BOYS! LET'S GET BUSY!
FLOWERS

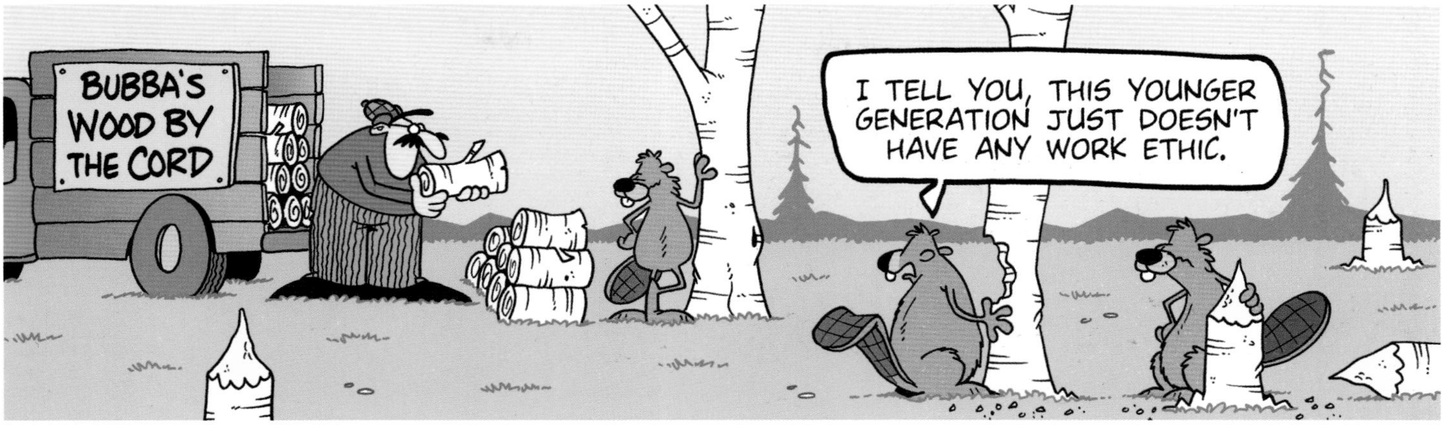
BUBBA'S WOOD BY THE CORD
I TELL YOU, THIS YOUNGER GENERATION JUST DOESN'T HAVE ANY WORK ETHIC.

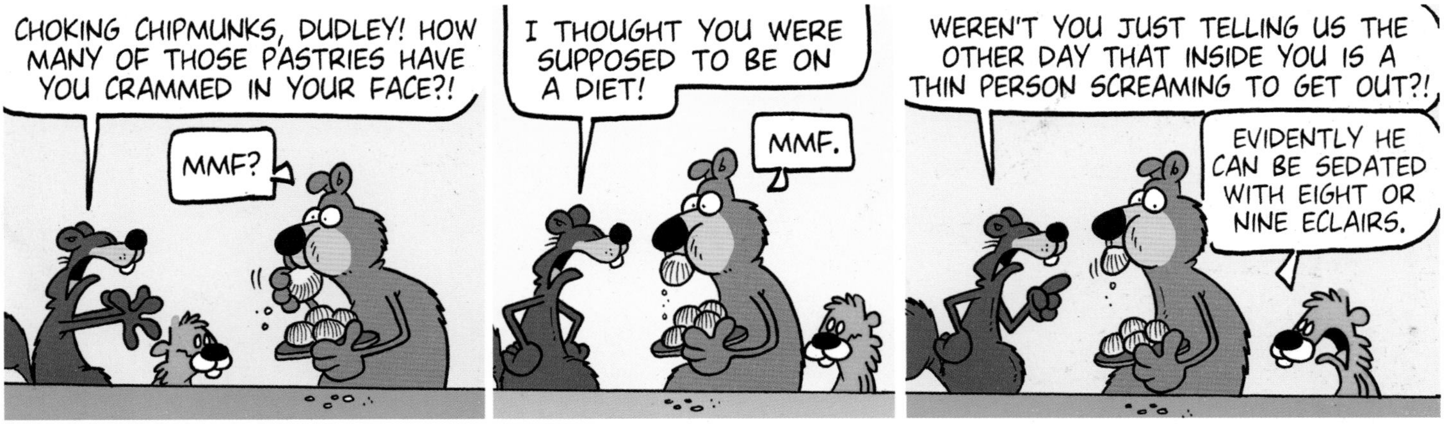
CHOKING CHIPMUNKS, DUDLEY! HOW MANY OF THOSE PASTRIES HAVE YOU CRAMMED IN YOUR FACE?!
MMF?
I THOUGHT YOU WERE SUPPOSED TO BE ON A DIET!
MMF.
WEREN'T YOU JUST TELLING US THE OTHER DAY THAT INSIDE YOU IS A THIN PERSON SCREAMING TO GET OUT?!
EVIDENTLY HE CAN BE SEDATED WITH EIGHT OR NINE ECLAIRS.

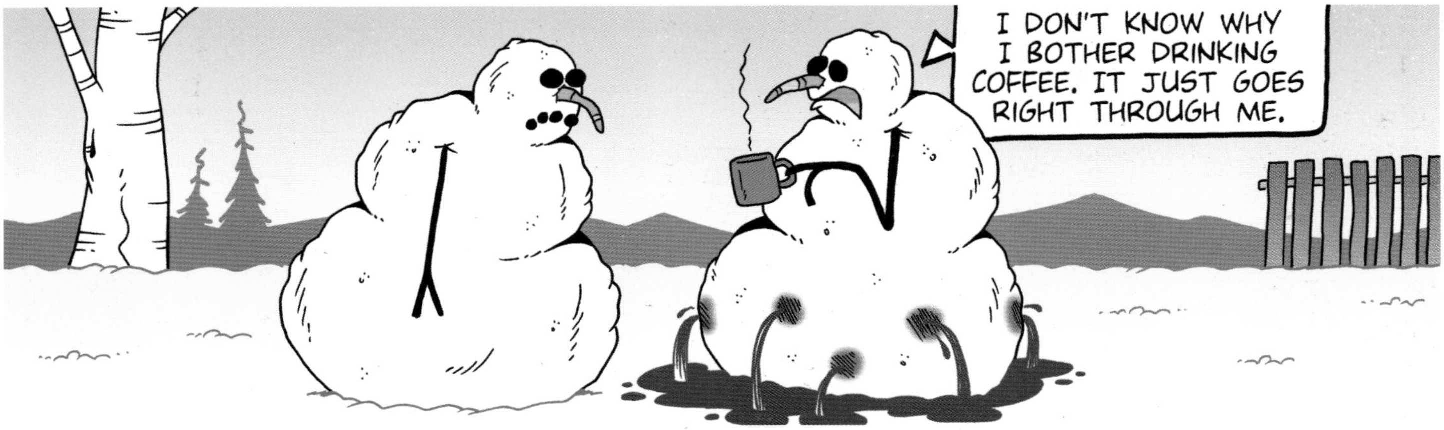
I DON'T KNOW WHY I BOTHER DRINKING COFFEE. IT JUST GOES RIGHT THROUGH ME.

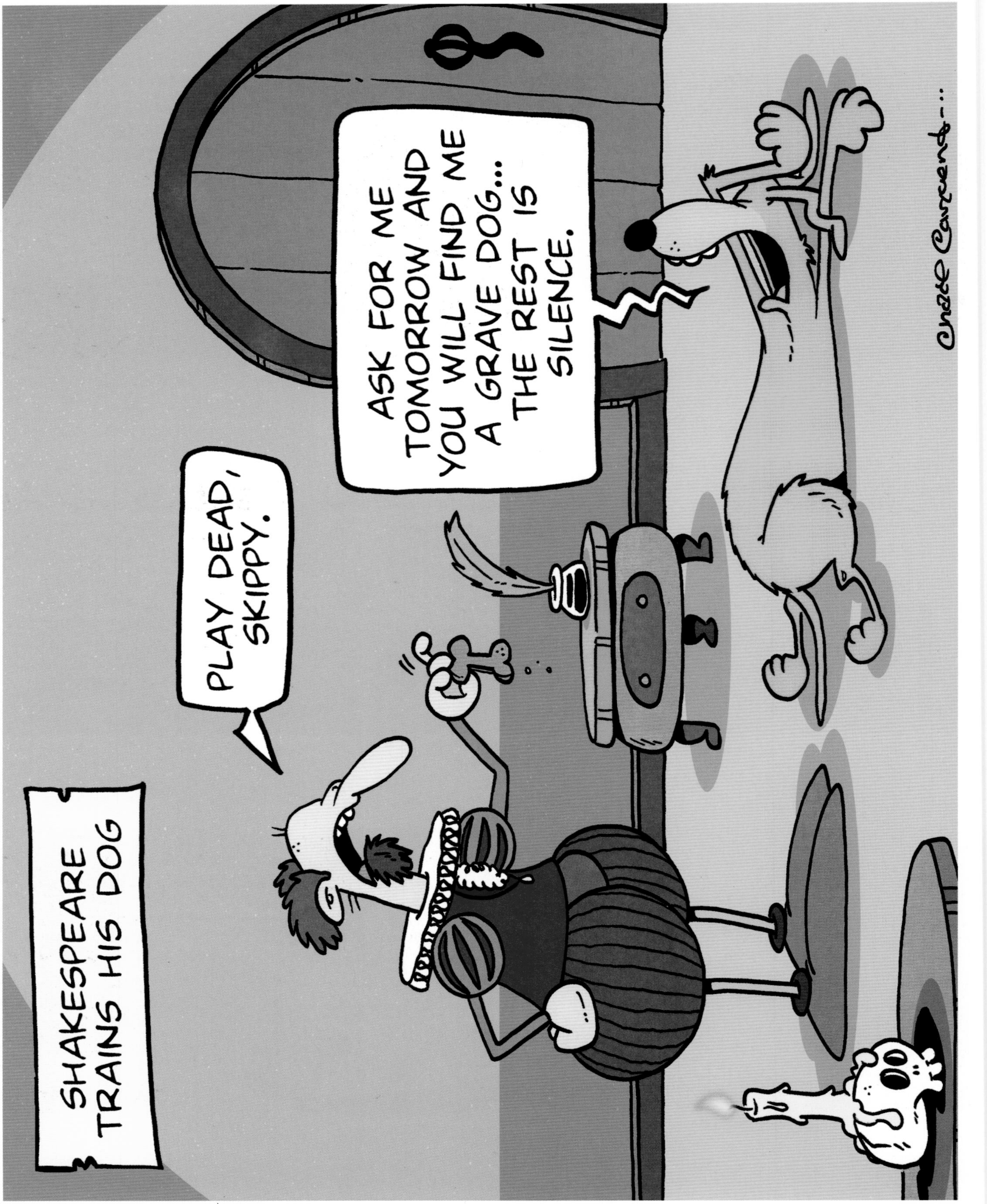
SHAKESPEARE TRAINS HIS DOG
PLAY DEAD, SKIPPY.
ASK FOR ME TOMORROW AND YOU WILL FIND ME A GRAVE DOG... THE REST IS SILENCE.

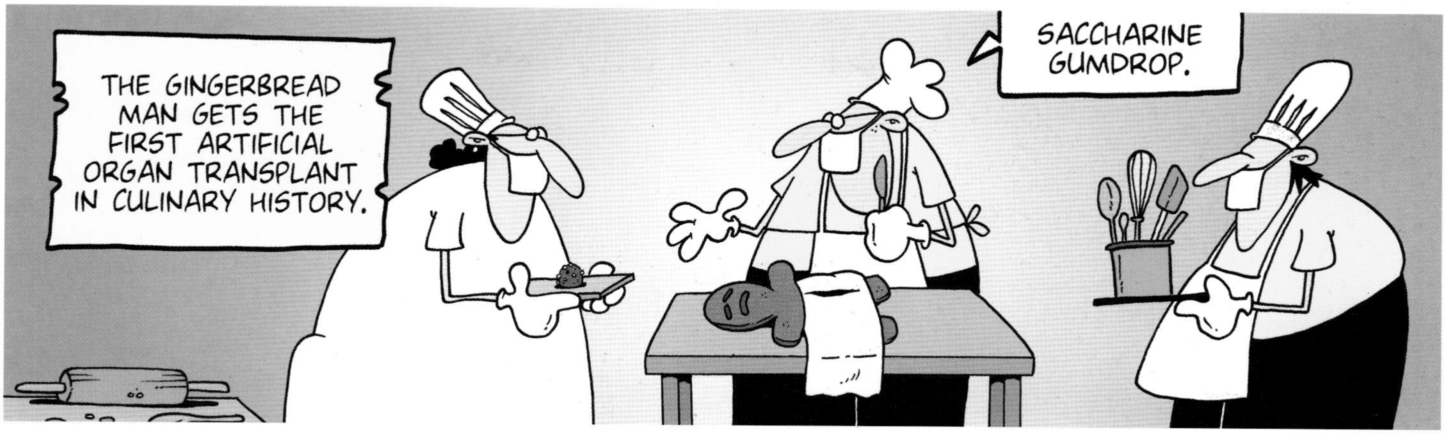
THE GINGERBREAD MAN GETS THE FIRST ARTIFICIAL ORGAN TRANSPLANT IN CULINARY HISTORY.
SACCHARINE GUMDROP.

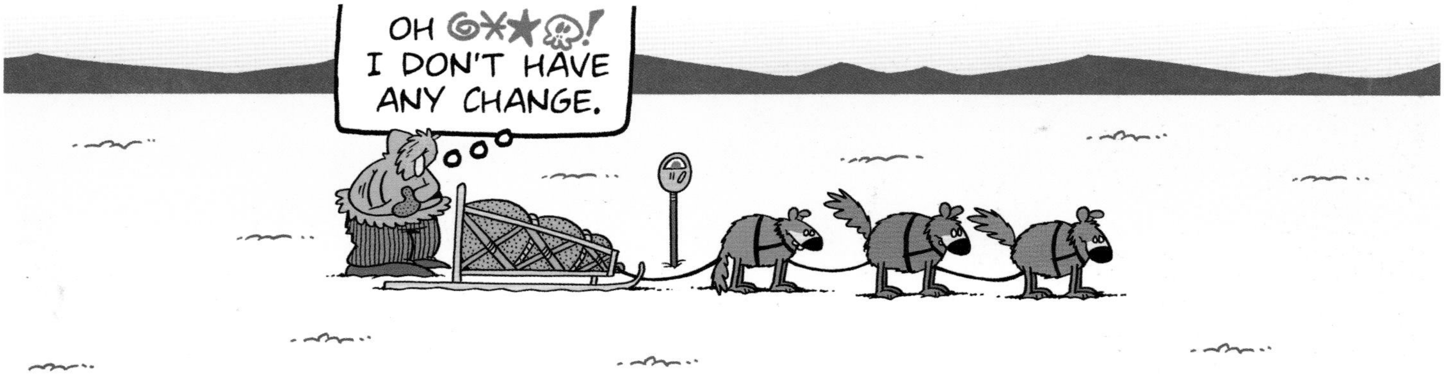
OH
I DON'T HAVE ANY CHANGE.

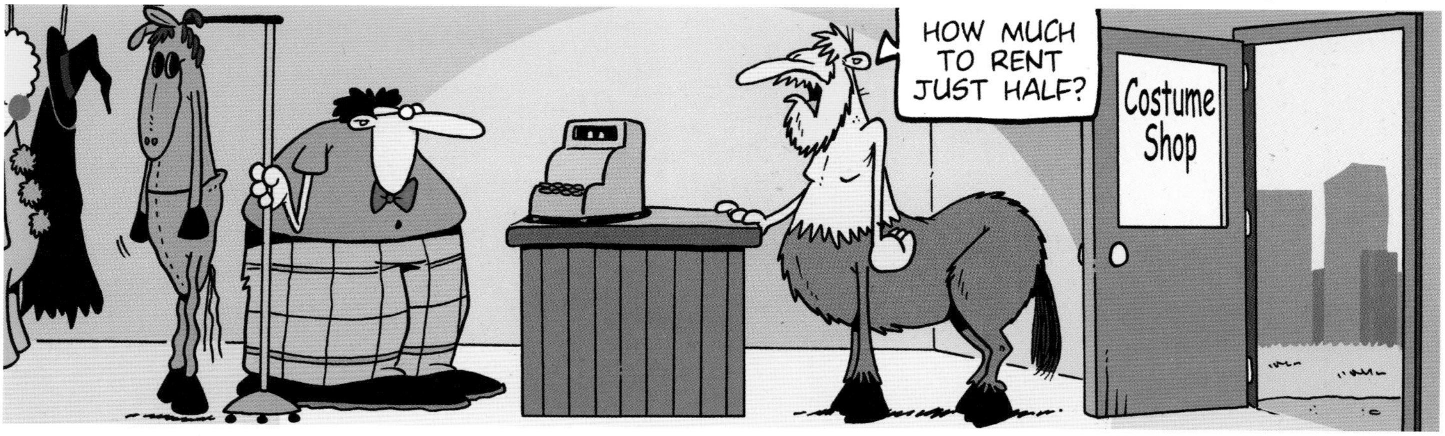
HOW MUCH TO RENT JUST HALF?
Costume Shop

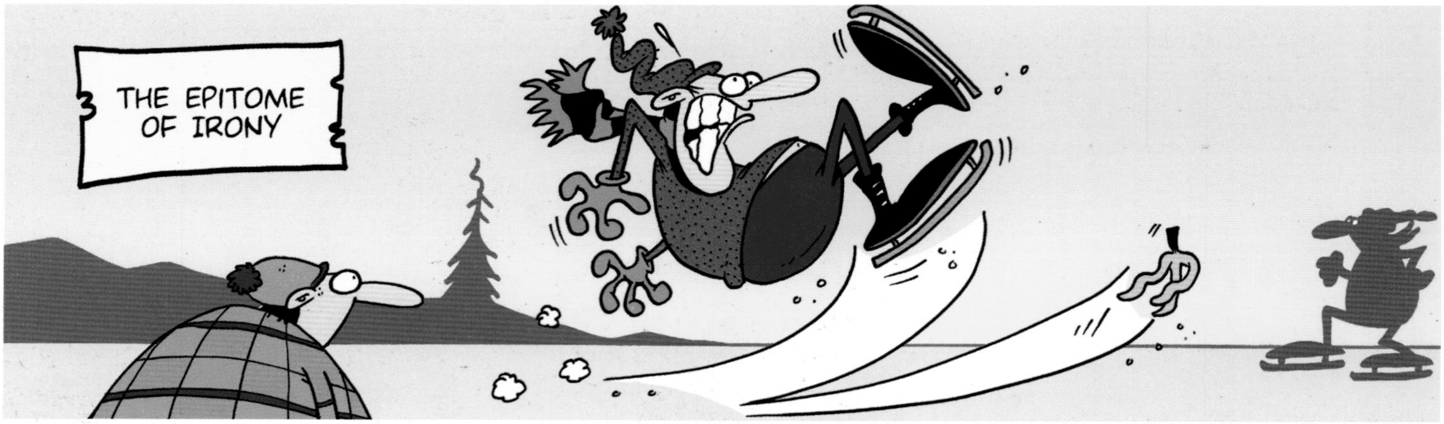
THE EPITOME OF IRONY

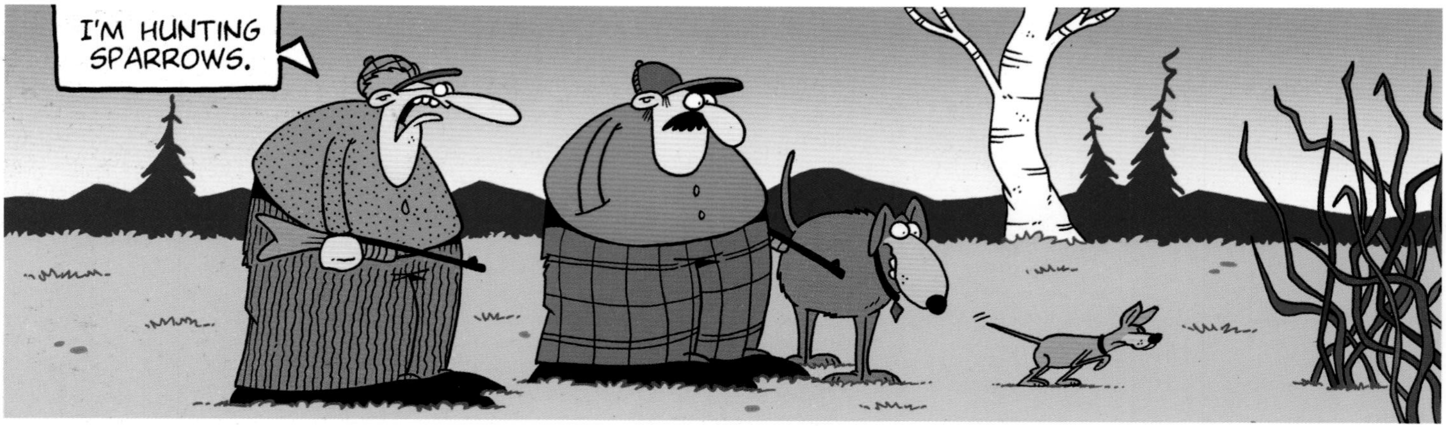
I'M HUNTING SPARROWS.

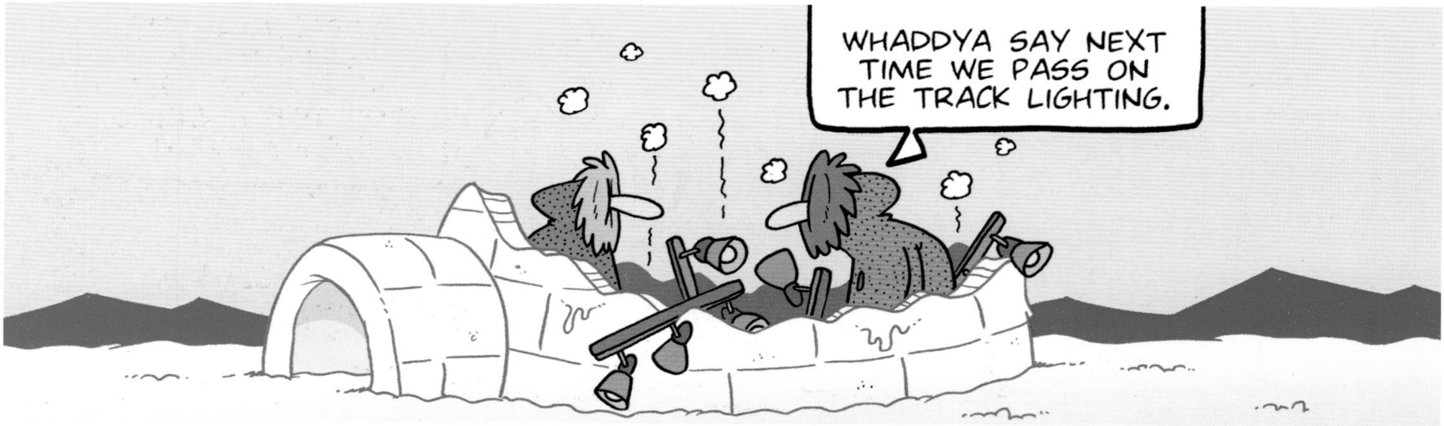
WHADDYA SAY NEXT TIME WE PASS ON THE TRACK LIGHTING.

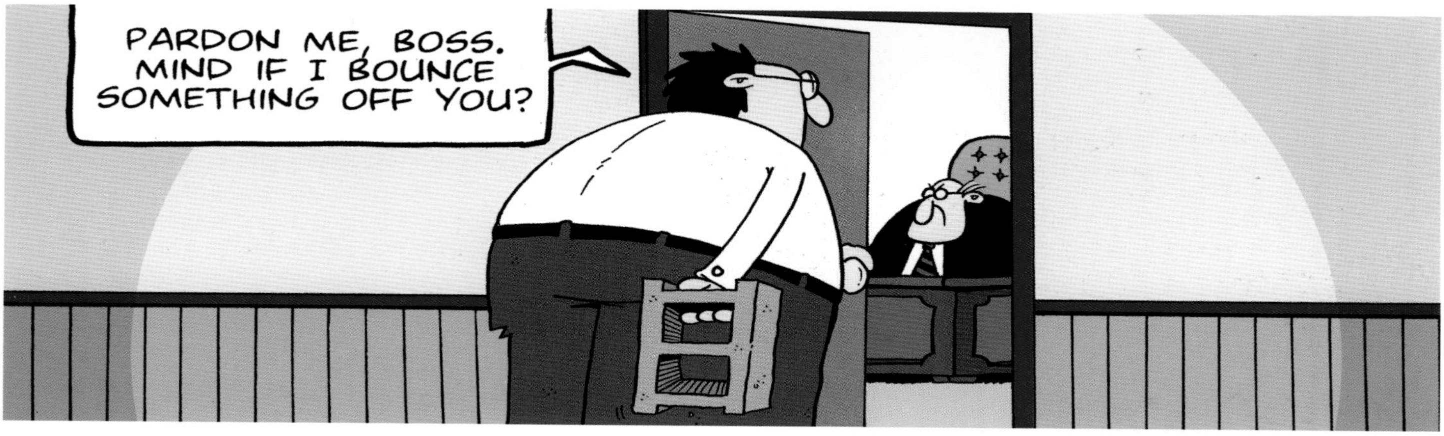
PARDON ME, BOSS. MIND IF I BOUNCE SOMETHING OFF YOU?

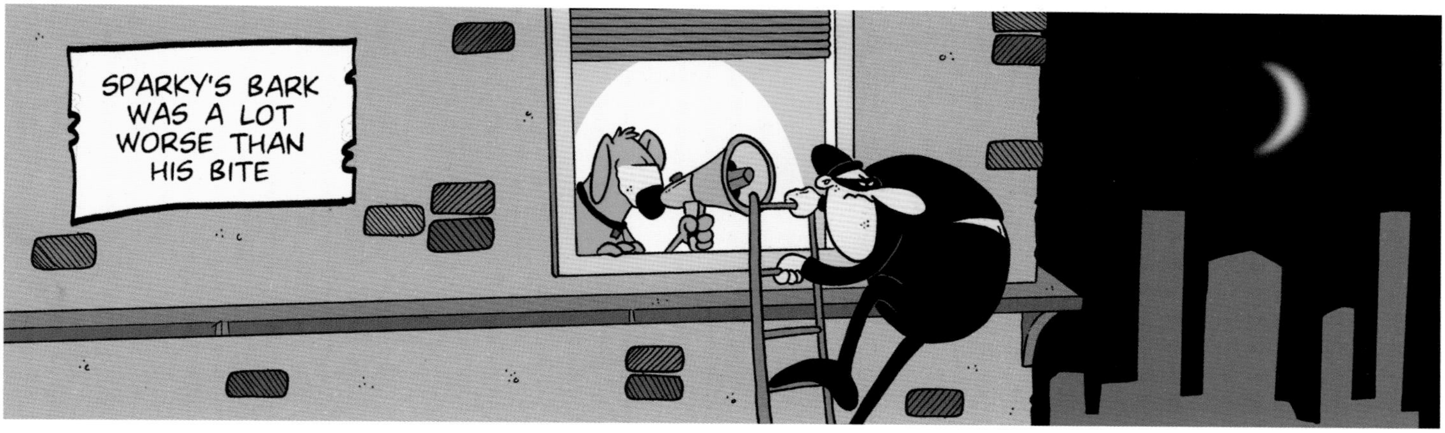
SPARKY'S BARK WAS A LOT WORSE THAN HIS BITE

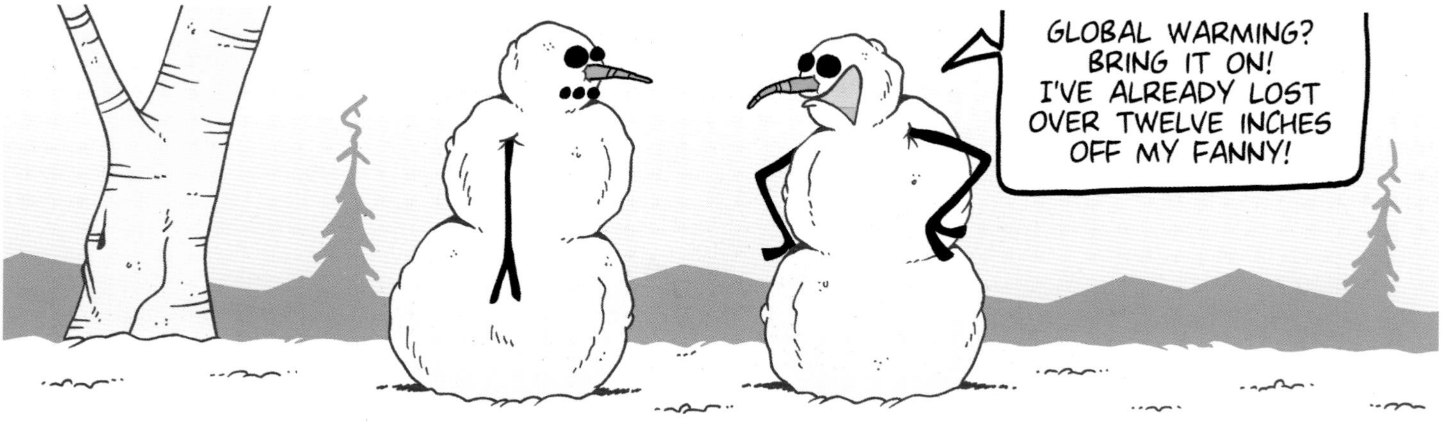
GLOBAL WARMING? BRING IT ON! I'VE ALREADY LOST OVER TWELVE INCHES OFF MY FANNY!

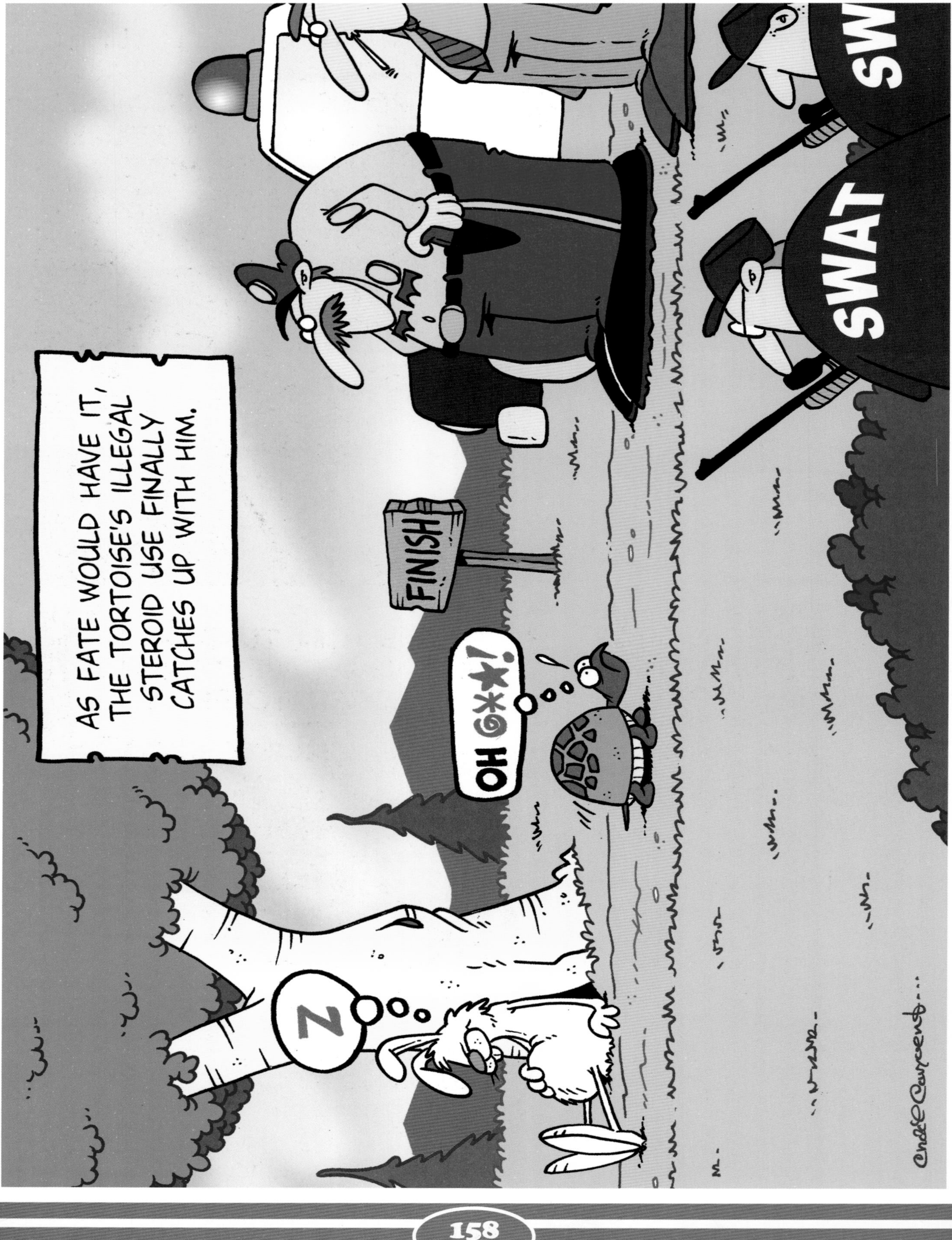
Z
FINISH
OH @**!
SWAT
SW
AS FATE WOULD HAVE IT, THE TORTOISE'S ILLEGAL STEROID USE FINALLY CATCHES UP WITH HIM.

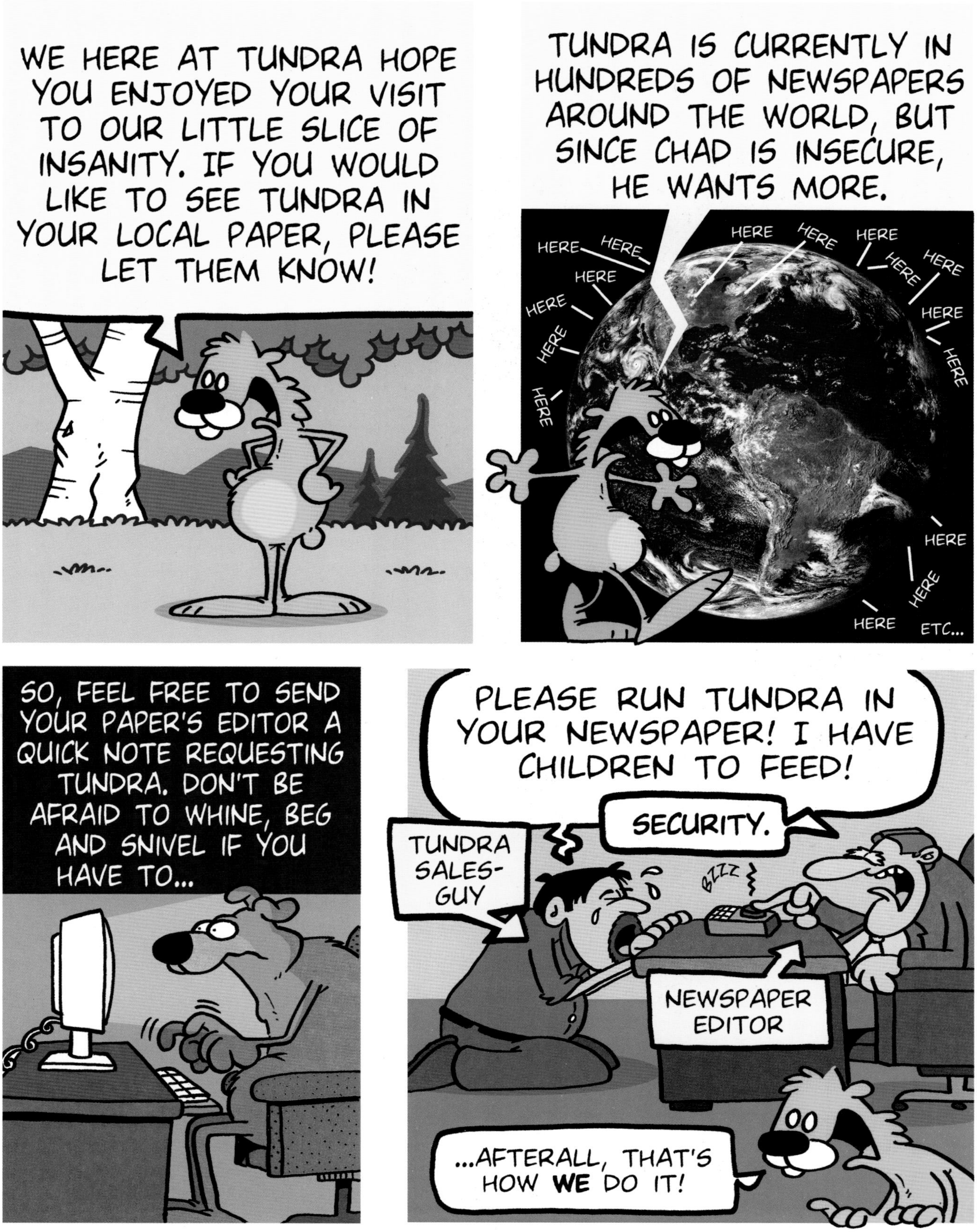
WE HERE AT TUNDRA HOPE YOU ENJOYED YOUR VISIT TO OUR LITTLE SLICE OF INSANITY. IF YOU WOULD LIKE TO SEE TUNDRA IN YOUR LOCAL PAPER, PLEASE LET THEM KNOW!
TUNDRA IS CURRENTLY IN HUNDREDS OF NEWSPAPERS AROUND THE WORLD, BUT SINCE CHAD IS INSECURE, HE WANTS MORE.
HERE
HERE
HERE
HERE
HERE
HERE
HERE
HERE
HERE
HERE
HERE
HERE
HERE
HERE
HERE
HERE
ETC...
SO, FEEL FREE TO SEND YOUR PAPER'S EDITOR A QUICK NOTE REQUESTING TUNDRA. DON'T BE AFRAID TO WHINE, BEG AND SNIVEL IF YOU HAVE TO...
PLEASE RUN TUNDRA IN YOUR NEWSPAPER! I HAVE CHILDREN TO FEED!
TUNDRA SALES-GUY
SECURITY.
BZZZ
NEWSPAPER EDITOR
...AFTERALL, THAT'S HOW **WE** DO IT!

FOR LOTS MORE INFO ABOUT **TUNDRA** AS WELL AS A MULTITUDE OF OTHER SILLINESS, PLEASE VISIT US AT **www.tundracomics.com**

ABOUT THE CARTOONIST

photo by Mark Dickerson

Chad, seen here in one of his more pensive moments.

Cartooning has been a part of Chad Carpenter his entire life. As a young child, when normal kids would be playing video games, watching TV or talking on the phone, Chad could be found scribbling on anything that didn't move (and a few things that did). This same geeky, antisocial behavior lasted well into young adulthood when Chad decided to move from his home of Wasilla, Alaska to Sarasota, Florida, on a quest to become a cartoonist.

It was on a Sarasota golf course that Chad met Dik Browne, the creator of the classic comic strip HAGAR THE HORRIBLE. Mr. Browne was gracious enough to allow Chad to hang out at his studio every now and then and learn some of the tricks of the cartooning trade. Tricks such as, what types of pens and paper to use, the correct format of a comic strip, and most importantly, that a well-organized drawing table is by no means a necessity.

Armed with some solid tools in his cartooning arsenal, Chad continued on his quest of avoiding gainful employment, and ventured on to seek yet more wisdom from another of the comic strip greats – Mike Peters, creator of MOTHER GOOSE & GRIMM. It was Mr. Peters who gave Chad the four all-important words that would eventually inspire him to develop TUNDRA. Those four words were "DRAW WHAT YOU KNOW." Mr. Peters also had a couple other four-word sentences to share with Chad, such as "Who let you in?" and "Get off my leg!" but those aren't important to this story.

Chad took Mike's words to heart and decided, having grown up all across the state of Alaska, that what he knew was the great outdoors and the creatures that dwell within its vast expanse. It was from this seed of an idea that the comic strip TUNDRA sprouted. Chad moved back to Alaska and began flinging out strips faster than an incontinent monkey flinging out stock tips.

Tundra is now featured in hundreds of newspapers around the globe. It has culminated in many books, calendars, T-shirts and anything else Chad can make a buck on.

Chad and his wife, Karen, live in Alaska with their three children, Zack, Pherrari & Sarah.

Chad's hobbies include chasing cars, shedding and rolling in dead things.